W9-CJD-550

The publisher and the University of California Press Foundation gratefully acknowledge the generous support of the Peter Booth Wiley Endowment Fund in History.

We Are the Land

We Are the Land

A History of Native California

Damon B. Akins and
William J. Bauer Jr.

UNIVERSITY OF CALIFORNIA PRESS

University of California Press
Oakland, California

© 2021 by The Regents of The University of California

Cataloging-in-Publication Data is on file at the Library
of Congress.
Names: Akins, Damon B., author. | Bauer, William J., Jr.,
author.
Title: We are the land : a history of native California /
Damon B. Akins and William J. Bauer, Jr.
Description: Oakland, California : University of
California Press, [2021] | Includes bibliographical
references and index.
Identifiers: LCCN 2020029628 (print) | LCCN 2020029629
(ebook) | ISBN 9780520280496 (hardback) |
ISBN 9780520280502 (paperback) |
ISBN 9780520976887 (epub)
Subjects: LCSH: Indians of North America—California—
History. | Indian reservations—California—History.
Classification: LCC E78.C15 A487 2021 (print) |
LCC E78.C15 (ebook) | DDC 979.004/97—dc23
LC record available at https://lccn.loc.gov/2020029628
LC ebook record available at https://lccn.loc
.gov/2020029629

25   24   23   22   21
10   9   8   7   6   5   4   3   2   1

Contents

Illustrations

Acknowledgments

This book began over a conversation at a Western History Association meeting in Oakland, California. It has been with us for a while. It has seen our oldest children go off to college and our youngest children develop into promising artists. As we put the final touches on this book, we are both proud, as with our youngest children, of its artistic nature. But, as with our oldest children, we are proud to see it leave the house.

The first person that we need to recognize is our doctoral mentor Albert Hurtado. Both of us worked with Al at the University of Oklahoma, where we wrote dissertations on aspects of California Indian history in the late nineteenth and early twentieth centuries. It was a great pleasure to work with Al and this book in some ways answers the question he used to ask us, usually in the margin of our seminar papers: what is the story here? His work and guidance showed us that stories can carry great explanatory or analytical power, but they do so better when people show up in them.

Niels Hooper has balanced his enthusiasm for the project with his patience and forbearance. We are grateful for both. We appreciate his faith in what we envisioned. As we came to the end of writing this book and preparing it for production, Robin Manley stepped in and guided us to the finish line.

Several people aided us in researching, developing, and fine-tuning this book. We are especially grateful to the five people who reviewed this manuscript for the University of California Press: Terri Castaneda,

Cutcha Risling Baldy, Nicolas Rosenthal, Khal Schneider, and Natale Zappia. They were generous with their time, and their insights have made this a better book. At the University of Nevada, Las Vegas, Stephen Bohigian, Neil Dodge, and Lee Hanover provided excellent assistance as graduate student research assistants. Willy thanks the students in a California Indian history class at the University of California, Los Angeles, for allowing him to tell some of these stories. That class remains a highlight of his teaching career. At Guilford College, students in Damon's writing-intensive California Indian course provided helpful feedback. Our friend and colleague Cheryl Wells gave this book a much-needed and helpful copyedit. We have presented portions of this book at various conferences: the Organization of American Historians, the Historians of the Twentieth Century United States, Western History Association, American Society of Ethnohistory, and Native American and Indigenous Studies Association. Thank you to panel commentators and participants.

At the University of Nevada, Las Vegas, Annette Amdal worked tirelessly as department administrator. Department chairs Andy Kirk and David Tanenhaus helped provide us with time to write this book. Deans Chris Hudgens, Chris Heavey, Jennifer Keene, and John Tuman helped to fund travel and production costs. Thanks to Raquel Casas, Carlos Dimas, Mark Padoongpatt, Marcie Gallo, Mike Green, Susan Johnson, Todd Robinson A.B. Wilkinson, and Tessa Winkelmann, among others, for making UNLV a vibrant place to teach and research Western and United States history. At Guilford College, faculty research funds supported travel to produce the book, and numerous colleagues provided helpful commentary—in formal presentations or in the hallways. Particular thanks go to Diya Abdo, Phil Slaby, Kathryn Shields, and Bob Williams.

Betty Matthews and Charlotte Bauer always showed up to hear Willy deliver a lecture on California Indian history, whether it was at the Sun House Museum in Ukiah or the California State Indian Museum in Sacramento. Willy's grandmothers, Anita Rome and Elizabeth Fritsch, passed away during the writing of this book. They are both deeply missed. His parents, William and Deborah, have never failed to support him in life's many ventures. This book could not have been written without their love. Kendra, Temerity, and Scout are probably among the happiest to see this book completed. Thank you, again and as always, for your love and support. Perhaps now, we might have more time for an evening at Hank's, a pickup basketball game, or a *Star Wars* marathon.

Damon's kids, Hollis and Reuben, have grown up with the book. Their growth has also helped him write it—they grew *it* up. They have both helped in ways they can't imagine. His parents, Judy and Winford Akins, have supported him throughout this project. Damon's conversations with Colleen Trimble, Byron Hutto, David Rosfeld, and Mandy Taylor-Montoya could fill a book. In some ways, they have here. He is particularly grateful for Colleen, for helping him learn how to see, how to listen, and how to write from that place.

This is *a* history. There are others, and we are grateful to the California Indians past and present who shared theirs.

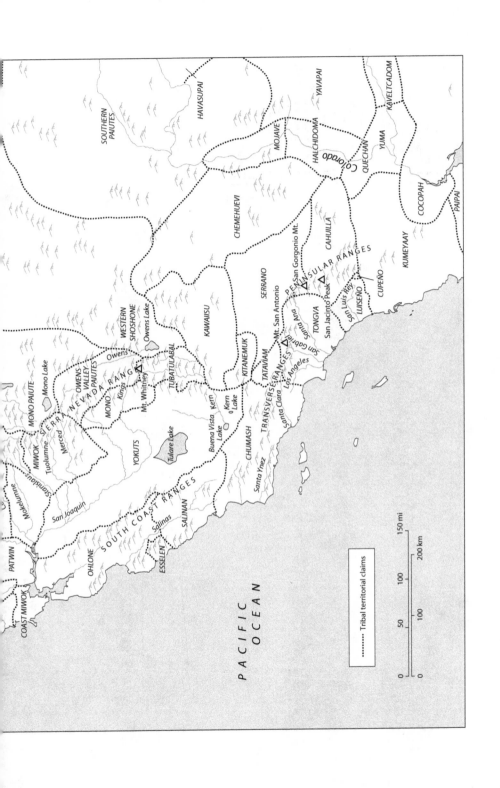

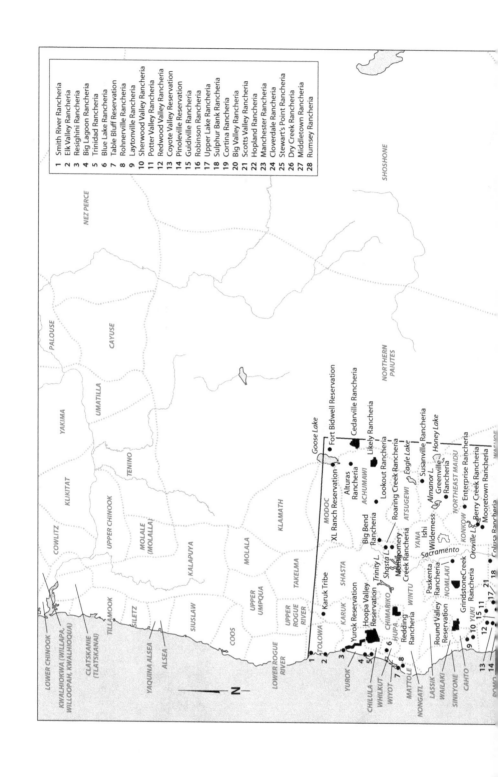

1 Smith River Rancheria
2 Elk Valley Rancheria
3 Resighini Rancheria
4 Big Lagoon Rancheria
5 Trinidad Rancheria
6 Blue Lake Rancheria
7 Table Bluff Reservation
8 Rohnerville Rancheria
9 Laytonville Rancheria
10 Sherwood Valley Rancheria
11 Potter Valley Rancheria
12 Redwood Valley Rancheria
13 Coyote Valley Reservation
14 Pinoleville Reservation
15 Guidiville Rancheria
16 Robinson Rancheria
17 Upper Lake Rancheria
18 Sulphur Bank Rancheria
19 Cortina Rancheria
20 Big Valley Rancheria
21 Scotts Valley Rancheria
22 Hopland Rancheria
23 Manchester Rancheria
24 Cloverdale Rancheria
25 Stewart's Point Rancheria
26 Dry Creek Rancheria
27 Middletown Rancheria
28 Rumsey Rancheria

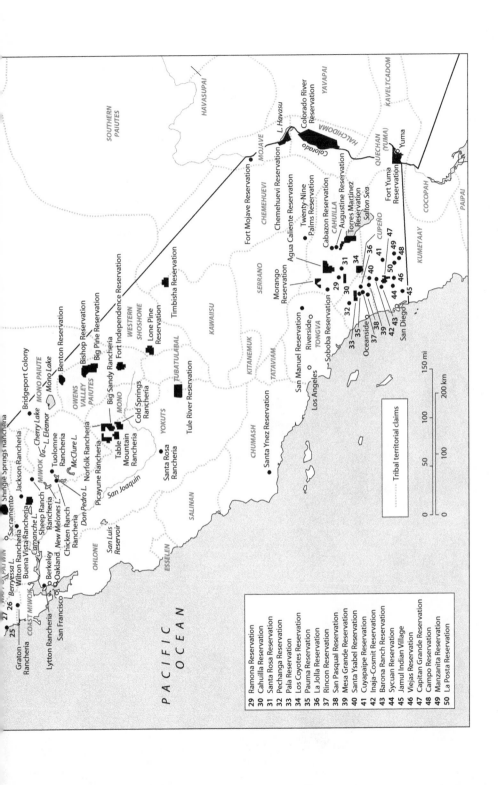

PACIFIC
OCEAN

SOUTHERN
PAIUTES

HAVASUPAI

YAVAPAI

KAVELTCADOM

Colorado River
Reservation

HALCHIDOMA

L. Havasu

MOJAVE

Fort Mojave Reservation

CHEMEHUEVI

Chemehuevi Reservation

QUECHAN
(YUMA)

Yuma

COCOPAH

PAIPAI

Fort Yuma
Reservation

Twenty-Nine
Palms Reservation

Agua Caliente Reservation

Cabazon Reservation

Augustine Reservation

CAHUILLA

Torres Martinez
Reservation

Salton Sea

CUPEÑO

Morongo
Reservation

SERRANO

San Manuel Reservation

Riverside

Los Angeles

TONGVA

Soboba Reservation

29
30
32
33
35
37–38
39
42 43
44 45
46
48
50 49 47
41 40 36
34 31
KUMEYAAY

Oceanside
San Diego

KITANEMUK

TATAVIAM

CHUMASH

Santa Ynez Reservation

KAWAIISU

Timbisha Reservation

WESTERN
SHOSHONE

Lone Pine
Reservation

TUBATULABAL

Tule River Reservation

YOKUTS

Santa Rosa
Rancheria

SALINAN

ESSELEN

OHLONE

San Luis
Reservoir

San Joaquin

Picayune Rancheria
Don Pedro L
New Melones L.
Chicken Ranch
Rancheria
Sheep Ranch
Camanche L.
Buena Vista Rancheria
Wilton Rancheria

MIWOK

Cherry Lake
L. Eleanor
McClure L
Tuolomne
Rancheria
Norfolk Rancheria
Table
Mountain
Rancheria

MONO

Cold Springs
Rancheria

Big Sandy Rancheria

Fort Independence Reservation

OWENS
VALLEY
PAIUTES

Big Pine Reservation

Bishop Reservation

Benton Reservation

MONO PAIUTE

Mono Lake

Bridgeport Colony

COAST MIWOK

Graton
Rancheria
25
26
27
Shingle Springs Rancheria
Berryessa L.
Jackson Rancheria
Sacramento

Lytton Rancheria

San Francisco
Berkeley
Oakland

PATWIN

Tribal territorial claims

0   50   100
0   100   200 km
0   50   100   150 mi

29 Ramona Reservation
30 Cahuilla Reservation
31 Santa Rosa Reservation
32 Pechanga Reservation
33 Pala Reservation
34 Los Coyotes Reservation
35 Pauma Reservation
36 La Jolla Reservation
37 Rincon Reservation
38 San Pasqual Reservation
39 Mesa Grande Reservation
40 Santa Ysabel Reservation
41 Cuyapaipe Reservation
42 Inaja-Cosmit Reservation
43 Barona Ranch Reservation
44 Sycuan Reservation
45 Jamul Indian Village
46 Viejas Reservation
47 Capitan Grande Reservation
48 Campo Reservation
49 Manzanita Reservation
50 La Posta Reservation

Openings

On August 4, 2011, Native and non-Native activists extinguished their "sacred fire" at Glen Cove, near Vallejo, California. Three months earlier, the land protectors built the fire to protest the city of Vallejo's proposal to bulldoze a burial site, which Ohlones call Sogorea Te, to make way for a city park. When the land protectors put out the fire, they marked the end of a long but successful campaign to claim Ohlone lands in the Bay Area. For twelve years, Bay Area Natives and their allies resisted the city of Vallejo's proposal to develop the land. When city officials finally decided to consult California Indians, they contacted the Yocha Dehe Wintun Nation and Cortina Indian Rancheria, whom the Native American Heritage Commission of California identified as the "most likely descendants" of those interred at Glen Cove. City officials did not reach out to Ohlones, who have lived in the Bay Area since their creation, in part because the Ohlones are not a federally recognized tribe, as the Yocha Dehe and Cortina Bands are. In April of 2011, Vallejo city officials announced their intention to go ahead with plans to build a public park, with a parking lot, restrooms, picnic tables, and paved walking trails. Chochenyo and Karkin Ohlone Corrina Gould led scores of Native and non-Native People to occupy Glen Cove and prevent the city from building the park. The land protectors' "sacred fire" burned at the center of tents and two tepees. Dozens of people kept up the vigil to protect the land and Ohlone ancestors. "Sogorea Te is one of the last burial grounds still on open land where we can actually touch our feet to the ground and say our prayers the way

FIGURE 1. Ohlone leader Corrina Gould at a protest of construction on top of a shell mound in Berkeley, 2016. Photo by Wendy Kenin. Licensed under Creative Commons Attribution-NoDerivs 2.0 Generic (CC BY-ND 2.0).

we're supposed to and pass that teaching on to the next generation," Gould said (see fig. 1). Protectors set up tables laden with food, sat down on the earth, and enjoyed one another's company. After nearly one hundred days of occupying the site, the Yocha Dehe and Cortina Bands brokered a deal between the protectors and the city of Vallejo. The three parties agreed to a "cultural easement," like a cultural right-of-way, that guarantees Yocha Dehe and Cortina Bands joint governance over the burial sites without transferring ownership. Protectors celebrated guarding one of the last visible burial sites in the Bay Area.

To many non-Indians, stories like the Ohlone protecting Glen Cove seem as if they came out of nowhere. Despite the long and rich history of Indigenous People in California, historians, anthropologists, and everyday people disconnected California Indian history from California history. Histories of California mention that Indigenous People lived within the current state boundaries and perhaps discuss the amazing diversity of languages, cultures, and political bodies. California histories recognize that Indigenous People lived in and worked at the missions established by Spanish colonists on the California coast. Yet California Indians often disappear from those histories after the demographic catastrophe of the California Gold Rush, in which the population of

California Indians declined from about 150,000 to 30,000. In the twentieth century, many people believed California Indians vanished. Some Californians expressed amazement, and sometimes anger, when California Indians seemingly reappeared on the political scene when fighting for gaming rights in Southern California, to protect land at Glen Cove, or to challenge cherished stories about the state's Catholic missions. Histories that ignore how California's Indigenous People lived within the state boundaries for centuries, maintained relationships with the land, and shaped the state's history undermine the sovereignty of contemporary California Indian communities. We hope this book contributes to efforts to correct the misperceptions that exist about California Indian, and California, history.

Rather than being peripheral to or vanishing from California history, Indigenous People are a central and enduring part of the state's history because of their relationship to the land. Before the arrival of Europeans, California's Indigenous People developed and maintained relationships with the land and other peoples across the region that was not yet California, Arizona, Nevada, Oregon, or Mexico. When Europeans first arrived, California Indians sailed out to meet and trade with them, striving to incorporate these newcomers into preexisting social, political, and economic relationships. Beginning in the 1760s, though, Spaniards, Russians, Mexicans, and, especially, Americans attempted to control California and divorce Indigenous People from the land. All four colonial nations sponsored policies that uprooted Indigenous People and communities from the lands in which they were created, and all four deployed violence, in the form of slavery, genocide, and an administrative state bent on eliminating California Indian people. Yet California Indian people, nations, and lands remain. California Indians have built and rebuilt communities, developed practices to maintain ties with the land, and remade policies intended to separate them from their homes. At times, California Indians hid to survive, but they never left.

By titling this book *We Are the Land,* we do not mean to hearken back to antiquated beliefs about Indigenous People as an intrinsic part of the natural world. Rather, the title evokes the two parallel arguments we put forth in the following pages: California is both a place and an idea. As a place, California has always been and remains Indigenous land, and Indigenous People are central to the history and future of the place. Creators made Indigenous People at specific locations. Indigenous People ground their ways of knowing in those places. They developed strategies to work on, with, and protect the land. One cannot separate Indigenous

People from the land that makes up California. But as an idea—or, as it was often described, a dream—that colonial entities brought with them, "California" represented a natural abundance of resources to be exploited; it could not be Indigenous land. Spain, Mexico, Russia, the United States, and the state of California extracted resources from Indigenous communities and appropriated the land. Colonists took the abundant resources often associated with California from the state's Indigenous People. In this sense, policies intended to dispossess Indigenous People of the land also directly attacked Indigenous Peoples' identity and existence.

For many Californians, the region's history stretches back only 150 years. People misunderstand the settler invasion of Indigenous California *as* California history rather than as an unsustainable and disruptive episode in it. This book recenters Indigenous People's fight to retain their land in the place that is California, as a way of challenging the idea of California. When we take a less compressed historical view, we see the continuity and persistence of Indigenous communities as they adapted to dramatic changes. We see the people of a specific place changing as the place itself changed. As "California" becomes California, Indigenous People become California Indians. We see a different California, and we see a future those communities are building there.

We Are the Land is divided into ten chapters. Chapter 1 describes the creation of California. Rather than treating Indigenous People as isolated and historically static "tribelets," this chapter examines how Creators made the land and the People, how the People worked with the land to survive, and how People lived with one another. Any examination of Indigenous Peoples before the arrival of Europeans is difficult. The chapter attempts to provide a holistic understanding of early California peoples by foregrounding Indigenous knowledge.

Chapter 2 explores the historical era commonly known as the "age of exploration." Rather than retelling the romanticized first encounters between "civilized" sailors and "savage" Indians, or dwelling on the brutal exploitation of Native Peoples, this chapter positions itself on beaches, hillsides, and riverbanks to examine Indigenous People as explorers and discoverers cautiously observing and then engaging with European travelers. In the early sixteenth and seventeenth centuries, Native Peoples studied newcomers to their land, such as Juan Rodriguez Cabrillo, Francis Drake, and Juan de Oñate. Following these initial encounters, Native Peoples scrutinized Europeans indirectly, as European manufactured goods followed consumer demand into Indigenous communities via preexisting trade routes that linked much of western North America. Diseases also traveled these trails, harming Native People. Often, Indigenous Peoples left their homelands and joined other peoples in response to these new illnesses. The discovery of new technologies and sicknesses produced conflict as well as cooperation. Some Europeans captured Indigenous People, causing them to prey on others for captives to replace the dead or to trade with other peoples. In the dynamic process of adaptation and resistance, Natives expanded into the territories of other native communities in an attempt to secure marketable goods. Far from being a static period in California history, the period immediate to the creation of the Spanish missions featured pulsating trade networks, cross-cultural encounters between different Indigenous nations, and technological innovations far beyond the purview of European witnesses.

Chapter 3 explores the relationship between Indigenous People and Spanish colonists. It avoids the perspective of looking over the shoulders of Spanish priests and soldiers who came to the area in the late eighteenth century, in favor of considering the Spanish missions from the perspectives of Indigenous communities. Missions posed significant risks to Indigenous People and their relationship to the land. Priests brought strangers to Native communities, disrupting established and delicately managed political relationships and contributing to the spread of the diseases the missions hosted. The missions' domesticated livestock devoured the People's food and trampled the places where the People harvested plants for their baskets. Despite these dangers, Indigenous People sometimes left their communities and moved to the missions and other Spanish settlements. At other times, Spanish officials forced Indigenous People to the missions and presidios. Other Native People created new social, economic, cultural, and political relationships with the Spanish at missions, presidios, and pueblos. Spanish communities offered new kinds of food and trade items, which Native leaders used to provide for their people. The priests, who did not become sick when many Indigenous Californians did, preached a different religion with an obvious power. From the viewpoint of the countless Indigenous communities along the California coast, the Spanish missions offered a host of risks and opportunities.

Chapter 4 focuses on the period of Mexican independence from Spain and the drive to secularize the missions. It begins by describing Native Peoples' relationships with Russian fur traders, American merchants, and Franciscan missionaries in the emerging regional market for trade goods. These new markets increased the demand for Indigenous labor, natural resources, and new commodities. The dynamic relationships among these various actors created new spaces in which Indigenous

People asserted their power. Some leveraged political instability to resist the pressures placed on their communities, such as the Chumash, who rebelled in 1824. Others, such as Pablo Tac and Pablo Apis, two Luiseños who followed very different paths, acclimated themselves to the new cultural and economic landscape and the markets it created. Most California Native Peoples fell somewhere between these poles, leveraging their labor power to resist increasing attempts to limit their freedom. Growing American interest and presence in the area hinted at further drastic changes on the horizon.

It is exceptionally difficult to see the middle of the nineteenth century as anything but horribly destructive to California's Native Peoples. But it is also critical to resist the victimizing tendencies implicit in such a focus. Indigenous People suffered greatly, but they are more than just victims. Chapter 5 tracks how they resisted attempts at their wholesale destruction. Native Peoples ultimately survived the transition to American rule and the Gold Rush by creatively asserting what power they had through their labor, limited acts of violence, and—less frequently, but importantly—the law. Despite the dynamic political and demographic changes to California, Indigenous Peoples' land and labor remained vital concerns in the new state. The Constitution of 1849 wrestled with Indigenous Peoples' citizenship, labor, and rights. The 1850 Act for the Government and Protection of Indians attempted to retain Indian labor while limiting Indian sovereignty and mobility through indenture. The State Land Commission and the eighteen federal treaties signed, but ultimately not ratified, in 1852 sought to quiet Indian claims to land in a way that advantaged settler society. The 1850s and 1860s were incredibly destructive times for Indigenous People in California, as they faced extermination campaigns and a system of slavery that eventually brought tens of thousands of them under its provisions. This chapter also focuses on collective acts of resistance, such as the Garra rebellion of 1851, and individual ones, such as Indigenous workers killing their employers. Other Indigenous People retreated from contact with Americans, turning the state's diverse geography into sites of refuge and resistance.

Chapter 6 explores the unmistakable direction of demographic changes that occurred in California in its first two decades after statehood. California would be an Anglo state. While California Indian labor remained critical in some industries, it declined in importance overall as Anglo interest shifted from *labor* to California Indian *land*. These changes forced Indians to deploy new strategies, such as pooling their resources to purchase land where they could resist and negotiate the demographic changes in the state or leveraging non-Indian benevolence to their advantage. High profile evictions, dispossessions, and disputes, such as those at Temecula, Round Valley, and Capitan Grande, brought California Indians to the attention of reformers across the nation. Change meant actively seeking rancherias and reservations as sites for temporary forays into the local wage-labor economy and as refuges from reliance on it. It also meant fighting dispossession in the courts and on the ground.

Chapter 7 traces the growth in California Indian–led political and legal activism in the early twentieth century to illustrate the changing power relationships California Indians faced across the state. Increased non-Indian awareness of the challenges they faced, as well as growing interest in their languages and material culture, gave California Indians traction in their efforts to assert control over land, labor, and citizenship. The impulse to mobilize refracted through the distinct circumstances Indigenous People faced across the state, producing divergent outcomes. California Indians fought the allotment of their land when it cut against their own landholding patterns, as it often did in the southern part of the state. Where allotment furthered Indian claims for land, they tended to support it, as often occurred in the northern part of the state. Chapters 6 and 7 together trace the long arc of Indian activism before it emerged into the public eye.

Chapter 8 tracks the emergence of a legal, political, and cultural California Indian identity. The forces that brought California Indians from all over the state and nation into contact with each other, and the legal challenges Indians mounted, meant that California Indians actively created a statewide identity that built on local communities without subsuming them. The "Indians of California" collectively sued the federal government for the loss of their land. While the victories they won were tokens in terms of actual compensation, the organizational work in which California Indians engaged paid bigger dividends. The federal government, through its termination policy, sought to break apart that identity to diminish California Indians' power.

Chapter 9 follows the experiences of California Indians from the onset of termination to the era of self-determination. It highlights the different path tribal nations—such as the Pit Rivers, Round Valley Indians, and the multinational protesters at Alcatraz—took to make claims on Indian land in California. Pit Rivers initially looked to the courts. Round Valley Indians hosted and negotiated with Governor Ronald Reagan to prevent a dam from flooding their reservation. Those at

Alcatraz occupied the former federal penitentiary, located in San Francisco Bay. Although all three groups experienced varying levels of success, they each influenced other California Indians as they argued for respect and self-determination. California Indians living on reservations and rancherias weighed the costs and apparent benefits of terminating their relationship with the federal government. The American Indian Historical Society, led by Cahuilla Rupert Costo, battled in the 1960s to alter the negative perception of California Indians that permeated statewide elementary textbooks. Pomo Tillie Hardwick successfully sued to reverse the termination of the Pinoleville Rancheria, winning a court decision that set a precedent for other tribes in the 1980s. Finally, a small, impoverished group of Indians in Southern California opened a bingo hall, ushering in a period of unprecedented political and economic growth for California Indians.

Chapter 10 examines the ways in which California Indians transformed their social, economic, political, and cultural practices after the development of Indian gaming. In 1980, the Cabazon Band of Mission Indians in Palm Springs opened a bingo and poker hall on their small reservation. This action produced two decades of conflict. State officials attempted to stop Indian gaming, while California Indians fought to expand their gaming operations. After successful lobbying, California Indians secured the right to operate casinos on their reservations. The resulting economic boom in California supported and expanded various programs of ethnic renewal, convinced many California Indians to return to their reservation homelands (reversing more than a century of diaspora), and enabled other groups to launch efforts to repurchase ancestral homelands. Meanwhile, other tribal nations have pursued the tortuous path of federal recognition to reclaim indigenous lands and assert their sovereignty. Yet the struggle over land continues. California Indians, recognized and unrecognized, have fought for indigenous land-use rights on off-reservation and off-rancheria sites across the state, such as the Ohlones' effort to protect gravesites at Glen Cove, which led to the establishment of the Sogorea Te Land Trust to act as a legal entity to represent Ohlone interests. As we move through the twenty-first century, empowered California Indian nations are returning to their homelands, invigorating their economies, and flexing their political power.

Spatial vignettes interspersed between each chapter make the California Indian presence more visible in some of the state's most populous, important, and iconic places. These short segments interpret Yuma, San Diego, Sacramento, Ukiah, the Ishi Wilderness, Riverside,

Los Angeles and the East Bay, and even Rome, Italy, as Native spaces across time. By emphasizing these places, we resist the erasure of California Indians. The vignettes connect the region's diverse geology, topology, ecology, climate, and flora and fauna to the institutions that wove the people and the land into a state.

Characterized by the twin themes of flux and abundance, the broad geological forces that formed California supported distinct forms of Indigenous life. In the Atsugewi, also called Pit River, creation story, Kwaw and Ma'Kat'da struggled with each other over the mist, the dough with which they kneaded a world. Kwaw created; Ma'Kat'da destroyed, and in that creative destruction, they created the California landscape. Thirty million years ago, the Pacific, North American, and Farallon tectonic plates collided and created the region's mountains and craggy coastline, as well as the region's climatic, topographic, and geological diversity. Mountains captured rain and served as barriers to migration. The interstitial spaces of the coast created refuges for peoples and animals. The climatic and topographic diversity facilitated and condensed seasonal rounds and trade routes, allowing Indigenous People to develop sedentary communities with distinct lifeways. In a Pomo creation story told by William Benson, Marumda formed the world out of wax, shaping specific habitats to support distinct life. Rivers served as thoroughfares for fish. Fire regimes regenerated oak groves and basket-making materials. The abundance of flora and fauna supported Pomo life. Scientists, however, point to the sedimentary settlement, which formed the Central Valley's rivers and wetlands and served as a source for food, as well as providing the grasses and forbs used for baskets. The grasslands and foothills nurtured the oak forests and acorns critical to native diets. Alluvial deserts in the south, and massive granite uplifts in the central and north, formed barriers to migration and shaped cultural patterns. The vignettes peel back the present to look into the past and examine how these forces shaped California Indian communities. They also bring the past into the present to emphasize California Indian persistence.

A NOTE ON TERMINOLOGY

The language used to refer to people, any people, is both arbitrary and powerful. It is created, and it creates. Words sit at the center of the contested terrain of cultural sovereignty. As many have pointed out, the term *Native Americans* is only slightly more accurate than the term

Indians. What does it mean to be native to a place called "America," a name imposed on an entire continent by a people who had never seen it, an appellation derived from the corruption of an Italian sailor's name? Is that any more accurate than a different Italian sailor's misidentification of a place as India, and its inhabitants, "Indians?" Likewise, what does the term *native Californian* mean, especially before the idea of California existed?

All aggregate or ascriptive names fail to capture the complexity of what they seek to name. The specific names all people have for themselves, however they define that grouping, capture the complexity and distinctiveness but fragment and disconnect the people's experiences. As much as possible, we have used the names people used for themselves instead of ascriptive terms. In writing on Indians of the Spanish Empire, some scholars have carried over the terms used by the Spanish to distinguish those Indians who had relocated to a mission ("neophyte," from *neófito*) from those who had not ("gentile," from *gentil*). Spaniards understood a neophyte as a recently converted member of a church, usually in a probationary period. We use *Mission* (or occasionally "affiliated") and "unaffiliated" because *neophyte* and *gentile* center the Catholic experience as the defining aspect of Indian life. Instead, we choose to emphasize, in many (but not all) cases, Indigenous People affiliated with a mission as a matter of strategy or choice.

Likewise, we have generally avoided using the word *California* and *Californian* to describe people, especially in the chronologically early sections of the book. The term is imprecise until California existed, sometime in the late eighteenth century. When we use the term, we do so in an inclusive sense, meaning all the people who live in and consider themselves members of the political or cultural entity of California. A big part of the story this book tells is about California Indians fighting to protect themselves and their land from settlers who tried to erase them. The settlers' idea of California, mythologized as "the California Dream," excluded California Indians. California Indians resisted that erasure and claimed a sovereign space for themselves within the state's politics, culture, and economy.

When we refer collectively to the region's Indigenous People, we have used that phrase, or variations on it. In the first few chapters of this book, we use the term *Indigenous People* or *People*. We have chosen these terms, in part, because the name that Indigenous People have for themselves is often some variant of *people*. For instance, Yukis call those who live in modern-day Round Valley *Ukomnom*, which translates into People in the Valley. They call their relatives who live near the Pacific Ocean

Ukhoatnom, or People on the Coast. Over time, of course, the names for Indigenous People changed, as will our use of terms. In the eighteenth century, the region's Indigenous People were not Californians. Today, they are California Indians, a critical part of the state's identity. The language we use in this book highlights that change, from "Indigenous People" to "California Indians," and, later, to the legally defined category "the Indians of California." These terms are not sequential. They do not supplant the terms that came before but layer and add precision to the communities they describe. And finally, a sense of deference drove our choices on word usage. In our varied experiences, most California Indians use that term, or *Native Californians,* to refer to themselves. There are exceptions, and we imagine those tendencies may shift over time. We remain alert to those changing patterns.

MAPS AND SOURCES

We have included two maps in the book. The first emphasizes the territoriality of Indigenous Peoples' claims to land. The territorial limits it describes are not meant to be definitive but rather to challenge the notion that Indigenous People moved loosely over the land without deep attachments and specific claims to it. The map also emphasizes the relationships between the state's topography, geography, hydrology, and Indigenous People.

The second map represents Native California today but retains the tribal territorial claims from the first map. It includes the cities and Native spaces discussed in the text, as well as the reservations and rancherias established in the nineteenth, twentieth, and twenty-first centuries. Our goal is to emphasize the ongoing nature of Indian territorial claims, to recognize the presence of Indian communities that the federal government has not, and to indigenize the cities where the majority of California Indians now reside. It is a crowded map, testament to all that is commonly erased, forgotten, or left off the maps.

At the end of each chapter, we offer a brief discussion of the sources used to construct our narrative. We hope these bibliographic discussions serve as a way to follow the stories back into the sources themselves but also as a way to address the challenges facing anyone seeking to capture the Indigenous past using sources often inimical to it. Government documents, Western written sources, and anthropological records all capture skewed and partial views of Indigenous People. As much as possible, we have sought to resist the biases they possess and to balance them against available Indigenous sources. In the case of this introduction, there was, and continues to be, regular news coverage on the issue of Ohlone land activism in local and special interest journals and newspapers around the Bay Area, such as *In These Times, East Bay Express, East Bay Times, San Francisco Chronicle, YES Magazine,* and the *Daily Californian,* as well as national and international news sources such as *Truthout, The Guardian,* and *Al Jazeera America.* The quote from Corrina Gould was taken from Jacob Simas, "Native American Activists Save Sacred Burial Ground from Bulldozers," *New American Media* 4 (August 2011). Will Parrish's article "Protecting Ohlone Heritage," which details the creation of the Sogorea Te Land Trust, can be found in the *East Bay Express,* March 4, 2015.

A People of the Land, a Land for the People

Nocuma, the Tongva Creator, held the world in his hands. He fixed the earth in place by anchoring it to Toshaawt, a large rock. A stream, over-crowded with fish, encircled this world. The fish wondered how to make more room for themselves. One fish broke open Toshaawt, and a bilious liquid, like the contents of one's stomach, spilled into the water. The water turned salty and fed the ocean. Nocuma then made first man and first woman. This couple had children, one of which they named Wewyoot. Eventually, Wewyoot lived at Povuu'nga, now located on the California State University, Long Beach, campus, where he matured into an ambitious and ruthless leader who attempted to conquer others. Wewyoot's followers grew restless with his leadership. They killed Wewyoot by grinding a piece of Toshaawt and applying the paste to Wewyoot's chest. The People burned his body at Povuu'nga. The People held a council to figure out how to feed themselves. Attajen, whose name means "man," appeared at this meeting and recognized the people's precarious situation. He taught ceremonies to religious leaders so they could produce rain, acorns, and bountiful animal populations. Then, Chinigchinich, the prophet, came to Povuu'nga. He taught Tong-vas ceremonies and laws, as well as how to build the *yovaar* (sweath-ouse). The Tongva People were now prepared to live with the land.

Indigenous People begin their history with creation stories like the Tongva's narrative of Nocuma, Wewyoot, and Chinigchinich. These stories define a people and a land. Yet historians, anthropologists, and archaeologists have questioned the historical validity of oral histories and oral traditions. Scholars have called these stories "myths" or "legends." They have privileged written sources, often produced by non-Indians, and material objects, such as stone tools and mortars, to tell the deep and long history of Indigenous People in California. This chapter uses creation stories to understand this history.

As the Tongva creation story illustrates, Indigenous People's creation stories described the relationship between Indigenous People and the land. First, Creators made Indigenous People with the land. Second, Indigenous People developed ways of working with the land. Although Indigenous People practice different economies, this chapter emphasizes the work and labor associated with harvesting acorns to illustrate this history. Finally, Indigenous People lived with the land in complex political and economic networks. They built towns, cooperated or fought with their neighbors, and extended trade routes to reach those farther away. Through their attachment to the land, and their engagement with each other, Indigenous People wove the region together. These histories and practices were not limited to the time before the arrival of Europeans. Rather, Indigenous People in California continue to tell these histories, harvest acorns, and perform the ceremonies necessary to relate to the land.

The history of Indigenous People in California began when Creators made the land and the People. According to the Tachi Yokuts, whose homelands sit in the southern San Joaquin Valley and who now occupy a rancheria outside of Lemoore, Ancient People, portrayed as animals, formed the land from the bottom of the ocean. Eagle and Coyote sat on a spit of land on a vast ocean. Turtle swam over to them. Eagle asked Turtle to dive to the bottom of the sea and bring back dirt. Turtle gulped as much air as he could and dove. He struggled to reach the ocean's floor and managed to grab only a handful of dirt. Turtle breached the water and flopped on the island with Coyote and Eagle. Much of the dirt washed out of Turtle's hand. Coyote inspected Turtle and nearly gave up hope of finding any when he spied a bit of mud underneath Turtle's fingernail. Eagle and Coyote mixed the dirt with chiyu seeds to make the earth. Then, Eagle and Coyote sent People throughout the world. They told one group, "You go to that place with your people. You go to that spring."

The People named the landscape and its features as they spread across the land. Nahachish, a Luiseño figure from Temecula, was poor and hungry. He sang a song about leaving his home, but he did not know where he would end up. Nahachish traveled until he met a group of people having a gathering, what California Indians call a "Big Time." These people gave Nahachish a light gray mush. Nahachish replied, "My stomach is *picha* [whitish]." Thus, Nahachish named the place Picha Awanga, now shortened to Pechanga. Next, Nahachish walked to where some of his relatives lived on Palomar Mountain. His relatives gave Nahachish some food. The food made his stomach burn, like from a nettle. Nahachish called this place Sukishva, which means nettle. Finally, Nahachish went to a small canyon to drink some water. He named this place Pala, from *páala* (water).

Creation stories situate Indigenous People in specific places, such as Picha Awanga or Pala. As such, Indigenous People understood themselves as People of a place. In the 1830s, Luiseño Pablo Tac called his People the Quechnájuichom, which means "inhabitants of Quechla," a town of five hundred Luiseños that sat near the San Luis Rey River. In the northern Paiute language, the term *witü* means "place." The Paiutes who lived near modern-day Bishop referred to themselves as Pitana Witü, People of the "south place."

Place and land structured how Indigenous People discussed their past. Oral traditions often began and ended at specific places. A Karuk story opens with a woman walking toward Ipputtatc, uphill from the Klamath River, to harvest wood. The story ended with the woman returning to Xavnamnihitc, her town located near modern-day Orleans. Where an oral history occurred mattered more than when the event occurred. Place names also structured songs. Chemehuevis, in southeastern California, used songs to describe and claim ownership of the land. The Salt Song Trail is a one-thousand-mile trail from the Bill Williams River to Las Vegas, Nevada. From there, one trail extends north toward Reno, Nevada, and another cuts south toward Twenty-Nine Palms and Blythe. Chemehuevi leader Matthew Leivas explains that the songs "tell about the different sacred sites on the thousand-mile journey . . . [and] the whole history of our people."

California has always been a densely populated and diverse place. Within the current boundaries of California, Indigenous People speak more than one hundred different languages, making it the most linguistically diverse area in North America. Scholars conservatively estimate at least 310,000 people lived in California's current boundaries when Spain began to establish missions in 1769, but some scholars have challenged these numbers. California's land and resources could have sustained far more than 310,000 people. Anthropologist Martin Baumhoff estimated an average annual acorn crop could have supported nearly two million people in California, although, as he and other anthropologists have noted, the enormous amount of work necessary to leach out acorns' tannic acids meant that they were a low-ranked resource. Still, there were land and resources available in California for an excess of 310,000 people. Additionally, epidemic diseases likely arrived in California before the onset of Spanish colonization in the late eighteenth century. Scholars have often used mission baptism records to extrapolate premission Indigenous populations. If, however, epidemic diseases arrived in California before the missions, those estimates could be low. California's resources and the possibility of epidemic disease convinced some scholars to estimate between seven hundred thousand and one million Indigenous People lived within the current state boundaries.

Archaeologists have identified Indigenous People's living sites throughout the current state boundaries. Quite often, Indigenous People chose to live on or near bodies of water. Between fourteen thousand and twelve thousand years ago, People fished and harvested shellfish on the Channel Islands, off the coast of Los Angeles. At roughly the same time, People hunted animals on the shore of Tulare Lake. They waited until animals, such as the enormous *bison antiquus,* bogged down in the swampy areas around the lake. The People used atlatls, hooked spear-throwers, to hurl spears equipped with Clovis points. Eight thousand years ago, as the climate warmed, People hunted dolphins in the channels off San Clemente Island. Meanwhile, People harvested grass seeds and hunted and fished on the shores of Borax Lake.

Indigenous People spread across California in densely populated settlements. At their peak, eighteen thousand to twenty thousand Chumash occupied a swath of territory from present-day Point Conception to Malibu and from the Pacific Ocean inland for about thirty miles, to modern-day Paso Robles. Chumash located their largest towns in the Goleta Slough, near present-day Santa Barbara. Chumash also lived on the Channel Islands. Approximately eight hundred Chumash lived at Helo' on Mescalitan Island. In the Sacramento and San Joaquin Valleys, Patwins clustered along the rivers that fed the valley. Patwin towns boasted populations of between twelve hundred and fourteen hundred people. The Southern California bight, a segment of the coast that stretches from Point Conception to the present-day California-Mexico border, was another densely populated area. Tongvas clustered their towns around coastal estuaries in the Los Angeles Basin, located at the center of the bight. Each community had a neck of land on the coast and a head of land in the interior. One Tongva town, of perhaps 150 people, had a village on the coast and satellite camps inland up the Palos Verdes peninsula. Tolowas occupied the town of Ta'giatun, located at modern-day Point St. George, a windswept plain near Crescent City. The town consisted of a living area, with homes and a sweathouse; a cemetery; and a workspace, where Tolowas knapped flint and made tools, butchered large mammals, such as sea lions, and cleaned fish.

As towns grew, Indigenous People established satellite communities in outlying areas. Along the rocky beach at Ta'giatun, Tolowas gathered mussels and seaweed from the rocks. In the early summer, they caught smelt in A-frame nets in the surf as the fish came toward the shore to spawn in the gravel. The smelt were dried at the beach on raised sand beds to take advantage of the sun and the salt air. When the smelt were dried, Tolowas left the coast to harvest acorns in the mountains. They stayed in the mountains, harvesting acorns and fishing for salmon until about November, at which time they returned to Ta'giatun.

Indigenous People worked with the land as they populated it. Coyote sent his five children out into the world. These children spoke five different languages and founded five rancherias, along the Salinas and Carmel Rivers. The People named their villages Ensen, Rumsen, Ekkheya, Kakonta, and Wacharon. Coyote provided the People with rabbit nets and bows and arrows to hunt rabbits. Coyote then told the People to go to the ocean to gather seaweed, abalone, and mussels to eat with acorn mush and acorn bread. In addition to acorns, Coyote instructed his children to gather grass seeds and carry them back to the rancherias in baskets. "I have shown you how to gather food," Coyote said, "and even though it rains a long time, people will not die of hunger."

As the Ensen story illustrated, Indigenous People considered acorns a vital part of their worldview. Many oral histories mention how and when Creators made oak trees and acorns. After the Maidu Earth Maker formed the world, asked the sun and moon to rise, and named the stars, he declared, "I am going to do more yet." Earth Maker created a tree on which twelve different kinds of acorns grew and planted it near the modern-day city of Durham, about eighty miles north of Sacramento. Exhausted by the enormous energy it took to create the world, Earth Maker sat down under the world's first oak tree and rested against its gray, craggy bark for two days. Cahtos, who live on Mendocino County's coast, tell that after a flood destroyed the first world, Earth Dragon came from the north and waded through the water. Tired, Earth Dragon lay in the water. Nagaicho, the Creator, traveled from Earth Dragon's head and made land on Earth Dragon's body. He turned the head into mountains, on which brush grew. People and animals appeared. Nagaicho caused seaweed, abalone, and mussels to grow in the ocean. He then planted redwoods on Earth Dragon's tail. Finally, Nagaicho made oak trees to provide the people with plenty of acorns to eat.

Acorns sustained Indigenous life. Fifteen species of oak trees, with varying productivity, grow within the current state boundaries. Acorns lack as much protein as wheat and corn, but they possess a high content of fat and vitamin B6. The high fat content enabled people to survive the lean winter months. Indigenous People stored acorns in caches made from wood and grass and placed on wooden platforms off the ground. The ability to store acorns was a boon. Indigenous People possessed a year-round food source, which allowed them to offset winter famine and balance fluctuating tree yields since acorn crops are notoriously volatile. Rain and frosts, especially in the spring, can decimate an annual crop. Tan and black oaks produce a good crop only every other year. Valley, Oregon, and blue oaks produce one good crop out of three.

Although acorns are plentiful, nutritious, and relatively nonperishable, they require a lot of work to be made edible. Work commenced in late summer. Yukis, who live in modern-day Mendocino County, called the month of August *lanl simimol* (acorn to ripe) and September *lanl hak'olimol* (acorn to wash). Indigenous communities owned specific oak groves and returned to them every year. Karuk families possessed special and defined places where they harvested acorns. To collect the seasonal bounty of acorns, men deftly climbed the trees and knocked the nuts off the limbs with sticks. Women and children spread out mats and blankets underneath the trees, picked up the acorns, and placed them in baskets. Men, women, and children carried the baskets to milling stations or bedrock mortars, large granite platforms located close to the oak trees. An experienced acorn grinder quickly took the gray cap off the acorn and cracked the brown shell with a rock pestle, revealing the nutritious meat. Women such as Pomo Elsie Allen (fig. 2) and an unidentified Paiute woman (fig. 3) used the pestle to pound the nuts into a meal. A woman could grind six pounds of acorns in about three hours. When finished, women buried their pestles and mortars to use the following season rather than carrying them home. People returned to some grinding areas so often that they made deep depressions into rock platforms, which are still visible.

At this point, people could not eat acorns. Coyote told his children at Ensen, "If the acorns are bitter, wash them." Acorns contain tannic acids that prevent the body from metabolizing protein and cause ulcerations of the mouth and intestines. These acids are especially high during

FIGURE 2. Elsie Allen pounding acorns into flour. Photo courtesy Sonoma County Library.

autumn. Over time, Indigenous People learned which trees possessed the largest and sweetest acorns; these required the least work to process. Oral histories explained how and why acorns possessed different traits. A long time ago, a Creator figure told the Acorn women to prepare to travel to the world. The Creator told the women to weave hats for their trip. Black Oak Acorn did not finish her hat. Tan Oak Acorn finished a hat but did not clean it. Maul Oak Acorn and Post Oak Acorn finished and cleaned their hats. The women fell from the sky onto Karuk land. Tan Oak Acorn expressed jealousy toward Post Oak Acorn and Maul Oak Acorn because they made nice hats. Tan Oak Acorn wished bad luck on her two rivals. Therefore, Post Oak Acorn and Maul Oak Acorn do not taste good, and the soups produced from them are black.

To make acorns palatable, women placed the acorn flour into a shallow pit and poured water over it to leach the bitter tannic acid. The

FIGURE 3. Paiute woman sitting on a small wooden crate grinding acorns on a metate stone in Yosemite, ca. 1900. Created by C. C. Pierce. Photo courtesy USC Digital Library. California Historical Society Collection.

process took less time if the water was hot, making hot springs ideal places to process acorns. Given that springs tended to bubble up amid rocks that could be used as bedrock mortars, the tools and harvesting sites for acorns placed Indigenous People in specific locations. Acorns from black oaks, which are among the most toxic varieties, require four to six hours of leaching. After the harvesting, pounding, and leaching, the acorns were ready to eat. Women baked acorn flour into bread or boiled it into a soup by placing water and acorn flour in watertight baskets and dropping in hot rocks.

Place-names reinforced Indigenous Peoples' ties to land, work, and acorns. Indigenous People named their landscapes after the work related to harvesting, pounding, and leaching acorns. Pomos called an acorn-gathering place near modern-day Ukiah *kca'kaleyō*, which translates as "under white oak tree." They also named an old town on Tule Lake *xaro'* or *xaro'malūgal*, which means "to bake valley oak acorn black bread homeward." Yukis called the area where they leached acorns *mamol sismol* (acorn soaking).

Acorn mush and bread served several roles in Indigenous Peoples' societies. Certainly, People ate acorns. They also considered acorns a symbol of an Indigenous woman's productivity. According to a Gashowu Yokuts story, Hawk gave acorn mush to Wolf and Coyote. She told the two men that if their children wanted more, they need only ask her. Thus, Hawk demonstrated that she could provide for other people and possessed the industriousness, or work ethic, to sustain a large population. Acorn mush also connected People in marriage. According to a Yauelumni Yokuts story, Prairie Falcon lost a gambling match to Coyote and Rabbit. After he left the match, Prairie Falcon traveled to a house in which an old woman and a young girl lived. The old woman served Prairie Falcon some acorn mush and fish. Then the young girl and Prairie Falcon married. Here the exchange of acorn mush sanctified the relationship between the two Peoples.

Man-made fires shaped the land and increased the productivity of acorns. Indigenous People told many stories about how their ancestors acquired this essential tool. Concows (also spelled Konkows) say that the Ancient People, led by Mouse, teamed up and stole fire from Eagle, who kept it hidden on Mount Lassen. The Pohonichi Miwok tell a similar story about acquiring fire. All the world was cold because Turtle lay on top of fire in his home in the Sierra Nevada. Coyote traveled to Turtle's home and disguised himself to look like a stick of wood. Someone put Coyote into the fire underneath Turtle. Coyote grabbed a burning stick and ran down the hill and gave the fire to his People.

Indigenous People built fires underneath oak trees to stunt the growth of weeds and limbs close to the ground. This type of burning made it easier for families to harvest acorns that had been knocked to the ground. Fires also promoted the growth of straight but pliable oak shoots and deer grass, materials Indigenous women used to make baskets. Fires controlled insects that might blight a year's crop. Burns took care of weevils and worms that feasted on decomposing acorns. Burning stimulated the growth of food near oak trees. Black morel mushrooms, for instance, thrive in black oak forests that have been burned. Burned-over landscapes were also easier to travel, to hunt on, and to see enemies approaching. Thus, Indigenous People worked with the land to ensure its productivity. They selectively burned the land to ensure oak tree growth, ease of harvesting acorns, and travel.

Although acorns are important, Indigenous People engaged in an array of economic activities. In the seemingly barren Mojave Desert,

Paiutes developed irrigation systems to grow food. At Pitana Patü, near the modern-day town of Bishop in eastern California's Owens Valley, Paiutes used irrigation ditches to increase the growth of plants, such as *nä'hävīta* (spike rush). In the spring, the town headman announced the beginning of the irrigation season, usually when snow runoff from the southern Sierra Nevadas caused creeks to rise. Residents of Pitana Patü then elected a *tuvaijü'u* (irrigator) to lead twenty-five men in building a dam out of rocks, brush, sticks, and mud. After people completed the dam, the tuvaijü'u directed the water into the ditch, which fed northern and southern fields in alternate years. Along the Colorado River, Cocopahs practiced floodplain agriculture, utilizing the natural annual cycles of rainfall and drought. In April, Cocopahs cleared their fields in anticipation of the late spring and early summer flooding. Snowmelt from the Rocky Mountains engorged the Colorado River, which overflowed its banks as it passed through Cocopah territory. After the River receded, Cocopahs planted their gardens of corn, beans, and squash. Men dug holes, into which women put seeds, which they then covered with dirt. They planted corn in one field and beans and pumpkins in another. In August and September, Cocopahs weeded their fields. In October, women picked and husked the corn, and men and boys carried the food into camp, where Cocopahs stored their agricultural surplus.

Indigenous People supplemented acorns and agricultural crops with the hunting of deer, elk, and sheep inland and sea mammals along the coast. In an Eastern Pomo creation story, an old man taught other men to hunt. The old man selected four men and told the others, "These men will take care of you. What I am teaching you, you must not forget!" The old man taught the four men to make arrows from sticks and flint. He then went hunting with the four men, all the while singing a Deer Song. After killing a deer, the old man instructed the four men, "Watch and learn! That's the way to skin. You will hunt deer for this village." As the Pomo creation story pointed out, Pomos considered hunting a communal enterprise. An elderly hunter remained in the town while his young protégé hunted for deer. The elderly man sang deer songs, hoping for a successful hunt. If the songs worked, and the young man killed a deer, the young man gave choice cuts to his mentor.

The evidence of hunting, in the form of stone spear- and arrowpoints, is spread throughout California. At Tulare Lake, archaeologists have found Clovis points—thin, fluted projectile points that could be eight inches long and date to about eleven thousand years ago. At Borax Lake, located in Lake County, archaeologists unearthed concave-based points without fluting, along with manos, metates, and other implements used to grind grass seeds. These artifacts date to about five thousand years ago.

Acorns, animals, and agricultural crops needed more than human work to make them productive. The land also needed supernatural forces to intercede. Indigenous People developed ceremonial cycles to ensure productive acorn harvests and maintain balance in their worlds. Yukis held two ceremonies that ensured a good acorn harvest for that year and in the future. First, they hosted a *hamnam wok,* a girl's coming-of-age ceremony. The three-part ceremony featured community singing and dancing after a girl came of age. After the second part of the ceremony, women brought baskets and prepared acorns to make into soup or bread for a feast. Yukis also hosted a *lanl hanp,* or "acorn sing," a biannual four-day ceremony. A head singer invited people to the round-house, where Yukis sang acorn songs and danced in a way that imitated the work of gathering and preparing acorns.

Indigenous Peoples' ceremonial cycles exhibit a close relationship among all aspects of the world. Humans, animals, and the land are alive, and all possess human characteristics. Mojave Robert Martin described how he created a cradleboard for an infant. He began by singing a song: "I am going to make a baby cradle now. I go, I go, I look for mesquite root, mesquite root. I dig anywhere up in the valley and I'll stay until I get one, if I'm lucky, if the tree gives it to [me]." To find the proper materials to make a cradleboard, Martin ensured that the tree would give the materials to him. Maintaining the relationship between the person and the tree (or animals when hunting or acorns when harvesting) required proper protocols.

Indigenous People developed procedures to take care of the land. For instance, Southern Sierra Miwoks harvested a variety of bulb plants, such as brodiaea, lilies, and onions, often referred to as "Indian potatoes." Miwoks uprooted the plants with digging sticks. Miniature bulbs, called "babies," clung to the plant's roots. Miwoks removed the babies from their mother and replanted them in the churned and aerated soil. Miwoks understood the relationship between the bulbs in kinship terms; the main plant was the mother, and its babies clung to the root system. Miwoks also understood that they played a role in the plant's reproduction and health. A Miwok woman recalled how "she would leave the babies behind to make more."

Across California, Native People developed three distinct religious traditions to ensure the proper balance among humans, plants, and animals.

In northwestern California, Native People, such as the Hupa and Yurok, practice world-renewal religions. Hupas call the ceremonies the White Deerskin, Jump, and Women's Coming of Age, and, collectively, they restore order to the world. Host communities invited people from across the region to participate in the annual ceremonies. Hupas and Yuroks continue to practice these ceremonies because it is their obligation to restore order to the world. In April of 2020, during the COVID-19 pandemic, the Yurok Nation held a small, socially distant Jump Dance to restore balance to an upset world.

In central and Northern California, Native People participate in forms of the Kuksu religion, named after an Eastern Pomo deity. Male and female religious leaders learned to lead these ceremonies through elaborate religious societies. As with the world renewal ceremonies to the north, host communities invited neighbors to participate in ceremonies, which featured the exchange of gifts between hosts and guests. In ceremonies, people imitated a deity, such as Kuksu. These ceremonies ensured productive acorn harvests or healed the sick. Northern Maidu Marie Potts described the Bear Dance, an aspect of the Kuksu religion. Maidus held the ceremony several times throughout the spring, when green shoots emerged from the ground. Maidus held the Bear Dance to give thanks for surviving the winter and to ensure that Bear and Rattlesnake, who were also emerging from their winter hibernation, looked favorably on the People. Maidu women sent out strings with knots tied on them to their neighbors, with each knot representing the number of days until the dance began. Invited guests brought food and items for gifts or trade. Host families provided meals consisting of acorn bread, acorn soup, seeds, and meat. The Bear Dance began after an evening meal. Potts said, "One person was designated to wear a bearskin and imitate a bear. He smelled and scratched the ground, pretending to look for food as he was a very hungry bear after hibernating all winter." At the end of the ceremony, the bear led the People down to a stream, where everyone washed their faces, symbolizing that they had washed away the bad feelings from the previous year and were ready to begin a new one with "love and friendship for all." Today, Maidus hold a Bear Dance on United States Forest Service land outside of Susanville.

To the south, Indigenous People participate in a ceremonial cycle that Luiseños call Chinigchinich, named after their Creator figure. As with the Kuksu religion, Indigenous People learned how to lead and practice the religion through societies. Among Chumash, boys consumed a tea infused with *datura* (jimsonweed), which tribal elders administered to young boys as part of a coming-of-age ceremony. After drinking the tea, the boys spent days fasting and seeking visions. The ceremonial system, which comprised many other ceremonies as well, ensured productive hunting in the future, as well as healing. An annual mourning ceremony initiated the yearly cycle of dances, feasts, and religious practices. Indigenous People continue to practice the Chinigchinich religion. Luiseños on the Rincon and Pauma Reservation participate in the ceremonial cycle.

Ceremonial cycles connected the People to the land and to each other. Oral traditions and oral histories explained how Creators taught the People how to live with one another. Nahachish brought the People to Quechla, situated on the San Luis Rey River. There, Nahachish identified places for the People to live so that everyone had access to food and water. He divided the People into clans, led by a hereditary headman called a *not*. Each not cared for a ceremonial bundle, signifying his relationship with the Creator. The not mediated disputes within the community, directed ceremonies, and acted as the town's liaison with outsiders. If the not developed good relationships with outsiders, he oversaw trade with them. If relations soured with their neighbors, the not led the People into battle. Luiseños understand the not's duties as original to creation and that they were not a People until Nahachish established the not's duties in that place.

Women and men who demonstrated their capacity for leadership by balancing internal and external social relationships led Indigenous towns. At creation, Marumda picked one man to serve as the Pomo's "Head-Chief." He exhorted the Pomo to be good people and follow the law, or the world would be destroyed. Chiefs, "Big Men," or nots possessed skills or knowledge that enabled them to act as good providers. Patwin leaders determined the timing and location of fishing weirs, used to harvest salmon during their annual spawning runs up the Sacramento River. Pomo men, meanwhile, collectively owned large fishing nets and distributed fish among the owners. Yuki chiefs possessed the ability to eloquently speak in public. Community elders chose a young man, renowned for his speaking ability, to groom as a chief. When the older chief died, the younger man assumed the role. Yuki chiefs mediated disputes in their towns. Men and women carried their status into the afterlife. Followers buried prominent men and women with luxury items, such as obsidian and shell beads. Among the Chumash, the brotherhood of the *tomol* (canoe) learned the skills and knowledge needed to create seagoing canoes. They used these canoes to sail from the mainland to the islands out in the Pacific Ocean to trade.

Town leaders created productive relationships with their neighbors. People traded raw materials for use as hunting implements or in craft design for goods they could not find in their own territories. Throughout the state, Indigenous People desired obsidian, a black or red volcanic glass used to make blades and arrowpoints. Obsidian from the Coso Mountain Range, south of Owens Valley, traveled along trade routes, which ran east to west and south to north, resembling in some ways the modern interstate system that connects California to the rest of North America. Indigenous People acquired these items via down-the-line trade. In other words, obsidian passed through many hands before reaching the destinations where archaeologists find it. Archaeological sites on San Nicholas Island contain obsidian from the Coso Range, chert from around present-day Monterey, soapstone from Santa Catalina Island, and fused shale from Happy Camp Canyon, north of modern-day Simi Valley. People who lived at a town near the mouth of Big Sur River acquired obsidian from the Coso Range; Casa Diablo, in eastern California; and Glass Mountain, in Napa County. The People exported sea otter pelts to their neighbors in order to acquire obsidian. In modern-day Napa County, Native People carried mollusk shell beads and obsidian between the San Francisco Bay and the Sacramento River Delta. Yokuts, who lived near Tulare Lake, acted as intermediaries in the obsidian trade. Yokuts acquired obsidian from Indigenous People living near a deposit at Coso Peak. Yokuts kept some of the obsidian to make blades, sometimes used in ceremonies. Yokuts also traveled to the coast and traded the obsidian for shell trade beads.

White shell beads functioned as a form of currency. Chumash and Pomos produced rounded, white shell beads. Chumash living on coastal islands exchanged the shell beads with mainland Chumash for food, bows and arrows, and baskets. Mainland Chumash then traded the beads to other People. Yokuts, for instance, arrived on the coast on yearly trade expeditions and took the currency to the Central Valley. Yokuts moved the beads inland on the same trails that brought obsidian from the east. Archaeologists found Chumash-made beads across the Southwest and Great Basin, and as far north as Oregon.

Marriage connected people across the region. Northern Maidu Marie Potts put it rather bluntly when speaking about her grandfather: "When a young man in our tribe needed a wife, he would often go over to the Hat Creek tribe, which lived on the north side of Mount Lassen, and bring back a young woman." Some Indigenous People married their immediate, linguistically related neighbors. Leaders married people from neighboring towns to create trade ties or acquire economic resources. Along the Sacramento River and its tributaries, Wintu men married Achumawi, Atsugewi, and Chimariko women. By marrying Chimariko women, who lived in towns situated along the Trinity River, Wintus gained access to new fishing and acorn harvesting sites. They shared their fishing equipment and skills with their new Chimariko families, enhancing everyone's ability to extract resources from the land. Marriages expanded territories by linking towns across California and establishing relationships that benefited everyone.

At other times Indigenous People did not get along with their neighbors. The growing size and density of Indigenous Peoples' towns sometimes led to conflict. In the San Francisco Bay area, cemeteries contain bodies with arrow wounds, suggesting increased conflict between Peoples. As populations grew, People expanded the areas in which they harvested acorns. Warfare often followed a common formula. For example, Kumeyaay sang "bad" songs, or songs about enemies, which named their dead, mocked their physical appearance, and claimed they were poor providers. Designed to provoke, the songs usually did. Generally limited in scope and purpose, some oral traditions document warfare, massacres, and other atrocities. It is unclear if these occurred before the arrival of Europeans or were postinvasion stories.

Indigenous People raided other groups and took captives. Hupa Minnie Reeves told a story of a young "handsome" man who attended a Brush Dance at Medildiñ: "Though there was no open warfare with the Mill Creeks [Yahi], they would sneak into our camps when the men were gone and kill or carry off the helpless ones." At the end of the dance, the man stole a girl and ran off with her. He took her to his home, and she eventually gave birth to a child. But the man did not trust his captive to stay at home and took her hunting. He owned a *na'wehch* (Jump Dance basket) that he pointed and wiggled at deer, after which they would die. One time he carelessly left the na'wehch on the ground after killing a deer. The woman picked up the basket, pointed it at the man and wiggled it. The basket did not kill the man immediately because he did not look at it. That night, however, the man complained of a head ache and died the next morning. The woman took the man's great wealth, which he had stolen from many People, and returned to Medildiñ.

Creators put Indigenous People in specific places, creating them as the People of that place. As such, Indigenous People tended the natural world to produce food, tools, and to strengthen their communities into increasingly complex towns. Towns, in turn, altered the political, economic, and cultural elements of Indigenous Peoples' lives, leading to increased specialization and even more complex systems of political organization and resource use. Towns tightened the ties to the land and connections with other towns through extensive trade networks. Indigenous oral stories recount the tension between persistence and change. Communities stretched, split, fused, and adapted. They came together for various reasons and shared languages, culture, and even kin. But they were independent. For the most part California looked like the sky, as many villages as stars, organized into constellations.

SOURCES

This chapter combines oral histories with archaeological and anthropological evidence to interpret the long history of Indigenous People in California. For an example of how one can use oral histories and oral traditions to narrate California history, see William J. Bauer Jr., "The Giant and the Waterbaby: Paiute Oral Traditions and the Owens Valley Water Wars," *Boom* 4 (Winter 2012): 104–17; and William J. Bauer Jr., *California through Native Eyes: Reclaiming History* (Seattle: University of Washington Press, 2016).

In the early twentieth century, anthropologists collected many of the oral histories and traditions used in this chapter. They did so to preserve what they considered a vanishing culture and people. They often looked for common traits in the stories to identify and categorize "California" cultural groups. Although oral histories were collected within colonial and exploitative frameworks, Indigenous storytellers shaped and molded the production of knowledge. For instance, they chose the stories they wanted to share with anthropologists. See, e.g., how Cutcha Risling Baldy discusses Hupas and sharing cultural knowledge with anthropologists in *We Are Dancing for You: Native Feminisms and the Revitalization of Women's Coming-of-Age Ceremonies* (Seattle: University of Washington Press, 2018).

Readers can find the oral histories and oral traditions used in this chapter in several edited collections and anthropological articles: Herbert W. Luthin, ed., *Surviving through the Days: Translations of Native California Stories and Songs* (Berkeley: University of California Press, 2002), which contains the Eastern Pomo Deer Song (288–89), the story of Robert Martin's cradleboard (524), and the story of Minnie Reeves and the *na'wehch* (112–13); William McCawley, *The First Angelinos:*

The Gabrielino Indians of Los Angeles (Banning, CA: Malki Museum Press, 1996); Malcolm Margolin, *The Way We Lived: California Indian Reminiscences, Stories and Songs* (Berkeley, CA: Heyday, 1981); Marie Potts, *The Northern Maidu* (Happy Camp, CA: Naturegraph, 1977, 2007), which contains the stories of Mill Creek captive taking (5–7) and the Bear Dance (29–33); John P. Harrington, *Karuk Indian Myths* (Washington, DC: Government Printing Office, 1932), which contains the story of Karuk Acorn Women (6); Edward Gifford and Gwendoline Harris Block, *California Indian Nights Entertainment* (Glendale, CA: Arthur H. Clark, 1930), from which the Maidu Earth Maker story (85–87) and the Cahto story of Earth Dragon (79–82) come. The story of Nahachish can be found in Constance Goddard Dubois, "The Religion of the Luiseño Indians of Southern California," *University of California Publications in American Archaeology and Ethnology* 8, no. 3 (1908): 151–52. In Alfred Kroeber, "Indian Myths of South Central California," *University of California Publications in American Archaeology and Ethnology* 4, no. 4 (1906), the Ensen Coyote story can be found on pages 200–201. The Gashowu Yokuts story of Hawk, Coyote, and Wolf can be found on pages 205–6. The Yauelumni Yokuts story of Prairie Falcon comes from pages 240–41. The Miwok story of Turtle, Coyote, and Fire can be found on pages 202–3.

For the historical and contemporary importance of Chemehuevi Salt Songs, and the quotation by Matthew Leivas, see Beth Rose Middleton, *Trust in the Land: New Directions in Tribal Conservation* (Tucson: University of Arizona Press, 2011); and Clifford Trafzer, *A Chemehuevi Song: The Resilience of a Southern Paiute People* (Seattle: University of Washington Press, 2015), 30.

Throughout the twentieth century, scholars debated the size of the Indigenous population of California. For an overview of this discussion, with citations to key works, see Albert Hurtado, "California Indian Demography, Sherburne F. Cook, and the Revision of American History," *Pacific Historical Review* 58 (August 1989): 323–43. Russell Thornton upwardly revised Indigenous California populations to seven hundred thousand in *American Indian Holocaust and Survival: A Population History since 1492* (Norman: University of Oklahoma Press, 1990). Writer and poet Deborah Miranda is a proponent of upwardly revising the number of Indigenous People in California to near one million. See her *Bad Indians: A Tribal Memoir* (Berkeley, CA: Heyday, 2013); and "Extermination of the *Joyas*: Gendercide in Spanish California," *GLQ: A Journal of Lesbian and Gay Studies* 16, no. 1–2 (2010): 253–84.

Several anthropological and archaeological surveys informed this chapter. See Lynn Gamble, *The Chumash World at European Contact: Power, Trade, and Feasting among Complex Hunter-Gatherers* (Berkeley: University of California Press, 2008); Brian Fagan, *Before California: An Archaeologist Looks at Our Earliest Inhabitants* (Walnut Creek, CA: AltaMira Press, 2003); Brian Dillon, *Archaeological Investigations at CA-TUL-1613, the Creighton Ranch Site, Tulare County, California,* edited by Judith Porcasi (Redondo Beach, CA: Tulare Lake Archaeological Research Group, 2000); Jeffrey Altschul and Donn Grenda, eds., *Islanders and Mainlanders: Prehistoric Context for the Southern California Bight* (Tucson, AZ: SRI Press, 2002); Christopher Chase-Dunn and Kelly Mann, *The Wintu and Their Neighbors: A Very Small World-System in Northern California* (Tucson: University of Arizona Press, 1997); Terry L. Jones, "Mortars, Pestles, and Division of Labor in Prehistoric California: A View from Big Sur," *American Antiquity* 61 (April 1996): 432–64; William J. Wallace and Francis A. Riddell, eds., *Contributions to Tulare Lake Archaeology I: Background to a Study of Tulare Lake's Archaeological Past* (Redondo Beach, CA: Tulare Lake Archaeological Research Group, 1991); Mark E. Basgall, "Resource Intensification among Hunter-Gatherers: Acorn Economies in Prehistoric California," in *Research in Economic Anthropology,* edited by Barry Isaac, vol. 9 (Greenwich, CT: JAI Press, 1987); Clement Meighan and C. Vance Haynes, "The Borax Lake Site Revisited," *Science* 167, no. 3922 (1970): 1213–21; Clement Meighan and C. Vance Haynes, "New Studies on the Age of the Borax Lake Site," *Masterkey* 42, no. 1 (1968): 4–9; Richard A. Gould, *Archaeology of the Point St. George Site and Tolowa Prehistory* (Berkeley: University of California Press, 1966); Mark Raymond Harrington, "An Ancient Site at Borax Lake, California," *Southwest Museum Papers,* no. 16 (Jan. 1948): vii–131.

For Pomo and Yuki place-names see Samuel A. Barrett, *The Ethnogeography of the Pomo and Neighboring Indians* (Berkeley, CA: University Press, 1908), 154, 155. The discussion of two Yuki ceremonies is based on George M. Foster, "Summary of Yuki Culture," *University of California Publications in Anthropological Records* 5 (1900–1947): 185–93. For the qualities in Yuki leaders see Virginia Peek Miller, "The Changing Role of the Chief on a California Indian Reservation," *American Indian Quarterly* 13 (Autumn 1989): 447–55.

M. Kat Anderson provides a compelling study of Indigenous land-use patterns in *Tending the Wild: Native American Knowledge and the Management of California's Natural Resources* (Berkeley: University of

California Press, 2005); the Miwok description of leaving the baby tubers behind comes from pages 297–99. For irrigation and floodplain agriculture see the helpful discussions in Julian Steward, "Ethnography of the Owens Valley Paiute," *University of California Publications in American Archaeology and Ethnology* 33, no. 3 (1933): 247–50; and William H. Kelly, *Cocopa Ethnography* (Tucson: University of Arizona Press, 1977), 30–32.

A succinct discussion of Indigenous People's ceremonial cycles is found in Lowell John Bean and Sylvia Brakke Vane, "Cults and Their Transformations," in *Handbook of North American Indians: California,* edited by Robert Heizer, vol. 8 (Washington, DC: Smithsonian Institute Press, 1977), 663–65. Readers should be careful with this text, as it refers to Indigenous religions as "cults."

Native Spaces

Yuma

The name *Yuma* comes from the O'odham word *yu:mi* and refers to the people we now call the Quechan (Kwtsaan). Yuma, Arizona, sits across the Colorado River from Winterhaven, California, just south of the confluence of the Colorado and Gila Rivers. Both flood-prone rivers drain vast arid landscapes and concentrate the silt of erosion in their floodplains. As such, the rivers are vital corridors of life, sustaining agriculture in a region otherwise inhospitable to it. For thousands of years, Cocopah and Quechan living along the river have engaged in floodplain agriculture, meticulously planting seeds in the rich soil deposited after seasonal floods, tending the plants that emerged, and harvesting them before the floods returned.

Geology has defined Yuma in other ways. The present-day city meets the Colorado River on the north at a point where the river bisects two pronounced granite outcrops. The narrows provide the best crossing in the lower Colorado River and therefore made Yuma a critical juncture for travel throughout the region. In addition to the Quechan and Cocopah, various indigenous communities sought to control the crossing: Kohuana, Halyikwamai, Halchidhomas, A-ha-yes, and Hamakhavas. In the sixteenth century, Spanish colonists tried to do the same. In 1540, Hernando de Alarcón encountered Cocopahs as he sailed up the river, attempting to connect with Francisco Vázquez de Coronado's expedition ranging across present-day Arizona and New Mexico. Nearly 250 years later, in 1774, Juan Bautista de Anza met the Quechans there on his first exploratory expedition to blaze a trail to California. The trail that came to bear his name carried sporadic traffic as the only effective crossing point to Southern California from the east.

The river crossing brought all travelers across the region through the narrow passage. The Spanish recognized the crossing's strategic benefit and established a permanent settlement on a hill on the north (now California) side of the river. But Spanish livestock interfered with Quechan agriculture, and Spanish Catholicism obstructed Quechan cultural practices. In the summer of 1781, the Quechan, with Mojave allies, attacked and killed Spanish settlers. Until 1852, Quechans retained control over the critical river crossing, closing it periodically to frustrate Spanish, Mexican, and American imperialist efforts.

Beginning with the Mexican War (1846–48), Americans challenged Quechan control over the Colorado River crossing. The subsequent Treaty of Guadalupe Hidalgo ceded the region to the United States on paper, and federal surveyors established a ferry-crossing operation as part of their surveying for the international boundary. Cave Johnson Couts led a detachment of the First US Dragoons in establishing a fort on the eastern side of the river. The fort became the end point of the Gila Trail from Santa Fe through Tucson. With the onset of the Gold Rush, and the flood in traffic to the gold fields along the trail, a frustrated miner who saw his chance to make an easy fortune picked up the abandoned ferry crossing. He soon fell in with the infamous scalp-hunting John Glanton gang, which terrorized the US-Mexico borderlands. Glanton took over the operations; kidnapped, raped, and extorted travelers; and eventually attacked the Quechan ferrying operations, which competed with him. In 1850, Caballo en Pello, a Quechan leader, led an attack on Glanton, killing him and ten others. Both the US Army and California militia shifted the blame from the Glanton gang to the Quechans and punished them for what they perceived as unprovoked attacks on innocent travelers.

The Quechans resisted the attacks by the California militia, forcing the hand of the federal government. In response, the United States established Fort Yuma atop the outcrop on the California side of the river in 1851 to bring the region more firmly under US control (see fig. 4). Fighting continued throughout 1852. The presence of the fort led to the growth of the American settlement there. Gold Rush travelers, the Butterfield Stage line, and the railroad utilized the crossing to connect the growing city to Los Angeles and San Diego to the west; Santa Fe, New Mexico, to the east; and Mexico to the south.

FIGURE 4. Drawing of Fort Yuma on the Colorado River, ca. 1850. Photo courtesy
USC Digital Library. California Historical Society Collection.

American settlement challenged the Quechans' grasp on the agricultural potential of the floodplain, and state and international boundaries
divided Quechan territory. In the twentieth century, the development of
Colorado River water for use in the Imperial Valley, and the militariza-
tion of the border during and after the Mexican Revolution, increasingly
marginalized and divided Quechans and others. The All-American Canal
runs diagonally through the center of the Fort Yuma Indian Reservation,
delivering water from the Colorado River to the Imperial Valley.

Agriculture, the military, and transportation still dominate the region.
Today, satellite images show clearly the green and brown checkerboard
of irrigated agriculture that occupies the historic floodplain. Rather than
relying on natural cycles of seasonal flooding, agriculture now occurs
year-round through irrigation, part of a massive, region-wide irrigation
network that has siphoned off the flow of the Colorado such that it no
longer flows to the sea. Northeast of the city is the Yuma Proving Ground,
one of the largest military bases in the nation and one of the largest
employers in the region. Interstate 8, the main thoroughfare between Tucson and San Diego, roughly follows the course of the Gila Trail.

Yet Quechan people retain control over the places around Yuma.
Capitalizing on the thousands of travelers passing through the region,

the Quechan opened the Paradise Casino on the Fort Yuma Indian Reservation, just up the road from the site of the first Spanish settlement. The Cocopah opened the Cocopah Casino just south of Yuma. The former Fort Yuma is now the site of the Fort Yuma Indian Hospital, operated by the Bureau of Indian Affairs for the benefit of the Quechans living on the reservation. The Quechan of the Fort Yuma Reservation, along with Cocopah, Mojave, Chemehuevi, and Colorado River Indian Tribes, are members of the Colorado River Basin Tribal Partnership, also called the Ten Tribes Partnership, and possess significant reserved water rights on the Colorado River, making them vital and powerful stakeholders in the region's future.

SOURCES

On the name of Yuma, see Victor Golla, *California Indian Languages* (Berkeley: University of California Press, 2011), 125. For other theories, see James M. Crawford, *Cocopa Dictionary* (Berkeley: University of California Press, 1989), 383. For Quechan efforts to control the river crossing, and resist Spanish incursions, see Florence C. Shipek, "A Native American Adaptation to Drought: The Kumeyaay as Seen in the San Diego Mission Records, 1770–1798," *Ethnohistory* 28 (Autumn 1981): 295–312; and Jack D. Forbes, "The Development of the Yuma Route before 1846," *California Historical Society Quarterly* 43 (June 1964): 99–118. For the context of Caballo en Pelo's attack on Glanton, see Brendan Lindsay, *Murder State: California's Native American Genocide, 1846–1873* (Lincoln: University of Nebraska Press, 2012), 139–42.

2

Beach Encounters

Indigenous People and the Age of
Exploration, 1540–1769

About a dozen People of the River, currently known as Cocopahs, lounged in the shade of their houses on the banks of Red Water, what the Spanish called the Colorado River. A month previous, the People of the River returned to Red Water to fish, farm, and harvest plants. Although still rushing toward the gulf at a fantastic rate, Red Water receded from its midsummer heights, leaving a fertile swath of land on which to plant corn, beans, and melons. By midmorning, men returned from Red Water with salmon. Women and children harvested mesquite beans and weeded their fields. A woman busily separated mesquite beans from their long, green fibrous pods; she hoped to complete this tedious task and make flour before the heat made the work unbearable. She looked up to see two boats coming from *mat chinanap* (downstream), struggling against Red Water's current. The woman pointed at the vessels, and the People of the River rushed to the shore. They yelled to the strangers on the boats to return to the gulf. The currents, everyone knew, were too strong at this time of the year to continue. As the boats neared, the People of the River noticed that no women or children traveled with the strangers.

The People of the River sprang into action. They heard of similar parties of men from their neighbors. The previous year, people from *inyaxsabah* (sun rising; i.e., east) killed a dark man. Other strangers had used sharp weapons to murder People mat chinanap. The men attempting to sail up Red Water might be related to those who brought violence and disease to their neighbors' lands. A couple raced to find the *shapai axany* (headman), who had already moved into the shade for the hot midday hours. Women hurried to their homes, grabbed as much food as possible, and fled toward the hills. Men picked up their bows and assembled on Red Water's beach. They looked warily as one of the boats, bobbing and fighting the currents, moved to the middle of Red Water and dropped anchor. A man in the boat began to speak, but the People of the River did not understand him. Another man disembarked and walked toward shore. The People of the River put stakes in the river to block the stranger's path to the beach. The People of the River had already planted a year's supply of food; they could not surrender this precious resource. A man approached the People of the River and handed over some beads. Different from the flat, round, white beads that the People of the River acquired from the people who lived *inyahap* (sun setting; i.e., west), these new beads were long, tubular, and blue, like the color of the stones that came from inyaxsabah.

The shapai axany arrived, carrying a staff adorned with shells from inyahap. Since the newcomers gave gifts to the People, the shapai axany handed his staff to the stranger. The invader lurched forward and embraced the shapai axany. Startled by the odd act of what seemed to be affection, the shapai axany patted the man on the back and separated himself. These newcomers, the People of the River reasoned, did not appear violent. Instead, they offered new goods that might be useful in trade with the People of the River's neighbors. Perhaps the newcomers should not continue their ascent of Red Water.

In the 1540s, Indigenous People, such as the People of the River in this historical reconstruction of their meeting with the Hernando de Alarcón expedition, encountered Europeans for the first time. Spanish explorers arrived from the south, either sailing up the Gulf of California or along the Pacific coast. Others arrived overland from Sinaloa or Arizona. Because of California's geography and Native Peoples' marine knowledge and skill, these encounters first took place on water spaces, such as the turbulent Red Water or the Pacific Ocean. Indigenous People and Europeans fit each other into their own understandings of human beings and the world. Sometimes, Indigenous People and Europeans misunderstood and mis-communicated with each other. At other times, Indigenous People and Europeans created peaceful relationships with one another, most often by exchanging goods. Throughout these encounters, Spanish and English sailors relied on Indigenous People's knowledge, resources, and labor to continue their journeys. For much of the sixteenth, seventeenth, and eighteenth centuries, Indigenous Californians lived in this new world largely without Europeans, who were merely sojourners, struggling against California's many waterways, as the People watched from the shore. Still, these encounters created a new world for everyone involved. Europeans, especially the Spanish, left behind harbingers of colonization in the eighteenth century: people, germs, trade goods, and Christian symbols.

Stories of first contact are popular in American history. They function as creation stories for the United States. Historians have used the stories of Juan Rodriguez Cabrillo, Sir Francis Drake, and, later, Junípero Serra to tell about the arrival of civilization in California. In early histories of California, writers depicted California Indians as cowering in front of the first Europeans that they encountered. In 1927, popular novelist Gertrude Atherton imagined the arrival of Franciscan priests in Southern California. Spanish soldiers and priests waded ashore at modern-day San Diego and held the first mass in California. "The Indians, who were hidden behind every rock," Atherton wrote, "ignored the invitation [to participate in mass], but felt sufficient awe of the impressive ceremonies to remain passive." Stories such as this one characterized Indigenous People as childlike, primitive, and docile and depicted them as waiting for the arrival of Europeans. Europeans and Americans repeated these myths to justify missionary efforts and colonization. In reality, Indigenous People rarely responded to Europeans out of fear; instead, Indigenous People demonstrated they knew about Europeans before they arrived.

Time and again, Indigenous People reached out to Spanish and English sailors who arrived on their shores and invited them to their communities. On October 7, 1542, Tongvas from the town of Nájquqar, located on the island of Pimunga (currently Santa Catalina Island), saw Spanish ships on the sea. Ten Tongvas boarded a tomol and rowed out to meet the Spanish, led by Juan Rodriguez Cabrillo. Antonio de Mendoza, the viceroy of New Spain, dispatched Cabrillo to explore the Pacific coast and look for trade opportunities or a route to China. The Tongvas and Spanish exchanged "beads and other articles," and the Tongvas escorted the Spanish to the island. Three days later, a fleet of Chumash tomols, carrying twelve or thirteen people each, left Muwu, a town near modern-day Oxnard, and sailed out to meet the Spanish. The Spanish gave "presents" to the Chumash, who brought the newcomers ashore. At the time, between three hundred and six hundred Chumash lived at Muwu. Cabrillo described their houses as "large like those of New Spain."

Indigenous People continued to engage with European sailors and explorers throughout the sixteenth century. On June 18, 1579, a Coast

FIGURE 5. Chumash tomol 'Elye'wun paddlers crossing at Santa Cruz Island, California, 2006. Photo courtesy of Robert Schwemmer. Licensed under Creative Commons Attribution 2.0 Generic (CC BY 2.0).

Miwok leader led a canoe out to meet the English captain Francis Drake, when he set his fleet in what later came to be called Drake's Bay. Queen Elizabeth I dispatched Drake, little more than an English pirate, to the Pacific Ocean to raid Spanish ships carrying gold. The Coast Miwok leader delivered a speech and gave to Drake "a bunch of feathers, much like the feathers of a blacke crow, very neatly and artificially gathered upon a string, and drawne together into a round bundle" and "a little basket made of rushes, and filled with an herb which they called Tabah." Drake reciprocated by giving the Coast Miwok leader a hat. In 1602, the viceroy of New Spain sent Sebastián Vizcaíno to explore the Pacific coast for safe harbors in which Spanish ships could dock as they traveled between Manila and Acapulco. On November 27, Tongvas from Pimunga again rowed tomols, made of "cedar and pine . . . planks very well joined and calked, . . . with eight oars and fourteen or fifteen Indians," out to meet Vizcaíno (see fig. 5). On January 10, 1603, the Vizcaíno expedition skirted Pomo territory, and "two canoes, with an Indian in each, came out from the bay calling to us to come to the port, and saying they were awaiting us." Vizcaíno opted to sail on because many of his men were sick and the seas were choppy.

American and European writers, like Atherton, prefer to depict Indigenous People as in awe of European technology and religion. These discursive strategies made it easier to conceive of Indigenous People as primitive and savage, lacking in political and economic power. Europeans considered them to be little more than heathen children—*niños con barbas* (children with beards). Rather than fearing Spanish and English sailors, Indigenous People boarded their own seagoing vessels and went out to greet the newcomers. They brought with them trade goods and offered them to the newcomers. Indigenous People possessed a long history of trading with oceangoing vessels. Tongvas and Chumash, for instance, carried on maritime trade between islands and the mainland. Although the size of the Spanish ships, their appearance, and the trade goods were novel, trading with maritime visitors was not.

Misunderstandings and the possibility of violence lurked behind every encounter. On June 19, 1579, Drake ordered his men to "build tents and make a fort" before repairing his leaky ship. Soon, Coast Miwok men arrived with "weapons as they had." Put simply, Drake trespassed. He failed to secure Coast Miwok permission to reside on the beach. Once the Coast Miwok discerned the English did not pose a threat, "a great number both of men and women" arrived on the beach to meet the English. At the turn of the seventeenth century, Ipais responded to the Spanish in a similar manner. On November 10, 1602, one hundred Ipais, armed with bows and arrows, stood on a hill overlooking San Diego Bay when Sebastian Vizcaíno and his men landed. Ensign Juan Francisco and Father Antonio de la Ascensión led six Spaniards to meet four Ipais, two men and two women. The two parties exchanged presents and fish, "whereupon the Indians became more confident and went to their Rancherias and we to our ships to attend to our affairs." Ipais had reason to suspect the Spanish intentions. The Spanish traveled in parties of all men, which signified hostile intent. Ipais demonstrated their peaceful intent by sending two women, as well as two men, to negotiate with the Spanish. Once the parties indicated their peaceful nature, both began to forge positive but tenuous relationships.

One reason for the Indigenous People's show of force was that they experienced difficulties communicating with the newcomers. In late September of 1542, Ipais could not understand Cabrillo and the other Castilian speakers. The Ipais turned to sign language and informed Cabrillo that they had heard of Spaniards passing through the interior, perhaps a reference to the Hernando de Alarcón expedition. Over time, Ipais found it easier to communicate with the Spanish. After Cabrillo, Ipais encountered the Spanish several times as various ships traveling between Acapulco and Manila stopped over in San Diego Bay. As a result, Ipais developed a proficiency in the Spanish language that greatly exceeded the Spanish capacity or willingness to learn Indigenous Peoples' languages. In 1602, Father Antonio de la Ascensión said the Ipai "pronounced so very well in our language that they heard us speak that anyone hearing them and not seeing them would say they were Spaniards."

Europeans attempted to demonstrate their peaceful intent by giving gifts to Indigenous People. On September 28, 1542, Spanish sailors gave presents to three Ipai leaders near present-day San Diego. On November 15, 1602, Ipais sent an elderly woman to negotiate with the Vizcaíno expedition. The Spanish explorers gave the woman some beads and something to eat. Afterward, the Ipais invited the Spanish to their town. Vizcaíno later complained, "I do not state, lest I should be tiresome, how many times the Indians came to our camps with skins of martens and other things." On November 27, Tongva women from the island of Pimunga presented a meal of "roasted sardines and a small fruit like sweet potatoes." The Spanish reciprocated by providing presents to children.

The exchange of gifts convinced Indigenous People that the Spanish could be viable trade partners. For three days in 1602, Tongvas exchanged goods with the Spanish. Vizcaíno described the Tongvas as "a people given to trade and traffic and . . . fond of barter, for in return for old clothes they would give the soldiers skins, shells, nets, thread and very well twisted ropes, these in great quantities and resembling linen." On November 30, Tongvas living at another town on Pimunga traded "prickly pears and a grain like the *gofio* of the Canary Islands, in some willow baskets very well made, and water in vessels resembling flasks, which were like rattan inside and very thickly varnished outside" for some beads.

Indigenous People shared their knowledge of the ocean, land, and people with the Spanish. In November of 1602, Vizcaíno wanted to land on Pimunga, but he lacked familiarity with the island's rocky shoreline. Tongvas judiciously guided Vizcaíno into a safe harbor. Indigenous People adapted their ships to the local waterscapes, unlike the bulky Spanish ships designed for the open sea. Native sailors proved far more adept at navigating their vessels through the shallow water. The Spanish desired this knowledge of the coast. Cabrillo recorded the names of Chumash towns, evidence that he relied on Chumash knowledge. Elsewhere, Indigenous People answered questions about other Spanish explorers. In 1602, Tongvas informed Vizcaíno that they heard of and encountered Spaniards. A Tongva woman presented two pieces of "China silk" to Vizcaíno, telling him that "they had got them from people like ourselves, who had negroes; that they had come on the ship which was driven by a strong wind to the coast and wrecked." Indigenous knowledge permitted Europeans to navigate the coast, map its terrain, and describe other European visitors.

The Spanish also wanted knowledge of the interior. Ipais informed the Cabrillo expedition that they had heard of violent bearded men who killed other Indians. It is likely that the Ipais learned of the Spanish from the Quechans. Using sign language, Tongvas from Nájquqar informed the Spanish that "clothed and bearded" men "were going about on the mainland." On October 10, 1542, Chumash from the town of Muwu informed Cabrillo that Spanish men were only seven days away. Cabrillo dispatched two Spanish sailors to take a letter to the Spanish in the interior. Chumash informed Cabrillo of many "pueblos" about three days away. Each pueblo possessed maize and many "cows," meaning either elk or bison. On December 16, 1602, the Vizcaíno party arrived at the town of Ichxenta, which they named Monterey. The Spanish held a mass and collected supplies to continue their expedition. "The land is thickly populated with numberless Indians," Vizcaíno reported, "of whom a great many came several times to our camp." The People of Ichxenta shared information about other People in the interior: "They said by signs that inland there are many settlements." The People of Ichxenta made little effort to trade with or spend more time with the Spanish. Perhaps because the Spanish showed signs of illness, or perhaps because of a devastating cold spell that arrived on the first of the year, or a combination of both, the People of Ichxenta left the coast. The Spanish explored south of Monterey via the Carmel River and Carmel proper, but "no people were found because . . . they were living in the interior." The expedition continued into the interior, which it "found . . . to be depopulated and returned." Far from being isolated, coastal Indigenous People possessed connections with interior Peoples, allowing them to traffic in desired information. In addition, Indigenous People knew enough to attempt to convince these newcomers to leave, with stories of their relatives or wealth further in the interior.

Throughout their encounters, Indigenous People forced the Spanish to adhere to social protocols. On the night of September 28, 1542, some of Cabrillo's men rowed ashore at San Diego Bay and attempted to catch fish with nets. The Spanish did not have permission to fish in Ipai waters. Ipais attacked the Spanish for intruding into their economic areas and wounded three. Over time, Ipais imposed their fishing rights on Spanish intruders. In 1602, Ipais exacted tribute from Spanish sailors. Fray Ascensión said, "Every day [the Ipai] would come in order that we might give them some of the fish we caught in the net, and they would go away quietly after they had helped to haul it in." Ascensión's deeply internalized assumptions about power make it easy to misread this encounter as friendly cooperation or Ipai reliance on Spanish fishing. Rather than Spanish generosity and Indigenous assistance, obligation and oversight are at play here. The Ipai allowed the Spanish to fish in their waters and supervised the haul to ensure they received what was rightly owed them.

Indigenous People attempted to incorporate Europeans into their political systems. In late June of 1579, "a great assembly" of Coast Miwoks appeared on a hill overlooking Francis Drake's camp. A Coast Miwok leader began a speech. When he ended, the rest of his people called out "Oh" in approval. The Coast Miwok men then came down the hill and gave the Englishmen "feathers and bagges [sic] of Tobah." Drake reciprocated with "[diverse] things." On June 26, another Coast Miwok leader, described by Drake as a "king," arrived with one hundred men. The Coast Miwok leader wore a crown made of "knitwork" and a rabbit-hide cloak. After entering Drake's encampment, the Coast Miwok leader gave Drake his "knitwork" crown and a necklace of beads. Cultural misunderstandings dominated the encounter between the Coast Miwoks and Drake. The English believed that the Coast Miwok considered them gods and the exchange of crowns indicated that the Coast Miwok "would resign unto [Drake] their right and title in the whole land and become his vassals." But the encounter conformed to Coast Miwok expectations. Coast Miwok leaders brought various gifts and displayed their wealth to the Englishmen, expecting the English to reciprocate. In front of one Coast Miwok leader walked a man carrying a staff, "made of a certain kind of blacke wood, and in length about a yard and a half." The leaders' attendant also wore "chaines" of magnesite beads. Men and women walked behind the Coast Miwok leader, carrying elaborate and ornate baskets, again symbolizing their People's wealth and status. Coast Miwok leaders, then, demonstrated they were good providers and sought to create ties with newcomers, who might enhance their ability to secure food and supplies for their people.

As much as the California beaches offered spaces for the exchange of goods and information, they could turn into violent places. On November 23, 1542, Cabrillo returned to Tongva territory with hopes of wintering at San Miguel Island. During the wet and cold winter months, food was scarce, and Tongvas did not want to share their limited resources. The Spanish described Tongvas as "very poor" and eating "nothing except fish." Tongvas attacked the Spanish who ventured onto San Miguel's beach and kept them under an assault of arrows. Cabrillo rushed from his ship to protect his sailors under siege and in the process broke his leg. He died a week later from his injury.

The Spanish took Indigenous People as captives. On September 29, 1542, Cabrillo ordered his men to abduct two Ipai children in hopes of using them as interpreters. Once on the ship, Cabrillo failed to communicate with the Ipai boys; he gave them each a shirt and returned them to the beach. In addition to their interpreting skills, the Spanish wanted information from captives. On October 8, 1542, the Spanish captured a Tongva man in a canoe, off modern-day Santa Monica. The man informed the Spanish that "toward the north there were Spaniards like them." The Cabrillo expedition continued to take captives throughout the expedition. In March or April of 1543, Spanish sailors, now commanded by Bartolomé Ferrer after Cabrillo's death, abducted four Chumash men from Pueblos de las Canoas, near Ventura. Later, the Spanish captured two more Chumash boys from San Miguel Island. Ten days later, the Spanish beached at San Diego and captured two Ipai boys "to take to New Spain as interpreters."

Although Indigenous People and Europeans attempted, and often succeeded at, establishing positive relationships with one another, Europeans laid the groundwork for the subsequent taking of Indigenous People's land. On October 10, 1542, after surveying the territory around the Chumash town of Muwu, Cabrillo "took possession" of California, likely by reading the *Requerimiento*. In 1513, the Spanish crown mandated that all explorers read this document to the Indigenous People of the Americas, informing them they were subjects of the Spanish crown. Across North America, the Spanish used the *Requerimiento* to justify colonization. They read the document in Latin, with no interpreters. The *Requerimiento* justified the conquests by channeling the authority of the Christian god through the pope to the king and queen of Spain and to their representatives abroad. The ridiculousness of it all was encapsulated in the claim that the authority on which it was based "is contained in certain writings which passed upon the subject as aforesaid, which you can see if you wish." It offered a welcome to those who embraced conversion and subjected themselves to Spanish authority but a warning for those who resisted or refused. The Spanish explorers claimed the authority to attack, kill, and enslave Indigenous People who acted like "vassals who do not obey," and they asserted that "the deaths and losses which shall accrue from this are your fault, and not that of their Highnesses, or ours, nor of these cavaliers who come with us." The ritualized readings of the *Requerimiento* granted, in European minds, legal rights over Indigenous People and their lands.

The Spanish performed discovery rituals on beaches along the Pacific coast. On November 28, 1602, Fray Antonio de la Ascensión ordered the construction of a makeshift church and held mass on Pimunga. Vizcaíno reported 150 Tongvas attended the ceremony. "They marveled not a little at seeing the altar and the image of our Lord Jesus crucified," Vizcaíno optimistically reported, "and listened attentively to the saying of mass, asking by signs what it was about." Vizcaíno continued: "They were told that it was about heaven, whereat they marveled more." The Spanish attempted to impose a religious order on North American lands by holding mass and attempted to eliminate Indigenous religions. Two days later, Vizcaíno observed a Tongva ceremony. He and his men traveled to a "level prairie," where Tongvas "were assembled to worship an idol which was there." Vizcaíno described the "idol": "It resembled a demon, having two horns, no head, a dog at its feet and many children painted all around it." Tongvas told Vizcaíno to stay away from the "idol," but Vizcaíno ignored their protests. Vizcaíno "approached it and saw the whole thing, and made a cross, and placed the name of Jesus on the head of the demon, telling the Indians that that was good, and from heaven, but that the idol was the devil." Vizcaíno, grossly misunderstanding the Tongvas' reaction, testified that his action positively affected relations with the Tongva: "At this the Indians marveled, and they will readily renounce [the idol] and receive our Holy Faith, for apparently they have good intellects and are friendly and desirous of our friendship." Discovery rituals assumed that Indigenous People consented to colonization. The Spanish believed that by allowing a mass and seemingly agreeing to learn about Christianity, the Indigenous People welcomed them to possess California and that Catholicism replaced Indigenous beliefs. Indigenous Peoples, however, simply added aspects of Catholicism to their existing religions.

Drake, too, attempted to incorporate California into the British Empire. In July of 1579, he and other men traveled inland from the coast and visited a Coast Miwok town. Drake performed two discovery rituals. First, he named the region "Albion." By giving the territory the alternative English name for England, Drake attempted to establish English power over California and erase the Coast Miwok name for their land. By naming the area Albion, Drake arrogantly assumed the Coast Miwok did not have names for their homeland. Second, Drake nailed a brass plate to a "great and firme post" to indicate the English were the first Europeans in the area, thus granting them a legal right to "discover" the adjacent lands. The plates challenged Spanish sovereignty over California and denied Coast Miwok sovereignty over their own lands, effectively attempting to envelop California within the nascent British Empire. England, however, failed to follow up on Drake's claim and curiously abandoned the Pacific coast until the eighteenth century.

Beaches on the Pacific coast were not the only places where Indigenous People encountered Europeans. Rivers also were meeting places. In 1540, Indigenous people met the Spanish on the banks of the Colorado River. A diverse group of Indigenous People lived in the Colorado River region. The inhabitants of the river spoke dialects of the Yuman language and lived in politically distinct communities. By the time the Spanish arrived, the region had already undergone social and economic upheaval. The Colorado River ran red because of the enormous amounts of sediment it carried downstream. As it slowed, the river dropped its sediment, creating a large delta fan that, over millions of years, pushed the northern shoreline of the Gulf of California farther and farther south. Eventually, the distance to the sea was so great that the river turned north, filling inland lakes such as the massive Lake Cahuilla, which stretched north more than one hundred miles into the Imperial Valley. Between 900 CE and 1400 CE, the Colorado River's course shifted back south toward its present-day location, and Lake Cahuilla began to dry up. Quechans and Kumeyaay fled the lake, with the Quechans moving into the Colorado River Delta and Kumeyaay moving to the Pacific coast, where they encountered Cabrillo. Quechans displaced Maricopas and Halchidhomas. In 1540, as the Cocopahs met the Spanish for the first time, the arrival of new people, especially from downriver, surely caused alarm.

On August 26, Hernando de Alarcón arrived at the mouth of the Colorado River. Alarcón led one of two expeditions that Viceroy Mendoza sent from central Mexico to the north. Francisco Vázquez de Coronado commanded the other expedition and traveled overland, eventually arriving in present-day New Mexico. Alarcón took the water route, surveying what is now the Gulf of California. Arriving at the mouth, Alarcón described the Colorado River as "a very mighty river, which ran with so great a fury of a stream that we could hardly sail against it." Alarcón's two boats, filled with twenty men and a Sobaipuri O'odham interpreter from near Sonora, sailed up the River.

Cocopahs did not immediately trust Alarcón and the Spanish sailing with him. Armed Cocopahs assembled on the banks of the River to meet them. Alarcón attempted to demonstrate his peaceful intentions to the throngs of Cocopahs on the beach. He put his sword and shield in his boat and stood on them. Alarcón then told his men to put down their banners. These actions failed to pacify the Cocopahs. A Cocopah shapai axany stepped out of the crowd. He carried a staff, adorned with shells, and wore a "girdle" around his waist. The shapai axany entered the water and handed the staff to Alarcón, who reciprocated by giving the shapai axany "beads and other things." Alarcón then embraced the Cocopah leader. As on the Pacific coast, exchanging goods transformed tense encounters into more peaceful ones.

Cocopahs and the Spanish continued to warily engage with one another. An "ancient" man invited Alarcón to meet with a council of "ten or twelve" Cocopah shapai axany. Cocopahs expressed concern when some of Alarcón's sailors attempted to disembark. Alarcón defused the situation by telling the men to stay on the boats. Alarcón "embraced" the Cocopah leaders and gave them "some trifles." In return, the Cocopah leaders gave them food. Alarcón ordered one of his men to fire an harquebus, which startled all but two of the Cocopah shapai axany. The old man instructed the other Cocopahs to grab their weapons. Alarcón offered the shapai axany a "silver girdle of different colors," but the gesture failed to mollify the shapai axany. He hit Alarcón in the chest with his elbow. Alarcón retreated to his boats and attempted to once more ascend the Colorado River. The firing of the harquebus ruined the encounter between Cocopahs and the Spanish. Alarcón claimed the Cocopahs wanted him to fire off the gun, and after he did, "they were all wonderfully afraid." Alarcón attributed the Cocopahs' response to Indigenous naiveté. But Indigenous People across North America, like the Cocopahs, responded in various ways to guns. Guns introduced new sights, sounds, smells, and avenues to power into their lives. Cocopahs may have heard about these weapons before seeing them. Cocopahs and other people of the Colorado River traded with neighbors to the east. These neighbors, who previously met the Spanish, may have witnessed how the Spanish wielded guns to capture peoples and may have shared the news with the Cocopahs and other people of the Colorado River.

Up and down the Colorado River, Cocopahs and their neighbors used food as a symbol of exchange. After Alarcón's nearly disastrous first encounter with the Cocopahs, he sailed up the river. He did not travel far before Cocopahs "entered the water with some cakes of maize." Once satisfied with Alarcón's peaceful intent, the Cocopahs brought food to open negotiations. Alarcón's report reads like a gastronomic journey up and down the Colorado River. He detailed the types of food that sustained Cocopahs, as well as the myriad ways they cooked, preserved, and stored their food. One group of Cocopahs brought Alarcón "some cakes of maize and a loaf of *mizquiqui* [mesquite bread]." In addition to "shells and beads," Cocopahs gave Alarcón "maize and a roll of the same, badly ground." The Cocopahs were generous with their prosperity. Merely three days into the voyage, Alarcón reported, "[Cocopahs] brought me such abundance that I was obliged twice to call for the boats to put it into them."

That Cocopahs provided food to Alarcón did not suggest that they supplicated themselves to the Spanish. Rather Cocopahs used food to establish relationships of power and reciprocal obligation with strangers. Food represented a shapai axany's power and prestige. A shapai axany gave away excess food, demonstrating his and his people's industriousness. Excess food proved Cocopahs maintained balance in their world and that the Colorado River provided enough water to sustain crops. Food functioned as a medium among a variety of worlds. Alarcón observed Cocopahs throwing food, likely maize flour, into the air toward the sun before giving some to Alarcón. Halyikwamais sprinkled maize on Alarcón as he entered their town.

Refusing to take food imperiled Alarcón's journey. Hearing of the arrival of strangers from downriver, a group of Cocopahs built an "arbor" and, as Alarcón passed up the river, invited him to shore by offering him some meat, perhaps rabbit or bird. Alarcón refused because he thought the place was "apt for an ambush." Shortly after passing the arbor, about one thousand men armed with bows, along with some women and children, appeared on the banks of the Colorado River forcing Alarcón to spend an uneasy night bobbing in the middle of the river. Several days after the suspected ambush, a community of Halyikwamais also set up an "arbor" and waited for Alarcón to come ashore. Alarcón again continued his ascent of the river. An "old" Halyikwamais man stood up and yelled out to Alarcón, "Sir, why do you not receive victuals to eat from us, seeing you have taken food from others?" The old man and Alarcón eventually defused the situation, but refusing to accept food on the Colorado River put newcomers in danger.

Alarcón reciprocated and gave Cocopahs and other Colorado River Indians his symbol of political and religious import. Alarcón kissed small crosses "of sticks and paper" and told Cocopahs to wear the crosses around their necks. A couple of days later, Alarcón made a "great cross" from a "piece of timber" for another group of Cocopahs up the river. He informed them that the cross symbolized their brotherhood and said that Cocopahs should pray to the cross every morning. Crosses, a ubiquitous aspect of Spanish colonization, signified the Catholic Church's authority to explore and exploit North America. Crosses represented a discovery ritual. Whenever the Spanish arrived in a new country, they erected a cross to indicate their arrival and to claim the land for the Spanish Crown. Some Spanish men might wear the cross on their clothing or person or make the sign of the cross before prayer.

Alarcón experienced difficulties teaching Cocopahs about the value of the cross, largely because he lacked an interpreter. Cocopahs understood that the cross possessed some import. They kissed the small crosses of paper and sticks and "lifted them aloft," in a manner similar to how they treated maize. They carried the cross to the center of their town, making certain not to allow it to touch the ground, and planted it. They then asked Alarcón "how they should join their hands and how they should kneel to worship the cross." Still, it is unlikely that they understood or accepted the religious and political meanings the Spanish invested in the cross. Alarcón reported that Cocopahs were pleased that he considered them "brothers." Cocopahs knew the crosses possessed religious meaning but in ways similar to their effigies and prayer sticks. One group of Kalyikwami asked Alarcón if they could or should hang anything from the cross's limbs, to which he replied no.

Cocopah mediators facilitated the exchange of food and crosses. Alarcón failed to record, learn, or understand these people's names, save for one. No doubt after hearing stories about the newcomers ascending the Colorado River, a man the Spanish named Naguachato came to the riverbank and invited Alarcón ashore with promises of "a great store of victuals" to give to the Spanish. An "old man" brought "rolls of maize and certain little gourds" to Alarcón when he finally beached. The "old man" said some words to the people and raised some maize to the sky. He then gave some food to Alarcón. Alarcón explained he did not bring many things to trade because his boats were so small. He promised to return, however, with more goods. After giving a large cross to the people, Alarcón took the old man. The following day, Naguachato and five hundred Cocopahs, armed with bows and arrows and bearing "certain conies and yuccas," met Alarcón at an apparently abandoned town. Alarcón returned the "old man," and the Cocopahs returned to their town. Mediators, such as Naguachato, were often the first face the Spanish saw. Mediators brought their leaders into contact with newcomers, setting the stage for Cocopahs and Colorado River

FIGURE 6. Rio Colorado near the Mojave Villages, California/Arizona. Created by J.J. Young and artist A.H. Campbell. Based on original by Sarony, Major & Knapp Lithographer. Photo courtesy Bancroft Library, University of California, Berkeley.

People and the Spanish newcomers to acquire what they desired from the other.

Indigenous Peoples' work and knowledge allowed Spanish explorers to travel the Colorado River. Alarcón complained that "the current of the river [was] exceedingly great and our men that drew the rope . . . [were] not well acquainted with the occupation." Alarcón requested Cocopahs pull his boats upstream. Without Cocopah work, "it would have been impossible for us to have gotten up the river against the stream." Alarcón also desired information from Indigenous people (see fig. 6). He asked Cocopahs if they heard of other Spanish, perhaps even Francisco Vázquez de Coronado. Alarcón inquired about the famed city of Cibola and what he called the Totonoac River, both requests influenced by Marcos de Niza's earlier expedition in the Southwest. Alarcón also sought ethnographic information about Cocopahs and other Colorado River Indians. He inquired about their political structures, religious practices, warfare, language, economies and homes.

Cocopahs and other Colorado River People likewise desired things from the Spanish. Some wanted trade partners and gave the Spanish "shells and beads." Others sought information about the Spanish, especially about their intent on ascending the Colorado River. A Cocopah leader sent two men to meet with Alarcón in order "to signify to him what my pleasure was." Cocopahs wanted mediators to quell the violence that plagued the region. One Cocopah leader proclaimed that he was going to war against a neighbor, but Alarcón's arrival stopped him. Up and down the river, Cocopahs and their neighbors expressed concern about the seemingly unending violence. They pointed out their enemies' locations. Some used Alarcón's arrival as a way to stem the violence and enlist an apparent mediator or ally.

The concern about the violence and warfare along the Colorado River continued to vex Indigenous People as they met more Spanish. A couple of months after Alarcón's visit, Captain Melchior Diaz arrived near Yuma. In September of 1540, Francisco Vázquez de Coronado placed Diaz in command of approximately eighty weak and tired men in San Hieronimo, located in Mexico's Corazones Valley. At the end of September, Diaz led twenty-five men in search of the Pacific coast. Diaz expressed amazement about what he saw near Yuma. "It is a mighty stream," he observed of the Colorado River, "more than two leagues across at the mouth." Diaz described the people who lived along the river in fantastic ways. Diaz named the River the Tizon, or Firebrand, after observing Cocopahs holding burning sticks on their abdomens and shoulders to warm themselves. Later, Diaz and his men encountered a group of "tall and muscular" Indigenous People. They carried three-hundred- to four-hundred-pound bundles on their heads. In another story, six Spaniards failed to carry a wooden log into camp. An Indigenous man "picked it up in his arms, put it on his head all by himself, and carried it quite easily."

Cocopahs informed Diaz that he missed Alarcón. Diaz retraced part of Alarcón's route, finding the tree on which Alarcón inscribed a message and stashed some letters. The letters left notice of Alarcón's arrival at the mouth of the Colorado River and stated that he returned to central Mexico because worms were eating his ships.

On discovering that he did not find the coast, Diaz determined to cross the river. This task required Cocopah knowledge and labor. Diaz marched for five or six days before finding a suitable place to cross. Cocopahs agreed to build rafts made of wicker baskets, caulked with bitumen, for the Spanish. Even this act concerned Diaz. He worried the Cocopahs would attack him and his party when they were in the middle of the river. After hearing rumors of armed Indians in the mountains, Diaz captured and tortured a Cocopah, who revealed Indigenous People planned to attack him. Diaz believed the Cocopah man, although testimonies acquired under torture often proved to be unreliable. Diaz ordered his men to kill the Cocopah informant and dump his body in the Colorado River.

Five or six Cocopahs guided the baskets, laden with Spaniards and their goods, across the river. Diaz continued into the interior for four days but turned back when he reached the southern edge of the Mojave Desert. The Spanish described the area beyond the Colorado River as a wasteland, with no water, "beds of burning lava," and ground that "resounded like a kettle drum." On returning to the Colorado River, Diaz and his men made camp. That night, a dog chased some of the sheep that accompanied the Spanish. Enraged, Diaz mounted his horse and chased after the dog with a lance. He threw the lance and missed the dog. Before he could rein his horse, Diaz ran into the spear, which punctured his groin. He suffered for several days and died before reaching San Hieronimo.

As on the Pacific coast, Indigenous People and the Spanish met sporadically during the following decades. In 1605, Spanish explorer Juan de Oñate entered the Colorado River region. Oñate, two priests, and forty soldiers left San Gabriel, in central New Mexico, and traveled, by way of the Gila River, to the Gulf of California. En route, the expedition encountered the eastern edge of Indigenous Peoples' trade networks. When Oñate was visiting a Hualapai town, a leader named Otata informed him that he was five days from an island, inhabited by the people the Hualapai called Zinogaba. Hualapais obtained pearl shells from these people, which they wore in their ears or around their neck. While camping along the Gila River, Maricopas informed Oñate that "they saw some good and sweet oak acorns, which the Indians said were from the other side of the river."

In December of 1604 or January of 1605, the Oñate expedition entered Quechan territory. Quechans came out to meet the Spanish travelers. "All came out to receive the Spaniards, and offered them their food," Geronimo Zárate, the expedition's chronicler, remembered. "Among these Indians were found many white pearl-shells and other shells, very large and shining. . . . These Indians said that on the coast toward the west there were many of those shells, and they indicated that the sea ran behind a very large mountain, on the skirts of which the Buena Esperanza River enters the sea." Zarate estimated that twenty thousand Indigenous People lived between the Gila and Colorado Rivers. He identified two thousand Halchidomas living in eight towns, the largest of which contained 160 houses. Quechans lived in nine pueblos. The Oñate expedition also met Cocopahs before descending the Colorado to its mouth. Oñate and others did not stay in the Colorado River area. They, like other European explorers, looked to colonize other places in North America.

Although the Spanish largely ignored California in the sixteenth and seventeenth centuries, their arrival helped create a new world for Indigenous People, one full of possibilities and dangers. Oral histories recorded one of those hazards. After the creation of the world, Sipa, a Cocopah deity, secretly exchanged his people for the ones made by Komat, another Cocopah deity. When Komat discovered this, he became enraged at Sipa. Komat reached into the sky and broke it open, exposing a hole to the earth. Smoke, air, lightning, and other things that cause death streamed through the hole and onto the earth. Sipa reached up and held the skies aloft in an attempt to prevent death from entering this world. Unfortunately, Sipa could not stop smallpox and trachoma from passing through the hole Komat made in the sky. Cocopahs have told a version of the story of Sipa and Komat for centuries; however, they altered their history to reflect the diseases introduced by the Spanish and other invaders.

Spanish maritime travelers were often ill and brought European diseases with them. In 1602, Sebastian Vizcaíno revealed on leaving Pimunga, "It was agreed that we should continue our voyage since our men were becoming ill." Later on the trip, Vizcaíno reported troubling news on arriving at Monterey: "we had so many sick, that the pilot of the admiral's ship and his assistant were very ill." Vizcaíno attempted to prevent sick sailors from interacting with the Chumash and other Indigenous People, but it is possible that the sick Spanish spread diseases. Throughout the seventeenth century, Spanish sailors continued to expose coastal communities to disease. Spanish galleons, traveling between Mexico and the Philippines, no doubt stopped along the California coast and encountered Indigenous People.

Old World epidemic diseases reordered Indigenous People's space, often outside the purview of Spanish explorers. In 1540, Hernando Alarcón encountered seven to eight native groups below Yuma. Sixty years later, Oñate met only five. The number of Indigenous towns on the Pacific coast also fluctuated. For fifteen hundred years, Chumash occupied Tecolte, west of Goleta, but abandoned it in the 1540s, shortly after Cabrillo's expedition. To the south, Tongvas concentrated settlements around Povuu'nga in the 1560s and 1570s. To the north, Native People left sites in the Sierra Nevada Mountains, White Mountains, and Morro Bay. The abandonment and concentration of communities resembled strategies other Indigenous People employed in North America as they adjusted to population decline with the onset of crowd epidemics.

Coastal communities, as with those on the Colorado River, integrated diseases into their oral histories. Narciso, a Chumash man, told of three pestilences that "cleaned out nearly all of the [Chumash]." The first started at the town of Simo'mo, which sent emissaries to meet with Cabrillo. Chumash abandoned Simo'mo and established a residence at Mitsqanaqa'n, near modern-day Ventura. Chumash thrived at Mitsqanaqa'n, which means low jaw place, a town nestled between two ridges that looked like Coyote's jaws and tongue. Chumash connected the name of their town to the spread of illness. According to oral tradition, Coyote visited the Chumash towns near Ventura, singing: "Clear away! Clear away! I have cramps in my belly. I have cramps in my belly and I have to retire." Chumash lived at Mitsqanaqa'n until another epidemic arrived; "People went about feeling sick until they fell backwards, dead."

Between 1600 and 1769, Indigenous People, especially those in the south and along the Colorado River, lived on the edge of an advancing wave of European disease and technology. After Vizcaíno and Oñate left California, Spanish officials made few efforts to explore or settle California. Instead, the Spanish slowly moved into modern-day Baja California and the state of Sonora. Indigenous People encountered the Spanish explorers, colonists, and pearl fishermen who served as the vanguard of colonial expansion. Diseases, originating in Mexico City, traveled with these ambassadors of colonialism. In 1593, smallpox and measles blighted Indigenous People in Sinaloa, the coastal province east of Baja. Between 1601 and 1618, a fever, called *cocoliztli*, took the lives of thousands of Indigenous People in Sinaloa. In 1641, smallpox erupted in Yaqui communities in Sonora, the province that currently borders the state of Arizona.

In Baja California and Sonora, Jesuit missionary activities exposed Indigenous People to crowd diseases. In 1697, Jesuits created Mission de Nuestra Señora de Loreto Concho, shortened to Mission Loreto, in modern-day Loreto, Mexico. Between Loreto's founding and 1769, when the Spanish Crown evicted the Jesuits from North America, Jesuits created nineteen missions, with the northern-most mission at Mission Santa María de los Ángeles, about three hundred miles south of modern-day San Diego. Jesuits brought the hunting and harvesting Indigenous groups in Baja to the missions, a process called *reduccion* (reduction). Priests concentrated Indigenous People into tight quarters and enabled crowd diseases to do lethal work. Smallpox, measles, and dysentery regularly struck Indigenous People living at the missions. The population of Indigenous People of peninsular Baja California declined from perhaps sixty thousand in 1697 to as low as one thousand in 1834, when Mexican officials secularized the missions. A similar story occurred in modern-day Sonora. In 1620, Jesuits established the first missions in the region. By 1700, Jesuits had planted a mission in modern-day Tucson, Arizona. During the eighty years of mission expansion, the population of Sonora declined from five hundred thousand people to five thousand. In modern-day southern Arizona, the Indigenous population declined from perhaps sixty-four thousand people to six thousand in 1767. Although evidence is scanty, it is likely that Indigenous People from missions in Baja California and Sonora carried their diseases to the Pacific coast and the Colorado River.

Although we lack definitive proof of diseases racing ahead of Spanish colonization, we know Spanish trade goods advanced into Indigenous California. Chumash and Kumeyaays reached out to the Colorado River nations of Mojave, Halchidhoma, Quechan, and Cocopah. One trade route that originated in Chumash towns, near modern-day Santa Barbara, went east to the Colorado River and ended in Taos or San Juan in modern-day New Mexico. Another, which originated in Kumeyaay towns, near San Diego, passed through Cahuilla territory to Halchidhoma towns and then through southern Arizona and southern New Mexico, concluding at Isleta. Two trade routes connected Tongvas to the People of the Colorado River.

In the seventeenth and eighteenth centuries, Spanish traders and merchandise intersected the west-to-east trade routes via the El Camino Real and the Pacific Coast Road, bringing new goods into the network. In 1701, Spanish missionary Eusebio Kino saw Indigenous People exchanging shell beads from the coast. Inland, Yokuts acquired Spanish glass beads and interred them with the dead. Livestock, too, moved into the Colorado River region. By the late eighteenth century, Cocopahs rode horses. Finally, people moved along these trade trails as captives. In Sonora, Indigenous people adopted as captives were called *nijoras*. People, livestock, and trade goods moved throughout the region. Maricopas traded horses to Halchidomas and Cocopahs who raided Southern Paiutes, Yavapais, and Quechans for captives.

For centuries, Indigenous people traveling these roads carried trade goods and information. After 1518, and increasingly after 1600, traders carried disease. Between 1518 and 1525, smallpox spread from central Mexico to the Gila River watershed along trade routes. Other diseases continued to move until 1620, when Jesuits established missions in Sonora.

Between 1542 and 1769, Indigenous People met European explorers and sailors on California's beaches. Each tried to make sense of the others as they exchanged trade goods and information. Europeans considered the People they encountered to be colonial subjects and potential sources of labor or resources. Indigenous People viewed the newcomers as sources of potentially valuable trade goods and, thus, power they could leverage and deploy within their own world. Sometimes, these encounters produced cordial outcomes, with fish and beads changing hands, or manufactured European goods contributing to indigenous systems of power and politics. When the delicate balance of power shifted, beach crossings produced violence. Indigenous People fired arrows at newcomers who transgressed land-use protocols or Spaniards abducted Indigenous People and took them south. Even though physical encounters remained close to the coast, glass trade beads and news about the newcomers traveled along well-worn Indigenous trade paths that linked the Pacific Ocean with the Great Basin and the Southwest. Franciscan priests in Mexico and Spain also heard about California Indians. Soon, imperial dictates and religious convictions brought the Spanish to California, this time intent on leaving the beach.

SOURCES

Scholars have looked for ways to analyze and interpret so-called first encounter narratives such as the one found on page 24 of Gertrude Atherton, *California: An Intimate History* (New York: Boni and Liveright, 1927). Anthropologist Greg Dening used the metaphor of the "beach" to examine colonial encounters. In *Islands and Beaches: Discourse on a Silent Land—Marquesas, 1774–1880* (Belmont, CA: Dorsey Press, 1988), he described the beach as a meeting place between two peoples and a boundary that neither Indigenous People nor Europeans successfully crossed. Anthropologist John Sutton Lutz and contributors ask us to think about the history of encounters and their usefulness in the present in *Myth and History: Stories of Indigenous-European Contact* (Vancouver: University of British Columbia Press, 2007). The reconstructed account that begins this chapter is taken from Albert Elsasser, "Explorations of Hernando Alarcón in the Lower Colorado River Region, 1540," *Journal of California and Great Basin Anthropol-*

ogy 1 (Summer 1979): 11–13. For Cocopah words and phrases see E.W. Gifford, "The Cocopa," *University of California Publications in American Archaeology and Ethnology* 31 (1933): 287 (directions), 298 (headman).

Useful overviews of this period include Natale Zappia, *Traders and Raiders: The Indigenous World of the Colorado Basin, 1540–1859* (Chapel Hill: University of North Carolina Press, 2014); and Jack Forbes, *Warriors of the Colorado: The Yumas of the Quechan Nation and Their Neighbors* (Norman: University of Oklahoma Press, 1965).

For material on the Indigenous People who encountered the Spanish, see Lynn Gamble, *The Chumash World at European Contact: Power, Trade, and Feasting among Complex Hunter-Gatherers* (Berkeley: University of California Press, 2008); Jeffrey Altschul and Donn Grenda, eds., *Islanders and Mainlanders: Prehistoric Context for the Southern California Bight* (Tucson, AZ: SRI, 2002); William Kelly, *Cocopa Ethnography* (Tucson: University of Arizona Press, 2015); Anita Alvarez de Williams, *The Cocopah People* (Phoenix, AZ: Indian Tribal Series, 1974); E.W. Gifford, "The Cocopa," *University of California Publications in American Archaeology and Ethnology* 31 (1933): 257–333; and John Peabody Harrington, Travis Hudson, and Francisco Librado, *The Eye of the Flute: Chumash Traditional History and Ritual, as Told by Fernando Librado Kitsepawit to John P. Harrington* (Santa Barbara, CA: Santa Barbara Museum of Natural History, 1977).

Scholars have transcribed and edited the reports of European explorers in California. See Harry Kelsey, *Juan Rodriguez Cabrillo* (San Marino, CA: Huntington Library Press, 1998); Albert Elsasser, "Explorations of Hernando Alarcón in the Lower Colorado River Region, 1540," *Journal of California and Great Basin Anthropology* 1 (Summer 1979): 8–37; Robert F. Heizer, *Francis Drake and the California Indians, 1579* (Berkeley: University of California Press, 1947); George P. Hammond and Agapito Rey, *Narratives of the Coronado Expedition, 1540–1542* (Albuquerque: University of New Mexico Press, 1940); George Parker Winship, ed., *The Journey of Coronado, 1540–1542* (Golden, CO: Fulcrum, 1990). Reports on the expeditions of Juan Rodriguez Cabrillo, Sebastian Vizcaíno, Fray Antonio de la Ascensión and Juan de Oñate have been reprinted in Herbert Eugene Bolton, ed., *Spanish Exploration in the Southwest, 1542–1706* (New York: Barnes and Noble, 1946).

For diseases and trade goods entering California during the seventeenth and eighteenth centuries, see William Preston, "Portents of Plague from California's Protohistoric Period," *Ethnohistory* 49 (Winter 2002):

69–121; Kent Lightfoot and William Simmons, "Culture Contact in Protohistoric California: Social Contexts of Native and European Encounters," *Journal of California and Great Basin Anthropology* 20, no. 2 (1998): 138–70; William Preston, "Serpent in Eden: Dispersal of Foreign Diseases into Pre-mission California," *Journal of California and Great Basin Anthropology* 18, no. 1 (1996): 2–37; and Robert H. Jackson, "Epidemic Disease and Population Decline in the Baja California Missions, 1697–1834," *Southern California Quarterly* 63 (Winter 1981): 308–46.

Native Spaces

San Diego

In December of 2003, alumni and current students of San Diego State University (SDSU) voted to replace the school's mascot, "Monty Montezuma," with a more "historically accurate" mascot generically named "Aztec warrior." Following the successful vote, a group of SDSU alumni met to celebrate the decision at the Padre's Pub, a hotel bar in Mission Valley along the bed of the San Diego River, four miles southwest of the site of the relocated Mission San Diego de Alcalá. Almost certainly an unintentional and, in fact, unremarkable choice given the ubiquity of Padre imagery across the city, including the "Swinging Friar" as the mascot of the San Diego Padres baseball team, the moment nonetheless highlights the convoluted and often ironic juxtaposition of San Diego's Spanish, Mexican, Indigenous, and American past.

San Diego is a sprawling American suburban city, a glimmering and iconic oceanfront paradise. It is also a richly diverse ethnic city with deep histories that stretch across the border with Mexico, immediately to its south, and into the wider world of Latin America, Asia, and Africa. San Diego wears its imagined Spanish past everywhere, from Balboa Park's grandiose Spanish colonial revival architecture to the municipal zoning regulations that drape McDonald's in fake mission roof tiles. Its place-names and mascots all attest to the region's Spanish heritage. At the same time, San Diego County has more Indian reservations than any other county in the nation. All of its eighteen Indian reservations lie inland from the city, in the mountains and deserts of the so-called backcountry or "North County" regions. During the last twenty-five years, a few of those reservations have developed profitable casinos that have, in effect, begun to recolonize San Diego, where shuttle buses ferry San Diegans and tourists from downtown to the casinos. Today, Native Americans and Alaskan Natives make up approximately 1.3 percent of San Diego County's population, but California Indian communities play a critical role in the region's development and are an iconic part of the region's image.

Kumeyaay settlements in what is today Mission Valley originally attracted Spanish colonists. In 1769, Franciscan priests established the first mission in Alta California along the San Diego River near the Kumeyaay village of Kosa'aay. Despite a weak Spanish presence and limited trade goods, initial contact between the Kumeyaay and the Spanish centered on trade. Five years later, Franciscan padres, with an eye to converting Kumeyaay and their neighbors, relocated the mission four miles upstream, adjacent to the Kumeyaay village of Nipaguay. Indigenous People, especially the Tipai or southern Kumeyaay living on the river, did not welcome the move. In November of 1775, frustrated by Spanish livestock grazing on Kumeyaay land, fearful of forced labor, and angered over rumors of rape, Tipais led a coordinated revolt. At least fifteen predominantly Tipai villages, both affiliated with the missions and unaffiliated, participated in the revolt. The leaders came overwhelmingly from the villages of Macate, Janat, and Abusquel, the same villages where many Tipai lived before they relocated to the mission. In the revolt, Tipai killed Father Luís Jayme and two others and looted and burned the mission. Kumeyaay, while initially interested in the technology and trade goods the Spanish offered, chafed at the cost associated with the growing Spanish presence.

Nonetheless, within two years, Spanish officials rebuilt the mission, which eventually grew to have one of the largest populations in California. Between 1797 and 1831, an average of fifteen hundred Indigenous People lived at Mission San Diego. The mission often lacked sufficient space for all affiliated Indians. In a rare move, the friars allowed Indigenous People to live in their traditional villages and visited the converts there.

Spanish, and later Mexican, officials expanded into the interior. Padres established ranchos in the backcountry to provide for the mission. Californios did as well, with a dramatic increase in the number of rancho land grants in the Mexican period after 1824. As the padres had done, Spanish and Mexican rancheros demanded that Native People work on the ranches. Where the Franciscans gave Indigenous workers Catholicism and diseases in exchange for their labor, rancheros provided meager and unreliable wages. Indigenous People tried to maintain a balance, but they faced malaria in 1832, smallpox in 1837–39, and occasional violent encounters with Spanish and Mexican officials and settlers.

The Mexican War, and the shift to Anglo-American rule, brought a new regime to San Diego County, embodied in Cave Johnson Couts, a Tennessean who came to the region as part of the boundary survey. In 1851, Couts married into a prominent Californio family and received Rancho Guajome, located east of modern-day Oceanside, as a wedding gift. Couts notoriously exploited the 1850 Act for the Government and Protection of Indians to enforce de facto Indian slavery through debt peonage and forced apprenticeship. As justice of the peace, county Indian agent, and *juez del campo* (similar to sheriff), Couts wielded almost unlimited power over Indian lives.

In response to American efforts to assert more control over Indian life and livelihood, Cupeño Antonio Garra led a revolt against Americans, centering on Juan José Warner, a rancher in northern San Diego County. Garra envisioned a widespread revolt well beyond the borders of Warner's ranch. Quechans at the Colorado River initially agreed to join Garra, but the revolt faltered. Couts organized a militia in San Diego and, aided by Cahuillas, captured Garra. A military tribunal tried and executed Garra in San Diego in 1852.

Although the revolt and its suppression did not quiet Indigenous resistance, it signaled a shift in the momentum of Anglo development of the region. San Diego grew in the post–Civil War years, following the 1885 arrival of the railroads and the completion of the Cuyamaca and Sweetwater dams a few years later. That growth rippled through the region, translating into additional work for Indigenous People in agriculture and construction.

During the twentieth century, Indigenous People generally resided inland while Americans generally sought to develop the coast. Kumeyaay Delfina Cuero recalled, "The Indians had to move around from place to place to hunt and gather enough food, so we knew lots of places to camp. Later on White people kept moving into more and more of the places and we couldn't camp around those places any more. We went farther and farther from San Diego looking for places where nobody chased us away." The integration of these two regions unleashed devastating effects on Native People. Water development, critical for growing cities, meant storing inland water sources and delivering it to coastal users. Speculators trailed inland, looking for sites to develop and putting increasing pressure on Indigenous land and water rights. Real estate, tourism, and water projects displaced and dispossessed Indigenous People and flooded their land. In 1903, after a long legal battle, John Downey, the former governor of California, secured a United States Supreme Court order to evict the Cupeño residents of Warner's ranch. Federal officials moved the Cupeños to Pala, forty miles to the northwest. In the 1930s, the Bureau of Indian Affairs cooperated with local real estate developers to remove the Kumeyaay residents from the Capitan Grande Reservation and to dam the valley, creating El Capitan Reservoir to store water for the city's supply.

At the same time that San Diego's growth dispossessed Indians in the interior, international expositions honed the city's public image. Both the 1915 Panama-California Exposition, and the 1935 California-Pacific International Exposition in Balboa Park contained stock images of Indians, yoked inevitably to the machinery of civilization and progress. The Second World War and the importance of San Diego Bay to the US Navy plotted San Diego as part of the nationwide trend toward sunbelt suburban growth in the 1950s. The city's population exploded between 1930 and 1960. The dynamic demographic changes it brought exacerbated the racial and ethnic tensions of the city. Perhaps no city in the nation was more divided in this particular way. The Spanish past rubbed up against the Mexican present in a place devoted to selling an American future by dispossessing Indians. Mexican-born, San Diego–based artist Rubén Ortiz Torres captured this tension in his piece *1492: Indians vs. Dukes* (1993) from the permanent collection of the Museum of Contemporary Art in San Diego. Two baseball caps sit side by side: on the left, a modified Cleveland Indians cap with "14" stitched on the front left panel; on the right, a cap featuring a smiling Spanish conquistador—the mascot of the former Triple-A Franchise, the Albuquerque Dukes—and the number "92" stitched on the front right panel. As in Torres's piece, San Diego wears its Indigenous, Spanish, Mexican, and American heritage conspicuously, aware of that past but perhaps not the colonial underpinnings of its history. Thanks in large part to the efforts of the county's Native communities, awareness of the colonial past is growing. In January of 2020, the Pala Tribe sponsored "Antonio Garra Day" at the Old Town San Diego Historical Park. Citing Garra's last words before being executed—"Gentlemen, I ask pardon for all my offenses, and expect yours in return"—promotional flyers for the event claimed, "This event is the celebration of Garra's life and others who fought to secure the future of the California Indians during the post–

Father Serra era. Come join us for the testimonies given for the celebration of life—and ask for your own offenses to be forgiven, although there are no guarantees for pardons!"

SOURCES

On the 1775 Kumeyaay Revolt, see Richard Carrico, "Sociopolitical Aspects of the 1775 Revolt at Mission San Diego de Alcalá: An Ethnohistorical Approach," *Journal of San Diego History* 43 (Summer 1997): 142–57; and Claudio Saunt, "'My Medicine Is Punishment': A Case of Torture in Early California, 1775–1776," *Ethnohistory* 57, no. 4 (2010): 679–708. On Cave Couts, see Michael Magliari, "Free Soil, Unfree Labor: Cave Johnson Couts and the Binding of Indian Workers in California, 1850–1867," *Pacific Historical Review* 73 (August 2004): 349–90. Delfina Cuero's comments come from Florence Connolly Shipek, *Delfina Cuero: Her Autobiography, an Account of Her Last Years, and Her Ethnobotanic Contributions* (Menlo Park, CA: Ballena Press, 1991), 26. On the flooding of Capitan Grande, see Tanis Thorne, *El Capitan: Adaptation and Agency on a Southern California Indian Reservation, 1850–1937* (Banning, CA: Malki-Ballena Press, 2012). On the iconography of public nostalgia, see Matthew Bokovoy, *The San Diego World's Fairs and Southwestern Memory, 1880–1940* (Albuquerque: University of New Mexico Press, 2005). Information about Antonio Garra Day can be found on the website of the Pala Tribe, www.palatribe.com/events/antonio-garra-day.

3

"Our Country before the Fernandino Arrived Was a Forest"

Native Towns and Spanish Missions in Colonial California, 1769–1810

Perhaps it was summer, before the Quechnåjuichom (also known as the People of Quechla) harvested acorns, when the *not* (hereditary leader) of Quechla observed eight *Sosabitom* (Spanish) approaching. The Sosabitom previously visited Quechla and convinced some of the not's relatives to move to new places, namely Mission San Diego de Alcalá, Mission San Juan Capistrano, and Mission San Gabriel Arcángel. Although the not's kin created ties with the Sosabitom, on this day, the not expressed concern about the Sosabitom's presence. The Sosabitom settled in Quichamcauichom ("those of the south," Kumeyaay) territory. Perhaps the Sosabitom allied with the Quichamcauichom and now planned to attack the Quechnåjuichom. After all, neither women nor children accompanied the Sosabitom. The not met the Sosabitom and demanded they leave Quechla. Communication remained difficult. The Sosabitom did not know the language of the land, and the not did not know the Sosabitom's language. Sign language offered a possible solution. The Sosabitom gave gifts to the not, transforming themselves from potential threats into allies.

Writing from Rome, Italy, in the 1830s, Luiseño Pablo Tac provided this account to linguist Giuseppe Mezzofanti. He described the encounter between his People, the Quechnåjuichom, now called Luiseños after Mission San Luis Rey, and more recently as Payómkawichum, and Spanish Franciscan missionaries, whom Tac referred to as Fernandinos, after the Iglesia y Colegio Apostólico de San Fernando in Mexico City, where Franciscans studied. The meeting resembled previous ones. Quechnåjuichom and Franciscans exchanged goods and information. They struggled to understand each other's language. Quechnájuichom and Franciscans attempted to create alliances and economic relationships necessary to thrive in California. But unlike encounters with Juan Rodriguez Cabrillo or Sebastian Vizcaíno, these Sosabitom planned to stay.

In the late eighteenth century, Indigenous People living in coastal California encountered Spanish missionaries, soldiers, and government officials who intended to settle the region. Initially, Indigenous People attempted to form customary political and economic relationships with the Spanish, much like how they had responded to the Spanish and English sailors who preceded them. But the Spanish who invaded California after 1769 differed from those who explored the coast or the Colorado River. Spanish settler colonial policies attempted to separate Indigenous People from the land and each other and, in doing so, altered California's social and ecological makeup. Spanish missionaries believed in "reducing" Indigenous People from their allegedly "wild and primitive" state to what the Spaniards considered more "civilized" missions. There, Indigenous People encountered new animals, germs, and social practices. Domesticated livestock destroyed customary Indigenous Peoples' food sources. European diseases took the lives of relatives and reduced the reproductive rate and lifespan of those who survived. Priests assaulted Indigenous Peoples' lifeways and punished those who defied their authority. Yet Spanish colonialism did not destroy Indigenous People or the land. Indigenous People adapted to and resisted Spanish colonialism. Furthermore, not all Indigenous People lived in the missions. Many more lived outside those adobe walls, resisting Spanish incursions into their lifeways, repurposing European merchandise for their own purposes and building alliances.

In 1769, Kumeyaay encountered the first Spanish who wanted to live permanently in their lands. Fearing an English or Russian invasion of New Spain from the north, the Spanish general José de Galvez ordered Captain Gaspar de Portolá and Fray Junípero Serra to settle Alta California. Later that year, the duo arrived at modern-day San Diego. They established a presidio and mission near Kosa'aay, a Kumeyaay town along the San Diego River. Although Spanish officials preferred military officials in its colonial endeavors, they worried about the cost of colonizing California. Missionaries offered a cheaper option for occupying distant lands. Serra and his successor, Fermín Lasuén, created twenty-one missions between San Diego and Sonoma. Each mission possessed ranchos in the surrounding areas, which raised livestock and agricultural crops for the missions. Fathers later extended the missions' reach with *asistencias* (outposts) among some of the ranchos. The Spanish crown supported religious institutions with four presidio districts: San Francisco, Monterey, Santa Barbara, and San Diego. Each presidio hosted a small body of soldiers tasked with protecting the colony from Indigenous and European attacks. Finally, Spanish citizens established the *pueblos* (towns) of Los Angeles, San José, and Branciforte, later renamed Santa Cruz. Missions, presidios, and pueblos grew together. In 1776, Spanish soldiers established a presidio on a high cliff overlooking San Francisco Bay. In October of that year, Fathers Francisco Palou and Pedro Benito Cambón founded Mission San Francisco de Asís, named for Saint Francis of Assisi. The following year, fourteen Spanish families formed the nearby town of San José. In the late eighteenth and early nineteenth centuries, Franciscans continued to expand their settlements. In the 1780s, missionaries established a rancho outpost named San Pedro y San Pablo, near modern-day Pacifica, to raise crops. From 1777 to 1823, Franciscans established Mission Santa Clara, Mission Santa Cruz, Mission San José, Mission San Rafael Arcángel, and Mission San Francisco Solano in the Bay Area.

From the outset, Indigenous Peoples attempted to establish customary economic and political relationships with the Spanish. Indigenous People demanded Spanish officials follow Indigenous protocols when building missions and other settlements in their territory. Pablo Tac wrote that Quechla's not had allowed Father Antonio Peyri to establish the mission near Quechla. The Luiseños could have wiped out the small group of Spanish, but they did not because of the not's "great mercy." He had acted in a familiar manner, much like he would have allowed another Luiseño headman or another tribe of Indigenous People to hunt, harvest, or live in Luiseño territory. Tac explained the not's actions were remarkable because he usually did not want outsiders to live in his People's territory. But the not expected the Spanish to reciprocate, perhaps providing assistance against the Quichamcauichom. Other Indigenous leaders forged similar relationships with the Spanish. In 1782, Yanonali, the leader of Syuxtun, one of the largest Chumash towns and center for the bead trade, provided Chumash workers to build the presidio at Santa Barbara in exchange for Spanish goods. Yanonali acted as a good provider for the Chumash by creating alliances with the Spanish, enhancing his own status among other Chumash leaders and raising the profile of Syuxtun.

The arrival of the Spanish caused tension among some Indigenous communities. In the 1770s, Yelamus lived in three towns on the San Francisco Peninsula and traded obsidian and other goods with Indigenous People throughout the Bay area. Guimas, a Yelamu leader, created kinship ties by marrying women from Indigenous People living along the eastern shore of the bay. In June of 1776, Fathers Francisco Palou and Pedro Bonito Cambón left Mexico, leading a group of Indigenous People, a mule train, and a herd of cattle to the San Francisco Bay Area to establish a mission in Yelamu territory. Palou built a shelter and chapel near the Yelamu towns and spent the next couple of months visiting the Yelamu and their neighbors. In August, with construction of the mission well under way, a group of Ssalsons, from the southern part of the peninsula, sacked the three Yelamu towns. Yelamu survivors boarded tule rafts and moved to the north side of San Francisco Bay. Ssalsons likely wanted to protect their position in the Bay Area and prevent the smaller Yelamu villages from having access to new economic and political allies. Yet the Ssalson response to the budding relationship between the Yelamu and Spanish was not unique. Across North America, Indigenous groups competed with one another for access to trade goods and military allies.

The Spanish missionaries and soldiers differed from the Spanish sailors whom Indigenous People previously met. These Spaniards came to stay. As such, Spanish colonial policies attempted to sever the relationship between Indigenous People and their relatives, as well as between Indigenous People and the land. Rather than visiting Indigenous communities to preach, Franciscans practiced *reduccion* (reduction) of Indigenous People from their home communities. Missionaries infantilized Indigenous Peoples for being unable to control their "brutal appetites." Missionaries reasoned that Indigenous People either needed to confess their sins or endure physical chastisement to correct sinful behavior and save their souls. The best way to do this was to bring Indigenous People into a mission, far from their homelands. Once the People were in the mission, Franciscans briefly taught them about Catholicism and then baptized them. After baptism, Indigenous People lived under the Franciscans' watchful eye in a state of what historian James Sandos calls "spiritual debt peonage." By accepting baptism, Indigenous People obligated themselves to live the rest of their lives in the missions in return for learning all aspects of Catholicism. Indigenous People could not leave the missions.

The practice of *reduccion* separated Indigenous People from their relatives. Besides Mission San Luis Rey, Luiseños moved to at least three other missions: San Diego de Alcalá, San Juan Capistrano, and San Gabriel Arcángel. Luiseño Eva Kolb said, "The Luiseño people were separated and sent to various missions, not together to one mission. . . . In this way, the family was broken up; not only that, but the tribe was broken up." Inside the mission, Franciscan fathers separated men and women. Missionaries sought to control unmarried Indigenous women's sexuality by forcing them to live in single-sex dorms, designed to prevent women's libidinous interactions with single Indigenous or Spanish men. In 1798, missionaries at Mission San Luis Rey directed the construction of a dormitory for women and girls. When missionaries established the *asistencia* at Pala, they also built separate dorms for men and women.

Franciscans also estranged Indigenous People from the land. Luiseños who went to Mission San Juan Capistrano, for instance, could no longer see the sacred mountains that oriented their world view. Franciscans attempted to eradicate Indigenous religions that connected the People to land and each other. In 1801, a Chumash woman living at Mission Santa Clara received a vision in which Chupu told her that to avoid death, the Chumash must renounce Catholicism and pour special water on their heads. The Chupu prophecy spread throughout the mission and surrounding Chumash communities. Franciscans suppressed the religion as soon as they heard about it. Historical records do not reveal how they put down the Chupu religion, but likely, they made the woman publicly renounce her vision. Within the missions' walls, Franciscans attempted to stamp out Indigenous religions, which connected Indigenous People to place, sometimes through visions, and replaced them with Catholicism.

The Spanish efforts to occupy the land precipitated what historian Steven Hackel calls a "dual revolution." First, the arrival of Spanish colonists altered and damaged California's environment. Spanish officials cleared the land for agricultural and pastoral production. "Our country before the Fernandino arrived was a forest," Pablo Tac remembered. "He ordered that the trees be cut down so as to make in this way a flat expanse of land." Clearing the land was often a first step in settler colonialism. Europeans believed that unused land was waste and that they must alter the land to make it productive. These beliefs, of course, ignored the myriad ways Indigenous People shaped and related to the land. In addition to clearing the land, Spanish colonists introduced domesticated livestock. In 1776, Father Palou brought 286 head of cattle to the San Francisco Bay area. Missionaries reported the cattle "astonished" Indigenous People. Europeans frequently wrote that their technologies shocked Indigenous People. By depicting Indigenous People in this way, Europeans supported their argument that Indigenous People were primitive and in need of civilization. But the manner in which livestock altered land and plants likely shocked Indigenous People. Kumeyaay Rosalie Robertson said that the Spanish "had all kinds of animals they brought in here . . . and they turned those animals loose on our land. . . . We had lots of stuff we planted and harvested through the year. But they brought in the sheeps [sic] and goats and different things and they started taking out all the good food that we had." Domesticated livestock multiplied rapidly on California's soil. At Mission San Carlos Borroméo, herds of cattle and horses grew unchecked. In 1785, missionaries complained that so many cattle grazed near the mission that they endangered the mission's gardens and fields. A similar pattern developed when Franciscans established missions in Chumash territory. Between 1784 and 1790, Spanish officials introduced 2,435 horses and cows to the area around missions San Buenaventura, Santa Barbara, La Purísima, and Santa Inés. During the next decade, the herds increased to nearly fifteen thousand head. By 1810, more than sixty-five thousand head of livestock grazed in the areas around the four missions. Rather than fence in their livestock, missionaries simply turned out the animals and caught them when needed. Free-grazing domesticated livestock consumed grasses and acorns on which Indigenous People subsisted. Livestock overgrazed areas, which allowed European plants to replace Indigenous ones, and scared away deer and other animals.

Indigenous People recognized how domesticated livestock damaged the environment and endeavored to regain control over their lands. Kumeyaay shot cattle at night and killed the animals when they ventured near their towns. Other Indigenous People acted more drastically. In 1784, Tongva Nicolas José, an *alcalde* (Indian magistrate) at Mission San Gabriel, went to the Tongva town of Japchavit and met the healer Toypurina to discuss the possibility of attacking the mission. José chafed at missionaries, who attempted to thwart his influence at the mission. Priests forbade mission Indians from leaving San Gabriel and attending ceremonies in their home villages. Meanwhile, Toypurina and Tongvas living in their home communities clashed with mission practices. Between 1780 and 1785, the number of relocated Indigenous People doubled, and many of the new baptized Indigenous People came from communities with a history of conflicts with the Tongva from Japchavit. Additionally, the number of livestock tripled at Mission San Gabriel. Domesticated livestock undermined Tongva economies by consuming grasses and trampling on ecosystems. Toypurina brought supernatural power to the Tongva rebellion. She prophesied that the soldiers and priests at Mission San Gabriel would be dead if the Tongva and their allies attacked. Following the successful assault on the mission, Toypurina foresaw the Tongva dividing the spoils of the mission, permitting the mission Indians to return to their towns, and continuing to practice their ceremonies. Events did not transpire as Toypurina hoped. On the night of the attack, someone betrayed the Tongva. The mission guards swept into Tongva towns and captured the ringleaders, including Toypurina and José.

Some Indigenous People moved to the missions because of these environmental changes. Initially, Indigenous People came to the missions and presidios to work, augmenting what they already harvested on the land. Tac wrote Luiseños brought "stones from the sea (which was not far) for the foundations, [and made] bricks, roof tiles, cut rafters, reeds and other necessary things" for Mission San Luis Rey's buildings and the priests' homes. Luiseños earned *panocha* (a bread or pudding made from wheat and sugar), chocolate, flour, and ham for working at Spanish colonial settlements. Over time, as livestock overgrazed lands, Indigenous People permanently moved to the missions. Esselen People left their towns for Mission San Carlos in three waves, corresponding to the increase of livestock in the missions' and towns' vicinity. Between 1773 and 177, missionaries at Mission San Carlos baptized people from Achasta, Tucutnut, Ichxenta, Socorronda, and Echilat, the towns located near the mission and along the Carmel River. Newly imported livestock affected these lands first. Between 1782 and 1785, People from the more distant villages of Excelen, Eslenajan, and Sargentaruc arrived at the mission, corresponding with livestock expanding onto their lands. Between 1790 and 1792, encroaching domesticated livestock pushed People from the most distant village of Ensen into the mission.

Simultaneous with changing environments, Europeans exposed Indigenous People to diseases, the second part of Hackel's dual revolution. Tac wrote, "In *Quechla* not long ago there were five thousand souls, with all the countries nearby; because of a sickness that came to California, two thousand souls died, and three thousand remained." After 1540, trade connections with northern Mexico and Baja California already exposed Indigenous People to European disease. Disease increased after 1769, however, and expanded into new areas. Sometime between 1775 and 1793, a disease, most likely cholera, ravaged the Tolowas of Ta'giatun, located near modern-day Crescent City. Amelia

Brown remembered, "Some kind of sickness come along out there on the Point, kill 'em off, dead. Gets 'em in the stomach, they'd pass blood." English sea captain George Vancouver's sailors, who set in at Ta'giatun in 1775 and 1793, may have spread the illness to the Tolowa. Tolowas offered an alternative explanation. Lydie George recalled a man who performed a dance with a "flounders wishbone" on his head: "Wasn't supposed to do that, so they all died off. That's what brought the sickness out there. They got stomach troubles and bled that way." Indigenous Peoples responded in similar ways to the onset of new diseases. Tolowas abandoned Ta'giatun and moved to Tatitun, located more inland from the Pacific Ocean, because of the disease and ceremonial mishap. A similar incident occurred in the Sierra Nevadas. Ahwahnechees lived in the small villages that dotted Ahwahnee, the valley today called Yosemite. Protected by the valley walls, Ahwahnechees lived in small, nonagricultural, mobile communities isolated from the coast. In the late 1780s, forty years before the first European entered the valley, disease struck. Oral histories describe a "black sickness," which entered the Yosemite Valley along the kin-based trade routes connecting Yokuts communities in the Central Valley to the Paiutes to the northeast. Also, Indigenous People escaping the missions on the coast could have also brought the illness to the Ahwahnechee. Like Tolowas, Ahwahnechees fled the valley to the east to escape the sickness and lived as refugees among the Mono Lake Paiute. While some Indigenous People, such as Tolowas and Ahwahnechees, responded to the new epidemics by moving to new towns, other Native People relocated to missions.

Moving to the missions failed to protect Indigenous People from disease. In fact, they frequently found the opposite. Missions congregated Indigenous People into unhealthy and crowded living conditions, fertile ground for the spread of contagious diseases. Missionaries required Indigenous People to move out of their tule grass homes and into adobe walled structures. The damp new dwellings lacked proper sanitation facilities. In 1797, California governor Diego de Borica reported the stench of a woman's dormitory overpowered him. Statistics show the missions were terribly unhealthy places to live. The life expectancy of a Native person affiliated with a mission ranged from ten to twelve years. At every mission, death rates exceeded birth rates, sometimes by a ratio of two to one. Between 1769 and 1810, outbreaks of typhus, typhoid, pneumonia, diphtheria, pleurisy, measles, and other diseases erupted in the missions. In 1806, for instance, an outbreak of measles struck Indigenous People living from San Francisco to Santa Barbara. At the end of

April, missionaries at the San Francisco presidio reported four hundred ill Indigenous People. A month later, the number of sick doubled. Approximately, 337 Indigenous People died at San Francisco, and sixteen hundred died in the measles outbreak there.

Women and children suffered disproportionately from disease. Pregnant women faced dangers at nearly every turn. Missionaries offered little to no prenatal care, attempted to stamp out customary midwife practices, and required pregnant women to work. Spanish soldiers and colonists spread syphilis—a New World disease that traveled to Europe before returning with the Spanish to California—and gonorrhea to Indigenous People. Sexually transmitted diseases produced low fertility and high infant mortality rates. A healthy Indigenous woman might give birth to six children in her lifetime. Yet women in England gave birth to an average of seven children in their lifetime, and women in France gave birth to eight. The infant mortality rate at the missions, however, compared to other parts of the world. Thirty-seven percent of children died before the age of one, 11 percent within the first month. But the 43 percent child mortality rate for those between the ages of one and five exceeded that of other parts of the world. Quite simply, Indigenous women and children faced horrible living conditions in the missions, often leading to premature deaths and low fertility rates.

Missionaries' beliefs about Indigenous People hindered treatment and exacerbated living conditions. Missionaries ignored forced sexual contact occurring within mission walls. Instead, they reasoned venereal disease simply resulted from promiscuous Indigenous behaviors. Other missionaries believed that Indigenous People's ignorance (and in many cases rejection) of the Christian god caused their susceptibility to and death from disease. This kind of fatalism prevented missionaries from treating Indigenous People with current medical knowledge. In Baja California, for example, Franciscans did not use the new technique of inoculating Indigenous People by variolation to reduce smallpox mortality.

The declining populations at the missions produced two outcomes. Between 1769 and 1800, the number of Indigenous People on the California coast declined by nearly 50 percent. Even with the persistent increase in new people coming to the missions, measured in baptisms, the affiliated Indian populations in the missions remained stagnant in the eighteenth and nineteenth centuries. Second, with mission populations suffering such high death rates, Franciscans looked inland for runaways and potential new converts, the third way in which Indigenous People came to the missions. At San Francisco, missionaries dispatched Raymundo, a Baja California Indian, and thirty affiliated Indians to return some runaways. When they reached the East Bay, Huchiuns attacked Raymundo and his party. The Huchiuns then attacked the Spanish soldiers who followed up on Raymundo's expedition. In the ensuing melee, Spanish soldiers killed seven Huchiuns and took captured Huchiuns and runaways to the mission.

Indigenous People had reason to run away. Priests assaulted their lifeways and identities inside the missions. Missionaries changed Indigenous Peoples' names. Maurice Magante, from the Pauma Reservation, said, "Our people lost their identity and were given Spanish surnames 'for the church records,' they were told. That is why today many of our people have Mexican surnames and registered with the Bureau of Indian Affairs as such to identify them. So our original, beautiful names in our own language, that distinguished our family, our band, our tribe, and linked us for generations and generations through a common blood line, were taken away."

Franciscans often changed Indigenous Peoples' names at the time of baptism. In 1797, Yanonali, a Chumash leader, came to Mission Santa Barbara to be baptized. The Franciscan priest bestowed a new name on Yanonali—Pedro—after conducting the ceremony. Spanish officials made Indigenous People legible by giving them new names. Franciscans recorded the new and old names, dates of birth, death and baptism, as well as the towns of origin of the Indigenous People. These baptismal registers survive and serve as the basis for much of the scholarly work on the Spanish colonial period.

Mission life similarly reordered Indigenous Peoples' labor. Indigenous People built the missions and produced all that Spanish officials needed to operate them. Chumash Eva Pagaling said, "I feel that the church was built by the blood of the Indians." In 1834, Pablo Tac highlighted the areas in which Luiseños worked, such as workshops, granaries, orchards, and pastures for livestock. Tac said, "Here is where the bricks are made, and roof tiles for the missions." The mission buildings themselves contained the shape and sweat of Indigenous bodies. Indigenous People gathered the straw, mixed the ingredients, and shaped the bricks in wooden molds milled by Indigenous People from trees they cut down. Indigenous People mixed the red clay, which made the roof tiles and initially gave them their distinctive curved style by shaping them over their thighs and shins. Indigenous men tended livestock, worked in the mission's fields, and tanned cowhides. Women made clothing and ground mission crops into a *pinole*. Indigenous People recalled that the labor system resembled slavery. Maurice Magante, from the Pauma Reservation, heard stories of Indigenous People cutting down logs at Palomar Mountain and carrying them on their shoulders to Missions San Diego, San Juan Capistrano, and San Luis Rey. "They couldn't sit or drop the timbers on the ground until they reached the mission grounds," Magante said. "If they did, they were severely whipped and punished."

Plainly, mission life exposed Indigenous People to violence. Franciscans and soldiers punished Indigenous People for various reasons. Luiseño Eva Kolb's grandfather passed down stories of Franciscan abuse: "[Luiseños] were flogged when they were too sick to work, and for any other reason. If they didn't want to do something, they were flogged again." Missionaries placed Indigenous People in stocks or hobbled their legs. At Pala, Franciscans built a "prison cell," with iron bars, where missionaries incarcerated Indigenous People. At Mission San Gabriel, Franciscans maintained an "underground dungeon" to hold those they considered wayward Indigenous People. In her memoir, *Bad Indians*, Deborah Miranda traces the multigenerational legacies of violence introduced by Franciscans. In a section of the book she calls "The Genealogy of Violence, Part II," she interweaves passages written by Franciscan padres in their mission reports with a narrative of her memories of her father's physical abuse:

> *"Toward their children they show an extravagant love whom they do not chastise. Nor have they ever chastised them but allow them to do whatever they please. We know now, however, that some are beginning to chastise and educate them due to the instructions they are receiving."*—Mission San Miguel

> "You want something to cry about? You want the belt?" our father yells, embarrassed by his cowardly son, this son he waited half a lifetime to have, this son who carries on the family name as none of his seven sisters can, this son whose tears break every rule my father ever learned about surviving in this world.

The military also punished Indigenous People. In 1775, soldiers rounded up Indigenous People whom they suspected of launching an attack on Mission San Diego. When the soldiers brought the Indigenous People in for interrogation, they gave them fifty lashes. Soldiers flogged one man so severely he died from his wounds. In 1785, Spanish soldiers arrested nearly twenty Tongvas for the failed attack on Mission San Gabriel. They put the conspirators of the Tongva Revolt on trial and sentenced five to receive twenty-five lashes and another twelve to receive fifteen to twenty lashes. Officials carried out these floggings in public so that the entire mission community could see the consequence of an attempted rebellion.

Spanish officials banished Indigenous People to Baja California or other parts of Alta California. In 1785, Spanish officials found Toypurina, José, and two other Tongva men guilty of leading the attack on Mission San Gabriel. They sentenced José to six years of hard labor at the presidio at San Francisco and exiled Toypurina to Mission San Carlos Borroméo. There, Toypurina lived without kin and far from her home.

If Indigenous People ran away from the mission, the priests asked soldiers to recapture them. Punishments continued when Indigenous People returned. Kolb said, "Those who fled from the mission were hunted down and brought back, and were flogged in public." Cahuilla Katherine Siva Saubel said, "My father told a story about a great-uncle of his who escaped from the mission confines, was captured and brutally beaten, made to kneel on the ground and received more whiplashes because he refused to salute the Cross."

Still, Indigenous People and cultures proved resilient. They adapted old customs to new circumstances and adopted new practices. For instance, some Indigenous People incorporated Christianity into their worldviews. Tac wrote, "Now that we are Christians we dance for ceremony." Although Indigenous People might accept baptism, so that they "are Christians," Indigenous religious practices and ceremonies persisted. Tac described the Luiseño dance cycle, which consisted of three male dances. He did not describe the women's dance cycle, likely because he lacked access to Luiseño women's ceremonies and practices. To the north, Indigenous People continued to dance and perform ceremony, even under the watchful and likely disapproving eye of the Franciscans. In 1816, Louis Choris, a Russian artist, visited Mission San Francisco. He drew hundreds of Indigenous People dancing in the foreground and a cross looming over the event, casting a figurative shadow over cultural practices the Franciscans sought to eradicate (fig. 7).

Other Indigenous People explored what it meant to be Catholic. Franciscans buried some Indigenous People with the *santo habito* (holy habit), the clothing worn by the Franciscans. That Native People wore habits at their death suggests they wanted to follow the Third Order Secular Franciscans, laypeople who devoted themselves to following the practices of Saint Francis of Assisi. A few took the eucharist, an additional step beyond baptism that often required a priest's approval and acted as a tacit indication of the perceived depth of the conversion

FIGURE 7. California Indian dance at Mission San Francisco, ca. 1815, by Louis Choris. Photo courtesy Bancroft Library, University of California, Berkeley.

experience. But these were infrequent, and there is little evidence most baptisms represented a thorough conversion experience.

Indigenous women also gravitated to certain aspects of Catholicism. Across North America, Indigenous women found Catholicism's emphasis on the Virgin Mary an empowering alternative to the patriarchy imposed by colonial society. At Mission San Francisco, Native women expressed a desire to become *monjas* (nuns). Chumash Maria Solares summed up these contradictory perspectives. She described her grandmother as "an esclava de la misión [a slave of the mission]." Solares captured the complex nature of mission life: her grandmother ran away from the mission and considered herself a "slave." She endured harsh punishments. Yet she and many other Indigenous People adopted aspects of the new religion that entered their lives. Solares's descendants considered themselves "good Catholics."

Native artists worked within and modified Catholic and Indigenous traditions. At Mission San Fernando Rey de España, a Native artist painted the Stations of the Cross, featuring a white-skinned Jesus and darker-skinned figures. Such a painting suggests that Indigenous Californians adopted a race-based understanding of social interactions. Yet the darker-skinned figures in the painting inflict pain on the white-skinned Jesus, a subtle statement of resistance against Franciscan authority. At

Mission Santa Inés, a Chumash artist painted a portrait of Saint Raphael, holding a fish in one arm, a staff in the other, and with enormous wings, blending Chumash and Catholic symbols. The fish, staff, and wings have Catholic roots: Raphael, the healer, cured blindness with a fish's gall bladder, and his wings suggest his position as an archangel. Yet Chumash possess corollaries to these symbols: the Chumash relied on fish for their subsistence; the wings may point to the enormous California condors that once swirled around California's skies; and Raphael was a healer, much like traditional Chumash doctors.

Although some Indigenous People remembered the assault on their naming practices, others recalled that their ancestors encoded cultural traits in their new surnames. A Chumash man from Santa Inés said, "Maybe they wanted a name that would still say they were part of Mother Earth, so they got together and chose names that had some connection with the sky or the earth. And so we have people by the name of *Robles*, which is the oak tree, which is strong and it has a very beautiful significance for the Indian people." He continued: "Then there's the name '*Pina*.' Pina means pine nut. That was one of the staple foods of the Chumash." Missionary practices might separate People from the land, but naming practices restored those connections.

Indigenous People incorporated newcomers into preexisting kinship relationships. In 1789, Toypurina, the spiritual leader of the Tongva attack on Mission San Gabriel, lived at Mission San Carlos Borroméo as an exile. She married a Spanish soldier named Manuel Montero, from Puebla, Mexico. Toypurina gave birth to three children: Cesario, Juana de Dios Montero, and Maria Clementina. It is possible that Toypurina married Montero because he protected her from the poor living conditions that plagued the missions. Furthermore, Toypurina and Montero were strangers in a strange land, far away from their natal towns. They were kindred spirits in a new place. Toypurina continued to move for the rest of her life. In 1799, she passed away at Mission San Juan Bautista.

Native People who lived year-round at the missions limited how Franciscans intruded into their daily lives. At many missions, Native People used the mission's spatial layout to insulate their communities from complete Spanish control. In one depiction of an idealized Spanish mission, a road and irrigation ditch separated Indigenous dwellings from the central mission quadrangle. Within their quarters, Indigenous ways of life endured. Indigenous People retained the use of stone and bone tools and refashioned Spanish items to their own purposes. Indigenous People ate customary foods, such as fish, birds, and game, in addition to domesticated livestock

FIGURE 8. California Indians at Mission San Francisco, ca. 1815, by Louis Choris. Photo courtesy Bancroft Library, University of California, Berkeley.

and European-introduced crops. Finally, Indigenous healers tended to the sick with ceremonies and medicinal plants.

Indigenous People maintained ties with the land and with family outside the missions. Affiliated Indians visited kin, and townspeople came to the missions to interact with relatives. Artist Louis Choris drew Indigenous People playing a gambling game. The presence of fully clothed and seminude Native People suggests that not everyone in the painting lived at Mission San Francisco. Priests gave Indigenous People clothing that accorded with Spanish beliefs about decency. Baptized Indigenous People might wear a blanket, work shirt, and a skirt or loincloth. But Choris depicted some of the Indigenous People without these items, which suggests that they lived outside the mission, beyond the reach of Franciscan missionaries. These men came to the mission for entertainment, such as a traditional gambling game, clearly not a part of the Franciscan conversion process (fig. 8).

Traditional work and labor practices persisted as well. Tac recounted that Luiseño men woke up every morning, took their bow and arrow, and hunted in the woods or cut firewood. Luiseño women still prepared food and attended to domestic chores. If anything, the children's lives changed substantially. Tac mentioned that priests selected some precocious children to sing in the choir and attend schools. Older boys worked in the fields, and girls went to the workshops to make clothing and blankets and sometimes lived in dorms, isolated from their families and unwed men.

Within the missions' walls, Indigenous People assumed important leadership roles. Spanish colonists integrated Indigenous leaders into political offices, including that of alcalde. Although the alcalde reported to the priest, he performed similar roles in the mission as in Indigenous towns. He announced work schedules and supervised the labor in the fields. He also exhibited emblems of status or wealth, such as wearing Spanish clothing and carrying a staff. Still, Indigenous People elected alcaldes, suggesting that alcaldes walked a delicate line between the Indigenous community and the Spanish priest.

Although missionaries and Spanish soldiers attempted to confine them, Indigenous People remained mobile. They moved back and forth between town communities and the missions. In part, missions could not sustain large Indigenous populations. Mission San Diego and Mission San Luis Rey could not grow enough food to support Indigenous People year-round, so Luiseños, Kumeyaays, Cahuillas, and Cupeños lived in their own towns, such as Quechla and Pala, and came to the missions for special events, such as festivals, mass, or communal labor. In the fall, Chumash lived in the mountains, not at Mission Santa Barbara. Missionaries explained that there were so few Chumash at the mission that a single kettle of soup could feed the entire population.

Indigenous People left missions for many of life's significant events. Some began their lives outside the mission walls. In 1786, Juuim gave birth to her son Pedro de Alcantara at the village of Ssalayme, among her husband's, Simmon, female relatives. In 1802, Cabachuliva, baptized as Elzeario, and his wife, Huiumutaca, baptized as Elena, left Mission San Francisco on a *paseo* (approved furlough) to Cabachuliva's town of Huimen, located across the North Bay on the Marin Peninsula. While there, Huiumutaca gave birth to the couple's child, a daughter named Elena. Missions were dangerous places for pregnant women and infants, making Indigenous towns a safer place to prepare for and recover from childbirth. Furthermore, Huiumutaca and Juuim could follow traditional birth protocols, such as burning the infant's umbilical cord and the afterbirth and bathing the child in the ocean or a nearby stream. Others ended their lives in their own communities. In 1799, María de la Assumpción fell ill and requested permission from the missionaries to go on *paseo* from Mission San Francisco. She wished to return home to family and friends and, perhaps, to seek the assistance of customary healers. Before leaving on her *paseo,* however, Maria made a confession. Her confession ensured her a death in the good graces of the Catholic god while her return home to friends, family, and traditional healing and burial practices ensured a different kind of salvation.

The persistence of Indigenous social practices and mobility at the missions points to examples of Indigenous resistance. Some Indigenous People relied on small acts of resistance, such as claiming to be sick, expressing confusion over instructions, or breaking agricultural tools. At other times, resistance escalated. In 1808, three Kumeyaay killed Mission San Diego's *mayordomo* (foreman) because he beat them. In 1811, Nazario, a cook at Mission San Diego, killed Father José Pedro Panto for giving him 124 lashes. In 1812, Julian and Donato led fourteen People in assassinating Father Andres Quintana at Mission Santa Cruz. Both were well respected men at Santa Cruz; the former was the mission's gardener, the latter a worker at the mission. The conspiracy also included the mission cook and page. Indigenous People expressed anger at Quintana for whipping Indigenous People with the *cuarta de hierro,* a horsewhip tipped with iron. One night, Julian pretended to be on his deathbed and asked for Quintana to deliver his last rites. After Quintana made the last sacrament with Julian, other Indigenous People ambushed him. They beat Quintana, crushed one of his testicles, and returned him to his quarters. Afterward, they freed single women from the *monjerios* (dormitories for unmarried women). Men and women celebrated the overthrow of Quintana late into the night. Sometime before morning, the conspirators went to Quintana's quarters and discovered that the beating and castration had not killed the priest. They then smashed his other testicle and the priest bled to death.

The killing of Quintana demonstrated several aspects of Indigenous resistance at the mission. Although some mission Indigenous men and women found ways to advance in the missions, not all of those at the top of the hierarchy agreed with the missionaries. Several prominent mission Indians played key roles in Quintana's assassination, including the mission's gardener, page, and cook. Affiliated Indians recoiled at the severity of some of the punishments administered at the missions. Some of the mission's defenders claimed priests merely spanked or mildly chastised mission Indians for sins and transgressions. Yet mission Indians recalled severe punishments, like those administered at Mission Santa Cruz. Gender and sexuality also shaped Indigenous resistance to mission life. Mission Indians castrated Quintana, and then they broke down the doors that separated single men and women. Indigenous People protested the sexual behavior of Spanish soldiers, who raped Indians at every mission. Although missionaries often came to Indigenous People's defense in cases of rape, they, too, violated Native understandings of sexuality. Missionaries sometimes broke their vows of chastity. Father Blas Ordaz, for example, apparently fathered two or three children with Indigenous women. After Franciscan officials removed Father Mariano Rubi from California, they concluded he suffered from syphilis. More commonly, Franciscans attempted to impose Catholic ideas about sexuality, gender, and marriage on Indigenous Peoples, emphasizing monogamy, heterosexuality, premarital chastity, and the permanence of marriage. Killing Quintana and allowing single men and women to mingle challenged the Spanish efforts to control the Indigenous body.

Indigenous People often chose the simplest form of resistance and avoided the mission altogether. Some California Indians ran away, sometimes in a slow trickle and other times as a deluge. In 1795, two hundred Indigenous People left Mission San Francisco with some of the mission's horses. Once in California's interior, absconding Indigenous People taught others how to ride horses and revealed the weaknesses in the mission's defenses. Indigenous People fled the missions for several reasons. In 1797, Spanish officials interrogated twenty-three Sacalans and Huchiuns, who escaped Mission San Francisco. They found three reasons for Indigenous People running away from the mission. First, Indigenous People resented punishments and violence. Timoteo explained that Luis, the mission alcalde, whipped him while he felt ill. Later, Father Antonio beat him with a "heavy cane." Second, Indigenous People fled the mission when family members died. Macario claimed he fled the mission after his wife and son passed away. Finally, Indigenous People lacked food at the mission. Liborato said that after his mother, two brothers, and three nephews died, he ran away from the mission because he feared starvation.

Indigenous People gravitated to what archaeologist Tsim Schneider calls "places of refuge," where they could collect traditional foods, share stories, dance, and carry out old practices while simultaneously integrating new ones. Three shell mounds sit on the grounds of China Camp State Park, near modern-day San Rafael. Indigenous People of the San Francisco Bay Area buried their dead under the shell mounds. They also frequented the site to clean fish and make baskets and obsidian tools. The three shell mounds at China Camp revealed evidence of Coast Miwok and Pomo cultural practices, as well as those borrowed from the Spanish missions.

In the interior, Indigenous People harbored those who escaped the missions. In 1782, the People of Eslenajan and Ensen, near modern-day Soledad, welcomed their friends and relatives who ran away from Mission San Carlos. Spanish officials gave gifts to town leaders in an effort to induce the leader to turn over current and future escapees. Chumash leaders refused to return runaways and fought Spanish soldiers over the fate of their newly returned people.

As Spanish officials looked for runaways and new converts, they increasingly encroached on Indigenous spaces. In the 1770s and 1780s, Miwoks and Yokuts in the San Joaquin Valley met Spanish officials with greater regularity. Initially, Miwoks and Yokuts hosted the newcomers and amicably exchanged trade goods. In early 1772, Yokuts living at Tulamniu, a town on Buena Vista Lake, welcomed Spanish soldiers, led by Pedro Fages. He described Tulamniu: "the natives live . . . in very large squares, the families divided from each other, and outside they have very large houses in the form of hemisphere[s], where they keep their seeds and utensils." In March, Miwoks on the northern edge of the San Joaquin Valley met Fages and Father Juan Crespí, southeast of Suisun Bay. Four Miwok men gave the visitors a "bow trimmed with feathers, the pelt of an animal and arrows" in exchange for some glass beads.

In the 1790s, however, relations soured between Miwoks and Yokuts and the Spanish. Increasingly, Spanish soldiers and priests entered the San Joaquin Valley to capture Indigenous People who ran away from the missions or to replenish mission populations with Miwoks and Yokuts. In July of 1797, Spanish officials accused Miwoks living at Sacalan, north of San Jose, of harboring runaways. Sergeant Pedro Amador took three soldiers and twenty-five civilians to the town and demanded their return. Miwoks refused to hand anyone over and opened fire on the soldiers, killing a horse and wounding two others. The Spanish fired guns at the Miwoks and, when that failed, dismounted and attacked with swords and lances. After a two-hour battle, Amador tersely reported that "some were killed," and the Spanish took thirty-two captives. The Spanish released the Miwoks but took the runaways to Mission San José. In December of 1803, Gachupa, a Yokuts leader of the town of Cholam, met with Father Juan Martin of Mission San Miguel. Gachupa refused to allow Martin to take Yokuts children to the mission. The next month, fifteen Spanish soldiers traveled to Cholam and captured Gachupa, his son, and four other Yokuts. Gachupa secured his release from Monterey by promising to return any runaway Indians living at Cholam. The next year, Martin made a similar request of Chape, the leader of the Yokuts town of Bubal. Chape also refused to hand over two hundred Yokuts children to the missionary.

By 1810, Yokuts and Miwoks openly resisted Spanish invaders. Bozants, a Chulamni Yokuts leader, informed Padre José Viader, from Mission San José, that no runaways lived in his town. Viader continued to travel along the river, looking for runaways. Yokuts harassed the Spanish invaders. Periodically, Yokuts and Spanish exchanged fire across the San Joaquin River. No one was killed, but the Yokuts and Spanish wounded one another. Two months later, Viader returned to Chulamni territory with a larger force. The Spanish attacked the town while the Chulamni performed a ceremony and captured eighty-four people. Viader allowed fifty-one Yokuts women captives to return home but took the remainder, fifteen runaways and eighteen Yokuts, to the mission.

North of San Francisco, disputes among the Spanish complicated the encounter with Indigenous People. In June of 1775, Yuroks at the town of Tsurai, located near Trinidad Bay, caught sight of ships, and two men in a canoe paddled out to greet them. The Yuroks gave the newcomers hide clothing and then followed the ships, which turned out to be from Don Bruno de Heceta's expedition. Heceta explored the Pacific coast and looked for Russian traders, who, according to rumor, were moving down from modern-day Alaska. On June 11, Heceta claimed Yurok land for Spain by planting a cross at Trinidad Head. While the Spanish understood the cross as a symbol of their discovery of Northern California, Yuroks likely understood this as a symbol of an alliance between the two parties. The Spanish quickly strained that relationship. On June 14, two Spanish sailors deserted Heceta. The following day Heceta took armed men into Tsurai to locate them, in the process capturing two Yurok headmen. When Heceta could not discern the whereabouts of the two men, he reluctantly released the Yurok captains on the advice of one of his lieutenants and the Franciscans. Eventually, one of the deserters returned and was punished, but the other apparently remained in Northern California.

After 1800, Indigenous People fleeing the Spanish missions set up their own towns in Miwok and Yokuts territory. The runaways brought new trade goods, religious ideas, and, perhaps most important, horses. In Southern California and along the Colorado River, Spanish glass beads replaced shell beads as a form of currency. Chumash, especially on the Channel Islands, where they previously made the shell beads, suffered population loss because of disease and mission relocations. In 1806, Father José María de Zalvidea and Lieutenant Francisco María

Ruiz began a tour of the lower San Joaquin Valley to find a suitable site for missions in the interior. As Zalvidea and Ruiz reached the Cuyama River, they saw wild horses. As in other parts of North America, the arrival of horses transformed relationships in California's interior. Initially, Yokuts and Miwoks ate horses to supplement declining food sources. Over time, though, they and the runaways rode the horses to raid Spanish missions and pueblos. In 1783, Indigenous runaways and Yokuts allies raided the Santa Clara Valley and stole horses. Yokuts and Miwoks traded the animals to their neighbors.

New items came from the north as well as the south. By the late seventeenth century, Indigenous People on the Plains traded horses to Native Peoples living in the northern Rockies. Once there, horses entered the Pacific-to-Plateau trade system, with a trade center located on The Dalles, on the Columbia River. By the late eighteenth century, Indigenous People and horses, acquired from Spanish missions, traveled, as commodities, north to The Dalles and east to the Humboldt Sink. In the early nineteenth century, Klamaths held trade fairs at Yainax Butte, about thirty miles east of Klamath Lake, Oregon. New trade goods arrived on the northern Pacific coast. The Yuroks who met Heceta wore iron knives, which they acquired on "the coast toward the north," around their necks. Another Yurok explained he "made [a knife] from a spike, which came from the fragment of a ship the sea had cast on the beach." Yurok women expressed interest in acquiring glass beads, perhaps as a replacement for dentalium shells. By the 1770s, metal implements remained status symbols rather than utilitarian tools. Beginning with the encounter with Sir Francis Drake, Indigenous People on the northern Pacific coast repurposed ship debris for utilitarian purposes and to demonstrate status. The new trade goods, infiltrating California from northern, Plateau, and Middle Missouri trade centers, recalibrated peoples' lives on the coast.

Some Indigenous groups entered alliances with their neighbors to create a more permanent barrier against the Spanish. Olleyquotequiebe, a Quechan kwoxot, recognized the value of a stronger alliance with the Spanish to deflect the eastern Maricopa alliance and to gain access to captive markets in Sonora. He hoped to acquire horses, metal tools, and wheat seeds from the Spanish. Olleyquotequiebe lobbied for a Spanish settlement at the Yuma crossing, traveling to Mexico City in 1776 to make his case to Spanish officials. He convinced both the Spanish and his fellow Quechan. The Spanish built Mission Puerto de Purísima Concepción and settled the area with one hundred people and their livestock. Olleyquotequiebe took the name Salvador Palma.

Relations quickly fell apart. Quechan killed Spanish livestock, perhaps in revenge for livestock ruining Quechan farmland in the narrow floodplain of the river. A power struggle emerged, fueling rumors of impending violence on both sides. By 1781, Palma renounced his pro-Spanish position and allied with his brother against the Spanish presence. A violent, quick, and decisive revolt ensued. Quechan and Mojaves killed more than one hundred settlers and seized around seventy prisoners and their livestock. In a clear instance of symbolic violence, Palma ordered men to club Father Francisco Garces to death. Furthermore, Palma ordered all Catholic icons of the mission placed in a box and set off down the river. While this marked the conclusion of Spanish settlement at the Yuma crossing, it in no way reflected the end of Spanish influence on life in the region.

With the Spanish gone, the Mojave-Quechan alliance strengthened and pushed the Maricopa to seek alliances with the Spanish farther east, particularly by supplying Spanish settlements at Tucson and elsewhere with captives. By 1801, one-third of the households in Tucson contained Quechan *nijora* (captives). As Maricopa raided Quechan for slaves, the Mojave raided farther west for horses. The missions were increasingly attractive targets as the Franciscans grew harsher in their treatment, and fugitive mission Indians brought disease, disturbing news, and intimate knowledge of the mission system into the interior. These connections between the coast and the Colorado River would undergo more changes in the future.

Beginning in 1769, the Spanish came to stay in California. Based on appropriating Indigenous land and labor, their settler colonization project hinged on the establishment of missions, presidios, and pueblos near Indigenous towns. The Spanish introduced new livestock and diseases, which forced Indigenous People to make difficult decisions. Some opted to leave the area of Spanish settlement to sustain their way of life, but others moved *to* the missions in an attempt to do the same thing. Inside the mission, Indigenous People retained aspects of their previous life, but they experienced more disease, violence, and slavery. Over time, Spanish officials increasingly forced Indigenous People to move to the missions. Yet Indigenous People and practices persisted. They acclimated to certain aspects of Spanish society and resisted other aspects. Yet by 1810, European intrusion into California Indian lives remained confined to the coast. After 1810, new people and products moved inland.

SOURCES

Scholars have poured more ink over the era of the California mission than any other period and with great controversy. Historian James Sandos summarizes these debates in his *Converting California: Indians and Franciscans in the Missions* (New Haven, CT: Yale University Press, 2004). In addition to Sandos, the following scholars offer helpful overviews of the Mission period, as well as individual missions: Lisbeth Haas, *Saints and Citizens: Indigenous Histories of Colonial Missions and Mexican California* (Berkeley: University of California Press, 2014); Steven Hackel, *Children of Coyote, Missionaries of Saint Francis: Indian-Spanish Relations in Colonial California, 1769–1850* (Chapel Hill: University of North Carolina Press, 2005); Steven Hackel, "Sources of Rebellion: Indian Testimony and the Mission San Gabriel Uprising of 1785," *Ethnohistory* 50, no. 4 (2003): 643–69; Steven Hackel, "Land, Labor and Production: The Colonial Economy of Spanish and Mexican California," in *Contested Eden: California before the Gold Rush,* edited by Ramón Gutiérrez and Richard Orsi (Berkeley: University of California Press, 1998), 111–46; Steven Hackel, "The Staff of Leadership: Indian Authority in the Missions of Alta California," *William and Mary Quarterly* 54 (April 1997): 347–76; Robert H. Jackson and Edward Castillo, *Indians, Franciscans, and Spanish Colonization: The Impact of the Mission System on California Indians* (Albuquerque: University of New Mexico Press, 1995); Randall Millikin, *A Time of Little Choice: The Disintegration of Tribal Culture in the San Francisco Bay Area, 1769–1810* (Menlo Park, CA: Ballena, 1995); Benjamin Madley, "California's First Mass Incarceration System: Franciscan Missions, California Indians and Penal Servitude, 1769–1836," *Pacific Historical Review* 88, no. 1 (2019): 14–47; Deana Dartt-Newton and Jon Erlandson, "Little Choice for the Chumash: Colonialism, Cattle, and Coercion in Mission Period California," *American Indian Quarterly* 30, no. 3/4 (2006): 416–30; and James Sandos, "Between Crucifix and Lance: Indian-White Relations in California, 1769–1848," *California History* 76, no. 2/3 (1997): 196–229.

Several scholars who examine the history of Indigenous People, women, sexuality, and gender include Quincy Newell, *Constructing Lives at Mission San Francisco: Native Californians and Hispanic Colonists, 1776–1821* (Albuquerque: University of New Mexico Press, 2009); Albert Hurtado, *Intimate Frontiers: Sex, Gender, and Culture in Old California* (Albuquerque: University of New Mexico Press, 1999); Chelsea Vaughn, "Locating Absence: The Forgotten Presence of Monjeríos in Alta California Missions," *Southern California Quarterly* 93 (Summer 2011): 141–74; and Jonathan Cordero, "Native Persistence: Marriage, Social Structure, Political Leadership, and Intertribal Relations at Mission Dolores, 1777–1800," *Journal of California and Great Basin Anthropology* 35, no. 1 (2015): 133–49.

The last two decades have seen significant development in the field of historical archaeology. Kent Lightfoot's *Indians, Merchants, and Missionaries: The Legacy of Colonial Encounters on the California Frontiers* (Berkeley: University of California Press, 2006) is an initial example of this work. Tsim Schneider has been at the forefront of these scholarly trends with "'Suffering the Hunger and a Thousand Labors in the Mountains . . .': The Archaeology of Indigenous Resistance, Runaways, and Refuge in Spanish Alta California," in *Franciscans and American Indians in Pan-Borderlands Perspective: Adaptation, Negotiation, and Resistance,* edited by Jeffrey Burns and Timothy Johnson (Oceanside, CA: Academy of American Franciscan History, 2018), 271; and Tsim D. Schneider, "Shellmounds and Colonial Encounters in the San Francisco Bay Area," *News from Native California* (Winter 2007/2008): 14–16, 18.

This chapter relies heavily on the writings of Pablo Tac and the oral histories collected in Rupert Costo and Jeanette Costo, *The Missions of California: A Legacy of Genocide* (San Francisco: Indian Historian Press, 1987), particularly those of Luiseño Eva Kolb, Kumeyaay Rosalie Robertson, Luiseño Maurice Magante, and Chumash Eva Pagaling. Born in 1822 at Mission San Luis Rey, Pablo Tac wrote "Conversión de Los San Luiseños" and a Luiseño vocabulary as a student in Rome, where he studied to be a priest in the 1830s. A Spanish text was published in 1930, and in 1952, Minna and Gordon Hewes translated it into English in "Indian Life and Customs at Mission San Luis Rey," *The Americas* 9 (July 1952): 1–33. More recently Lisbeth Haas offered a new edition and interpretation of the writings in *Pablo Tac, Indigenous Scholar: Writing on Luiseño Language and Colonial History, c. 1840* (Berkeley: University of California Press, 2011). Since Tac wrote the history and vocabulary in Italy, scholars questioned its interpretations. Historian Steven Hackel writes, "He was anything but an independent or objective informant. His account was penned by an Italian linguist in Rome . . . and it was only later assembled into its current form. Nevertheless, the narrative is a very valuable source, especially since it is confirmed by other evidence" (*Children of Coyote,* 241n32). Haas places Tac's work in the canon of Indigenous writers in areas of

Spanish colonization and argues that he wrote within Indigenous and colonial frameworks.

For California beyond the mission, see Natale Zappia, *Traders and Raiders: The Indigenous World of the Colorado Basin, 1540–1859* (Chapel Hill: University of North Carolina Press, 2014); Kathleen Hull, *Pestilence and Persistence: Yosemite Indian Demography and Culture in Colonial California* (Berkeley: University of California Press, 2009); George Harwood Phillips, *Indians and Intruders in Central California, 1769–1849* (Norman: University of Oklahoma Press, 1993); Richard A. Gould, *Archaeology of the Point St. George Site and Tolowa Prehistory* (Berkeley: University of California Press, 1966); and Robert Heizer and John Mills, eds., *The Four Ages of Tsurai* (Berkeley: University of California Press, 1952).

Native Spaces

Rome

In 1834, two young Luiseño men, Pablo Tac and Agapito Amamix, enrolled at the Collegio Urbano de Propaganda Fide in Rome, Italy. They arrived in Rome from Mexico, where they had studied for two years after leaving their home at Mission San Luis Rey, near modern-day Oceanside, California. It might seem curious to consider Rome an Indigenous space. Yet Rome and many other European cities figure in how Europeans and Americans dispossessed Indigenous People of their lands, as well as how Indigenous People, such as Pablo Tac, resisted those efforts. In 1493, after Christopher Columbus returned from what we now call the Caribbean with six Indigenous People and stories of his journey, Pope Alexander VI issued a papal bull that served as the foundation for the Doctrine of Discovery. Kings and queens sent people and policies from European cities, such as London, Madrid, Moscow, Paris, and Rome, across the Atlantic and Pacific Oceans to colonize California and other parts of North America. For more than one thousand years, beginning with the ancestors of the Beothuk traveling to Norway, Indigenous People left the Americas, crossed the Atlantic, and traveled to Europe. They came as slaves, diplomats, and students. Objects made the journey as well: baskets, beaver pelts, tobacco, tools, weapons, sacred objects. Some made the long voyage back to the Americas, but many, many more remained in Europe. All, though, transformed places like London, Madrid, Moscow, Paris, and Rome into Native spaces.

Kinship and connection to the land linked both boys' lives. In January of 1822, Tac was born at Mission San Luis Rey. He was the second of six children born to Pedro Alcantara Tac and Ladislaya Molmolix. Tac's father came from Quechla and his mother from the Luiseño town called Pumusi, located south of San Luis Rey. On January 15, 1822, a Franciscan priest baptized Tac. On August 6, 1820, a Franciscan priest baptized Agapito Amamix. Geronima Atuma Mainamman, his mother, came to San Luis Rey by way of Quechla and Mission San Juan Capistrano. In 1820, Geronima married Vicente Amamix. Both had been previously married. Geronima perished shortly after Agapito's birth, and his father passed away sometime before 1824. An orphan, Agapito grew up in the *monjerio*.

Tac and Amamix, likely extraordinary students, caught the eye of Father Antonio Peyri. At the age of eight or nine years, Tac and Amamix began to assist Peyri with his duties. On January 17, 1832, Tac, Amamix, and Father Peyri boarded a ship named *Pocahontas* and left Mission San Luis Rey for Mexico City. The boys studied at the Iglesia y Colegio Apostólico de San Fernando to prepare for the priesthood. In February of 1834, Tac, Amamix, and Peyri departed Veracruz, Mexico, for Italy (via New York, France, and Barcelona) to enter the seminary established to train priests from among colonized populations around the world.

Although Peyri physically separated the boys from their homelands, Tac and Amamix retained their Luiseño identities. They enrolled in the Collegio Urbano de Propaganda Fide as "people from Quechla." Looking at the etching of the Pallazo di Propaganda Fide by Hendrik Elandt (fig. 9), one can imagine Tac and Amamix strolling across the grounds of what today would be Via di Propaganda. The Collegio is the building on the left of the image. Tac and Amamix entered the school, along with Albanian, Cypriot, Persian, and three other non-California Native students, as part of a twenty-nine-person class. The other Indigenous students included Patritus Lynch (a Cheraw from South Carolina) and two unnamed students from the Ohio Territory. At the College, Tac received a classical education, comprising four years of Latin, two years of rhetoric, and one year each of humanities and philosophy. Tac used that knowledge to impart a legacy of Luiseño culture, history, and identity.

Sometime after beginning his studies, Tac worked with Giuseppe Mezzofanti, the chief custodian of the Vatican Library. Mezzofanti had an ear for languages and translated many languages from colonized people into Latin and Spanish. He produced an Algonquian-language catechism and a grammar for Aymara, a language from Indigenous

FIGURE 9. The Collegio di Propaganda Fide (Holy Congregation for the Propagation of the Faith) in Rome, depicted under a cloudy sky and with pedestrians, horsemen, and dogs on the street, by Hendrik Elandt, ca. 1700. Photo courtesy Rijksmuseum, Amsterdam.

People of the Andes. Tac and Mezzofanti collaborated on two projects. First, they produced a twelve-hundred-word Luiseño vocabulary. Tac's vocabulary focused on words related to Luiseño religious practices, dances, and illnesses. Second, Tac dictated a history of the Luiseños and Mission San Luis Rey entitled *Conversion de los San Luiseños de la Alta California*. Representing the only contemporaneous document written by an Indigenous author about California mission life, Tac's history has been the subject of debate among scholars, some of whom have questioned its usefulness as a source. They have questioned the work's reliability because a teenage Tac produced the history and word list from memory and in Rome, thousands of miles from San Luis Rey. Born after Mexican Independence, Tac only knew the end of the Spanish mission period, leaving California at the time the Mexican government secularized the missions. Yet Tac interpreted and told a Luiseño history of their encounter with Spanish people and colonialism in the late eighteenth and early nineteenth centuries. Furthermore, he drew pictures of Luiseño dancers and sketched a map of Mission San Luis Rey. Today, like other artifacts left behind by Indigenous travelers, these documents exist out of context, residing in an archive in Bologna.

Tac and Amamix left behind more in Rome than archival sources; they left their bones. On September 26, 1837, Amamix died, perhaps of smallpox. Church officials buried him in a subterranean crypt at the monastery church. Tac, like Amamix, died in Rome at the age of nineteen on December 13, 1841. There are reports of lingering smallpox from the previous year, which may have compromised his respiratory system. Their deaths while they were enrolled in the Collegio were not uncommon. As was the case in the missions themselves, the living arrangements in Rome encouraged the transmission of disease. Of the fourteen students who enrolled in the Collegio from present-day Canada between 1829 and 1840, four died in Rome, two died on the return voyage, two left the college for health reasons and remained in Rome, and two struggled with health issues such that they never finished their studies but returned home. Only four completed their studies and returned home to serve as planned.

In this way, Tac and Amamix resemble other Indigenous people who left the Americas and ventured into Pacific and Atlantic spaces. The six Taino slaves who accompanied Columbus to Madrid died in Spain. Mataoka (Pocahontas) traveled to London with a delegation of Powhatans in 1616. She died in England the following year, while her kinsman Uttamattomakin returned to Virginia. In the late 1840s, Pomo women accompanied their Aleut husbands to Alaska, after the Russians sold Fort Ross to John Sutter. Few returned to their homeland.

One wonders what might have happened had Tac or Amamix completed their studies and returned home to California. Uttamattomakin used his experiences in London to carry important information back to Powhatan, contributing in part to the 1622 uprising against the British. A closer example comes from Ottawas William Blackbird's and Augustin Hamlin's experiences. Blackbird, the son of Ottawa leader Mackadepenessy, traveled with his cousin Hamlin to Rome to enroll in the Collegio two years before Tac and Amamix. Blackbird died within the year. Hamlin remained at the Collegio until the spring of 1834, when he returned home to present-day northern Michigan. Once there, Hamlin turned not to the priesthood but to politics, becoming an important spokesperson for the Ottawa. He vigorously advocated for the protection of Ottawa land. In December of 1835, he wrote on behalf of the Ottawa leaders: "It is a heart-rending thought to . . . think of leaving our native country forever, the lands where the bones of our forefathers lay thick in the earth; the land which has drank [sic], and which has been bought with the price of, their native blood, and which has been there after transmitted to us." Hamlin was part of a delegation that met with President Andrew Jackson in March of 1836, to protest Jackson's Indian Removal policy. It is easy to see Pablo Tac following a similar line of action, using the colonizer's language to resist colonization, but hard to imagine all he might have accomplished had he been able to do so.

Indigenous objects traversed the oceans as well. Between 1792 and 1794, George Goodman Hewett, English navigator George Vancouver's surgeon, acquired a Chumash-made basket from Santa Barbara. The description of the basket is rather stale. The basket is ten centimeters high, made of sedge root and redbud, and decorated with abalone shells. In the early twentieth century, an unknown Pomo woman sold a basket, adorned with black, white, and red feathers, glass beads, and abalone shell, to the Austrian artist Wolfgang Robert Paalen, who lived in San Francisco. By 1946, Paalen moved to Mexico and sold the basket to an anthropologist, who in turn sold it to the British Museum in 1976. The Pomo and Chumash baskets remain in London, sometimes on display and other times in storage.

Objects traveled out of context, as souvenirs, curiosities, artifacts. Collectors did not use baskets *as baskets*. The British astrologer and mathematician John Dee did not use the polished obsidian sixteenth-century Mexica mirror he had in his collection *as a mirror*. In a similar fashion to the way Indigenous People repurposed European goods, breaking cookware to use as adornment, in rituals or as tools, Europeans repurposed Indigenous objects. Their purpose was cataloguing, organizing, controlling. In 1952, Minna and Gordon Hewes published an edited translation of Tac's narrative in the American Academy of Franciscan History's journal, *The Americas*. They had been "kindly assisted" in their translation by the Reverend Maynard Geiger, who "suggest[ed] improvements in the wording." In a sense, Tac's narrative was treated like one of those objects. The translators broke up his text into fragments, which they rearranged according to their expectations. They repurposed it. Tac himself repurposed his own experiences. He was not in Rome for the same reasons Peyri or the rector of the Collegio imagined.

Indigenous People were common visitors to Europe. Many returned. Yamacraw leader Tomochichi led a delegation to London to negotiate with King George and representatives of the Georgia Colony in 1734. Other Indigenous People went as performers in Buffalo Bill's Wild West show and did a command performance for Queen Victoria in 1887. Others went as soldiers, like Muwekma Ohlone brothers Toney and Fred Guzman, who voluntarily enlisted in the United States Army in 1918. The draft applied only to American citizens. Many California Indians only gained citizenship in 1924, making them ineligible for mandatory service. During World War I, the Guzman brothers saw action in several campaigns in France. Both men survived the war and returned to California. On their deaths, they were buried at the Golden Gate National Cemetery, in San Francisco. Atsugewi Oscar Grant served in Germany and France, and his parents, Sampson and Mary Grant, raised money for the Red Cross among the Atsugewi near Burney. In May of 1919, the *Redding Searchlight* celebrated his return. Beginning in 2012, Kashaya Pomos and Coast Miwoks traveled to Russia. The Su Nu Nu Shinal dancers performed at various locations across the country. They visited the Kunstkamera Museum, where they viewed Kashaya artifacts. Yuri Berezkin, curator at the museum, said after seeing them that he "would never see the objects the same way again."

Since 1769, California Indians and objects remade Rome, London, and other European cities. California Indian culture arrived in Europe as part of various colonial projects—as young men training for the priesthood or fighting in world wars and as artifacts sold as part of the tourist trade. The reach and continued presence of Indigenous People in Europe points to the ways in which California Indians and objects remade the world.

SOURCES

On the movement of Indigenous People across the Atlantic, see Jace Weaver, *Red Atlantic: American Indigenes and the Making of the Modern World, 1000–1927* (Chapel Hill: University of North Carolina Press, 2014); and Coll Thrush, *Indigenous London: Native Travelers at the Heart of Empire* (New Haven, CT: Yale University Press, 2016), which devotes an interlude to John Dee's mirror. On Pablo Tac, see Lisbeth Haas, *Pablo Tac, Indigenous Scholar: Writing on Luiseño Language and Colonial History, c. 1840* (Berkeley: University of California Press, 2012). On the cultural power of objects, see Les Fields, *Abalone Tales: Collaborative Explorations of Sovereignty and Identity in Native California* (Durham, NC: Duke University Press, 2008). For details on the conditions in the Collegio di Propaganda Fide in particular, and Rome in general, see Luca Codignola, *Blurred Nationalities across the North Atlantic: Traders, Priests, and Their Kin Travelling between North America and the Italian Peninsula, 1763–1846* (Toronto: University of Toronto Press, 2018); and Theodore J. Karamanski, *Blackbird's Song: Andrew J. Blackbird and the Odawa People* (East Lansing: Michigan State University Press, 2012), from which our account of William Blackbird and Augustin Hamlin was drawn. To see some of the items discussed here, consult the online search functions of the British Museum website, www.britishmuseum.org.

4

Working the Land

Entrepreneurial Indians and the Markets of Power, 1811–1849

In the summer of 1839, Western Ute leader Walkara led 150 Indigenous People, known as the *Chaguanosos,* and "adventurers of all nations," through the Tejon Pass separating the Great Basin from Alta California's coastal plain. Already well known for their raids, Walkara and his group attacked the secularized ex-missions at San Luis Obispo, San Gabriel, and San Juan Capistrano. The raiders captured between four thousand and six thousand horses and led them on a five-hundred-mile trip through the San Gorgonio Pass and into the high desert. Mexican officials in Los Angeles quickly organized an informal force, which included convicts freed from jail, to follow and recover the horses. They tracked the raiders into the desert near present-day Joshua Tree, where a contingent of the Ute raiders ambushed the posse, stole their horses, and forced the pursuers to walk back to Los Angeles.

By 1839, groups of Indigenous People like Walkara's, exceptional in size and brazenness, regularly raided former Spanish missions. For at least three hundred years, what historian Natale Zappia calls the "interior world" supported a vibrant and far-reaching trading and raiding network stretching across inland California, Arizona, New Mexico, southern Colorado, Nevada, Utah, and parts of Sonora, Mexico. In the early nineteenth century, Mexican independence disrupted the political and economic connections between California, Mexico, and Spain. Europeans and Americans arrived to fill the void left by the waning Spanish Empire. Russians encroached from the north, and Americans moved in from the north and the east. The Russians and Americans introduced new trade goods and trade partners into established interior world networks. Horses and Euro-American goods warped and twisted the markets of power already at play in the interior world. To understand how and why, we have to follow the trade back over the coastal range, into the worlds of the Indigenous People in the interior. Despite living far away from European and American incursions and settlement, interior Indigenous People actively engaged with the power that traveled through things: livestock, agricultural products, diseases, and manufactured trade goods.

Horses emerged as a highly valuable, iconic, edible, and invasive currency that transformed the region's physical landscape into fuel and power. Horses enhanced Indigenous Peoples' ability to hunt for food and trade with their neighbors. Indigenous People also used horses as food and trade goods themselves. Horses altered relationships on the California coast and in the interior world, but they did so unevenly. Tribes that went to missions often left with horses, licitly or illicitly. At the same time, tribes that remained distant in the interior often acquired horses through existing trade networks. Therefore, some Indigenous People—from the Utes in the Utah Territory to the Chumash along the coast and the Yokuts and Miwoks in the San Joaquin Valley—acquired horses, which increased their political and economic influence. Other groups found themselves in between Peoples with access to horses. For example, the Colus Patwins and some Nisenan communities found themselves blocked in by Yokuts to the south, who obtained horses from the coast, and Maidu, Washo, and Miwoks to the east, who acquired horses from the Great Basin trade network. As a result, they saw their status erode. Where they could, Indigenous People utilized these changes to deploy new identities to negotiate this dramatically opportunistic and dynamic regional market of power (see fig. 10).

In 1810, a priest launched the Mexican War for Independence in Guanajuato, east of León, and initiated a decade of insurgency and war. Several global political factors contributed to the collapse of Spanish California. Primarily, Napoleon Bonaparte invaded Spain and placed his brother on the throne. People living in the Spanish colonies did not believe the Spanish crown possessed a legitimate form of government and therefore had no right to rule over them. Mexican Independence separated Alta California from the centers of power in Mexico City and Seville. Before 1810, Spain adhered to restrictive, mercantilist economic policies. All trade, for

FIGURE 10. A California Indian riding a horse on the plain between the San Joaquin and King's River, California, by Charles Koppel, ca. 1854. Photo courtesy Bancroft Library, University of California, Berkeley.

instance, passed through Spanish ports, and Spanish authorities promoted manufacturing of goods in Spain rather than the colonies. All of these policies left California in a precarious place. Take the example of a shirt. If a missionary desired a shirt, he waited until a manufacturer in Spain made the shirt, a Spanish ship transported the shirt from Spain to Veracruz on the Gulf coast, someone then carried the shirt overland to San Blas on the Pacific coast, and someone else then reloaded it onto a ship bound for Monterey. Furthermore, Spanish officials attempted to prevent other European ships from docking at Spanish ports. Thus, Franciscans could not shop for shirts in other markets. These policies made it difficult for Spain's colonies to acquire goods and increased their price.

Indigenous People vied with Europeans to move into the power vacuum created by Spanish and Mexican weakness. In the early spring of 1812, Kashaya Pomo along the coast of the land they called Métini, west of present-day Santa Rosa, met at the outer edge of a massive trade network stretching across the Russian steppe, Siberia, and the northern Pacific. Approximately one hundred Undersea People, so called because the Kashaya believed their boats brought the sailors from under the water where they lived, came ashore north of Point Reyes. Made up of approximately twenty-five Russians and three times that many Aleuts and other Alaska Natives, the Undersea People hoped to expand the Russian American Company's (RAC) work in North America. Based in Pavlovskaya, and later Novoarkhangelsk (New Archangel), present-day Kodiak and Sitka, Alaska, the RAC built forts and agricultural outposts in California and Hawai'i to grow food for its colonies and enlarge the areas in which to hunt sea otter. Russians built the fur trade network with Indigenous laborers. Russians forced Aleuts and Alaska Natives into three-year contracts to hunt sea otters. RAC officials paid these hunters a salary, which they used to buy items from the company store. The sea otter trade connected Indigenous Peoples to remote markets of power. A decade earlier, a small contingency of Aleuts traveled thousands of miles to the capital of the Russian fur trade at Irkutsk, Siberia, to better understand the trade.

Now the Undersea People and their network of trade reached Métini, and while they threatened the changing nature of the regional landscape, they also provided opportunities. Kashaya Pomos and Coast Miwoks knew all sorts of newcomers, as well as their accompanying problems and possibilities. More than two hundred years previous, Francis Drake spent time on their shores. Since then, Kashaya Pomos and Coast Miwoks saw Spanish, English, and American ships traverse their coast and, at times, went out to meet them. Kashaya Pomos and Coast Miwoks also met Indigenous People who had fled from the Spanish missions located on the southern edge of their territories, from whom they learned all about the new material culture and unhealthy living conditions at the missions. Kashaya Pomo and Coast Miwoks understood a productive relationship with the Undersea People could provide access to new trade networks and offer protection from the increasingly assertive Spanish military expeditions into the interior, driven by the pressure of mission expansion closer to home. Unlike the Spanish, the Undersea People did not attempt to convert Indians to the Russian Orthodox faith. More practical concerns weighed on the minds of the Undersea People. Valenila, a Bodega Miwok leader, contrasted the attitudes of the Spanish and Russians by telling a visiting Russian naval officer they were "very glad of the settlement of the Russians near them . . . because the Russians did not offend and oppress them" as the Spanish did, who "catch them with lassos, like wild beasts, put them in irons and force them to work."

Kashaya Pomo and Coast Miwok leaders worked with the Undersea People and strengthened their position. To simplify interethnic relations, Russians chose one Kashaya Pomo and Coast Miwok leader with which to negotiate. The Russians named these figures *toions,* after the

Yakut (an ethnic group in eastern Russia) word meaning "leader." In 1817, Russians invited Pomo and Miwok leaders to Fort Ross. There, Russian leaders thanked the Pomos for allowing them to build Fort Ross and gave a silver medal to Chu-Gu-An, a Pomo leader. Chu-Gu-An and other Pomo and Miwok leaders consolidated power and influence through relations with the Russians. According to Kashaya Pomo oral tradition, the first Kashaya Pomo "chief," likely the aforementioned Chu-Gu-An, used the name, "Toyon." To secure and strengthen kin-based trade alliances, Miwok and Kashaya leaders created kinship ties with the Undersea People. Valenila, along with Chu-Gu-An, Amat-tan, and Gem-Le-Le, Kashaya Pomo leaders, offered their daughters as potential wives to Ross employees.

Pomos and Miwoks found limited opportunities at Colony Ross, which consisted of the fort, nearby ranches, sealing stations on the Farallon Islands, and a port at Bodega Bay. A few worked as company employees. Iik, a Kashaya man, worked in the Fort Ross kitchen. Kashayas Zakharov Irodion and Murav'ev Ieromin assumed Russian names, labored for wages on the ships, and eventually traveled to New Archangel. More commonly, Kashaya Pomo and Coast Miwoks worked temporarily at the colony. Pomos and Miwoks aided in the building of the fort by hauling clay for making bricks and cutting timber. Pomos and Miwoks tended fields of vegetables and grain, harvested wheat or barley, and watched over livestock. Pomos and Miwoks earned food, tobacco, beads, and clothing for these temporary services.

Early on, the Undersea People's demand for Pomo and Miwok labor remained fairly low. To supply their hunting outposts farther north, the Undersea People traded manufactured goods to the Spanish missions for grain. Trade with the missions for their surplus grain reduced the agricultural demand on Fort Ross. RAC employees, and their Native spouses, met these labor demands. Pomo and Miwok women who married Alaska Natives, Creoles (children of Russian men and Aleut, Pomo, or Miwok women), or, later and less frequently, Russian men made up a slightly different class of employees. The RAC drafted the women into service, working to support their husbands, and integrated their Creole children into the colony's economy.

The Spanish government's trade embargo legally restricted Alta California's trade to the infrequent official supply ships from San Blas. After Mexican Independence, the missions depended on illegal Russian trade to make up the difference. Franciscans traded agricultural surpluses, produced by Indigenous workers at the missions, to the Russians for manufactured goods, such as ticking used to make clothes for Indigenous People. In the early 1820s, newly independent Mexico lifted the Spanish trade embargo, allowing English and American trade in Alta California.

By the second decade of the nineteenth century, increased competition undermined the de facto Russian monopoly and forced the RAC to turn toward more on-site manufacturing and agriculture to maintain the colony's profitability. This economic change put more demands on Pomo and Miwok labor. Simultaneously, however, insufficient pay and increasingly harsh efforts by the Russians to impose sovereignty over Métini made Pomos and Miwoks less inclined to provide agricultural labor to support the Fort Ross colony. The Russians resorted to kidnapping, intimidating, and coercing Pomos and Miwoks. Russians raided Indigenous communities some distance from the fort, not the communities they worked with for years. In 1833, Russians attacked a Pomo town; captured men, women, and children; tied their hands; and drove them seventy kilometers back to Fort Ross. Additionally, the Russians punished Pomo and Miwok employees for what they considered crimes. By 1821, the census of Fort Ross shows eight Indigenous prisoners. Some served their sentences at Ross, others at the Farallon Islands outpost. Occasionally, Russians sent prisoners to serve out their sentence at New Archangel, as in the cases of Chilan and Yogokoiy, whom the Russians convicted of killing horses. By the end of the 1830s, most native field hands worked at Ross by force.

As the colony expanded its agriculture and ranching, it transformed the landscape in ways that harmed Pomos and Miwoks. RAC cut redwoods to build ships, houses, and other buildings, as well as fencing to keep livestock from trampling agricultural sites. Livestock, in turn, ranged farther into the interior looking for fodder, eating grasses and acorns critical to Pomo and Miwok foodways. Kashaya Herman James remembered that the Undersea People's crops of wheat "covered" and "blanketed" the land.

Although tensions between Indigenous People and the Undersea People grew, Pomos and Miwoks refrained from outright violence. In part, the presence of the Russian militia and the lack of livestock herds at the colony made Indigenous raids unreasonable. Additionally, Pomos and Miwoks partially incorporated the Russians, their tools, and their food into their world. They butchered and processed cattle the same way they had elk and deer. Pomos and Miwoks broke European ceramic, glass, and metal and used them to make projectile points, pendants, and fishhooks. Pomo and Miwok women wove invasive European plants into their baskets. The shortages of food at the colony ensured Pomos and Miwoks continued to rely on traditional foodstuffs, and they redistributed European goods inland through gift-giving, gambling, and trade. Pomos and Miwoks strengthened connections with the interior and asserted a modicum of control over their affairs.

As the missions declined and closed in the 1830s, Russians changed their raiding practices. Indigenous People, who formerly affiliated with the missions, were now free to meet the colony's labor needs without fear of upsetting the Franciscans. Russians, Mexicans, and Americans observed Indigenous People from Missions San Rafael and San Francisco Solano working at Fort Ross. In fact, Indigenous People and Russian administrators built an adobe house at Khlebnikov Ranch, one of Fort Ross's agricultural outposts in the Salmon Creek Valley, for Indigenous workers rather than the timber structures they previously built.

In some cases, Kashaya Pomo and Coast Miwok developed and strengthened a sense of collective tribal identity in comparison to traditional village identity after interacting with the Russians. In other cases, indirect contact with Europeans realigned politics and transformed Indigenous culture.

As Mexican Independence disrupted trade between Mexico and the California colony, Franciscans stepped up the intensity of agricultural production as a way of offsetting the loss of manufactured goods coming from Mexico. Since California was cut off from Mexico, presidios and pueblos depended on the missions to grow food and produce goods. As labor demands increased, Franciscans sent more expeditions into the interior world to capture unaffiliated Indians for mission salvation and labor. In doing so, Indigenous People exchanged information, trade goods, and disease between the coast and the interior.

Epidemic disease was nothing new to California. The early nineteenth century was a particularly virulent time. From 1800 to 1810, the concentration of diverse individuals into the missions' tight quarters with a shared food and water supply, and the proximity in which these people lived to domesticated animals, made outbreaks of disease common. The increase in "fugitives" fleeing the missions turned those outbreaks into waves of epidemics. Pneumonia, diphtheria, diarrhea, and unnamed fevers swept Missions San Diego, San Juan Capistrano, and San Gabriel. Measles and syphilis continued to debilitate Indigenous men and women. Diseases did not respect the boundaries of the mission walls. Instead, the spread of diseases reveal the extent of the networks linking the affiliated Indians to their interior, unaffiliated kin.

Around 1790, Tenaya, a future Yosemite leader, was born near Mono Lake. His father led the Ahwahnechee people during a disruptive moment in their lives. The Ahwahnechee fled Ahwahnee, currently the Yosemite Valley, to Mono Lake to escape what they called the "black sickness." While living there, Tenaya's father met his mother, a Mono Lake Paiute woman. In the early 1820s, Tenaya led the remaining Ahwahnechee, approximately three hundred people, back into the valley. Given the reduction in population, the Ahwahnechee could not return to their previous way of life, clustered in small villages connected by language, trade, and kinship ties with outsiders. Instead, the Ahwahnechee consolidated into larger settlements, which represented a political and cultural change significant enough that the Ahwahnechee assumed a new name: "Yosemite," from the Miwok for "Grizzly Bear." Twenty-five years later, the American Mariposa Battalion entered the valley and "gave" the valley the name. The battalion found a people already well-versed and adept at managing colonial invasion. While a new encounter for the Americans, Indigenous People had already struggled with their arrival for almost a lifetime.

As the example of the Ahwahnechee-Yosemite shows, the coastal Spanish missions altered the lives of people in the interior world. At the same time, colonial encounters across the region altered indigenous markets of power. A vast indigenous trade network connected the coast with the San Joaquin Valley, the Mojave Desert, and the Colorado River. For hundreds of years before the Spanish arrived, this trade network functioned like a river, circulating goods and captives from place to place. Mojaves determined how goods moved through this network.

Spain, and later Mexico, attempted to connect Sonora and Tucson with California. Colonial competition introduced new trade goods and altered the location and scope of demand for those already present. Indigenous People integrated these changes into the network, although they did so unevenly, realigning the politics of the Colorado River Valley. Maricopa, Cocopah, and Akimel O'odham forged an alliance seeking closer ties with the Spanish in Arizona. Quechan, Mojave, Yavapai, Kumeyaay, Chemehuevi, and some western Tohono O'odham united in response. Mojaves traded *nijora* (captives) and horses taken from coastal communities with the Quechan. Demand for nijora increased in Spanish settlements to the east, and the Quechan met that desire to strengthen their position vis-à-vis Maricopas. The trade, and extensive intermarriage, led to a very tight alliance between Mojave and Quechan communities.

After the 1781 Quechan revolt against the Spanish, the Mojave-Quechan alliance strengthened. Mojave raiders found the missions increasingly attractive targets. In 1810, approximately one thousand raiders, mostly Mojave, traveled from the Colorado River to the Tongva village of Wa'aachnga, near current Redlands. They planned to attack Mission San Gabriel, fifty miles to the west, but they abandoned their effort, likely because of unreliable reconnaissance. Instead of stealing horses and destroying the mission, the raiding party captured three thousand sheep from the mission ranchos. Historian Natale Zappia argues that during this era, Indigenous People pursued new strategies and created "a new Indian economy that harnessed (rather than destroyed) the products of missions, *pueblos,* and ranchos." In other words, Indigenous People living in the interior saw missions and ranchos as a supermarket of sorts, a place where they could shop for desired items, such as livestock and captives. When Spanish, and later Mexican, power faltered, the market of power turned trading partners into targets.

In 1821, after a chaotic decade of fighting against the Spanish, the short-lived Empire of Mexico formed. Three years later, the Republic of Mexico replaced the empire. Political upheaval in Mexico City reduced support and attention to the missions in Alta California and coincided with stronger resistance by Indigenous People. In 1819, Father Mariano Payeras, the father-president of the California missions, wrote, "A considerable number [of neophytes] have withdrawn from the mild rule of the friars and have become one body with the savages with whom they carry out whatever evil their heart and malevolent soul dictates. From day to day the danger of an attack from united apostates and gentiles is growing." Liberals in Mexico hoped to throw off the shackles of the aged colonial order and free individuals and resources, especially land, from state control. In California, nothing appeared to control people and land more than the missions.

Although the padres saw fugitives as apostates, slipping back into a state of savagery, the reality of the refugee interior was far more complex. Missions altered interior communities through trade and disease. Some interior communities sheltered mission refugees. After many escapes from Mission Soledad, the Esselen fugitive Gonzalo was captured by soldiers and sentenced to die. While shackled and awaiting execution, Gonzalo cut off his own heels to escape the chains and fled. After recovering from his wounds, Gonzalo joined with a group of insurgents led by Coast Miwok Lupugeyun, who had been baptized at Mission San Francisco at age four and given the name Pomponio. In

1818, Pomponio fled the mission and led a group of insurgents made up of formerly affiliated Indians, who had sought shelter in the interior, and the unaffiliated Indians who had sheltered them. For the next five years, the insurgents raided the Bay Area's missions and ranchos. One account claims that in fleeing from authorities, Gonzalo's horse fell, and he was injured. To avoid capture, Pomponio killed Gonzalo. Nonetheless, in 1824, Mexican officials captured and executed Pomponio.

In late February of 1824, a well-coordinated revolt took place across the three missions in the heart of the Chumash world. Chumash affiliated with Mission Santa Inés, angry over a harsh flogging, burned the mission buildings and fled to nearby La Purísima Concepción. There, Andres Sagimomatsse, an alcalde from Mission Santa Barbara, and José Pacomio from La Purísima, organized a rebel force, which built on existing connections between missions and towns. The rebels sought assistance from interior Yokuts groups and sent them shell beads to encourage participation. Some Yokuts joined; others refused. Yokuts and Chumash communities in the interior sheltered fugitives and sent fighters to the missions, where their combined force of between four hundred and twelve hundred people occupied the mission compound for more than a month.

Chumash religion organized and inspired the revolt and connected those within the missions to the interior communities. Chumash believed talismans provided power to protect rebels from Mexican bullets; to make water, rather than cannonballs, shoot from their cannons; and to make the holder invisible or capable of changing shape. Additionally, the 'antap religion, an elite religious order with members in all the major Chumash villages and followers in the missions, facilitated communication across communities and transcended the divide between those in the missions and those in the interior.

When Mexican soldiers retook the mission compound at La Purísima, the rebels capitalized on those existing relationships and relocated to a camp in the San Emigdio Valley and later to the Buena Vista Lake region. Sagimomatsse's relationship with the unaffiliated Yokuts leader Hilarón Chaaj and Chumash leaders José Venadoro and Luis Calala enabled the retreat. Under Sagimomatsse's leadership, approximately 450 unaffiliated Indians and fugitive mission Indians formed a new community in the San Emigdio Valley. By April, a Mexican military force found their camp mostly deserted but with clear signs that the Chumash had recently occupied the area. In June, padres from two missions and soldiers found the rebels' new settlement, Mitochea, on an island in Buena Vista Lake. The location gave the rebels a clear tactical advantage, and negotiations ensued. Eventually, some Indigenous People surrendered and returned to the missions. Sagimomatsse returned to serve as an alcalde in Santa Barbara, helping the padres locate others who fled. Mexican officials captured and executed approximately seven Indigenous People for murder and sentenced Mariano, Pacomio, Benito, and Bernabé to ten years in prison.

Indigenous People in the interior absorbed changes emanating from the coast by reconfiguring spatial relationships. Tashlipun, perhaps the largest Emigdiano Chumash village, sat in the northern foothills of the western Transverse Ranges. In the late mission period, unaffiliated Chumash resettled the area to escape the mission and, much like the Underground Railroad, to facilitate the freedom of others who fled from the missions. Chumash settled in places where they could assist refugees, and those settlements faced different directions. Tashlipun faced north and toward interior Yokuts towns, such as Tulamniu, located on the southern shore of Buena Vista Lake. Only two hundred meters south, "Runaway Camp" faced south and toward the coastal world of missions and ranchos. The Chumash towns connected the coastal and interior worlds and a protected site of refuge.

Similarly, during the mission period, unaffiliated Chumash repurposed Pinwheel Cave, a Chumash religious space known for its rock art, as a site of refuge. The cave is a rock shelter and bedrock mortar site with a commanding view of the San Joaquin Valley. Chumash who ran away from the missions left behind glass beads, iron-needle-drilled *Olivella* wall beads, and mission pottery. Pinwheel Cave's remote location protected runaways from recapture. Indigenous People in the interior used existing political and cultural systems to protect themselves from the destructive elements of the mission system, as well as to welcome those who fled from it. Those strategies also altered aspects of their own society.

Just as missions altered life far beyond mission walls, the trade economy of American and European merchants altered life beyond the marketplace. In the 1820s, American fur trappers penetrated California's interior, competing with the Hudson's Bay Company farther north, and availing themselves of the political chaos and economic changes in Mexico. While their initial forays into the Sierra Nevada were numerically insignificant, they connected regional trade to another network stretching across the continent and facilitated the transmission and spread of disease and goods throughout the interior.

As with the Spanish, the arrival of Americans altered the political landscape. Indigenous People viewed Americans in light of their own needs. American Jedediah Strong Smith traveled from Utah to San Gabriel. From there, he moved north into southern Yokuts territory, near Kern Lake in early 1827. Yawelmani Yokuts and Sukuwutnu Yokuts accepted Smith, but Miwoks along the Mokelumne and Cosumnes Rivers rejected him, in part because he shot at them because he suspected them of stealing some of his traps. Along the American River, another encounter turned violent when Smith killed several Nisenan. His expedition returned south to the Stanislaus River, northeast of present-day Modesto, in territory traditionally held by the Lakisamne Yokuts. Smith found the area largely empty owing to disease and Spanish officials' removal of Yokuts to Mission San José.

Muquelemne Miwok sought a closer relationship with Smith because they worried about northern Miwoks encroaching on their territory. Muquelemne chief Te-Mi made overtures to Smith's party. On learning this in May of 1827, Narcisco, a Lakisamne Yokuts at Mission San José, led four hundred mission Indians to their traditional territory. They remained in the interior for the summer, living among the Muquelemne and fending off attacks from Mexican forces. Part of their interest in returning may have stemmed from the desire to avail themselves of the potential trade opportunities Smith's presence provided. In addition, Narcisco and other Lakisamne Yokuts worried that other communities might also be attracted into their territory. The American arrival functioned as both a magnet and a threat, and Indigenous communities forged separate and distinct relationships with them in response.

Along the Sacramento, Trinity, and Klamath Rivers, Indigenous People reacted to Smith with hostility. Many of these groups either lacked sustained encounters with Europeans or Americans or experienced negative interactions with them. By the first decades of the nineteenth century, Spanish expeditions to capture Indigenous People stretched far into the northern part of the state. Indigenous People in this region had more to protect by keeping Smith out than to gain by availing themselves of the connections and trade goods he offered.

As Smith traveled inland, Spanish and later Mexican landholders turned to cattle ranching to take advantage of the booming hide and tallow industry. Manufacturers in New England needed cattle hides for shoes and other leather products. Silver miners in Peru, meanwhile, used tallow, rendered beef fat, for candles and soap. American and

Spanish merchants traded manufactured goods for the cattle by-products. The hide and tallow trade also increased demand for Indigenous labor. Indigenous People herded and slaughtered cattle, preserved hides, and tendered tallow. All were very messy jobs.

Indigenous resistance, partly emboldened by new opportunities for trade and increasing collaboration with unaffiliated interior communities, helped to bring down the mission system. In the summer of 1826, California governor José María Echeandía issued a partial proclamation of emancipation, which allowed Indigenous People to petition for their freedom. Many did and received documentation freeing them from the missions. This effort to emancipate Indigenous People, however, became entangled with secularization, a process to shift ownership of the mission properties from the Franciscans to joint control by civil and secular clergy.

People in California possessed distinctive opinions on how to approach emancipation and secularization. Mexicans and Indigenous People disagreed on who should own the mission lands and control Indigenous labor. The Mexican government promoted settlement of the territory and therefore wanted former mission lands open to Indigenous People, soldiers to whom the Mexican government owed money, Mexican residents of California, foreign families who agreed to settle, entrepreneurs *(empresarios),* and convicts. The idea of opening lands led to colonization efforts in 1833. Californios saw things differently. They expressed concern about access to labor and generally believed Indigenous People should acquire the missions' land and property but should be obligated to perform common labor. In short, Mexican officials wanted settlement by a broad array of people. Californios wanted to secure and control Indigenous labor.

Unsurprisingly, Indigenous People saw things differently. They understood emancipation to mean freedom rather than the more technical disaffiliation understood by Californios. The desire for freedom caused many to disregard Echeandía's process of petition, especially in large groups. In November of 1828, while leading a group of Indigenous People from Mission San José on a visit home to Lakisamne, Estanislao, the Yokuts alcalde of the mission, notified the priest that they were emancipated and in revolt. He claimed not to fear the Mexican soldiers, who were "few in number . . . very young, and do not shoot well."

Estanislao sought alliances with disaffected Indigenous People from Missions Santa Clara, Santa Cruz, San Juan Bautista, and among the unaffiliated Yokuts along the Stanislaus River. Eventually, more than five hundred Indigenous People joined Estanislao at a fortified village in the San Joaquin Valley. Several leaders emerged from those alliances: Lakisamnes Yokuts Cipriano; Yozcolo, from Mission Santa Clara; and Chowchilla Yokuts José Jesús, whose raids cast shadows across the region for decades.

During the spring of 1829, the rebels traded horses stolen from the missions with American traders. In this way, Yokuts used the American presence to resist the Mexican military. Increasingly desperate and fearful of further uprisings, the Mexican forces murdered cooperative affiliated Indians, Indian auxiliaries, and rebel prisoners. By summer, Estanislao secretly returned to San José to seek a pardon from the priest. Once he secured his freedom, Estanislao resumed his duties as alcalde and vaquero. Cipriano refused to return and died in the interior. José Jesús, however, dominated the trade network in stolen horses throughout the Mexican-American War.

In addition to Indigenous People fleeing and resisting the missions, decreasing support coming from Spain and, later, Mexico undermined Franciscan efforts. With independence from Spain, Indigenous Peoples' fate and the land they developed at the missions were deeply intertwined and swept up into the powerful political battles within the Mexican government. The disputes, not entirely ideological, became rooted in assumptions each side made about Indigenous Peoples' capacity to manage their own affairs. Liberal politicians, who in the early years of the Mexican Republic identified with the ascendant Enlightenment ideals of human equality, sought to diminish the power of the Catholic Church, which they associated with colonial Spain. Toward that end, they argued for the return of all mission land to the public domain, as well as the emancipation of Indigenous People from the missions. In 1830, Governor Echeandía proposed a tentative compromise between liberals and church sympathizers, who wanted to retain some aspects of protective oversight. Echeandía planned to convert mission lands to *pueblos,* or towns; secularize the missions into parish churches; and emancipate Indigenous People, with the possibility of receiving land and former mission property, particularly livestock. Economic and political instability left the plan largely unfulfilled, but Indigenous People often took up the plan's promise on their own. Even before Echeandía's plan, Father Narcisco Durán had complained that neophytes from Mission San José ran away because they lacked respect for Mexican soldiers. After Echeandía's proposal, Indigenous resistance grew, and the People increasingly demanded emancipation.

Revisions to Echeandía's plan maintained much of the mission system but replaced religious with civil authority. Indigenous People could organize together and request emancipation, in which case civil administrators oversaw the ex-neophytes' work. Mexican officials then restored undistributed mission lands to the public domain. The process proved difficult to navigate and the boundaries unclear. A group of mission Indians asked Tomás Tajochi, the Luiseño overseer at Mission San Luis Rey's Rancho Santa Monica, to represent them to Echeandía. In February of 1833, Tajochi met with mission alcaldes and captains of unaffiliated communities. Authorities did not understand what the Luiseños hoped to accomplish, particularly by involving those outside the mission. Mexican officials feared a rebellion and arrested Tajochi and four others for trying to "be independent and govern themselves," which was, to the Luiseños, the essence of emancipation. Mexican judges sentenced Tajochi to two years labor.

In 1833, Governor José Figueroa responded to the confusion and half-hearted efforts with the "Provisional Steps for the Emancipation of Mission Indians," which provided for the emancipation of married Indians who had been Christian for twelve years and knew how to cultivate the soil or had a trade. The act, however, obligated those Indigenous People to develop mission lands as pueblos, to continue to work and care for the livestock, and to cultivate their land or face being placed back under mission control.

All the competing interests in the state converged on the issue. The president of the mission system, Narciso Durán, described it this way: "The government wants the Indians to be private owners of lands and of other property; this is just. The Indians, however, want the freedom. . . . The [Californios] want the absolute liberation and emancipation of the neophytes without the command to form civilized towns, in order that they may avail themselves of their lands and other property, as well as of their persons. I do not see how these opposing interests can be harmonized." At Mission San Luis Rey, neophytes proclaimed, "We are free! We do not want to obey! We do not want to work!" In 1834, thousands left the mission and returned to their communities.

In August of 1834, Governor Figueroa issued his second set of regulations, the "Provisional Regulations for the Secularization of the Missions of Upper California." The chaos of Mexican politics also swept up these regulations. The presidency alternated between two people seven times in twenty-one months, producing competing and contradictory plans for California. In the ensuing standoff, Figueroa accused José Maria Híjar, the newly appointed governor, of trying to enrich himself at the expense of the region's Indigenous population by seeking their full emancipation, which would make land available for settlers. Híjar cynically responded that Indigenous People were equal to any Mexican, a proposition Figueroa thought preposterous. Euro-Americans' thoughts about Indigenous People had more to do with how they could benefit from them than with a realistic assessment of their situation in society.

Clearly, Mexican officials separated secularization from emancipation. A few Indigenous People were emancipated before secularization, but most were not. After secularization, some Indigenous People remained close to the mission, working for food and housing. They asserted their freedom through work stoppages and holding previously prohibited celebrations. Indigenous People continued to work in the same capacity in some instances until formally emancipated, as late as the 1840s.

It is difficult to track Indigenous People during this time because they were highly mobile. The breakup of the missions also produced a decline in the rigor of record-keeping. Finally, the ongoing population decline, which had begun before secularization and emancipation, made it difficult to estimate how many Indigenous People left the missions because of emancipation (or their belief that they had been freed) or secularization. In general, Indigenous People, who could, left. One study suggests 60 percent of the Indigenous population living in the missions left between 1834 and 1842, with more leaving in the first few years than the last few. Others suggest even larger numbers: by 1835, only 1 percent of the mission Indian population remained at San Francisco Solano. By the early 1840s, 3 percent of those at Mission San Francisco de Asís remained. In the southern part of the state, the numbers appear slightly higher: 9 percent remained at Mission San Juan Capistrano by 1838, and 20 percent remained at Mission San Luis Rey by 1841 (fig. 11).

Many Indigenous People moved to the region's growing cities and towns. Between 1825 and 1828, six years before secularization, the number of Indigenous People in Los Angeles increased from 23 to 311. By the mid-1830s, two major Indigenous settlements existed near Los Angeles. Pipimares, the smaller of the two settlements, consisted of a cluster of houses occupied mostly by Chumash and Nicoleño migrants from San Nicolas Island. Trappers working for the Russian American Company attacked residents of the island and, in the 1830s, took all but one to the mainland. Juana Maria, the island's lone resident, lived alone for two decades.

Transplants from the missions to the south and Tongva, who abandoned the site of Yaanga, constituted a larger settlement just south of the

FIGURE 11. Ruins of the church and buildings of the Ex-Mission of San Luis Rey, from rear, May 1865. Photo courtesy USC Digital Library. California Historical Society Collection.

present-day site of Union Station. The polyglot Indigenous communities supplied critical labor to Los Angeles's incipient wine industry. Between 1837 and 1842, Tongvas and Chumash planted more than one hundred thousand vines. The residents of these settlements faced a legal system created to exploit their labor. Without documentation of employment, Los Angeles Indians were arrested by Mexican officials for vagrancy. Ranchers bailed them out of jail, forcing them to work off the debt. By 1845, settler communities in Los Angeles destroyed the settlements and forced the former residents to move across the river. By the following year, Los Angeles settlers destroyed those new settlements and forced Indigenous People to live with their employer or face arrest as vagrants.

Most of those who left the missions remained close by, often in their traditional tribal homeland, and worked on ranchos, which sat on property previously belonging to the mission. As they had in the missions, Indigenous People developed several strategies to thrive. Former affiliated Indians attempted to recapture earlier subsistence strategies by hunting and harvesting. Some stole livestock, while others formed armed groups to protect themselves and resist recapture for labor. Many People moved and sought work on the ranchos because mission livestock devastated food-harvesting areas and scared off deer and other game. While the land and the nature of work remained essentially the same, these new jobs paid wages and offered some degree of worker control over labor. Employers offered meager wages (less than a dollar a week) and occasionally paid in goods rather than cash. In one case, Bay Miwoks around Suisun Bay suffered from malaria. Their employer, a Harvard-trained doctor, offered them quinine as opposed to cash wages. The Bay Miwok accepted.

Many other Indigenous People worked in more exploitative labor systems. Approximately two thousand to four thousand Indigenous People worked in a system of unfree labor, bound to their employer by debt, or worse. Labor relations at Rancho Petaluma, General Mariano Guadalupe Vallejo's rancho, located outside of modern-day Petaluma, illustrated these trends. First, Vallejo used debt to secure Indigenous workers. Former affiliated People grazed their cattle on Vallejo's land in return for herding and butchering cattle. Over time, Vallejo charged the Indigenous People far more than what they earned. Indigenous People either gave their cattle to Vallejo to pay off the debt or, increasingly, fell into indebtedness. Second, Vallejo ordered small- and large-scale military attacks on Indigenous communities. Vallejo accused Indigenous People in the interior of stealing horses and ordered expeditions to recapture his livestock and take captives, whom he kept as ranch workers. Finally, Solano, a Suisun Patwin leader, made an alliance with Vallejo and provided him with workers. In 1810, Franciscan priests at Mission San Francisco baptized Solano. After Solano and other Patwins left the mission and returned to their homeland, they worked for Vallejo to fulfill their part of the alliance.

Indigenous People continued to resist abuse by protest and flight. In 1838, at the former Mission Santa Clara, thirty field hands drafted a public notice protesting the cruelty of their administrator: "We give our administrator 8 days to remove him and put another in his place. . . . If this is not done as we state, one of two things will happen: Either this man will experience some misfortune or 30 of us men will walk off."

Others left for new opportunities in distant places. The story of Crespin and Policarpio illustrates these trends. Baptized in 1816 at Pala, the asistencia northeast of Mission San Luis Rey, Crespin's parents raised him in the interior. Policarpio, baptized in 1811, grew up in a village outside Mission San Juan Capistrano. Between 1833 and 1834, both of them, independently, headed east from Southern California on the Old Spanish Trail. Crespin traveled with a non-Indian trader, stealing horses along the way. Policarpio journeyed with another Indigenous person. They both arrived at Abiquiu, a major trading hub between

Santa Fe and Taos in New Mexico. Crespin remained for more than a year, where he observed other California Indians passing through Abiquiu. Meanwhile, Policarpio visited pueblos in the area. By 1835, Crespin and Policarpio participated in regional trade networks stretching from their home base of Ysleta Pueblo to El Paso. At the conclusion of one such six-day journey in 1836, the men were arrested in El Paso on suspicion of trading weapons with the *indios bárbaros,* the Spanish name for Indigenous People who remained outside their control. Before their case went to trial, Crespin and Policarpio escaped from jail and disappeared from the historical record.

Indigenous People sought land as well as mobility. Indigenous People argued they earned land through their labor. The alcaldes at Mission San Juan Capistrano demanded Mexican officials hand over mission lands to those who had worked them. One alcalde claimed, "To stand by and watch these men [the appointed administrators] take over the missions which we have built, the herds we have tended, and to be exposed incessantly, together with our families, to the worst possible treatment and even death itself, is a tragedy!" He further threatened to take the livestock with them as they fled to the Tulares.

For those few Indigenous People who received land grants, the opportunities were tenuous. Kumeyaay Cristina Salgado was born at San Luís Obispo in 1777. Her parents came from Baja California and moved with the missionaries into Alta California. Salgado married Esselen Gaspar María Talatis from San Carlos, where they resided briefly. They left San Carlos sometime between 1819 and 1820, eventually moving to the pueblo of San José, then to the ranchos in the Salinas Valley. Talatis died in 1827, and Salgado received title to the twenty-two-hundred-acre Rincón de las Salinas at the mouth of the Salinas River, where she lived in 1834. Along with the labor of another widow from San Carlos and seven children who moved to the rancho, Salgado entered the hide and tallow trade. In 1844, in an effort to secure her situation for the last years of her life, she sold the land to a caretaker at the Monterey customs house with the proviso that she be allowed to live on it for the rest of her life.

Luiseño Pablo Apis leveraged his position within the mission to leadership in Temecula and eventually procured land for his family. He was born ca. 1792 near Guajome, and baptized at Mission San Luis Rey in 1798, where he eventually became an alcalde. When Mexican officials secularized San Luis Rey, Apis attempted to retain the mission's land for Luiseños, work that pitted him against Pio Pico, the first civilian administrator of the former mission. Pico reinstated many of the Franciscans' practices that had divided Luiseño men and women. According to Luiseño Julio Cesar, who lived at San Luis Rey in the 1830s and 1840s, "the system that the priests had followed was continued by Señor Pico during his administration. There was a nunnery [dormitory] for single girls. . . . There were separate quarters for unmarried men." Pico sought to acquire land in the area, provoking fierce Luiseño resistance by 1836. Luiseños selected Apis to travel to San Diego and represent their interests in their protest against Pico. Mexican military officials, under Pico's orders, arrested Apis. Approximately one thousand Luiseños, many armed, gathered to object to Apis's arrest, eventually resulting in his release. Pico subsequently rearrested Apis and other Luiseño leaders. Luiseño defiance grew fierce, and Pico abandoned his position and claims on Temecula, in favor of land elsewhere.

In 1843, Pablito Apis, Pablo's son, received a grant of approximately two thousand acres surrounding the village of Temecula. He built an adobe with extensive vineyards and orchards and used ranchlands nearby for his livestock. In 1845, Governor Pico confirmed the Little Temecula Ranch, but, in 1853, around the time of his father's death, the Public Land Commission rejected the claim. Between 1843 and the mid-1850s, father and son acted as the informal leaders of the region's Luiseños. The adobe functioned as the center of the Temecula Village and the location for the 1851 treaty signing with the American commissioners.

Similarly, María Juana de los Angeles petitioned for and received a grant for Rancho Cuca, part of Mission San Luis Rey's holdings. In May of 1845, Governor Pico granted the land to her. Casiano Sobenish, Angeles's husband, was a Luiseño captain, who obtained some land in the late 1830s but without formal title. He died by the time Pico granted Cuca to Angeles. In November of 1852, María Juana de los Angeles filed her formal claim under the Public Land Commission, which confirmed and later patented the land.

In the early years of American control in California, contradictory California Supreme Court and United States Supreme Court decisions obscured the legality of Indian land grants. In one case, the California Supreme Court held that Roberto, an emancipated Indian, did not have the right to sell or transfer his land grant to a Californio because contracts involving Indians resembled those of "infants, idiots, lunatics, spendthrifts and married women." All of the aforementioned people were citizens but required the "intervention of [a] tutor, curator, committee or guardian." The court upheld the claims by American settlers that the land remained in the public domain and thus open to settlement. Three years later, the United States Supreme Court heard arguments on another case involving the ability of a California Indian to sell or transfer a Mexican land grant. A Mexican military official assisted the Patwin leader Solano in obtaining a land grant near Suisun Bay. Solano later sold the land to the official, who, in turn, sold it to an American settler. In this case, the question was whether Solano was "competent" under the law to have received the grant in the first place. In this instance, the judge wrote:

> But as a race, we think it impossible to deny, that, under the constitution and laws of [Mexico], no distinction was made as to the rights of citizenship, and the privileges belonging to it, between this and the European or Spanish blood. Equality between them, as we have seen, has been repeatedly affirmed in the most solemn acts of the government. . . . Our conclusion is, that [Solano] was one of the citizens of the Mexican government at the time of the grant to him, and that, as such, he was competent to take, hold, and convey real property, the same as any other citizen of the republic.

In both cases, the courts ruled that Indigenous People had been citizens of Mexico, yet the courts came to that conclusion for different reasons and with different consequences. One court decided that Roberto could *not* sell his land. Another court ruled that Solano *could* sell his land. The courts' legal distinctions hewed closer to the American claimants' desires for Indigenous land than to the cases' legal logic.

Most Indigenous attempts to obtain land from the missions failed. By the 1840s, Pueblito de las Flores, near San Luis Rey, grew to include thirty-two families with sheep, oxen, milk cows, and cultivated fields. By 1843, for unclear reasons, but almost certainly under duress, the village alcaldes transferred all village land and buildings to Pio and Andres Pico. In 1844, the Dominican missionary Joseph Sadoc Alemany received land grants on behalf of the formerly affiliated Indians of *all* of the missions. These grants were for small tracts of ungranted lands near the missions. It is unclear whether Indigenous People occupied the grants, but in 1853, the Public Land Commission rejected the claims.

During the late 1830s and early 1840s, marketplaces of power played out in an untended garden. Local Indigenous power, which had followed communities *into* the missions as alcaldes, moved back out into the interior world, linking communities and reinforcing surviving power structures. But Indigenous People deployed power in a dramatically changing environment. Russians moved the fur trade to more lucrative hunting groups, taking Fort Ross's livelihood with it. RAC workers and some of their Pomo spouses gradually relocated to New Archangel. In 1841, Russian officials closed the fort and sold its equipment and buildings to John Sutter, a colorful and rapacious settler from Switzerland. The hide and tallow trade ascended along the coast and animated the interior's ranching industry. Mexican ranches proliferated and Indigenous labor proved vital to the booming business. Indigenous men worked as vaqueros, rounding up and slaughtering cattle, skinning and salting the hides, and rendering the tallow that was carried in two-thirds of all foreign vessels leaving California ports by the 1830s. Indigenous women performed domestic work in the homes of Mexican citizens.

Americans saw these changes and the myriad possibilities available. The Pacific trade brought more and more Americans to California. John Sutter disassembled Fort Ross for lumber to build Sutter's Fort, the administrative heart of New Helvetia, his forty-eight-thousand-acre claim around the confluence of the Sacramento and American Rivers. Sutter established a baronial fiefdom based on Miwok and Nisenan labor. He convinced Miwok and Nisenan leaders to organize labor crews in return for exemptions from his efforts at strict social control. Indigenous men constructed an eight-foot-high corral wall, inside which horses trampled the grain to thresh it. Indigenous men winnowed the grain by tossing shovels full of wheat into the air on windy days.

Sutter cracked down on traditional Indigenous practices. He banned polygamy at New Helvetia. Sutter enforced discipline gruesomely and recruited his own personal army of two hundred soldiers and cavalry. They conducted raids on interior villages, bringing orphan survivors of their attacks to New Helvetia to work. Often, Sutter rented those children out to others as payment for debt. Miwok and Nisenan workers lived at Sutter's Fort in disease-ridden barracks and relied on Sutter for food. A Nisenan man later described eating gruel of boiled barley and corn from a hollowed-out log, "like a hog's feeding trough."

By 1845, California buckled under internal fissures and external pressures. Mexico largely left California to its own defense. Governor Pio Pico, operating out of Los Angeles, contested power with the commanding general José Castro, operating out of Monterey. The presence of, and pressure from, American expansion grew. Early American settlers made uneasy alliances with Californio elites. The prospect of Pacific ports, ranching, and the hide and tallow business drew attention to the region, as Mexico grew increasingly unable to govern from Mexico City. Indigenous raids, such as Walkara's described at the beginning of this chapter, illustrate Indigenous People did more than survive. The raids call to mind what Anishinaabe literary theorist Gerald Vizenor has termed *survivance:* "more than survival, more than endurance or mere response; the stories of survivance are an active presence. . . . Survivance is an active repudiation of dominance, tragedy, and victimry." The raids also demonstrate Indigenous efforts to lay claim to the wealth of the missions, wealth Indigenous People created. Americans, though, viewed Indigenous People as an obstacle to their advancement, as well as a potential lever in their struggle with Californios. Thomas Larkin, an American diplomat and businessman, claimed that many Californios wanted American control: "a considerable portion of the Californians are well aware, that their land and property would increase in value, by change of Flags! . . . They are convinced that a proper administration of affairs would put down the Indians."

In 1846, the Mexican War reached California, bringing new military forces to the region and altering the marketplaces of power. The war increased demand for horses from California to Colorado. It increased demand for labor and produced opportunities for Indigenous People to fight. Sutter claimed he had work for two hundred Indigenous People at New Helvetia but not enough workers on hand to meet it. A massive corral in Tulare Valley contained approximately one thousand horses and demanded considerable Indigenous labor. José Jesús, who previously stole horses, assisted Americans in pursuing Yokuts horse thieves and now turned his attention to labor contracting.

With the American victory, a new regime arrived that borrowed more from the model of the former mission than the language of emancipation. Early proclamations by the military government sought to control Indian labor and movement. In 1846, John B. Montgomery, US Naval commander of American forces at San Francisco, issued the "Proclamation to the Inhabitants of California," which outlawed slavery but compelled all Indians to work. Subsequent proclamations clarified the process: Indians had a right to choose an employer, but, as historian James Rawls described it: "Indians were free . . . [but] not free to be idle."

SOURCES

Indigenous People have always been a presence in the documents on California and the Great Basin in the nineteenth century. They are usually there peripherally, however, as a generic threat to westward progress or victims to inevitable settler violence. Indigenous power is far less common in the sources. On the raid by Walkara and the Chaguanosos, see

Ned Blackhawk, *Violence over the Land: Indians and Empires in the Early American West* (Cambridge, MA: Harvard University Press, 2006), 139; Eleanor Lawrence, "Mexican Trade between Santa Fe and Los Angeles," *California Historical Society Quarterly* 10 (March 1931): 33. Natale A. Zappia, *Traders and Raiders: The Indigenous World of the Colorado Basin, 1540–1859* (Chapel Hill: University of North Carolina Press, 2016) provides a theoretical and geographical framework—the Interior World—connecting histories that have often been kept separate. Zappia's quote about harnessing rather than destroying missions is from page 55.

Kent Lightfoot's *Indians, Missionaries, and Merchants: The Legacy of Colonial Encounters on the California Frontiers* (Berkeley: University of California Press, 2006) addresses the Russian experience in California alongside the Spanish and Indigenous. Recent translations have made material on the Russian American Company more widely available. Valenila's comments comparing Russian and Spanish treatment of Miwoks is from V. M. Golovnin, "A Note about the Present Condition of the Russian-American Company, 1819," in *Russian California, 1806–1860: A History in Documents*, edited by James Gibson and Alexei Istomin (Burlington, VT: Ashgate, 2014), 370. A related, but far more readily available, collection is James Gibson, *California through Russian Eyes, 1806–1848*, vol. 2 (Norman: University of Oklahoma Press, 2013).

While the literature on the Franciscan missions in California is extensive, the immediate postmission period is far less so. The story of Cristina Salgado comes from Steven Hackel, *Children of Coyote, Missionaries of Saint Francis: Indian-Spanish Relations in Colonial California, 1769–1850* (Chapel Hill: University of North Carolina Press, 2005). The quote "we are free . . ." and the alcalde's lament, "to stand by and watch . . ." are from Lisbeth Haas, *Conquests and Historical Identities in California, 1769–1936* (Berkeley: University of California Press, 1996), 38–39. The account of Tomás Tajochi's arrest comes from Lisbeth Haas, *Saints and Citizens: Indigenous Histories of Colonial Missions and Mexican California* (Berkeley: University of California Press, 2013), 151. The account of Julio Cesar is taken from Rose Marie Beebe and Robert M. Senkewicz, *Lands of Promise and Despair: Chronicles of Early California, 1535–1846* (Norman: University of Oklahoma Press, 2015), 468–75. Father Payeras's letter on neophytes withdrawing from the missions comes from Zephyrin Engelhardt, *The Missions and Missionaries of California*, vol. 3, *Upper California, Part II—General History* (San Francisco: James H. Barry, 1913), 33–34. Engelhardt was a prolific, impassioned, and deeply biased Franciscan historian who wrote individual histories of more than a dozen missions, as well as general histories of the mission system in Alta California, Baja California, and Arizona. Other works we relied on include Robert Howard Jackson and Edward Castillo, *Indians, Franciscans, and Spanish Colonization: The Impact of the Mission System on California Indians* (Albuquerque: University of New Mexico Press, 1995); and Deborah Miranda, *Bad Indians: A Tribal Memoir* (Berkeley, CA: Heyday, 2012).

Estanislao's claim that Mexican soldiers could not shoot well and the quote about a hog's feeding trough come from Albert Hurtado, *Indian Survival on the California Frontier* (New Haven, CT: Yale University Press, 1990), 43, 58. Narciso Durán's description of the competing viewpoints of Indian emancipation comes from David Weber, *The Mexican Frontier, 1821–1846: The American Southwest under* Mexico (Albuquerque: University of New Mexico Press, 1982), 43. The quote threatening a "misfortune" if a cruel administrator is not removed comes from Richard Steven Street, *Beasts of the Field: A Narrative History of California Farmworkers, 1769–1913* (Palo Alto, CA: Stanford University Press, 2004), 89–99.

The two legal cases discussed in this chapter are *Suñol v. Hepburn*, 1 Cal. 254 (1850); and *United States v. Ritchie*, 58 U.S. 525 (1854). Roberto's story and the quotes about "infants, idiots, lunatics . . ." come from *Suñol*, pp. 279, 284–85. Solano's story and the long quote on the rights of citizenship of Mexicans and competency come from *Ritchie*, p. 540.

Gerald Vizenor's description of survivance is from his *Fugitive Poses: Native American Indian Scenes of Absence and Presence* (Lincoln: University of Nebraska Press, 2000), 15. On Larkin's claims that Californios wanted American control, see George Harwood Phillips, *Indians and Intruders in Central California, 1769–1849* (Norman: University of Oklahoma Press, 1993), 135. The quote about being free but not free to be idle is from James Rawls, *Indians of California: The Changing Image* (Norman: University of Oklahoma Press, 1986), 4.

Native Spaces

Sacramento

Sacramento sits at the confluence of the American and Sacramento Rivers. Today, it serves as the state capital. Before that, at least fifteen Nisenan towns existed within the current city boundaries. The Notomusse, Bushumnes, and Pawenan Bands of Nisenans occupied the Sacramento area, with the Pawenan living north of the American River, the Notomusse south of it. Nisenans established towns on natural knolls or made dirt mounds along the rivers to protect against seasonal flooding. Pujuni, one of the largest towns, possessed a population of between seven hundred and eight hundred in the early 1830s and a *k'um* (roundhouse). Before the California Gold Rush, Tawec served as the *h'uk* (chief) of Kademah, located upriver from Pujuni, which had two k'um. Nisenans and other Indigenous People lived along the entire stretch of the Feather, Sacramento, Bear, and American Rivers. The Sacramento River served as the border between Nisenans and Patwins, their western neighbors.

The area provided an ideal environment for Nisenans. Lilly Williams remembered gathering clams from the American River. Nisenans took fish, waterfowl, and mussels from the river and harvested roots and seeds on the banks. The American and Sacramento Rivers allowed easy transportation to trade with their Nisenan and Miwok neighbors. Nisenans traversed the river using dugout canoes and tule boats. Those who lived nearer the Sacramento River traded basket materials, such as *puitaw*, a white root, and shells to their mountain kin for redbud and bear skins. Nisenans also intermarried with their Miwok neighbors to the south.

Nisenans rarely interacted with the Spanish, although they accepted the People fleeing the missions. In the 1830s, Americans and Mexicans pushed Nisenans out of their villages along the rivers and into the mountains. After Mexican Independence, the Hudson's Bay Company and American fur traders ventured into the Sacramento Valley. In 1833, a malaria epidemic swept through Nisenan villages, killing perhaps 75 percent of the population. *Anopheles* mosquitos spread malaria by biting an infected person and then carrying the parasites to new hosts. The disease traveled from Oregon by way of Hudson's Bay Company traders. Fur traders brought the sickness into the wetlands of the Sacramento River, an ideal location for mosquitoes to spread the disease. Fur traders observed abandoned villages along the Sacramento River. Nisenan survivors fled the river areas into the mountains to escape the ravages of the disease.

In the 1830s and 1840s, American, British, and Mexican invaders exposed Nisenans to disease, violence, and slavery. Beginning in 1839, John Sutter established outposts in Nisenan towns along the Sacramento and American Rivers. Sutter located New Helvetia in between the Nisenan towns of Pujuni and Yalisumni. Sutter invited Nisenans to work for him by offering food, clothing, and Hawaiian sugar. As with the arrival of fur traders, Sutter's presence imperiled Nisenans. Sutter also convinced Miwoks to live and work at New Helvetia, thereby increasing the number of people encroaching on Nisenan territory. Additionally, Sutter attracted Mexicans and affiliated Indians from the missions. In October of 1840, Miwoks from Mission San José asked to pass through Sutter's territory to visit interior Miwoks. Once given permission, however, the Miwoks attacked the town of Yalisumni while the men worked at New Helvetia. The Miwoks killed the elderly and very young and took Nisenan women and children captive. Nisenans and Sutter recaptured some of their people, but the losses were significant.

During the California Gold Rush, more Americans flocked to the area. Merchants understood that the best way to make money during the Gold Rush was to sell pans, food, and clothing to the miners foolish enough to spend hours swirling water and dirt in search of gold. John Sutter Jr. moved to California to manage his father's business operations. He enlisted the support of several merchants and laid out the plans for the city of Sacramento. Merchants easily accessed the miners along the American River, as well as up the Sacramento to the Feather. In 1854, state leaders moved the capital to Sacramento. Yet Americans did not learn from the Nisenans, who built their towns on elevated knolls. Flooding attempted to wash away Sacramento, like the debris in a miner's pan. In 1850, for instance, snowmelt and heavy rains swelled the Sacramento and American Rivers. The *Alta California* described a "vast lake of water" from the city of Sacramento to Sutter's Fort. The water covered everything but the tops of trees, and all sorts of merchandise, such as lumber, bales and cases of goods, boxes and barrels, tents and small houses, bobbed on the water covering the city. To compound matters, cholera, a bacterial disease contracted by drinking contaminated water, which causes diarrhea and dehydration, spread throughout the waterlogged city. City politicians erected levees in hopes of protecting the city from future floods, but the great floods of 1860 and 1861 proved again the folly of Americans living in Sacramento. The levees failed, and water again inundated the city.

In Sacramento, politicians debated, crafted, and enacted laws that affected California Indians. In 1861, the state voted to extend and modify the notorious Act for the Government and Protection of Indians. The amended law enabled Americans to indenture orphaned Indigenous children without the parental consent the law had previously required. It also extended the term of Indian indentures from twenty-one to twenty-five years old for men and eighteen to twenty-one years old for women. Throughout the late nineteenth century, the state government passed vagrancy laws aimed at California Indians and prevented California Indian children from attending public schools.

Yet Nisenans persisted in the Sacramento area. During the early nineteenth century, Nisenans abandoned Kademah but returned after the beginning of the Gold Rush. They cut wood, washed clothes, and harvested acorns, mixing wage labor and traditional subsistence. In 1857, a group of Nisenans leveraged their work for a rancher named Norris into the right to hold dances on his land. In the late nineteenth century, Paiutes from Nevada and Chinese immigrants lived with Nisenans while they picked hops in the Sacramento Valley. In the early twentieth century, anthropologists C. H. Merriam and John P. Harrington interviewed Nisenans living in Sacramento. A Nisenan woman named Lilly Williams, who lived in Broderick (present-day West Sacramento), worked with Harrington. Thomas Charles, who lived at Kademah, sat down and shared Nisenan culture and history with Merriam. Today, Kadema Drive runs parallel to the American River.

California Indians continue to carve out space in Sacramento. In 1940, the State Indian Museum opened on the grounds of Sutter's Fort. The museum helped to make the indigenous presence visible in the state capital but did so by attaching it to the overdetermined story of Sutter. Over the years, California Indians visited Sacramento to lobby against state policies and advocate for themselves. Recognizing the value of publicity, Maidu Kitty Flores arranged a "peace pipe ceremonial" with Governor Earl Warren to take place at the State Indian Museum to coincide with the Centennial Celebration of the gold discovery. In the 1950s, her mother, Maidu Marie Potts, wrote and produced the newspaper *Smoke Signal* out of her Sacramento home. In 1969, Round Valley tribal council members Norman Whipple and Joe Russ Sr. met with Governor Ronald Reagan to protest a dam on the Eel River that threatened to flood their reservation. Federal and state offices in Sacramento remind the United States of its ongoing fiduciary responsibility to California Indians and American Indians who have migrated to the state. The Sacramento Native American Health Center is located on J Street, a couple of blocks from the state capital.

In the 1970s, California Indians began to press for a new museum to replace the State Indian Museum and honor California's Indigenous People on their own terms. Years of advocacy, pressure, and fundraising have moved the project closer to reality. In 2009, the California Indian Heritage Center Foundation was formed. The City of West Sacramento donated a site for the new museum at the confluence of the Sacramento and American Rivers, just upstream and opposite the historic waterfront. The center will present "a statewide perspective on California's Indian cultural legacy, honoring the contributions of California Indians, providing educational opportunities, enhancing public understanding of traditional and spiritual beliefs, and enriching public life."

In September of 2015, Sacramento State University student Maidu-Navajo Chiitaanibah Johnson sparked a viral national debate about historical memory when she spoke out publicly about her confrontation with the professor in her United States History class. Johnson challenged the professor's claims that what happened to California Indians did not constitute genocide by reading from the United Nations definition of genocide. The professor dismissed her claims and accused her of "hijack[ing]" his class. The viral coverage of her protest contributed a brief moment of national attention to the growing push for state officials to recognize its own genocide. In June of 2019, Governor Gavin Newsom held a ceremony with tribal leaders on the grounds of the future California Indian Heritage Center. There, he issued an executive order apologizing to "all California Native Americans" on behalf of the citizens of the state for the "many instances of violence, maltreatment and neglect California inflicted on tribes . . . [during] a century of depredations and prejudicial policies against California Native Americans." The executive order pledged to form a Truth and Healing Council to explore the historical relationship between the state and its tribes. Although the executive order did not use the word *genocide*, and in fact explicitly clarifies that it does not, Newsom said in his spoken remarks, "It's called genocide. . . . That's what it was, a genocide. No other way to describe it. And that's the way it needs to be described in the history books." Tribal leaders responded gratefully but cautiously. Yurok Abby Abinanti, chief judge of the Yurok Tribal Court described the event as "important because it's a first step in a process that has been a long time coming. We need to take a serious look as a state, as a country, about how we address these issues."

As this book was nearing completion, the Crocker Art Museum held an exhibition entitled *When I Remember, I See Red: American Indian Art and Activism in California*. The museum's prominent location in the city, Governor Newsom's apology, and the exhibit gesture to the way history haunts the present at the same time that it points to change.

SOURCES

Sherri Jean Tatsch's 2006 PhD dissertation at the University of California, Davis, "The Nisenan: Dialects and Districts of a Speech Community," traces the ongoing presence of Nisenans in Sacramento. Peggy Badovinac and Wendy Nelson's poster presentation at the 2013 California Indian Conference offered additional evidence of Nisenan persistence. Peter Aherns discussed the spread of malaria to Nisenan by American fur traders in "John Work, J. J. Warner and the Native American Catastrophe of 1833," *Southern California Quarterly* 93 (Spring 2011): 1–32. Historians have spent considerable time and effort discussing the history of John Sutter. The most recent and complete biography is Albert Hurtado, *John Sutter: A Life on the North American Frontier* (Norman: University of Oklahoma Press, 2006). Andrew Isenberg explored the environmental changes that occurred because of the creation of Sacramento in *Mining California: An Ecological History* (New York: Hill and Wang, 2005). Coverage of Governor Newsom's apology and executive order was widespread. On its relationship to genocide, see Jill Cowan, "'It's Called Genocide': Newsom Apologizes to the State's Native Americans," *New York Times,* June 19, 2019.

5

"The White Man Would Spoil Everything"

Indigenous People and the California Gold Rush, 1846–1873

In early 1873, the United States Army and 150 Modocs remained locked in a tense standoff. The previous year, Kientpoos (also known as Captain Jack) led the Modocs off the Klamath Reservation to the lava beds in northeastern California, where they fended off the army and volunteer citizen militias. Now both sides wanted to negotiate for peace. Modoc Toby Riddle was uniquely positioned to carry messages back and forth between the two combatants. Born sometime in the late 1830s or early 1840s, Riddle possessed the skills, knowledge, and relationships to help mediate the conflict. She married Frank Riddle, an American from Kentucky, which troubled her father but enabled her to develop bilingual and bicultural skills. As Kientpoos's cousin, Riddle could enter Modoc camps. California Indians considered women like Riddle emissaries of peace, not war. Yet not everyone trusted her. Despite her knowledge, skills, and relationships, many Modocs observed her warily when she came to camp. Americans did, too. The army ignored Riddle's warnings of a Modoc attack the next time Americans ventured into the lava beds to negotiate an end to the war. As a result, Modocs ambushed and killed General Edward Canby and Reverend Eleazar Thomas and wounded Alfred Meacham, the chairman of the Modoc Peace Commission. Later, Riddle toured the nation as part of Meacham's traveling show and lecture, often under the name Winema. Her portrait was taken when the group visited Washington, DC, in 1875 (fig. 12). At the time, though, Modocs and Americans suffered as

FIGURE 12. Tobey Riddle (or Winema), Modoc Indian. Photograph by C. M. Bell. Photo Courtesy Huntington Library.

the so-called Modoc War lingered. Foolish men failed to heed the advice of knowledgeable Modoc women.

The tensions animating the conflict had begun twenty-five years earlier when, in 1848, Americans discovered gold in the American River. The ensuing Gold Rush reordered lands and imperiled Indigenous People. Young men immigrated to California from all corners of the world to cash in on the find. Ranches and farms developed to feed the newcomers. The hydraulic mining industry, which quickly replaced individual prospectors panning for gold, tore open mountainsides and clogged streams and rivers. While Spanish and Mexican colonists used Indigenous People as laborers, most Americans adhered to the settler colonial "logic of elimination," in which Indigenous People must disappear. Americans almost succeeded. According to most estimates, before the Gold Rush, 150,000 Native Peoples lived within the state's boundaries; only 30,000 survived the following maelstrom. Americans caused the demographic catastrophe through genocide, ethnic cleansing, and the enslavement of Indigenous People. The Modoc War, which required Riddle to carry messages and information across the cold, windswept lava beds, represented one of the last efforts, of many, to exterminate Indigenous People.

Indigenous People shaped and brokered the violent policies of California and the United States. Between 1846 and 1873, they negotiated with the United States and defended their communities from American violence. During the Mexican-American War and early days of the Gold Rush, Yokuts José Jesús transformed from a horse raider to a labor contractor. Indigenous People negotiated treaties with the United States to blunt the demographic and ecological damage of the Gold Rush. When the federal government failed to ratify those treaties, Indigenous People experienced ethnic cleansing. In Southern California, Indigenous People found work and violence in the towns of Los Angeles and San Diego. During the Civil War, Hupas resisted the American invasion of their lands. At the same time that Modocs and Americans squared off in the lava beds, a religious message of hope swept through California Indian communities.

After the California Gold Rush, Americans, bent on taking Indigenous Peoples' land, imagined them as "California Indians." Statehood in 1850 fixed the state's boundaries, and the federal and state governments asserted their authority over that territory and its people. Treaty commissioners arrived with orders to meet with *California* Indians, not those in Oregon or Nevada. The United States Congress created the *California* superintendency to monitor the Indigenous People of the state. Of course, the Indigenous People did not see themselves as a homogenous population of "Indians," nor did they accept the administrative boundaries of "California." They retained ethnic identities that connected them to place and their kin.

In April of 1846, United States troops invaded Mexico, using the flimsy excuse of the presence of Mexican forces on Texas soil. In actuality, Texas and Mexico disputed the location of their border. Americans in California soon rebelled against the Mexican government. In June, Americans overtook Sonoma and, in July, occupied Monterey and San Diego. Americans declared California an independent republic. Commodore Robert F. Stockton appointed John C. Frémont commander of the California Battalion and tasked him with monitoring the California coast. Americans briefly held coastal California. In September, Californios recaptured Los Angeles and, later, forced US soldiers to abandon the fort at Santa Barbara.

In the early days of the war, little changed for California Indians. With the onset of fighting, interior Indigenous People increased raids on the coast. In July, Indigenous People carried off more than one hundred horses from Mission Santa Clara. In part, Indigenous horse raids prompted Americans to rebel against Mexico. Americans accused the Mexican government of failing to prevent Indigenous People from stealing horses and claimed they could do a better job. Americans and Californios expected Frémont and the California Battalion to fulfill that promise. Frémont performed with mixed results. The battalion tracked the raiders to the Santa Cruz Mountains, attacked the Indigenous People, and recaptured the horses, but the counterattack failed to stop the raiding.

Indigenous People from outside the territory elicited a different kind of alarm. In September of 1846, Americans spread rumors that Piupiumaksmaks was leading one thousand Walla Wallas, who lived near the Cayuse and Umatilla, from southern Oregon to New Helvetia, to seek revenge for the death of his son. In 1844, Elijah Hedding, Piupiumaksmaks's son and named by missionaries who taught him in Oregon, arrived at New Helvetia to trade. John Sutter attempted to adjudicate a dispute between Hedding and an American, but the American shot and killed Hedding. The rumor of Piupiumaksmaks was only partially true. Piupiumaksmaks arrived at New Helvetia but with only fifty Walla Wallas, intending to hunt and trade for horses and cattle. Piupiumaksmaks wanted to foster relationships with his neighbors, not strike vulnerable Americans. "When I came to California I did not know that the Boston men had taken the country from the Spaniards," Piupiumaksmaks said, using a common term among Pacific Northwest Indians for Americans. "I am glad to hear it."

With rumors of Indigenous invasions from Oregon, several horse raids to the coast, and a Californio uprising in Southern California, Americans needed as many allies as they could muster. Some turned to Indigenous People to defend their territories and protect their property.

Fifty Indigenous People, commanded by Lieutenant John Sutter, served as a cavalry and infantry at New Helvetia. But Sutter needed more soldiers to defend his fort and livestock, as well as to march on Southern California to make war on Mexican forces. Sutter persuaded Piupiumaksmaks and Walla Walla men to join the California Battalion. He then invited José Jesús and other Yokuts to negotiate terms under which to join the war on the side of the California Republic.

José Jesús cut a stark figure at six feet tall and dressed like a Mexican ranchero, with sombrero and serape. Likely born in the early nineteenth century, Jesús grew up at Mission Santa Clara, where he ascended to the rank of alcalde. In 1829, he left and joined Estanislao to raid the missions for horses and trade them to American fur traders. After Estanislao returned to San José, Jesús assumed leadership of Yokuts who lived at Chaspaiseme, located along the Tuolumne River. In 1846, Jesús attacked Muqueleme Miwoks, who stole John Sutter's horses and cattle, in return for gifts and "passports" issued by Sutter, who claimed they enabled uncontested travel throughout California.

Jesús and Piupiumaksmaks joined the battalion because service promised twenty-five dollars pay for three months in the field. Frémont also ordered United States military officials to provide beef and flour to the Walla Walla women and children who remained at New Helvetia. Meanwhile, a Sutter associate lent thirty-two horses to Jesús. Rewards continued while in the field. Indigenous People took livestock, clothing, and other valued items as war spoils. Cash, food, clothing, and, especially, horses promised to enrich Yokuts in the San Joaquin Valley and Walla Wallas linked to the Indigenous Columbia Plateau's fur trade.

Indigenous People acquitted themselves well in the campaign against Californios. Jesús and the other Yokuts and Miwoks in Company H scouted for the battalion, camping three miles on either side of them, "so that no traveler on the road escaped falling into [the battalion's] hands." They also undermined the Californios' ability to resist Americans. Jesús led horse raids, which gave the United States an advantage over the now-riderless Californios. Because of their effectiveness in stealing horses, Californios called Company H the "forty thieves," a reference to the story from *Arabian Nights*, which circulated widely in the American West in the early nineteenth century. Furthermore, Californios in San Luis Obispo refused to join the uprising against Americans because they feared that Indigenous People would steal their horses.

On January 13, 1847, Californios surrendered at Cahuenga Pass. Company H disbanded a month later. When Yokuts and Walla Wallas returned to their families, they realized how much the Mexican-American War had disrupted life in Indigenous communities. The war interrupted trading routes connecting the coast and the interior. The absence of men led to a decline of food and other resources. Jesús and Yokuts were mistaken if they thought the pay from the United States would augment lost resources. The United States issued receipts, instead of cash, to all members of the California Battalion, which they could exchange for cash when Congress authorized funds. Jesús and other Yokuts probably traded these receipts for food and clothing.

Immediately after the war concluded in California, Americans and Californios worried that Indigenous People would renew horse raids. Americans heard rumors that Indigenous People in the San Joaquin Valley formed alliances with those in the Sierra Nevada to launch raids on the coast. Reports surfaced that six Americans from the California Battalion took trade goods from Los Angeles to the San Joaquin Valley to acquire horses from José Jesús and an ally named Felipe. The stories about Jesús flabbergasted some settlers. The *California Star* refuted the story and informed readers Jesús was "entirely and wholly friendly to the Americans." Other settlers, though, believed Jesús was up to his old tricks and had renewed his horse raids. Nevertheless, Americans and Californios demanded a stronger military presence to prevent raiding.

Rumors soon turned to action. In March of 1847, raiding parties of between one hundred and two hundred Indigenous People swept along the California coast, stealing horses. Other Indigenous People raided San Juan Bautista and fired arrows at the settlers, who lacked guns and ammunition after the war. In April, Indigenous People raided San Francisco Bay daily. In one such attack, they made off with two hundred horses.

Americans attempted to curb horse raiding. In December of 1846, General Stephen Watts Kearny arrived in California from New Mexico and assumed command of the state. He appointed John Sutter, Mariano Vallejo, and Jesse Hunter as federal Indian subagents and tasked them with ending Indigenous raiding through diplomacy and gift-giving or by force if necessary. Kearny also issued orders preventing Indigenous People from traveling in crowds and requiring passports or certificates of employment to travel. Kearny catered to Californio and American rancheros who needed Indigenous workers and relied on punitive action, more than negotiation, to calm relations between peoples.

As during the war, Americans failed to prevent Indigenous People from raiding the coast. In December of 1847, Locolumne Yokuts struck ranches in the Livermore Valley and Mount Diablo. Since the military failed to prevent raiding, Charles Weber, an associate of John Sutter and the founder of Stockton, reached out to Jesús to stop the raids. In February of 1848, Jesús and two hundred Yokuts attacked a group of raiders under Polo, a Locolumne, on the Calaveras River. Jesús and his men killed some Yokuts and returned the stolen horses.

Californios and Americans soon attacked Indigenous communities in an effort to prevent raids. In July of 1847, a Californio and two Americans attacked a Nisenan or Maidu town north of New Helvetia. They killed thirteen and took thirty-seven women and children captive. The three men marched the captives to New Helvetia. En route, they killed the children who were too weak to make the trip. Later that month, Californios went to a Yalesumne Nisenan town twenty miles northeast of New Helvetia. The invaders took some horses and whipped Shulule, the town's headman. Increasingly, then, Californios and Americans targeted Indigenous People who had little to do with the raids. They hoped that the attacks would serve as a lesson to those who thought about attacking coastal or interior ranches. Of course, the Americans and Californios in these examples targeted communities who did not participate in raids. They did so because the Nisenan and Maidus represented more vulnerable communities.

Indigenous People faced more troubles. In the summer of 1847, measles struck the Sacramento Valley. The illness arrived either from immigrants migrating from Southern California via overland routes or coming on ships from Mexico. Measles spread along the networks weaving communities and people together. In late June, Walla Wallas left California for Oregon, stealing horses en route. When they arrived at Fort Nez Perce on July 23, they brought measles with them. From there, Indigenous People and Americans spread measles north to the Thompson River in Canada, west to Fort Vancouver, and up the coast as far as Sitka, Alaska. In November, Cayuses, suffering from measles, killed thirteen people at the Whitman mission near Fort Nez Perce, in part because they blamed the missionaries for the disease. Back in California, measles reordered labor relations at New Helvetia. Sutter complained he needed two hundred Indigenous People to harvest his wheat crop, but only twenty to twenty-five showed up. When Indigenous People grew too sick to continue working in the fields, Sutter ordered them to recuperate in their home villages. Sutter's directives spread measles throughout the region. In September, he learned Shulule succumbed to the disease. Nisenan ceremonies to stem the tide of the disease outraged

Sutter because he believed they kept Nisenan workers from his fields. He therefore burned down the Nisenan's k'um outside New Helvetia.

On January 24, 1848, American and Indigenous workers discovered gold in what is now Coloma, located on the American River. Initially, Indigenous People allowed miners on their land. Northern Maidu Marie Potts explained: "The Maidu shared their land with the miners and ranchers who followed . . . intending only to loan them the land." After verifying the discovery of gold at the mill, John Sutter met with Yalesumnes Nisenan leaders Gesu, Pulpule, Colule, and Sole. The four men agreed to lease several square miles to Sutter for twenty-five years so he could build a sawmill, cut timber, cultivate the land, and open silver and lead mines. In exchange, Sutter promised to provide $150 per year in clothing and tools and to grind the Nisenan's grain. Sutter later claimed Yalesumnes would benefit from the merchandise required in the lease and "learn habits of industry." The lease was problematic: it failed to mention the gold strike, offered a pittance for the land, and was signed by the wrong people. Yalesumnes lived downriver from the discovery site. Sutter should have made the agreement with the Koloma Nisenan. Nevertheless, Sutter forwarded the lease to Governor Richard Mason, who denied his request, replying that in the United States, "private individuals" could not lease or buy lands from Indigenous People and that the United States planned to settle Indigenous land claims after the war. The lease had no chance to stand up legally.

As soon as word spread about the discovery of gold, Indigenous People dashed off for the American River. Sutter abandoned the property and retired to another farm because so many Indigenous workers left New Helvetia. In mid-1848, Governor Mason estimated Indigenous People made up about half of the four thousand miners in the mining districts. Sutter and John Bidwell, who arrived in California in 1841, hired out Indigenous People who worked on their farms to other Americans who wanted to make their fortunes in the Gold Rush. Some Indigenous leaders worked as labor contractors as well. José Jesús stopped raiding horses and arranged for Yokuts to work for Charles M. Weber. These unnamed Indigenous People washed out gold on Weber Creek. The men dug dirt out of the creek and put it in baskets. Children took the mud-filled baskets to women, who repurposed traditional crafts for new purposes. They washed the gold out in grass baskets. The coiled base of their baskets made it easier to catch the denser gold flakes as they swirled around with water, like cleats on a sluice. Americans who either hired large numbers of Indigenous workers or contracted for them could reap enormous profits in the early days of the Gold Rush. Perry McCoon and William Daylor, who previously worked at New Helvetia, employed one hundred Indigenous People. In one week, McCoon and Daylor made $10,000. Fifty Indigenous People worked for John Sinclair, washing out gold in woven willow baskets. Sinclair netted $16,000.

Mining exposed Indigenous People to exploitation and racism. A White woman living on the Bear River noted that she "give 'em a hankecher for a tin-cup full [of gold]." Other traders exchanged merchandise for an equal weight of gold. Still others used a "Digger Ounce," a lead slug that weighed more than the weights used for gold and was named after a common and offensive epithet for California Indians. American newspapers depicted Indigenous miners as uncivilized and savage. One such image, entitled "An Indian Woman Panning Out Gold," depicted an Indigenous woman panning for gold. Behind the woman, a naked child peers into the distance (fig. 13). The picture played on well-worn stereotypes and created new ones. On one hand, Europeans and Americans frequently showed Indigenous People as partially clothed in order to connect them to savagery. On the other hand, Americans increasingly equated California Indians with African Americans. The term *digger* ostensibly derived from California Indians' practice of digging for roots, but its popularity undoubtedly resulted from the fact that it rhymed with another well-known epithet. Americans used these pictures and practices to justify their taking of Indigenous Peoples' lands.

California Indians in the north described the impact of the Gold Rush in ways that resembled how Southern California Indians discussed the missions and the dual revolution. In the summer of 1851, Indigenous People along the Merced River informed federal subagent Adam Johnston that "their people were starving, [and] they must die of hunger or return to their hills." Marie Potts recalled the Gold Rush changed Maidu land: "As more white men came, they drained the land." Mining disrupted and damaged Indigenous economic areas. Silting from mining activities clogged streams and prevented annual salmon runs. Miners cordoned off land and prevented Indigenous People from accessing important economic spaces. Americans also chopped down trees. Yurok Lucy Thompson remembered that in the fall, an Indigenous woman, captured by an American man, harvested pine nuts from a sugar pine. The American chopped down the trees, then mocked the woman. "There they are," he sneered, pointing at the downed tree and pine

FIGURE 13. Illustration of a Native woman panning for gold, May 1850.

nuts; "what are you going to do about it?" The woman concluded that "the white man would spoil everything."

As with the lack of food and spread of disease, violence became endemic to the mining areas. Caporatuck, a leader of the Oppeo Band of Yurok who lived near the junction of the Klamath and Trinity Rivers, noted that "the whites would threaten to shoot them and steal their women, and that now an Indian was afraid to go on the mountains after game and nuts alone." Civilians invading California initiated violence against Indigenous People. In early 1849, a group of prospective miners from Oregon arrived at Coloma, the site of the initial discovery of gold, and attempted to rape Nisenan women. Nisenans responded by killing seven Oregon miners. The surviving miners attacked a Nisenan town, killed four, took "several prisoners," burned the town, and stole gold dust. Two days later, twenty "mostly Oregon men" attacked another Nisenan town on Weber Creek, killing thirty and taking forty to sixty prisoners. Reciprocal attacks continued. Nisenans killed another Oregon miner, and Oregonians resumed their killing spree. Fifteen men killed three Indigenous miners and chased another eleven to a cabin owned by an Englishman. After initially refusing to surrender the Indigenous miners, the Englishman relented and turned them over. The Oregonians lynched the miners and continued to scour the area around Coloma and the Cosumnes River, killing sixty-six Nisenans. One Oregonian estimated they killed "more than a hundred" Nisenans in about a month.

Americans appeared all too willing to deploy violence against Indigenous People. In 1847, Andrew Kelsey and Charles Stone bought fifteen thousand head of cattle, twenty-five hundred horses, and the right to pasture those animals near Clear Lake. Kelsey and Stone then forced Eastern Pomos and Clear Lake Wappos to work for them on their ranch under the Mexican tradition of transferring workers with the land. The duo imprisoned and whipped Pomo and Wappo workers and raped Pomo and Wappo women. When Kelsey and Stone heard of the discovery of gold, they took twenty-six Pomos to the Feather River. In one month, the Pomos produced "a bag of gold as large as a man's arm." In return, Kelsey and Stone paid the Pomos a pair of overalls, a shirt, and a handkerchief. The next year, Kelsey and his brother took one hundred Pomos to the mines; however, they often neglected to feed and clothe them. When malaria swept through the mining camps, Kelsey rushed back to Clear Lake suffering from the disease. There, he told the Pomos waiting for their family members that they would return shortly. Only three Pomo men came back to Clear Lake, where they found terrible conditions. Cattle consumed Pomo food, and Kelsey withheld the Pomo and Wappo's hunting equipment for fear that they would use them against the Americans. Rather than find ways to provision the Pomos near Clear Lake, Kelsey decided to ship Pomo workers to New Helvetia to work for John Sutter. This plan was the last straw. A Pomo woman poured water down Kelsey and Stone's gun barrels, and the next day, the Pomos shot Stone and Kelsey with arrows.

The United States Army responded immediately. On May 15, 1850, seventy-five soldiers arrived at what is now called Bloody Island in Clear Lake. Brevet Major General Persifor F. Smith had ordered them there to, in the words of Captain John B. Frisbie, "exterminate if possible" the Pomos and Wappos they held responsible for Kelsey and Stone's deaths. Pomo leader Ge-Wi-Lih attempted to negotiate with the soldiers. Smith ordered Brevet Captain Nathaniel Lyon, the soldiers' commander, not to bargain, so the soldiers opened fire on the assembled Native People. Pomos fled the island by jumping into the lake and swimming toward the shore. But when the Pomos arrived on the banks of Clear Lake, soldiers, stationed there by Lyon, cut them down. Bloody Island stands as the site of the largest massacre in US history. Historian Benjamin Madley estimates the United States Army murdered as many as eight hundred Pomos, exceeding the number of Pequots that Puritans and their Native allies butchered at Mystic in 1637, Northern Shoshone the US Army murdered at Bear River in 1863, or Lakotas that the army murdered at Wounded Knee in 1890.

Throughout the twentieth century, Indigenous People and academics have called the atrocities of the Gold Rush "genocide." They reference the United Nation's 1948 Convention on the Prevention and Punishment of the Crime of Genocide. First, "perpetrators must demonstrate an 'intent to destroy' a group 'as such.'" Second, genocide criminals must commit one of five acts against that group: killing its members; causing serious bodily or mental harm to them; deliberately inflicting on them conditions of life calculated to bring about their physical destruction in whole or in part; imposing measures intended to prevent births within the group; or forcibly transferring children of the group to another group. Americans, aided and funded by the United States and the state of California, waged a campaign to exterminate California's Indigenous People.

Between 1850 and 1851, California politicians created what historian Benjamin Madley calls a "killing machine." The governor authorized citizens to form compulsory and volunteer militias to hunt down and kill Indigenous People. Senators and assemblymen paid the militias with state funds, loans, and bonds. When financial resources ran dry, politicians asked the federal government to pick up the tab. In the 1850s and the 1860s, the United States paid more than $1 million to California to fund these militias. Politicians praised their actions as "pedagogic killing," claiming that murdering Indigenous People taught the survivors a lesson.

Between 1846 and 1873, vigilantes, militias, the state of California, and the United States initiated hundreds of campaigns that killed between 9,492 and 16,094 California Indians. Some attacks were large-scale massacres, like Bloody Island. In the summer of 1853, Tolowas living at a town called Yontocket, which means "center of the world," on the south bank of the Smith River, held a Needash, a biannual ceremony to maintain balance in the world. They invited People from Taa-'at-dvn, outside current Crescent City, and Tututnis, from what is now southern Oregon. As the Tolowas and their kin played hand games and celebrated, Americans, seeking revenge for the deaths of some miners, surrounded the town. Sometime during the night, Americans set fire to the buildings and shot Tolowas and their kin who attempted to escape. When the massacre ended, the Americans burned the bodies of the dead. Between 450 and 500 Tolowas and their kin died in the massacre. Two Tolowa men survived by jumping into the slough and swimming away.

Other killings were local and small-scale. Hupa Minnie Reeves remembered Americans indiscriminately killing her family. When her grandfather was a boy, his mother fell ill. Chilula healers, also known as doctors, could not heal her, so they told him to go to Hoopa and fetch a doctor. The Hupa doctor and the boy left the Hoopa Valley, crossed Pine Creek at qos-ding (Soaproot), and went up the Bald Hills. The boy looked back and saw Americans on horseback following them. As he tried to surrender, the Americans shot the boy and the doctor. The doctor died, but the boy dragged himself to a cedar-bark hunting shelter, where he fell into a coma. While asleep, he dreamed of a white grizzly bear pouncing on him and tearing at his wound. His family found him and took him home.

The state of California made Indigenous People vulnerable to these genocidal attacks. Politicians crafted laws that denied rights to Native Peoples. Under the terms of the Treaty of Guadalupe Hidalgo, all Mexican citizens in the recently acquired territories could become United States citizens. The Mexican Constitution of 1824 included provisions whereby Indigenous People were Mexican citizens. But the Mexican Constitution did not provide universal suffrage for citizens; rather, one needed to own substantial property. Under Mexican law, a few California Indians owned enough land to vote in elections. In 1849, the California constitutional convention took up these issues. By a vote of twenty-one to twenty, the California constitutional convention denied California Indians the right to vote, whether or not they owned property. Subsequent California legislatures passed laws that prevented California Indians from testifying against Whites, serving on juries, or working as lawyers. In 1854, the California legislature passed the Act to Prevent the Sale of Fire-Arms and Ammunition to Indians, which remained a law until 1913. Effectively, then, the state of California denied rights, voting, legal recourse, and gun ownership to California Indians.

Nisenan William Joseph remembered the consequences of these laws. Two American miners left their cabin door open when they went to work. A Nisenan boy entered the cabin looking for food and stole two buckskin sacks full of gold and silver. When the miners discovered the theft, they tracked the boy to a Nisenan town, abducted him, and took back their gold and silver. The following day, the Americans invited the Nisenan chief to a gathering, where they put the captive boy on a mule, placed a noose around his neck, and lynched him. The extralegal violence convinced Nisenan leaders that their people needed to be careful around the newcomers. Leaders told other Nisenans not to steal or commit violence against White miners: "That is the way [they] will treat us if they catch [us]." A year later, another Nisenan boy found gold in a mountain stream. He informed other Nisenans about the discovery, and they began to mine. When they took their gold to town and exchanged it for food and supplies, Whites in town tracked the Nisenans back to their claim. The following day, Nisenans found Whites working their claim, which they called "Indian Digging." Nisenans understood the lessons imparted in Joseph's story. Nisenan thieves faced lynching; American thieves faced no punishment. Nisenans could not testify against them.

Those Indigenous People who survived the genocide lived in a state that exploited them for labor. Between 1849 and 1870, Americans and Californios in Los Angeles expanded agricultural and pastoral production to take advantage of the state's growing population. Between 1850 and 1860, the amount of improved lands in Los Angeles increased from 2,648 to 20,600 acres. Americans and Californios focused their energies on two industries: cattle and wine grapes. Americans and Californios raised cattle because of the high demand for meat in the mining areas, where beef cattle fetched between twenty-five and thirty-two dollars a head. Meanwhile, farmers in Los Angeles increased the number of grape vines from 450,000 to 1,650,000, making Los Angeles the most important wine region in the United States.

Indigenous People found numerous opportunities for work in Los Angeles and surrounding areas. There were simply too few American and Californio workers to sustain the growing agricultural enterprises. Indigenous workers tended cattle and drove the animals to the mining districts. Indigenous workers gathered grapes in baskets and brought them to the press, where they processed the grapes for wine. A resident of Los Angeles observed, "The grapes were placed in huge shallow vats placed near the 'sanja' *[zanja]* or water ditch. The Indians were made to bathe their feet in the sanja and then step into the vats where they trod rhythmically up and down on the grapes to press out the juice. Quite a number of Indians were in the vat at one time."

Indigenous People maintained and revitalized economic and cultural practices in and around Los Angeles worksites. Since so many ranchers raised cattle, Indigenous People possessed a virtual monopoly on the growing of vegetables and other crops in their gardens. They raised melons, onions, corn, and potatoes, some of which they kept for themselves and some of which they sold or bartered to settlers in Los Angeles. Indigenous People practiced hybrid cultural activities at feast days, attending mass and sporting events, such as horse races, rodeos, and bullfights. When those events ended, Indigenous People from Tehachapi and San Jacinto descended on the modern-day San Fernando Valley to dance and burn the belongings of people who had passed on during the previous year. Other Indigenous People reoccupied places in Southern California.

Despite Indigenous Peoples' economic, cultural, and social innovations, Los Angeles remained a dangerous place. During the Gold Rush, large numbers of people arrived there but looked to quickly move on to the mining districts. Dr. John Griffith said of Los Angeles, "Gambling, drinking and whoring are the only occupations, and they seem to be followed with great industry." Inter- and intra-Indigenous violence plagued Los Angeles. Accounts of murdered Indigenous People littered the *Los Angeles Star.* Cahuillas and Luiseños who came to Los Angeles to work frequently confronted one another. In January of 1850, Cahuilla Juan Pelon stabbed Luiseño Calletano at a card game. Traditional hand games, often lubricated with copious amounts of aguardiente, a liquor made by distilling wine, turned deadly. In 1851, headmen for the Cahuillas and Luiseños put up a game of churchurki, in which people bet on which player concealed a stick in their hand. The next day, city officials found thirteen dead Indians. The city stepped in and banned the playing of the game within town limits.

Indigenous leaders negotiated with town officials to mitigate further violence. In October of 1851, Cahuillas gambled near the home of Californios José Maria and Guadaloupe Ybarra. A Cahuilla man named Coyote argued with Ybarra over the high price of aguardiente. Coyote attempted to wrest a bottle of liquor from Ybarra, when José Maria intervened and captured him. Several Cahuillas attempted to free Coyote, as the disagreement flared into a battle between Cahuillas and Californios. The county sheriff arrived as the Cahuillas prepared to set fire to Ybarra's house. The sheriff ordered his men to open fire on the assembled Cahuillas, killing eight and forcing twenty-one to seek shelter in Ybarra's house. The sheriff arrested twenty-one Cahuillas on charges of rioting and attempted arson. The justice of the peace sentenced the men to twenty-five lashes. Before the justice could mete out the punishment, Cahuilla leader Juan Antonio arrived. He demanded the release of the prisoners and, when his demand was met, left Los Angeles.

To compel Indigenous People to work in agriculture, state laws and local ordinances sanctioned slavery. In 1850, the state of California passed the Act for the Government and Protection of Indians. As many historians have noted, this act did more governing than protecting. It included provisions for the indenture of California Indian children with parental consent; outlawed vagrancy, stealing horses, and setting fire to the prairie; and prevented Indians from testifying against White Americans. It also empowered local justices of the peace to monitor Indigenous People and their crimes. In 1860, the California legislature amended the act, doing away with the requirement of parental consent and allowing Americans to indenture orphans. Furthermore, the amended act lengthened the terms of the indenture contract from twenty-one to twenty-five years old for men and from eighteen to twenty-one years old for women.

Los Angeles officials augmented the act with city ordinances that allowed private employers to purchase incarcerated Indigenous People. On Saturday nights, local law enforcement officials swept through the town, picking up Indigenous People on the charges of intoxication and vagrancy. City officials then displayed the inmates, either chaining them to a wood beam in front of the city jail or locking them in a corral, for potential employers. On Monday morning, farmers and ranchers bid on the Indigenous People and placed them at work in vineyards. At the end of the week, farmers might compensate Indigenous workers with aguardiente, ensuring that the process repeated itself. Observers noted that the practice resembled other forms of unfree labor and slavery in the world: "Los Angeles had its slave mart, as well as New Orleans and Constantinople, only the slave at Los Angeles was sold fifty-two times a year as long as he lived."

Americans used the act's provisions to hold Indigenous People in bondage. In 1851, Cave Johnson Couts, a slaveholder from Tennessee, acquired the 2,219-acre Rancho Guajome, near Mission San Luis Rey, from his brother-in-law Abel Stearns after Couts married Ysidora

Bandini. Couts used his political connections in California to secure political offices, such as justice of the peace and federal Indian subagent. By the Civil War, Couts expanded the size of the rancho to twenty-three thousand acres, on which he raised cattle, horses, and sheep. Luiseños and Kumeyaay made up more than half of the rancho's workforce. About eighteen worked year-round, with women and children employed as domestic servants and men and boys working in the gardens and tending livestock. Additionally, Indigenous People sheared sheep, drove cattle, and temporarily performed day labor.

Couts used the 1850 law to enslave Indigenous People. Many workers found themselves indebted to Couts. In 1852, Antonio began working for Couts for eight dollars per month, which, in June of 1853, increased to twelve dollars per month. However, Antonio purchased his day-to-day items, such as soap, thread, and clothing, and his work supplies, such as spurs, bridles, rope, and saddle, from Couts's *tienda* (company store). By the end of 1853, Antonio owed $55.63. In November of 1855, Antonio finally worked off his debt, but many other workers simply fled the rancho, leaving behind large debts. Couts routinely and aggressively pursued runaways and, when they were found, flogged them. In September of 1867, Couts captured Olerio, who had run away from the rancho, and "whipped and discharged" him. Couts also forced Indigenous People into indentured servitude. In January of 1854, acting as justice of the peace, Couts bought Sasaria, an Indigenous girl, and bound her to his wife until Sasaria was at least eighteen.

Couts also found an ally in Luiseño Manuelito Cota. Cota was born in 1818 at Mission San Luis Rey to Luiseño Maria Concepcion and José Manuel Cota, a Spanish soldier. Eventually, Cota moved to Pala and emerged as a spokesman between Luiseños and outsiders. Couts named Cota a capitán-general, a largely made-up title, and tasked him with policing criminal cases involving Luiseños in several villages. Cota enforced vagrancy clauses in Luiseño communities; if he found any Luiseños without work, he either put them to work for himself or contracted them to Couts or other ranch owners in San Diego County. In 1854, for instance, seventeen Luiseños built Couts's hacienda.

It is difficult to know exactly how many Indigenous People Americans enslaved. Between 1850 and 1863, Americans held at a minimum ten thousand California Indians under the terms of the 1850 act. Some scholars believe the number is closer to twenty thousand. In 1860 alone, Mendocino County farmers held 1,057 Indigenous People as "apprentices" or "indentured servants." Indigenous People worked year-round as farmworkers or domestic workers. As such, women and children formed the bulk of unfree workers in the northern part of the state. American men enslaved Indigenous women for domestic work and sex. In 1862, Colusa County rancher Thomas McClanahan and a group of Americans ambushed and killed fifteen Achumawis and Atsugewis fleeing the Round Valley Reservation. After the attack, McClanahan found two girls hiding in the brush. McClanahan and his partner took the girls. McClanahan named his captive girl "Kate," and she cleaned his house and cooked meals. According to a local historian, Kate soon "began to have babies." The careful syntax of this sentence masks the power structure and coercive nature of Kate's relationship with McClanahan. Kate gave birth to four children. In 1876, Kate and McClanahan formally married. At this point, Kate was on her deathbed and wanted to ensure the legitimacy of her offspring.

In addition to sexual violence, the Act for the Government and Protection of Indians sanctioned genocide. In 1862, a group of mountain men approached federal superintendent George Hanson seeking to indenture nine Indigenous children between the ages of three and ten. They informed Hanson that they had taken the orphan children from the Eel River country in Humboldt County. When Hanson asked them how they knew the children were orphans, one mountain man replied, "I killed some of [their parents] myself."

Indigenous People attempted to shape indentured servitude to their best interests. In Mendocino County, elderly Pomos voluntarily entered into indenture contracts with American ranchers to avoid removal to reservations. Pomos found more reliable sources of food and clothing with local farmers than on reservations and remained in their Indigenous homelands. Other Indigenous People resisted the violence and dislocation that attended their enslavement. Many ran away. In 1859, Henry Bailey, a Colusa County rancher, acquired two Pomo girls from the Clear Lake area. The girls fled and tried to return to Clear Lake before Bailey recaptured them. Lopez, another of the children Bailey enslaved, also ran away. The first time he did so, Lopez ended up with a group of young men from his town, but Bailey recaptured him. The second time, Lopez eluded Bailey for good. If running away did not work, Indigenous People resorted to more deadly forms of resistance. In 1862, Indigenous workers in Round Valley attempted to kill an employer by lacing his coffee with strychnine. Although they failed, the next year a group of Yuki workers killed their employer with axes.

As the state government built a legal system hostile to California Indians, the federal government took tentative steps to help them. In

1850, the United States Senate dispatched Oliver Wozencraft, George Barbour, and Redick McKee to California. Initially, the Senate did not grant the men treaty-making authority, but a subsequent act provided $25,000 "to enable the President to hold treaties with various Indian tribes in California." The confusion regarding treaty making, as well as statewide opposition to granting Indigenous People land titles, undermined the federal government's role in California and opened the way to ethnic cleansing.

Throughout 1850 and 1851, Native People living along an arc running through the spine of the state—from the Trinity-Klamath Rivers in the far northwest, through the Cascade and Sierra Nevada foothills, the Sacramento and San Joaquin River basins, and the arid interior of Southern California—met with US commissioners. Indigenous People and Americans clashed in these areas because dense populations of Indigenous People lived in them, whereas Americans extracted economic resources, whether gold, land, or labor. Federal officials intended the reservation system to pacify American and Californio ranchers, who still depended on Indigenous People to work. Agents largely ignored meeting Indigenous People along coastal areas, where extensive land grants from the Spanish and Mexican eras kept that land out of the public domain.

Treaty making in California followed a formula—part Indigenous, part American. Dances initiated and closed diplomatic talks. On March 19, 1851, three Miwok Bands—the Apangasse, Apalache, and Awalache—met the US treaty commissioners at Camp Gibson, located on the Chowchilla River. The visiting Miwoks held a dance and feasted before discussing the treaties with the commissioners. Native Californians expected the agents and military officials visiting their lands to act as generous hosts. While negotiating with Pack-wans, Sca-goines, and Moo-ris, Yurok Bands who lived at the junction of the Klamath and Trinity Rivers, agent Redick McKee killed a bull and provided "hard bread and sugar" for a feast. When commissioners failed to provide food and gifts, Native People were uninterested in treaty making. At Rancho Chico, Wozencraft parsimoniously distributed food and clothing. He gave Maidu chiefs a jacket but did not give clothing to anyone else. When Maidu leaders discovered the lack of clothing or blankets, they left the treaty council.

After dancing, feasting, and distributing gifts, Indigenous diplomats and United States agents performed the play of diplomacy. Speeches opened the show. At a meeting with Pomo leaders near Clear Lake, agent McKee declared, "Brothers listen to my talk. We come among you as friends to learn the cause of your troubles, if you have any, and your condition generally. What I say comes straight from the heart, and there shall be no crook in my path, no fork in my tongue; listen attentively and give me your minds after you have heard." McKee related that the "Great Father, the President, at Washington, the most powerful and the richest chief on this continent," had sent him and had "conquered this country and you are his children now, and subject in all things to him." Pomo leaders responded with similar stylistic flourishes. They said that "they were happy to see [the McKee expedition] as friends. . . . This is what we want, and we will deal fairly with you; speak the truth only; we are glad to learn that you will speak the truth."

Indigenous People negotiated with federal agents using protocols honed over nearly a century of treaty making. Giving gifts, distributing food, hosting dances, and making speeches festooned with kinship terminology and declarations of peace were common to treaty negotiations since the American Revolution. Yet treaty making fit within established Indigenous social practices as well. Treaty negotiations resembled so-called big-time celebrations, which brought Indigenous People together to feast, perform ceremony, trade, and conduct diplomacy. Indigenous People expected the people calling the "Big Time," in this case the agents, to sponsor dances, generously provision feasts, and act as good hosts.

Indigenous People carried messages between their communities and the agents and conducted the hard work of treaty negotiations. On February 14, 1851, Cipriano and other Miwok leaders met with federal agents at Horr's Ferry, on the Tuolumne River. "After much persuasion and promises of reward," Cipriano agreed to take messages to Miwok Bands on the Mariposa, Merced, and Tuolumne Rivers and invite them to meet. Agents doubted Cipriano's success because of ongoing conflict between valley and mountain Indians. On February 25, though, Cipriano convinced Wilouma and Potawaekata, two Miwok leaders, to meet with the agents at their camp on the Tuolumne. Wilouma and Potawaekata heard the agents' message but appeared reluctant to meet as a large group, perhaps because they did not trust the assembled Miwoks or feared being an easy target for the state militias operating in the area. After discussing the matters among themselves, Cipriano, Wilouma, and Potawaekata left the agents to meet with Hawhaw and Newmasseeawa, Miwok holdouts, and invite them to a grand council scheduled for March 9. Cipriano's words and actions brought in some reluctant Miwok leaders.

Native diplomats benefited from their experience. Federal commissioners compensated Indigenous People for their hard work. Leaders, such as Cipriano, enhanced their stature in their own communities and gained access to food, clothing, and vaccinations via their negotiations with the United States. More important, though, Native runners and other go-betweens, such as Cipriano, possessed several advantages, which enabled them to influence the treaty process. They knew California's physical geography better than the agents. Runners understood where it was safe to travel and where it was not. They also understood California's social and political worlds. Runners performed these diplomatic roles for centuries before the arrival of Europeans and knew which village might better function as go-betweens. Go-betweens also knew California's varied languages. By midcentury, people spoke hundreds of languages in California. In the Central Valley, runners knew Miwok and Yokuts, in addition to English and Spanish, which many learned at the missions or working on Mexican ranchos. Farther north, people spoke Yurok, as well as the Chinook jargon, the language of the fur trade, which melded Indigenous and European languages to enable economic encounters. Indigenous runners utilized their geographical, political, and linguistic knowledge to shape and determine the outcome of treaty negotiations in California.

Indigenous People signed eighteen treaties with the United States, reserving 7.5 million acres of land. Non-Indians representing agricultural interests argued the treaties reserved too much land for Indians. Several of the treaties secured lands for Indians in the fertile San Joaquin and Sacramento Valleys. In 1852, bowing to non-Indian pressures, the United States Senate rejected the treaties in a secret session and prohibited their reproduction, essentially burying them in the Senate archives.

After the federal government refused to ratify the treaties, President Millard Fillmore appointed Edward F. Beale as superintendent of Indian Affairs. Modeled after the Spanish missions, Beale proposed to gather Native Peoples on five temporary reservations of no more than twenty-five thousand acres, instruct them in the benefits of work and labor, and keep them under federal agents and the United States Army's watchful eye. Reservations appealed to a cross-section of non-Indian society for a variety of reasons. To those who sought to promote American settlement, reservations promised to remove Indigenous People but retain their labor power locally. To those who were more critical of American society and saw Indigenous People as trapped in the past and unable to resist the onslaught of American settlers, reservations offered a form of protection. Both of these views looked to the missions as models of social control and orderly labor or protection and guidance toward civilization. In 1852, Benjamin Wilson wrote that the missions, which "flourished" in California until the 1830s, pursued "a successful course of tuition in the arts of civilized life and the duties of morality and religion." He went on to claim that their closure represented the "failure of one of the grandest experiments ever made for the elevation of this unfortunate race." Those advocating reservations on the mission model ignored the destructive nature of the mission system.

In 1853, Beale established the first reservation at Tejon, on the southern end of the San Joaquin Valley. The following year, President Franklin Pierce replaced Beale with Thomas J. Henley because of Beale's corruption. As California superintendent, Henley increased the number of reservations, establishing the Nome Lackee, Mendocino, and Klamath Reservations and several Indian farms at Nome Cult, Fresno, Kings River, and Tule River. Allegations of fraud and embezzlement also hounded Henley. An investigation found several improprieties with how he administered California reservations, and President James Buchanan fired him in 1858.

The early reservations, like the tenure of the superintendents, were tenuous and insecure. The government envisioned them as temporary. Henley rented the five-hundred-acre Fresno River Farm for $1,000 per year. Henley also hired the owner of the land as an assistant overseer of the farm, with a salary of one hundred dollars per month, ensuring him a tidy sum in rent money, and a salary from the United States. Tejon was a military reservation, chosen because officials believed that restricting Yokuts to a reservation would protect Los Angeles area ranchers from their widespread horse raids. The Yokuts were the most populous indigenous group in California at the time of first European contact, but their population was in steep decline, and reservation life contributed to that. From approximately fourteen thousand in 1848 the population of Yokuts fell to around six hundred by 1880. Similar patterns characterize the removal to reservations elsewhere in the state. In 1855, disregarding their opposition, the superintendent of Indian Affairs removed 150 Nisenans from their home in Grass Valley, present-day western Nevada County, to the Nome Lackee reservation, which the federal government created for the Nomlakis. Of those making the three-month journey, 20 percent died or escaped en route.

By 1859, the federal government had abandoned most of the reservations, and the following year, Congress abolished the California superintendency itself. During the Civil War, the United States cut funding for California reservations by 60 percent and reduced the number of reservations in the state to three: Round Valley (Yuki, Pit River, Pomo, Nomlaki, Concow, and Wailacki), Tule River (Yokuts, Wukchumnis, Western Mono, and Tubatulabal), and Hoopa Valley (Hupa). The so-called Four Reservations Act of 1864 reestablished the state superintendency, authorized the creation of no more than four reservations, and abolished all previous acts in conflict with the new law, officially returning previous reservations to the public domain to be sold or open to entrance by settlers. In 1865, the federal government added a fourth, the Colorado River Reservation, which straddled the river in Arizona and California.

The lack of treaties left Indigenous People vulnerable to the capricious nature of state and federal Indian policy. California settlers consistently called for a policy of ethnic cleansing, petitioning the state and federal government to forcibly relocate Indigenous People from their homelands to reservations. In 1859, agriculture and mining industries in Tehama and Butte Counties pushed Concows into the rugged Mill and Deer Creek Canyons, where they allied with the Indigenous Yahis. From this remote corner of California, Concows and Yahis raided farms and ranches, stole horses and cattle, and burned houses and crops in the Sacramento Valley. In 1859, Tehama County settlers complained to Governor John Weller that Indigenous People had driven off and killed livestock and burned houses. Weller dispatched General William Kibbe to northeastern California to raise a militia to quell the violence. Kibbe organized a company of about one hundred men, who scoured northeastern California's mountains and canyons and killed or took captive Concow, Yahi, Mountain Maidu, and Pit River women and children. One of the militiamen wrote, "I will say nothing further on this expedition except to say that we were gone four months and that we brought away more than 1500 Indians."

The army removed Indigenous People to the Mendocino Reservation, near Fort Bragg. Removal took two different paths. Some traveled overland. The army gathered the Concows at Concow Valley, twenty-five miles north of Oroville, and marched them to the Mendocino Reservation. The army and Kibbe's Guards marched another group of Concows and Pit Rivers from Fort Crook, about seven miles from the Fall River ferries, down the Sacramento River, through the Delta, and to San Francisco. The army put Pit Rivers and Concows on a boat and sailed them to the Mendocino Reservation and later Round Valley.

Concows and Pit Rivers refused to remain at Round Valley for long. About a year later, leaders decided that conditions on the reservation could not sustain them, and Concow Tome-ya-nem led the Concows from Round Valley to present-day Paskenta, where California Volunteers intercepted and escorted them to the nearby Nome Lackee Reservation. Concows returned to their homeland at an inopportune time. Americans blamed Indigenous People for killing a handful of children in the Sacramento Valley. Angered settlers demanded the army remove Concows. In the fall of 1863, the United States Army responded, imprisoning 460 Concows and Maidus in a corral outside Camp Bidwell to await removal. Malaria swept through the People waiting for the forced march. On September 4, 1863, the army began to march the Concows and Maidus the one hundred miles from Camp Bidwell to the Round Valley Reservation. Two weeks later, only 277 Concows and Maidus arrived at the reservation. The rest remained behind on the trail, too sick to continue. Oral histories of the ethnic cleansing recalled soldiers killing the elderly, women, and children.

Indigenous People transformed reservations into places in which they could avoid genocide and ethnic cleansing. In the San Joaquin Valley, Monos incorporated the Fresno River Farm into their seasonal economic practices, much like Native Peoples at missions and on ranchos did previously. Monos worked on farms and ranches, mined, harvested, and hunted. In between these times, Monos worked for food and clothing at the Fresno River Farm. The economic activities associated with reservation life enabled Monos to maintain their social and political practices. Monos lived in communities led by Native leaders, such as Wuemekana, and in households headed by Native People. Captains served as labor contractors, arranging jobs and negotiating wages and temporary living conditions for other Indians.

The California Gold Rush unsettled Native lands and peoples. Policies of genocide, ethnic cleansing, and slavery divorced Indigenous People from the land and one another. Throughout the Gold Rush era, though, Indigenous People resisted these incursions. San Diego County officials levied taxes on Cupeños, Cahuillas, and Luiseños, even though the California Constitution denied Indigenous People the right to vote. In 1850, San Diego County officials assessed Indigenous Peoples' lands at a tax rate of $600. Although leaders of the state militia informed southern Indigenous People that they would not have to pay the tax, the San Diego County sheriff, with permission from the state attorney general, visited Indian communities, collected $250 in cash, eighteen cows, and five horses and mules.

Antonio Garra, a Cupeño leader, bristled at the Americans and their laws. Garra was likely a Quechan, but Spanish officials took him to mission San Luis Rey while young. There, he learned Latin, as well as numerous regional Indian languages. He was eventually appointed as the headman of the two prominent Cupeño villages, Kupa and Wilakal. Garra attempted to create a pan-Indian alliance in Southern California to combat the invaders and reached out to other Cupeño, Cahuilla, and Luiseño communities in San Diego County; Quechans, Cocopahs, and Kumeyaay in the vicinity of the Colorado River; and Native People in modern-day Baja California. Garra informed Juan Antonio, the Cahuilla leader, "If we lose this war, all will be lost—the world." Garra proposed a coordinated attack on Americans, with Garra and his Quechan allies taking Camp Independence, followed by Yokuts striking Santa Barbara, Cahuillas and Cupeños attacking Los Angeles, and Quechans targeting San Diego. Americans foiled the plan. Garra and the Quechans failed to take Camp Independence and severed ties after they disagreed about the fair distribution of sheep they took from Americans.

To the east, Cahuilla leaders Chapuli, Panito, and Francisco Mocate left the Los Coyotes Canyon and traveled toward J. J. Warner's rancho. Cahuillas disliked Warner because he stole horses from them and whipped Indigenous workers. People warned Warner of the imminent attack, and he sent his family to San Diego. On the night of November 21, 1851, about twenty Cupeños attacked Warner's ranch. Warner and one of his Indigenous servants escaped, but the Cupeños stripped his home and stole all of his cattle.

Garra continued in his attempt to build a coalition to oppose the American invaders. His son contacted Manuelito Cota, but Cota refused Garra's entreaties, claiming to be loyal to Americans. Garra then renewed his contact with Cahuilla Juan Antonio. Antonio and his wife had accepted baptism at Mission San Luis Rey in 1828, but they lived in the San Jacinto Mountains, where Antonio was born. Antonio united several Cahuilla groups and in the 1840s built an alliance with Mexican ranchero Antonio Lugo, whereby some Mountain Cahuillas lived on Lugo's rancho to protect it from horse raiders. Antonio's role in the Garra uprising is open to some debate. He reached out to Tulareño leaders to rally to Garra's cause. But in late 1851, at a meeting he had requested, Antonio ordered his men to capture Garra. He subsequently turned him over to American officials.

On January 8, 1852, American officials paraded Garra into San Diego. Two days later, Garra was put on trial for "levying war against the government, of murder and robbery." At his trial, Warner was not only the star witness against him but, in a common practice at the time, served as his interpreter as well. Convicted and sentenced to death by firing squad, Garra was executed by Americans that afternoon.

Indigenous People resisted American invaders in the north as well. Hupas primarily lived in three towns in Natinook (the Hoopa Valley). In the northern part of the valley, Hupas stayed at Tseweñaldiñ and Takimildiñ. In the southern part of the valley, Hupas settled at Medildiñ. Each of these towns hosted annual ceremonies to maintain balance with the world and ensure productive hunting, fishing, and harvesting. Natinook was isolated from European explorers who skirted the Pacific coast and the Spanish missions to the south. In the 1820s and 1830s, however, *kiwamil* (fur traders, lit. "creatures with fur") passed through Hoopa. In 1849, three thousand *misah kititlut* (miners, lit. "their mouths flap") invaded Natinook following the discovery of gold in the headwaters of the Trinity River. Misah kititlut destroyed Hupa food sources, introduced disease, and killed Hupa people. Hupa resisted the arrival of misah kititlut by stealing horses and killing miners. In the mid-1850s, farmers invaded Natinook. Unlike the misah kititlut, Hupas attempted to create relationships with these newcomers. They worked on farms, traded goods, and married some invaders.

Outside of Natinook, Indigenous People resisted American invaders. In 1855, Yuroks and Karuks battled miners and the United States Army in the so-called Red Cap War. After most Yuroks and Karuks retreated to the recently established Klamath Reservation, Wiyots, Wintuns, Chimarikos, Chilulas, Whilkuts, Nongatls, and holdout Karuks and Yuroks continued the fight. Hupas did not overtly participate in these battles. Instead, they supplied the insurgents with arms and food and hired mercenaries to fight for them.

In 1859, the United States Army established Fort Gaston in the middle of Natinook in an effort to quell violence in the region and keep an eye on Hupas. The creation of Fort Gaston and the presence of soldiers exacerbated tensions between Hupas and Americans. In 1859, a group of soldiers attacked a Hupa woman from the town of Tseweñaldiñ. She killed one of her assailants with an elk horn used for cleaning eels. The following fall, a soldier and farmer killed a Hupa man from the town of Takimildiñ. The soldier fled to Fort Gaston, and the farmer fled the valley; courts prosecuted neither man for the crime. Quite clearly, the creation of the fort exposed Hupa women and men to more violence. This incident also aggra-vated relationships among Hupas. The residents of Takimildiñ blamed people from Tseweñaldiñ for the killings and demanded compensation for their loss. Tseweñaldiñ refused, and tensions escalated between the two prominent Hupa towns. These relationships exploded when Tseweñaldiñ John killed Bill Hostler, the brother of Charley Hostler, the leader of Takimildiñ.

On the morning of Friday, April 12, 1861, Confederate forces bom-barded the Union army, holed up at Fort Sumter, South Carolina. This event famously initiated the American Civil War. Despite California's distance from the bulk of the fighting, the rebellion reverberated in San Francisco and Los Angeles. Some United States Army officers aban-doned their posts and joined the Confederacy. Americans worried that without a strong military presence, California Indians would attack their communities. The new commander of the Department of the Pacific called up volunteer regiments and dispatched them to forts in the areas with the hottest conflicts. Colonel Francis J. Lippett took com-mand of the newly created Humboldt Military District and turned his attention to Natinook to put down what he believed to be recalcitrant and belligerent Hupas. During the Civil War, Lippett sent six volunteer units to Natinook.

Lippett blamed the Hupas, not the invasion of miners, farmers, and soldiers, for the violence in northwest California and recommended removing recalcitrant Hupas from the Humboldt District to Owens Val-ley or the Santa Barbara islands. Failing that, Lippett intended to force Hupas to relocate to the Klamath Reservation. Despite these threats, Hupas continued to aid allies outside of the valley. In April of 1862, a multiethnic group of Indigenous People attacked a pack train near Fort Anderson. The skirmish resulted in the deaths of three Americans and an unknown number of Indigenous People, including a Hupa leader. On learning of the role of Hupas in the attack, Americans in Hoopa Valley worried that Hupas would attack them. In the spring of 1862, Lippett responded to the Americans' concerns and ordered more volunteers to occupy Fort Gaston. When the new men arrived, Captain Edmund Underwood, Fort Gaston's commander, demanded that Hupas surren-der their guns. Most Hupas refused to comply, and many resented those who did. A Hupa leader named Captain John agreed to a peace with the soldiers and promised to scout for the army. His actions angered other Hupas and failed to mollify Americans, largely because the scouts con-veniently failed to find anyone.

In 1863, violence continued to tear apart northwestern California. In January, settlers complained that Indigenous People had killed thirty settlers, burned fifty buildings, and destroyed $500,000 worth of stock and property. Settlers likely exaggerated these losses, but they succeeded in bringing more military personnel into the Hoopa Valley. Hupas responded by attempting to resurrect alliances with their neighbors. In April of 1863, Hupa runners failed to convince Ca-pekw (or Hrkwr), a Yurok town at Stone Lagoon, to join the war against the settlers. As a result, Hupas and Redwood Creek Whilkuts attacked Ca-pekw, killed thirty Yuroks, and razed the town. Facing the invasion of settlers and miners, as well as the intrusion of the United States Army, Hupas displaced violence on their Yurok neighbors, who attempted to remain neutral in the Civil War–era battles.

The absence of allies did not deter Hupas from attacking Americans. Hupas and Whilkuts attacked pack trains traveling between the Hoopa Valley and Arcata. Other Indigenous People struck American trade posts, farms, livestock, and sawmills on the Trinity River. In August of 1863, Hupas and Whilkuts attacked an American family living on New River. Three of the Hupa men who participated in this attack went to the town of Medildiñ, located on the east bank of the Trinity River and neutral in the surrounding conflicts. The volunteers at Fort Gaston learned of the men's presence in the town and attacked Medilding. The army took 116 captives and forced the residents of the town to relocate to the fort. The attack failed to pacify the region. Big Jim, from Medilding, led forty Hupas in attacks along the Trinity River and attempted to rally support from Karuks. Another Hupa leader, Tseweñaldiñ John, joined Big Jim, increasing their numbers to more than one hundred.

Hupas established a fort east of Bald Mountain, described as "four solid log buildings which formed a square around a spring." On Christmas, soldiers surrounded and laid siege to the fort, but all Hupas escaped. The standoff continued through January of 1864. The army enlisted Hostler as a scout, but the Hupas consistently eluded capture. With the addition of 250 more volunteers that spring, the decision by the Karuk and Yurok not to become involved, and the capture of two of their important followers, John and Big Jim decided to negotiate a peace.

Settlers in the area urged the government to remove the Hupa. Recognizing the weakness of its position, the federal government appointed Austin Wiley, an erstwhile opponent of reservations while serving in the state legislature and later the publisher of the *Humboldt Times,* as the single superintendent of Indian Affairs for the state. The commissioner of Indian affairs authorized Wiley to establish no more than four reservations. Wiley offered Santa Catalina Island as a possible site to move Hupas. The commissioner suggested Round Valley instead. The Hupa refused both, especially Round Valley. Wiley remarked, "It would take a soldier for every Indian to keep them [there]." The superintendent arranged to meet with Hupas at Fort Gaston. Hupas arrived armed and determined not to surrender weapons if the government pursued removal. They negotiated a treaty that set aside the "whole of Hoopa Valley" for a reservation and secured Hupa rights to hunt, fish, and gather on their lands. By resisting the United States and American invaders, Hupas secured a measure of control over the valley.

By the late 1860s, California Indians' world was out of balance. The Gold Rush brought American invaders to Indigenous homelands; these invaders killed and enslaved Indigenous People and destroyed trees and rivers. Then positive news came from Nevada. In 1869, Wodziwob, a northern Paiute prophet from Nevada's Walker River Reservation, fell into a trance and dreamed of the return of the dead and transformation of the world into a paradise. Wodziwob urged followers to perform a Paiute Round Dance, in which men and women held hands and shuffled in a circle from left to right to hasten that transformation.

The Ghost Dance spread throughout Nevada, southern Oregon, and Northern California, like new growth following in the wake of the fire of the last twenty years. Weneyuga, one of Wodziwob's followers, took the Ghost Dance to Paiute communities at Surprise Valley, Reno, and Pyramid Lake. From there, Paiutes took the religion to the Klamath Reservation in Oregon, where Modocs heard it. Doctor George, a Modoc man, took the Ghost Dance from Klamath to Tule Lake, the home of Modocs led by Captain Jack, who had fled the Klamath Reservation and ultimately killed General Canby. Jake Smith, a Shasta man, attended a Modoc Ghost Dance and brought it back to his home on Bogus Creek, near Montague. A Shasta prophet named Sambo took the Ghost Dance to the Karuk at Orleans. Klamaths carried the Ghost Dance to the Siletz Reservation in Oregon. From Siletz, Native People brought the Ghost Dance to Tolowas. The Ghost Dance traveled easily, as it was intended for all Native People.

The Dreamers, as they came to be called, who practiced the Ghost Dance reclaimed a world that colonization and violence disrupted. Modoc Harrison Brown remembered, "[Weneyuga] told that all the dead were coming back, even the wild animals, like bear, deer, wolf, etc. Everyone who was dead was marching back in rows. All were to rise." Henry

Joseph, a Karuk man from Happy Camp, said, "[Sambo] said dead relatives were coming back and we must dance. All the old people believed and painted and danced." In a little more than a generation, Americans outnumbered Indigenous People in the state. The Ghost Dance promised to reverse those trends, with the return of the dead and animals.

The Ghost Dance traveled through kinship relationships. Tolowa Emma Villastra said, "Word came from [the] Siletz [Reservation] that people must put on Indian clothes and dance so that the dead would come back. The two men who brought the word were Depot Charlie and Port Orford Jake. Depot Charlie could talk Tolowa, so he did not need an interpreter. His sister, or half-sister, had married a Smith River [Tolowa] man." Depot Charlie was not a stranger to the Tolowas. He could speak their language and came to preach to relatives. Yuroks also remembered the kinships that brought the Ghost Dance: "There was an old Tolowa from Burnt Ranch between Crescent City and Smith River [who] started the movement. From him, his nephew, a Yurok living at Staawin, ten miles from the mouth of the Klamath, learned to dream." Religious leaders taught relatives the proper way to perform the ceremony, and then they went on the road. In fact, the Ghost Dance fostered relationships with the dead. Henry Joseph remembered: "Dead persons told them songs and the next morning the dreamers would sing them. They might hear a song for four or five nights."

The Ghost Dance challenged industrialization in California. Pit River people shared the message with the Wintu. A Wintu and Yana man named Norelputus adapted the Ghost Dance into the Earth Lodge Religion, whereby dancing in subterranean houses protected participants from the end of the world. Near Grindstone, a Pomo prophet named Santiago McDaniel heard the Earth Lodge Religion. McDaniel may have been an indentured servant as a young boy, but he was reclaimed by his community. After hearing the Ghost Dance, McDaniel traveled throughout Mendocino County, preaching the message. Round Valley Indians flocked to off-reservation worksites, whether hop workers' camps or sheep-shearing camps, to hear the message. Yuki Ralph Moore remembered that his father, George, heard Santiago McDaniel preach: "Santiago lighted a pipe, smoked and passed it to my father. He smoked, too, then Santiago took the pipe and shook out [a] fifty-cent piece. That is the way to get money, he told my father." That spring, George heeded McDaniel's advice and quit his job shearing sheep to dance because he wanted to see his mother, who had died. Other Round Valley Indians followed suit by refusing to plant gardens or work for ranchers.

McDaniel made labor and economic relations central to the message he brought to the reservation. He went further than exhorting Indians to quit their jobs, promising an economic revolution. "If you do as I tell you, it will happen so," McDaniel told Round Valley Indians. "We shall live in good houses. We shall hire white men to work for us. Your wife won't have to cook. White women will cook for you." Heard at off-reservation workplaces, McDaniel's Earth Lodge Religion pledged to provide cash to Indians and invert Mendocino County's economic hierarchy. There was no more popular, or hopeful, message than that for Mendocino County Indians. Round Valley Indians believed they could change places with White men and women and return California to Indian country. Indigenous People carried these hopeful messages to workplaces during the following decades.

Between 1848 and 1860, the state of California disenfranchised, disarmed, and legalized the indenture, if not outright slavery, of Indigenous People. The United States failed to ratify treaties, reducing the ability of Indigenous People to protect themselves. The United States Army and state-authorized militias massacred California Indians. All told, the population of California Indians declined about 80 percent from an estimated 150,000 to 30,000 people. Those California Indians who survived the violent colonization and genocide looked for ways to reverse and blunt what they had endured, to put their world back in order.

SOURCES

The years between 1846 and 1873 have attracted a disproportionate amount of attention from scholars, journalists, and popular historians. Despite that, much of the reality of the era for Indigenous People remains hidden. This chapter pulls back some of the well-known events to look at their relationships with lesser known histories. Our discussion of sources here does likewise.

On the Modoc War, see Jim Compton, *Spirit of the Rock: The Fierce Battle for Modoc Homelands* (Pullman: Washington State University Press, 2017); and Boyd Cothran, *Remembering the Modoc War: Redemptive Violence and the Making of American Innocence* (Chapel Hill: University of North Carolina Press, 2017). On the encounter between Riddle and Meacham during the ambush, see Rebecca Bales, "Winema and the Modoc War," *Prologue* 37 (Spring 2005): www.archives.gov/publications /prologue/2005/spring/winema.html.

Several works have been crucial in our discussion of the transfer of control from Mexico to the United States and how it played out, particularly in the Central Valley, as well as the Mexican-American War: Albert Hurtado, *Indian Survival on the California Frontier* (New Haven, CT: Yale University Press, 1988); Albert Hurtado, *John Sutter: A Life on the North American Frontier* (Norman: University of Oklahoma Press, 2008); and George Harwood Phillips, *Indians and Intruders in Central California, 1769–1849* (Norman: University of Oklahoma Press, 1993). The story of Piupiumaksmaks, also known as Yellow Serpent, Yellow Bird, Pio pio mox mox, and Peopeo Moxmox, can be found in these books. José Jesús appears throughout them as well. The quotation "so that no traveler on the road escaped falling into [the battalion's] hands," can be found in *Indian Survival*, page 82. See also Lisbeth Haas, "War in California, 1846–1848," *California History* 76 (Summer-Fall 1997): 331–55.

An extensive literature exists on the Gold Rush. In addition to the above-mentioned sources, we have relied on Marie Potts, *The Northern Maidu* (Happy Camp, CA: Naturegraph, 1977), from which the quotation about Maidu "intending only to loan them the land" can be found on page 10. The quotation used as the title of this chapter, "the white man would spoil everything," comes from Lucy Thompson, *To the American Indian: Reminiscences of a Yurok Woman* (Eureka, CA: Cummins Book Shop, 1916), 29.

Other important works on the Gold Rush include Andrew Isenberg, *Mining California: An Ecological History* (New York: Hill and Wang, 2006); Susan Johnson, *Roaring Camp: The Social World of the California Gold Rush* (New York: Norton, 2000); and Brian Roberts, *American Alchemy: The California Gold Rush and Middle-Class Culture* (Chapel Hill: University of North Carolina Press, 2000).

On the treaty process, much of that story remains in the primary sources. The *Report of the Secretary of the Interior, Communicating in Compliance with a Resolution of the Senate, a Copy of the Correspondence between the Department of the Interior and the Indian Agents and Commissioners in California*, Senate Executive Document, No. 4, 33rd Congress, Special Session (1853) contains a wealth of information, including the locations, goals, protocols, and McKee's entreaties—"Brothers listen to my talk . . ." on page 137. Cipriano's words can be found on page 251. The quotation about "now an Indian was afraid to go on the mountains after game and nuts alone" comes from page 164.

On the treaties, see the brief discussion in the note on sources for chapter 6.

On the question of genocide, see Benjamin Madley, *An American Genocide: The United States and the California Indian Catastrophe, 1846–1873* (New Haven, CT: Yale University Press, 2017). References can be found as follows: Oregonians, pages 87–91; Clear Lake, pages 103–15, 127–32; "killing machine" and "pedagogic killing" pages 178, 48. On use of the term *genocide,* see Benjamin Madley, "Reexamining the American Genocide Debate: Meaning, Historiography and New Methods," *American Historical Review* 120 (Feb. 2015): 98–139; Brendan C. Lindsay, *Murder State: California's Native American Genocide, 1846–1873* (Lincoln: University of Nebraska Press, 2012), x, 14–17; Gary C. Anderson, *Ethnic Cleansing and the Indian: The Crime That Should Haunt America* (Norman: University of Oklahoma Press, 2014), 6, 193; and Jeffrey Ostler, *Surviving Genocide: Native Nations and the United States from the American Revolution to Bleeding Kansas* (New Haven, CT: Yale University Press, 2019), 383–87. The full title of the United Nations' definition of *genocide* is "Convention on the Prevention and Punishment of the Crime of Genocide" (Dec. 1948).

On the Tolowa massacre of 1853, see Richard A. Gould, "Indian and White Versions of the 'Burnt Ranch Massacre': A Study of Comparative Ethnohistory," *Journal of American Folklore* 3 (June 1966): 30–42. For Minnie Reeves's story, see Luthin, *Surviving through the Days,* 110–11.

Any study of Indian slavery in California starts with the work of Michael Magliari, particularly "Free Soil, Unfree Labor," *Pacific Historical Review* 73 (August 2004), 349–90; and "Free State Slavery: Bound Indian Labor and Slave Trafficking in California's Sacramento Valley, 1850–1864," *Pacific Historical Review* 81 (May 2012): 155–92. Much of the information on Cave Johnson Couts comes from "Free Soil, Unfree Labor." On the larger context and demise of Indian slavery in California, see Stacey L. Smith, *Freedom's Frontier: California and the Struggle over Unfree Labor, Emancipation, and Reconstruction* (Chapel Hill: University of North Carolina Press, 2013), 182–92. See also William J. Bauer Jr., *We Were All like Migrant Workers Here: Work, Community and Memory on California's Round Valley Reservation, 1850–1941* (Chapel Hill: University of North Carolina Press, 2009), 45–51. The quotation "I killed some of [their parents] myself" comes from *The Congressional Globe,* Feb. 16, 1863, 1008. The account of the Nisenan boy lynched for stealing gold, and his community leaders' response, including the quote, "That is the way [they] will treat ... ," comes from Hans Jørgen Uldall and William Shipley,

Nisenan Texts and Dictionary (Berkeley: University of California Press, 1966), 177–81.

On Los Angeles in the 1850s, and the challenges facing California Indian workers, see George Harwood Phillips, *Vineyards and Vaqueros: Indian Labor and the Economic Expansion of Southern California, 1771–1877* (Norman, OK: Arthur H. Clark, 2010), including the quotation "Gambling, drinking and whoring are the only occupations . . . ," from page 263; John Mack Faragher, *Eternity Street: Violence and Justice in Frontier Los Angeles* (New York: Norton, 2016), details on the churchurki game, 248–50; Kelly Lytle Hernandez, *City of Inmates: Conquest, Rebellion, and the Rise of Human Caging in Los Angeles, 1771–1965* (Chapel Hill: University of North Carolina Press, 2017), information on the Los Angeles slave trade, and the quotation "Los Angeles had its slave mart . . . ," from 36, 38–39.

On the origins and establishment of reservations, see George Harwood Phillips, *"Bringing Them under Subjection": California's Tejón Indian Reservation and Beyond, 1852–1864* (Lincoln: University of Nebraska Press), 142–46; Gelya Frank and Carole Goldberg, *Defying the Odds: The Tule River Tribe's Struggle for Sovereignty in Three Centuries* (New Haven, CT: Yale University Press, 2011), 24; Donald Lindsay Hislop, *The Nome Lackee Indian Reservation, 1854–1870* (Chico: Association for Northern California Records and Research, 1978); *Indians and Indian Agents: The Origins of the Reservation System in California, 1849–1852* (Norman: University of Oklahoma Press, 1997).

Benjamin Wilson's belief that the mission system provided "a successful course of tuition in the arts of civilized life and the duties of morality and religion" comes from Benjamin. D. Wilson, *The Indians of Southern California in 1852*, edited by John Walton Caughey (Lincoln: University of Nebraska Press, 1995), 3.

On Kibbe's rangers and the removal of Concow and others to Round Valley, see Frank Baumgardner, *Killing for Land in Early California: Indian Blood at Round Valley, 1856–1863* (New York: Algora, 2005), 78, 79; Michele Shover, "The Politics of the 1859 Kibbe Campaign: Northern California Indian-Settler Conflicts of the 1850s," *Dogtown Territorial Quarterly* 38 (1999): 3–39. Bauer, *We Were All like Migrant Workers Here*. The claim of one of the rangers that ". . . we were gone four months and that we brought away more than 1500 Indians" is from William J. Bauer, *California through Native Eyes: Reclaiming History* (Seattle: University of Washington Press, 2016), 91. On the Round

Valley trail of tears, see Pamela A. Conners, *The Chico to Round Valley Trail of Tears* (Willows, CA: Mendocino National Forest, 1993), 14, 18–40.

On Garra's revolt, see George Harwood Phillips, *Chiefs and Challengers: Indian Resistance and Cooperation in Southern California, 1769–1906*, 2nd ed. (Norman: University of Oklahoma Press, 2014). Garra's claim that "If we lose this war, all will be lost—the world" can be found on page 105.

On the violence in Hoopa Valley, see Byron Nelson Jr., *Our Home Forever: The Hupa Indians of Northern California* (Salt Lake City, UT: Howe Brothers, 1988), where you can find the quotation, "it would take a soldier for every Indian to keep them [there]," 86–91. Alvin Josephy Jr., *The Civil War in the American West* (New York: Alfred A. Knopf, 1991); David Rich Lewis, *Neither Wolf nor Dog: American Indians, Environment and Agrarian Change* (New York: Oxford University Press, 1994); Jack Norton, *When Our Worlds Cried: Genocide in Northwestern California* (San Francisco: Indian Historian Press, 1979); A. J. Bledsoe, *Indian Wars of the Northwest: A California Sketch* (Oakland, CA: Biobooks, 1956); Owen C. Coy, *The Humboldt Bay Region, 1850–1875: A Study in the American Colonization of California* (Los Angeles: California State Historical Association, 1929).

On the Ghost Dance, see Cara Du Bois, *1870 Ghost Dance* (Lincoln: University of Nebraska Press, 2007). The quotations by Harrison Brown and Henry Joseph are on pages 36 and 40; Emma Villastra's is on page 41. McDaniel's promises can be found on page 244. Ralph Moore's memories are on page 243. For Santiago McDaniel, see Magliari, "Free State Slavery," 179–80n55.

Native Spaces

Ukiah

One hundred sixteen miles north of San Francisco, the town of Ukiah, population sixteen thousand, sits in a narrow valley, snuggled up to the Northern Coast Ranges to the west and looking out on farmlands, watered by the Russian River, to the east. There is a bit of a "blink and you'll miss it" character to the town, especially for those speeding along Highway 101 en route to the redwoods to the north or the Bay Area to the south. As with many places in North America, the town of Ukiah derives its name from an Indigenous word or phrase, in this case, the Pomo term *yō'kaia,* which means "lower valley" or "deep valley," a reference to the Pomo People who lived on the southern portion of what is now called the Ukiah Valley. Yet Ukiah was not always an isolated place in California. Colonization made the Ukiah Valley remote and rural. Settlers, bent on transforming the land for ranching and farming economies, dispossessed Pomos of their lands. Despite that, Ukiah Valley remained Pomo space in the minds of the Pomos, and they worked to protect their identity, reclaim the land, and create unique land bases, some of which exist only in California.

The Ukiah Valley sits at the center of Pomo territory, which stretches from the Pacific coast to Clear Lake and from the Russian River to the Eel. The people known as Pomo spoke seven distinct and mutually unintelligible dialects of the Pomo language. Speakers of the central and northern Pomo language dialects live in the Ukiah Valley. The Yokaya Pomos lived at Co'kadjal, which means "east flint place," in the southern part of the

Ukiah Valley. The town was an important site, often hosting ceremonies in its roundhouse. The Komli Pomo lived in the northern part of the valley at a town called Komli (drinking place). Sometime in the 1830s, perhaps because of the increasing intrusions of Russians to the west and Mexicans to the south, Yokayas forced Komlis to leave the valley.

Soon after Yokayas assumed control over the valley, Europeans intruded on their territories. Yokayas and Komlis had had little direct contact with Europeans, although they certainly knew about them from their neighbors. Russians established Fort Ross in Kashaya Pomo territory, and Spanish and Mexican officials forced southern Pomos into missions and onto ranchos. The lack of direct contact changed in the mid-1840s. In 1846, Governor Pio Pico gave Rancho Yokaya to Cayetano Juarez. The Mexican-American War prevented Juarez from developing the rancho, and the subsequent United States occupation threw the grant's legitimacy into question. As soon as the war ended, Americans invaded the Ukiah Valley. In 1850, after the United States Army wiped out other Pomos at a place currently known as Bloody Island, the army attacked Co'kadjal and killed seventy-five Yokayas. The following year, Americans drove cattle into Ukiah, initiating the agricultural pursuits that continue to sustain the valley's economy. Euro-American ownership of the valley remained contested until the 1860s, when California courts finally verified Juarez's land grant. By that time, however, Serranus Hastings, the namesake for the University of California Hastings Law School, and business associates had purchased much of the old land grant.

American farmers and ranchers quickly adopted provisions of the Act for the Government and Protection of Indians to create a workforce from the Pomo communities. D. H. Woodman, one of the most notorious human traffickers, operated out of Ukiah. Woodman frequently traveled to the Round Valley area, abducted Indigenous children, whom he called "quail," and sold them in Sonoma County. In 1861, county officials arrested Woodman and fined him one hundred dollars for trafficking Indian children.

Pomos recognized how they could exploit loopholes in law. The United States government removed Pomos from Ukiah and Potter Valley to the Mendocino Reservation, located on the coast near Fort Bragg. Rather than go, however, Pomo leaders voluntarily entered into an indenture contract with Aurelius O. Carpenter, an American photographer and the father of artist Grace Hudson, so that they could avoid removal and remain in their homeland. Federal Indian agents removed other Yokayas, however, to the reservation. When the government disbanded the reservation, the Yokayas returned to Ukiah to find much of their old lands occupied by American farmers and ranchers. Yokayas occupied new sites, often near ranches, to find work. For instance, Yokayas from Co'kadjal moved to a Canē'neū (sweat house place), suggesting the persistence of Pomo ceremonies.

After the American Civil War, farmers introduced a new agricultural crop, which revolutionized the Ukiah Valley. In 1868, L. F. Long planted hops, a plant used to flavor and preserve beer, along the Russian River. Hops thrived in Northern California's climate. Until the Great Depression, hop production centered on Ukiah and the surrounding area. American farmers put up hop kilns and barns throughout the Ukiah Valley, including on the site of Co'kadjal. Native People from throughout Northern California traveled to Ukiah to train and to pick and dry hops. Others sought out benevolent American ranchers, much like the elderly Pomos had done the previous decade. By 1881, 135 Pomos lived on J. H. Burke's ranch.

Soon, Pomos saw opportunities to buy back land in the Ukiah Valley. In 1878, Captain Jack led a northern Pomo group from the Round Valley Reservation to fifty-one acres of land near Ukiah that he and others purchased by pooling their wages. When the Round Valley agent attempted to bring them back to the reservation, he found they hired an attorney who threatened the agent with charges of kidnapping if he tried to remove any of the residents. In 1881, four Yokaya leaders—Bill (who was born at Co'kadjal), Dick, Lewis, and Charley—urged fellow Pomos to pool their money to buy land. The Pomos raised $800, which they used to make a down payment for 120 acres located east of the Russian River. For the next couple of years, the Pomos combined their wages made from farmwork, picking hops, and selling baskets to pay off the entire amount. By the turn of the twentieth century, Pomos had acquired 145 acres on the eastern side of the valley. Eighty people lived on the land, which also held an octagonal roundhouse, a hop kiln, and six barns. Pomos raised hops on fourteen acres of land. In 1908, the California Supreme Court affirmed that the four Pomo leaders intended to hold the land as a trust for all the Pomos living there.

Pomos reestablished a permanent presence on the land. Throughout Mendocino and Lake Counties, Pomos pooled wages and bought land in a similar fashion. There were six such communities in and near the Ukiah Valley and four more in Lake County. Certainly, the lands were small in acreage and conveniently near American employers, yet Pomos

FIGURE 14. Dancers performing at the Pomo weekend in Ukiah, 1978. Photo courtesy Meriam Library, California State University, Chico.

owned the land and used it to unite their people. In the 1870s, Ghost Dance preachers established spaces to lead the new religious ceremony. In 1911, Pomos in Coyote Valley hosted a three-day Christmas celebration. In 1978, Pomos gathered for the Pomo Weekend (fig. 14).

In 1906, the federal government stepped in. San José lawyer Charles Kelsey conducted a census of nonreservation Indians in California. Kelsey found 831 such Indians in Mendocino County. Furthermore, he noted only 213 owned land while the remaining 618 did not. Based on Kelsey's census, the federal government began buying small plots of land, often adjacent to Pomo lands they owned in common. These land bases, and others like them across the state, came to be called *rancherias,* from the term used to describe small, rural Indigenous villages in the Spanish and Mexican era. Rancherias, as federally recognized sovereign Indigenous spaces, exist nowhere else in the United States.

The census also raised questions about the identity of these nonreservation Indians. In 1929, Pomo Stephen Knight captured the ambiguity in a statement before a United States Senate committee. When asked if he was "a California citizen and an Indian," Knight replied, "Yes; and an Indian." Pomos in the Ukiah Valley, as well as other parts of Mendocino and Lake County, claimed citizenship rights since they did not live on reservations and were not considered wards of the government. They faced racial discrimination in the form of segregated schools and hospitals. Indeed, hospitals in Ukiah refused to treat California Indians who fought in World War I. Additionally, county officials refused to allow Pomos to vote, which Pomo Ethan Anderson successfully challenged in California courts. Yet, as Knight stated, Yokaya Pomos and others remained Pomo.

Twelve Pomo rancherias exist in and around the Ukiah Valley, though not without some contestation. In 1958, the federal government terminated five Pomo rancherias in Mendocino County and six more in Lake County. In 1988, Tillie Hardwick, of the Pinoleville Rancheria, successfully challenged termination in federal courts. Courts ruled the federal and state governments failed to provide the services to the terminated rancherias that the termination legislation required and restored their trust status.

Today, several Pomo rancherias operate lucrative gaming establishments, off Highway 101. In addition to casinos, the Pinoleville Pomo Nation took the lead on the development of large-scale cannabis operations. In December of 2014, the Department of Justice asserted that tribes possess a sovereign right to produce and distribute marijuana on tribal lands, even in states where it is illegal. Some viewed this decision as the "new casinos." In January of 2015, the Pinoleville Pomo Nation entered into a contract with a Colorado-based cannabis grower to build a $10 million, 110,000 square foot greenhouse and processing facility on tribal land. The operation placed them as major players in the region's cannabis industry, a role that many previously assumed big tobacco would play. That summer, they began planting. In September, the Mendocino County sheriff's office raided the facility and destroyed plants and equipment. The Pinoleville Pomo responded, citing Public Law 280 and the Justice Department memo, by filing a claim for $25,000 in damages against the sheriff's office. The issue languished in the courts until, in January of 2018, Attorney General Jeff Sessions issued a memo rescinding the previous memo and directing US attorneys to enforce federal laws. As California Indians and other Indigenous People in the United States understand all too well, certain political administrations actively attempt to put up roadblocks in front of tribal sovereignty.

Ukiah's "blink and you'll miss it" quality resulted from a historical project. Colonization made the Ukiah Valley, and much of the lands north of the Bay Area and Sacramento, remote. Pomos, using all the tools available to them, ensure that the Ukiah Valley remains Pomo.

SOURCES

On Pomo place-names and territorial claims, see Samuel A. Barrett, *The Ethno-geography of the Pomo and Neighboring Indians* (Berkeley, CA: University Press, 1908), 1–132; and Sally McLendon and Robert L. Oswalt, "Pomo: Introduction," in *Handbook of North American Indians*, edited by Robert Heizer, vol. 8 (Washington, DC: Smithsonian Institute, 1978), 282, 284. On D. H. Woodman's human trafficking, see William J. Bauer Jr., *We Were All like Migrant Workers Here: Work, Community and Memory on California's Round Valley Reservation, 1850–1941* (Chapel Hill: University of North Carolina Press, 2009), 52. On Aurelius Carpenter, see Marvin Schenck, Karen Holmes, and Sherrie Smith-Ferri, *Aurelius O. Carpenter: Photographer of the Mendocino Frontier* (Ukiah, CA: Grace Hudson and Sun House Museum, 2006), 99–100. On hops, see Charles Kasch, "The Yokayo Rancheria," *California Historical Society Quarterly* 26 (Sept. 1947): 209–15. On pooling wages to purchase land, see Khal Schneider, "Making Indian Land in the Allotment Era: Northern California's Indian Rancherias," *Western Historical Quarterly* 41 (Winter 2010): 429–50. See Stephen Knight's comments, from United States Senate, *Survey of the Conditions of the Indians in the United States: Hearings before a Subcommittee of the Committee on Indian Affairs,* 70th Cong., 2nd Sess., 1928, vol. 2: 559. The Pinoleville Pomo Nation's attempts to enter the cannabis business can be found in newspaper coverage: Glenda Anderson, "Ukiah Pomos to Establish State's First Tribal Pot Operation," *Press Democrat,* Jan. 8, 2015; "Pinoleville Pomo Nation Starts Planting Marijuana on Reservation," Indianz.com, June 4, 2015, www.indianz.com/News/2015/06/04/pinoleville-pomo-nation-starts.asp; "Pinoleville Issues Response to Marijuana Raid," *Ukiah Daily Journal,* Sept. 26, 2015; German Lopez, "Why a Native American Tribe Can Open a Marijuana Resort in a State Where Pot Is Illegal," *Vox.com,* Sept. 29, 2015, www.vox.com/2015/9/29/9417871/santee-sioux-marijuana-resort; and Brooke Staggs, "Could Cannabis Be the New Casinos for Southern California Native Americans?" *Orange County Register,* Feb. 14, 2019. The two memos in question are Monty Wilkinson, "Policy Statement Regarding Marijuana Issues in Indian Country," Oct. 28, 2014; and Jeff Sessions, "Memorandum on Marijuana Enforcement," Jan. 4, 2018.

6

Working for Land

Rancherias, Reservations, and Labor,
1870–1904

The story of Pomos pooling resources to purchase land in the Ukiah Valley appears more often in the *experiences* of California Indian communities than in the *story* of California Indian history. As had been the case during California's Spanish and Mexican periods, Indigenous Peoples' labor made American California possible. More than that, Indigenous People blunted the devastating effects of land loss and, in some cases, acquired and kept control over land and culture by entering wage labor markets. In the recovery from the catastrophe of the mid-nineteenth century, California Indians *worked* the land, and they worked *for* land. They also worked the law, or *against* the law, to protect their land and their right to use it. California Indians utilized the relationships connecting land, labor, and the law to carve out spaces to preserve sovereignty and culture throughout the state.

During the period historians call the "Gilded Age" (ca. 1866–1900), Indigenous People in California built on earlier efforts and entered the agricultural and industrial workforces. From Yreka to San Diego and San Francisco to Susanville, Indigenous People picked hops, laid railroad tracks, and cleaned homes. They understood that these efforts were necessary to develop a standard of living in California, as well as to secure and acquire land. They also sought the assistance of the federal government and new reform organizations to aid in their efforts to work for land. Both proved less than helpful. Federal officials failed to assist California Indians, either for want of resources or desire.

Reformers, meanwhile, pushed an assimilationist agenda on California Indians, culminating in the disastrous policy of allotment. By the start of the twentieth century, Indigenous Peoples' work for land had failed to universally protect resources, although not for their lack of trying. In those efforts, there may be no more devastating a story of land loss than the one that occurred at Warner's Ranch.

After the near collapse of the first reservation system, most California Indians lived tenuously on private land, working as ranch hands, farmhands, seasonal agriculture laborers, or domestic servants. The 1860 census found 17,798 Indians in such conditions, while approximately 13,500 resided on reservations. Nearly half of those living off-reservation were in Southern California. Often Indigenous women worked as domestic servants, while men performed agricultural or ranch labor.

During the Gilded Age, California changed dramatically. Between 1860 and 1920, the state population grew nearly tenfold, from fewer than four hundred thousand to 3.5 million. Those dramatic changes brought new opportunities and threats to Indians. During the Civil War, Republican politicians, nationwide and in California, slowly dismantled the laws that allowed Americans to enslave California Indians. In 1867, the United States passed the Anti-Peonage Act, which prohibited voluntary and involuntary servitude. As California's economy expanded, Indigenous People found ready work as skilled vaqueros, shepherds, shearers, and agricultural laborers. In the Ballena Valley, near Ramona, Kumeyaay earned fifty to seventy-five cents per day for herding, and four and a half cents a head for shearing sheep. But agricultural work often came at a high cost as settlers expanded agricultural production into Kumeyaay land.

Similar pressures operated on Indigenous People without a reservation to be removed to or to leverage on their behalf. Yana-Maidu Sam Batwi's story illustrates this trend. He was born around 1850 in Yana territory north of Mount Lassen, California. Prospectors traveled to the gold fields along the Lassen Cutoff through the heart of Yana territory. Between 1850 and 1866, local White militias and the United States Army led steady extermination campaigns, which killed most of the Yana. In the 1880s, folklorist Jeremiah Curtin worked in the area and described the violence. He claimed the "entire land of the Yana had been cleared. The few who escaped were those who happened to be away from home . . . and about twelve who were saved by Mr. Oliver and Mr. Disselhorst [sic]." While Curtin described the American farmers' motives as humanitarian, it is likely that both worked to protect the

FIGURE 15. Men and women playing hand game at Grindstone Rancheria. Photo courtesy Meriam Library, California State University, Chico.

labor supply critical for their livelihood. Oliver and Diestelhorst owned neighboring ranches in Redding, and the presence of the railroad adjacent to their properties facilitated their commercial operations. Both men needed workers and almost certainly viewed settler violence in economic terms.

On several occasions, Batwi worked with Curtin, who claimed Yanas were "distinguished beyond others for readiness to earn money," working particularly in ranching, haymaking, harvesting, hops, and vineyards. Batwi and others used their labor to carve out Indian spaces, in their cases informal spaces within the settler landscape. These spaces brought people together around their work and the social life that encircled it. They facilitated cultural preservation through food, stories, and traditional games (fig. 15).

After the 1870s, many Indigenous People traveled to burgeoning California cities to find permanent work and created new urban Indian spaces. They found jobs characteristic of "boom towns," working in foundries, slaughterhouses, and lumberyards or as launderers, domestic servants, masons, carpenters, shoemakers, tanners, blacksmiths, and millers. Around San Diego, Indians diverted the San Diego River with the Derby Dike in the 1850s and many other similar informal infrastructure projects in the years that followed. For their work, employers paid Indigenous People fifteen dollars per month, or one-quarter of the sixty dollars White workers made.

In the 1870s and 1880s, work as cooks, laundresses, and domestics grew increasingly common. In 1860, 20 percent of Indigenous People in Los Angeles County lived as servants in non-Indian homes. Nearly forty Indigenous People lived on William Wolfskill's rancho, employed as farmworkers, washerwomen, and servants. The Spence family near Monterey employed three Indigenous servants, ages twenty-five, twelve, and eight. Indigenous People integrating into non-Indian households made the reproduction of Indian communities difficult.

The railroad was a big part of the changes taking place in California. When the Central Pacific Railroad met the Union Pacific in northern Utah in 1869, California connected even more closely to the extensive rail network of the eastern United States and thus the national economy. In 1876, the Southern Pacific Railroad reached Los Angeles, linking it to the eastern US via New Orleans. Six years later, the California Southern Railroad joined the Atchison, Topeka and Santa Fe Railroad at Barstow, joining Southern California to Chicago. Not only did the railroads attach the state to the nation's marketplace, altering the market for agricultural and other goods, but they also helped to export the image of the state to a larger population.

Each of the main lines included complex systems, comprising multiple tracks, many smaller spur lines, switch stations, and hump yards. Beginning in the 1860s, California Indians left reservations and rancherias for long stretches of the year to follow railroad work. In 1881, the *San Diego Union* reflected the prejudices of the time in praising Indian workers as "far superior to either white or Chinamen. . . . They work harder and more persistently during the working hours of the day and move more earth than the same number of white laborers do, all other things being equal, on any other section of the line."

In part, Indigenous People's participation in the railroad workforce illustrates their particular presence in the regional landscape. Non-Indians understood rancherias, reservations, and other Indian communities, even those that were threatened or tenuous, to be Indian places. In short, they were places employers knew they could go to find ready workers at regular points in the annual work cycle. Indians could deploy their labor power by leveraging non-Indians' understanding of their land claims to their advantage.

The railroads radiated and reflected infrastructural development. Rail transport expanded the market for agricultural products, which in turn increased demand for those same commodities. Agriculture spread across the state, necessitating infrastructural development, particularly in regard to road construction and securing sources of water. The cycle fed on itself and on Indian labor.

By the 1880s, with a stronger connection to the national economy, the state's ports expanded their involvement in global trade. Overall, American California coincided with the industrialization and expansion of the economy, rapid urbanization, and dynamic demographic changes for Indians. Those changes were deeply paradoxical: industrialization and the market economy crowded Indigenous People and initiated a series of disputes over land that pushed many out of their traditional territory. But what land remained in Indian hands provided a base for entry into the expanding wage labor economy in support of cultural preservation. Indigenous People used their reservations and rancherias to deploy their labor power, moving in and out of Gilded Age California's economy. At the same time, Indian labor facilitated the acquisition of new tribal lands.

Indigenous People recognized the precarious nature of landowner-ship in California and demanded federal action to protect it. In 1870, President Ulysses S. Grant established two small reservations at Pala and San Pasqual that federal officials intended to meet the needs of *all* of Southern California. The reservations attempted to secure land for Indians and to formalize and clarify the Indians' relationships with the federal government through reservation-based tribal governments. Local non-Indians opposed the reservations because they believed they reserved too much land, and thus power, to Indians. In 1871, President Grant rescinded the executive order and disestablished both reserva-tions because of fierce American opposition.

Yet, moving to reservations did not appeal to all Indigenous People, especially when they rationally lacked confidence that the federal gov-ernment would deliver on its promises. Using legal measures, political appeals, and physical resistance, they sought to retain control over land. Between 1870 and 1873, Olegario Calac, a well-respected Luiseño *not* who spent years working for several Americans in the Los Angeles area, emerged as a leader in this fight. Elected general by twelve prominent Luiseño villages in 1871, Olegario led efforts opposing the reservations because they evicted Luiseños from their lands and relocated them to distant and tenuous territories. He urged his followers to refuse to move to the new reservations until they had seen proof of the deeds. Olegario traveled to San Diego, Los Angeles, and San Bernardino regularly to seek confirmation of the reservations' status. In those travels, he witnessed widespread squatting by settlers on the newly promised reservations, particularly at Pala and San Pasqual. Convinced that the reservations were paper promises, Olegario prepared for armed resistance.

The prospect of fighting frightened many settlers in the area, and they began to mobilize in response. Olegario sought peace by traveling to Los Angeles and giving an interview to a newspaper there. Over the next four years, Olegario met with journalists, lawyers, federal officials, and Luiseño leaders. The eviction at Temecula in 1873 spurred him to action again, and he petitioned federal officials, including the president. In November of 1875, he traveled to Washington, DC, and met with President Grant. That visit, and the pressure Olegario was able to bring, is credited with moving Grant to establish new reservations by executive order in 1875 and 1876 to replace those he rescinded in 1871. Olegario effectively pushed for change such that, when he died in 1877, many of his followers suspected foul play.

In the north, Indigenous People faced similar attacks on their lands. Yukis lost title to their lands in Mendocino County when the Senate refused to ratify the treaties negotiated with California Indians in 1851. In 1856, the Bureau of Indian Affairs established the Nome Cult Farm on Yuki lands. Four years later, the Land Office surveyed the 250,000 acres renamed the Round Valley Reservation. In 1870, President Grant confirmed the Round Valley Reservation by executive order. Three years later, an executive order quadrupled the size of the reservation. By that point, Yukis, Nomlakis, Huchnoms, Nisenans, Concows, Achumawis, Wailackis, and Pomo all lived on the Round Valley Reservation. Several very powerful and aggressive American trespassers also claimed land included within the 1873 expansion. The trespassers brought a deep sense of White privilege and home rule, which animated the Democratic Party and the American South at the time, to bear on their claims in California. These men disdained federal power and saw the occupation of land, especially land claimed by non-Whites, as a purview of White privilege. One of those was Thomas Jefferson Henley, former Democratic congressman from Indiana and the California superintendent of Indian affairs. Influential in designing California's Indian reservation policy, Henley was responsible for reserving Round Valley and viewed the area as his and his sons' bailiwick.

Federal and state officials disagreed about what should happen at Round Valley, but they agreed on their low opinion of Indians. The Indian Office saw Indian racial inferiority as the reason for federal protection. State officials, and the settlers whose views they embodied, saw

Indian racial inferiority as the reason they were unfit to hold territory. Furthermore, settlers saw Indian labor as a critical part of non-Indian possession of Indian land. In 1860, trespassers in Round Valley, including Henley's sons, held approximately 50 percent of the county's Indian apprentices.

Despite the Indian Office claim that Indians needed federal protection, by 1870, settlers claimed 80 percent of the reservation's land. The expansion of the reservation in 1873 further aided the settlers by removing much of the good valley land claimed by non-Indians from the reservation. Illegitimate preemption claims by non-Indians dotted the new acreage reserved north of the valley. In the end, the federal government agreed to pay trespassers for the improvements to their claims, as historians Kevin Adams and Khal Schneider point out, effectively "paying the trespassers for their crimes." Settlers, however, refused to accept the payments, allowing them to prolong their occupation without jeopardizing their claims.

Clearly, Round Valley needed a strong, decisive display of federal power to expel settlers and quiet their claims. The Indian Office requested help from the War Department. General O.O. Howard, the commander of the department of California and nationally known for campaigns against Cochise and Chief Joseph, sent a detachment of approximately forty men to Round Valley. Howard charged the soldiers with evicting settler cattle, but they possessed no horses, making the task nearly impossible on foot.

The War Department saw its task in clear terms: assert federal authority on federal land. Locals saw it very differently. The Mendocino County sheriff issued an injunction against the commanding officer and attempted to arrest him. The officer "respectfully declined" to be arrested, and the issue went to the courts. Having built no barracks, the troops waited in tents as the court challenge proceeded. When winter arrived, Howard recalled the soldiers to San Francisco. Negotiations eventually resulted in a reduction in the size of the reservation, a clear victory for trespassers. Indigenous People, such as those in Round Valley, expected federal officials to fulfill their responsibilities and protect Indigenous land. Federal officials, however, either lacked the resources necessary to keep squatters off Indigenous lands, or they lacked the desire.

On the Capitan Grande Reservation in San Diego County, the boundaries established in 1875 omitted much of the best river-bottom land and many of the Kumeyaay settlements. This well-known bureaucratic error encouraged non-Indian settlers to move to Capitan Grande.

Some leased land from Kumeyaay; other settlers threatened Kumeyaay residents with false claims in an attempt to force them to sell their land. A number of non-Indians married into Kumeyaay families, often with suspicious motives. President Chester A. Arthur added sections to the reservation to include more of the land already occupied by Kumeyaay, but the trespassing did not stop just because the boundaries moved. In fact, trespassing increased after 1882 because of strong local support for non-Indian settlement and reticence on the part of the federal government to evict Americans from Kumeyaay land.

The trespassers wanted Kumeyaay grazing and beekeeping land. But Americans considered the speculative value of the land for future water development even more desirable. San Diego was growing fast, and the headwaters of the San Diego River flowed through the reservation. As early as 1883, city officials arranged to construct a dam and flume to transport San Diego River water to the city. By 1886, the San Diego Flume Company built the dam and was beginning construction of the flume without the Kumeyaay, the Indian agent, or the Bureau of Indian Affairs' permission.

In 1887, at the Kumeyaay's behest, and with the help of Charles Painter, a member of the assimilationist Indian Rights Association, the commissioner of Indian affairs authorized the use of force to evict the trespassers. They negotiated a contract with the Flume Company to provide an ample supply of water for Kumeyaay needs and to pay them one hundred dollars per mile per year for the thirteen-mile right-of-way across the reservation. Despite the clear assertion of federal force, the contract produced murky results. The Indian agent relented and allowed several trespassers who married Kumeyaay women to remain on the reservation, and the federal government later renegotiated the contract, removing the payments. Even victories turned into disappointments, contributing to Indian skepticism and distrust of the policies of the federal government.

Nationwide, the late nineteenth century brought dramatic changes to federal Indian policy. President Grant's so-called Peace Policy (1868–69) essentially turned over the management of Indian affairs to the Board of Indian Commissioners (BIC), which consisted of representatives from various Christian denominations—Quakers, Methodists, Presbyterians, Catholics, and Episcopalians prominent among them. The BIC sought to end both violence against Indians and the rampant corruption of the Indian Office. The well-known case of Standing Bear brought attention to the issues. He was arrested for leading a group of Ponca from the reservation in Oklahoma, where he and his people had been forced to relocate, in order to return to their homeland in Nebraska. His successful lawsuit demanding a writ of *habeas corpus,* and resulting in his release, launched him on a multiyear national speaking tour in 1879.

The outrage that many felt at Standing Bear's treatment in particular, and the conditions of Indians in general, found a ready audience in organizations such as the Women's National Indian Association (WNIA), founded in 1879, and the Indian Rights Association (IRA), founded in 1882. Both groups were based initially in Philadelphia, possessed deep Quaker ties, challenged US Indian policy, and worked directly to "civilize," assimilate, and "protect" Indians. In Northern California, the WNIA-affiliated Northern California Indian Association (NCIA) organized to address the conditions of "landless" Indians. In their mind, land made Indians more sedentary and thus more open to their civilization programs. To the degree that this meant working to secure land, Indians worked with them.

Standing Bear's story moved author Helen Hunt Jackson to action. In 1881, she wrote a scathing critique of US Indian policy, entitled *A Century of Dishonor.* Jackson sent a copy to every member of Congress, but her call to reform Indian affairs failed to move senators and representatives in Washington, DC. Jackson subsequently moved to Southern California and took on more specific, local issues. In 1883, Jackson, along with Abbot Kinney, the developer of Venice Beach, wrote the *Report on the Conditions and Needs of the Mission Indians of California.* The report, like *A Century of Dishonor,* failed to move public opinion or federal policy. In addition to attempting to raise the profile of these issues through her research and writing, Jackson also played a direct role in legal challenges. At Soboba in Riverside County, Luiseños faced eviction at the hands of a settler. José Jesús Castillo, grandson of the Soboba captain, brought the issue to the attention of Jackson and the IRA, who got involved. They brought a lawsuit, which eventually made it to the California Supreme Court. In 1897, the court ruled on behalf of the Luiseños, protecting their land. This case represented a major victory for Indian rights, but it did not eventuate the same outcome for other Indigenous communities facing eviction, nor did it make an impact in a larger sense on federal policy. Frustrated by the lack of traction, Jackson turned to fiction, using the raw material from her report as inspiration.

Jackson's novel *Ramona,* published in 1884, was immensely popular. Like Harriet Beecher Stowe's *Uncle Tom's Cabin,* Jackson hoped to force federal officials and popular opinion to act, in this case to defend

Indians' land tenure and protect them from the oppressive power of local racism. In some ways, the book failed in the same way Stowe's did: both novels freighted the subjects the authors sought to help with blatantly racist stereotypes. Jackson's novel fictionalizes the dispossession of the Luiseño from Temecula in 1873. Into that, she wove the story of Ramona, a Luiseño-Scottish orphan under the somewhat heartless care of her *californiana* godmother. Ramona falls in love with Allesandro, a Luiseño from Temecula. They elope and struggle against encroaching White settlement. Eventually, a settler kills Allesandro for purportedly stealing a horse, and Ramona returns to marry the son of the woman who raised her.

The novel's popularity brought national attention to the condition of Mission Indians, but it did so by popularizing powerful and inaccurately idyllic images of Spanish and Mexican California as a counterpoint to the harshness of the American era. The novel ends with Ramona "redeemed" by marriage to a Californio. By presenting the Americans as greedy and venal, and the Indians as helpless, Jackson contributed directly to the nostalgia of California's Spanish past. All over Southern California, Americans transformed Ramona into a cultural icon. Both Rancho Camulos in Ventura County and Rancho Guajome in San Diego County claimed to be the site of Ramona's home. The Estudillo adobe in Old Town San Diego developed into a tourist attraction as the site where Ramona and Allesandro married. Fairs and festivals often included Indian women playing the part of the "real Ramona," the most famous of which, the Ramona Pageant in Hemet, began in 1923. Seventy years later, in 1993, California designated it the state's "official outdoor play."

The strange career of Ramona illustrates the challenges California Indians faced when they solicited help from Americans outside their communities. Reformers pressured the federal government to reassert its trust relationship with California Indians by securing land in the face of powerful local resistance and aggression. But their ambivalent efforts froze Indians in a dismissive set of manufactured stereotypes while they sought to help them. California Indians agreed with reformers that they needed land, secure water supplies, and the obligations promised by the federal government. They disagreed radically on how to get them, what to do with them, and who would direct their efforts. In addition to reformers, Indians found others interested in their affairs. They attempted to leverage that interest to their advantage.

The recorded California Indian population fell to its lowest point, just below twenty-five thousand, in 1900. Violence, disease, starvation, and intentional disappearance into other populations contributed to the decline. To some non-Natives, it looked like California Indians might disappear. Occurring at the same time as the rise of a commercial marketplace for Indigenous culture, the perception of Indian disappearance spurred collectors of all types into action. Americans' interests ran the gamut, including weekend hobbyists interested in Indian "lore," collectors of Indian crafts, ethnographers, popular authors, and anthropologists, who worked to salvage Indian culture before it disappeared entirely.

In 1896, Franz Boas established the nation's first anthropology department at Columbia University. In 1901, Alfred Kroeber received the first PhD granted by the program. That same year, Kroeber founded the anthropology program at the University of California. From the beginning, California Indians were imbricated in the discipline. Kroeber pursued salvage anthropology, documenting, in his words, "uncorrupted" "specimens" before industrialization and urbanization changed them. Others followed similar paths. Curtin's work on folklore, and J. P. Harrington's extensive work on California Indian languages are two prominent examples. All three were serious scholars who thought California Indians were disappearing and felt an urgency to document elements of Indian life before they were gone. They sympathized with Indigenous People, but as a part of settler society, they participated and benefited from the process of dispossession. When given the choice between documenting or acting to help protect Indigenous People from the pressure of settler society, anthropologists chose to document, often with disastrous consequences for the people they studied.

Others chose different ways to profit off their knowledge of or access to the artifacts of Indian culture. Journalist Charles Fletcher Lummis positioned himself as an expert on and spokesman for California Indians. He sparred with others, such as fellow journalist George Wharton James, who also sought to assert expertise on baskets and language through public lectures, magazine articles, and books. Popularizers such as these benefited from the transformations of California brought about by the railroad. The attention and infrastructure produced markets for both Indians and those who wanted to profit off them.

The popular Harvey House chain of restaurants and hotels along the Atchison, Topeka and Santa Fe rail lines included gift shops selling Indian baskets, blankets, and other artifacts. Indigenous People sold their wares at stations along the Southern Pacific and other lines. In this way, the railroads served as important marketing arms of the "southwestern style" of décor and architecture that popularized an imaginary vision of the region to the rest of the nation.

Industrialization and the railroads changed the land in dramatic ways. One of the more devastating consequences of the late nineteenth-century industrialization of the state was the impact on its water sources and supplies. In general, in the southern part of the state, water was scarce, and the arid climate could only produce its agricultural bounty by harnessing distant sources of water. In the central and northern portions of the state, water was abundant. The rich Sacramento–San Joaquin Delta promised great agricultural and ranching potential but only if it could be drained. All along the foothills and mountains across the entire state, surveyors and engineers identified sites on Indian land to build dams for water storage for agricultural and increasingly urban use. Irrigation infrastructure radically reshaped the land while offering opportunities for work. At the Pala Reservation, Cupeños and Luiseños provided the primary labor force for the irrigation system the BIA built to control floods and support agriculture.

The wetlands surrounding Tulare Lake, Buena Vista Lake, and Kern Lake across the San Joaquin Valley were early victims of the changes under way. Settlers eyed the valley early on for its ample water supply and fertile soil, but Yokuts maintained significant control over the region well after statehood. In conjunction with efforts to establish reservations, and the expansion of wheat south into the reclaimed tule marshes, Yokuts gradually lost control of the region to settlers.

Floods in the 1860s altered the courses of Kings River and Kern River, bypassing Tulare Lake and Kern Lake. Gradually, private irrigation efforts reduced the lakes' size, and the state turned the soil over to agriculture and ranching operations, irrigated through extensive canal systems. Between present-day Stockton and Fresno, industrialists engaged in extensive hydrological engineering, diminishing the water supply to Tulare Lake and other bodies of water and eventually altering the Sacramento–San Joaquin Delta's natural landscape beyond recognition.

Simultaneously, the federal government moved Yokuts, who relied on the water and fauna of Tulare Lake, to the Tule River Reservation, where they built a five-mile-long water ditch for irrigation and a twenty-five-mile wagon road into the mountains to facilitate harvesting timber. The Indian agent estimated the ditch alone represented more than two thousand days' worth of Yokuts labor and praised their "industry." But subsequent draws on the delta waterscape turned Tulare Lake putrid and salty by the 1870s. Gradually the water life died, and the surround-

FIGURE 16. Two Yokuts men on horseback, Tule River Indian Reservation, near Porterville, California, ca. 1900, created by C. C. Pierce. Photo courtesy Huntington Library.

ing wetlands, the lake, and eventually the underground aquifers dried up. By the 1930s, a lake that had sustained Yokuts and their ancestors for more than ten thousand years vanished, visible only as a ghostly outline in satellite images. The changing landscape challenged their culture in another way as well. Yokuts, who had readily adapted to the horse in the late eighteenth century, now found the grasslands of the southern San Joaquin Valley drying up (fig. 16).

South of the Tehachapi and San Gabriel Mountains, irrigation work followed rivers inland from the coast. Indigenous work similarly rendered ambivalent results. Irrigation projects provided a steady source of income through wages, while often simultaneously limiting Indigenous People's access to the water vital to agricultural pursuits. In the late 1880s, private land and water companies claimed water rights and began to construct dams and flumes across San Diego County. Los Angeles, Orange, and Riverside Counties followed. The federal government left protecting Indian water rights to the Indians themselves.

By the 1880s, settler violence shifted from overt assaults on Indigenous bodies—by this we mean statements of genocidal intent, state-sponsored body-part bounties, and militia and United States Army massacres—to assaults on Indigenous People's relationships with land, water, and culture. The federal government's trust relationship with Indigenous People collapsed. The trust relationship consisted of two principles: the federal government's plenary or absolute power over Indian affairs, which derived from its responsibility to protect Indian land and people. Power was lashed to the responsibility to protect, the second principle. But rather than targeting the threats posed by local governments, White settlers, and trespassers, Congress often trained its plenary power against Indian sovereignty itself. This was not the protection Indians demanded.

Nationally, the federal government reasserted its plenary power over Indian sovereignty in the 1885 Major Crimes Act, which made it an exclusively federal crime for an Indian to commit murder, manslaughter, rape, assault with intent to kill, arson, burglary, or larceny against another Indian on a reservation. The Supreme Court of the United States reaffirmed the plenary power doctrine in a case that began on a California reservation. In 1886, the case of *United States v. Kagama* tested the Major Crimes Act, a response to a Supreme Court decision, which overturned the conviction of Crow Dog, a Lakota, for the murder of Spotted Tail, another Lakota, on the Great Sioux Reservation. Kagama killed Iyouse, both Yuroks, near the Hoopa Valley Reservation's boundaries. The federal government prosecuted the case as a test case of the law's constitutionality. The Supreme Court's decision reinforced the wardship of Indian tribes, calling them "communities dependent on the United States. Dependent largely for their daily food. Dependent for their political rights." The Court reasserted the necessity of federal preeminence in relations with Indigenous People. While the Supreme Court upheld the constitutionality of federal jurisdiction, the trial determined that the murder occurred just beyond the reservation's boundaries. The federal government, therefore, lacked jurisdiction. The state prosecutor refused to prosecute and released Kagama.

In legal terms, the decision's significance served as the justification and foundation for taking sovereign rights from Indigenous People and nations. By reasserting the necessity of the plenary power of the federal government, the Supreme Court cemented the wardship status of Indians. *Kagama* also introduced a false binary: Indian crime *must* fall under either federal or state jurisdiction. The decision explicitly stated: "these Indians are within the geographical limits of the United States. The soil and the people within these limits are under the political control of the Government of the United States, or of the States of the Union. *There exist within the broad domain of sovereignty but these two*" (emphasis added). The language foreclosed the possibility of concurrent jurisdiction in which Indian tribes and the federal government share jurisdiction over crimes, a critical precedent for later court decisions.

Indigenous sovereignty faced further challenges in a less well-known but equally illustrative California district court case. On Christmas Day, 1886, Bill Whaley, Salt Lake Pete, Juan Chino, and Pancho Francisco, four Yokuts from the Tule River Reservation, carried out the tribally sanctioned execution of an Indian doctor who the tribe believed had killed its *tiya* (captain). The belief that Indian healing practices could be used for good or for evil was widespread. In fact, many believed a doctor might poison someone so that this same doctor might then be paid to heal the victim. When, after repeated warnings, and other suspicious illnesses, the captain died under the doctor's care, the tribe met and determined the doctor should be killed. They selected the four men to carry out the execution. They ambushed the doctor with a shotgun and recorded how he flew through the air in an attempt to escape, testifying to his power.

Yokuts at the Tule River Reservation distrusted the Indian agent there for his well-known desire to sell off portions of their land and his recommendation to the commissioner of Indian affairs to sell the entire reservation. Motivated in part by that enmity, the agent tried several times to prosecute the four men for their act. First, the agent filed a complaint with the Tulare County justice of the peace. The superior court dismissed those charges because the state of California lacked jurisdiction in the matter. Angered by the release of the four, the agent, who by that point had moved to a new position elsewhere, nonetheless filed a complaint with federal officials in Los Angeles, causing charges to be brought. The case went to the district court.

No one questioned the events of the execution. Instead, at issue in the trial were two points: first, was the meeting in which the tribe decided to kill the doctor a tribal meeting, that is, representative of a functioning tribal government? If so, then it was a legitimate exercise of tribal sovereignty and would fall under the jurisdiction of the tribe's own court. The court found it was not. Second, the defense challenged that the Yokuts had not been properly informed of the change to the law and therefore could not be held liable. The court found that they had been informed, based on the former agent's self-serving testimony that he himself had informed them. In essence, ignorance of the law was no excuse, an established legal principle within a specific, agreed-upon jurisdiction but dubious in an instance such as this, when jurisdiction was unclear. That is, it is one thing to accept the consequences of the law when one accepts jurisdiction. But the Yokuts had not accepted the expansion of federal jurisdiction. They were not even aware it had occurred. The court convicted the four on charges of manslaughter, and the judge sentenced them to five years in the state prison at San Quentin, arguing, "While the offense committed by the defendants would, if committed by a white man, have of course been murder . . . in view of the Indian nature, their customs, superstition, and ignorance, that in the circumstances attending the killing . . . there was wanting the malice that is essential to constitute the crime of murder." This was neither the first nor the last time Indians were sent to San Quentin under unjust circumstances.

Indigenous communities in California demanded the federal government honor its responsibilities by asserting its power to protect Indians or to support their efforts to protect themselves. The power the government asserted was not what Indigenous People hoped. Congressional plenary power and trust status were supposed to work in tandem through allotment, which emerged nationally with the Indian Homestead Act (IHA) of 1883 and the Dawes Severalty Act of 1887. Allotment attempted to break up tribally held land into privately held Indian farms. The BIA and reformers presented allotment as a way to simultaneously protect Indian land while "civilizing" the Indians who lived on it. Many doubted the plan, seeing it for what it was: a way to make Indian land available for non-Indian settlement. A few Indians took individual homesteads under the IHA and Dawes Act. To do so, they physically separated from tribal communities. Some had already been pushed out of their homelands, and homesteading was a way to secure their places of refuge.

Some Indians and reform organizations criticized homesteading because it isolated Indians. As an alternative, they pushed for allotment, seeing it as a way to protect Indian communities. California Indians living on reservations threatened by settler encroachment and dispossession often saw allotment as potentially helpful in securing Indian land against trespassers and settlers. On the Round Valley Reservation, for instance, Indigenous People expressed support for allotment because they believed the policy would enable them to secure their land from trespassers and squatters. Round Valley Indians hoped to use their allotments to raise livestock, hunt, and fish rather than farm, as the government planned. At the same time, the federal government tried to create a land base for some California Indians by diminishing the landholdings of others. National reformers believed private property and individual autonomy plotted the proper paths to civilization and, therefore, sought to break up the communal reservations with the policy of allotment.

In 1891, the Act for the Relief and Allotment for Southern California Indians brought allotment to Southern California, established additional reservations, and belatedly secured water supplies. The combination set the stage for major disputes across the region and the state. The first step was to survey the boundaries of Indian land and issue trust patents to the tribes and bands for the reservations located on public land. That began in 1892, and mistakes and stiff Indian opposition plagued the process. A clerical error inadvertently located the San Pasqual Reservation in the wrong township. Cosmit was located in the general area but away from the water where the Indians lived and that was necessary for agriculture. Officials left some Indian groups, such as the San Juan Capistrano and San Luis Rey, out of the process entirely.

The second step was to survey individual plots within the reservations for allotment. Under Dawes, allottees were to receive 160 acres. The reservations in Southern California, and many of the reservations across the state, proved insufficient to provide that amount of land. Instead, each head of family was allotted a homesite and irrigated farmland up to twenty acres. Single Indians received only up to ten acres. The allotments were to align with the General Land Office's (GLO) cadastral grid organized around townships and ranges, but that proved very difficult with such small allotments in such uneven and variegated terrain. The first surveyor requested permission from the BIA to survey plots in an older, metes-and-bounds fashion, which was granted. But the GLO and the BIA did not agree. The GLO rejected the surveys for failing to conform to its policy requirements. Subsequently, Cave Couts Jr. started the allotment surveys again but left them incomplete, and when there were disputes, he leaned heavily on settling in favor of non-Indian claims.

Across the state, allotment disrupted some land-tenure practices while strengthening and securing others. On the Hoopa Valley Reservation, allotment surveys in 1889 showed 2,475 acres of land for 450 residents. This was simply too little acreage for commercial farming. Recognizing this, Hupas configured their individual holdings to ensure that every family possessed access to multiple subsistence areas: a place to have a small garden and to build a frame house, as well as entry to the Trinity River for fishing. But federal officials did not move forward with those initial surveys. In 1895, they resurveyed and reallotted the reservation. This time federal surveyors provided each Hupa family with four acres of valley land for farming but failed to ensure that each family possessed access to the Trinity River, along with twenty acres of rough mountain land for grazing. The reallotment destroyed the Hupas' multisource land-use system, reduced the amount of land Hupas held, and forced tribal members to rely almost entirely on wage labor for their livelihoods. The Bureau of Indian Affairs, however, again failed to approve those surveys. In 1918, the federal government repeated the allotment process.

Reallotment also exacerbated internal tensions on other reservations. In 1909, Tom Arviso of Rincon, north of San Diego, asked the superintendent about the prospect of increasing the size of his twenty-acre allotment from 1895. In so doing, he learned that the federal government had failed to approve his original allotment, even though he had been using it for fifteen years. When the BIA began a new round of surveys, there were more people eligible for allotment. The ensuing uncertainty and eventual reallotment of smaller plots polarized the reservation, dividing those who sought to protect what they thought they had received from the earlier allotments, from those who had not received land in the earlier allotments and supported the new surveys.

Early leaders of the opposition efforts in the southern part of the state visited the Paiute Ghost Dance and brought that organizational structure back south. Their opposition was not to ownership itself but to the way it was carried out, which reduced size of Indian landholdings and often meant the loss of improvements, such as buildings, fences, and wells that Indians had made. Opposition in the south was particularly strong at Morongo, Santa Ysabel, and Mesa Grande. Pala was the only Southern California reservation the federal government allotted before 1920.

In 1893, former California governor John G. Downey filed an ejectment suit against the Indians living on Warner's Ranch, land he owned surrounding Warner's Hot Springs in northern San Diego County. Rancho grants in the Spanish and Mexican period typically included provisions respecting the Indian right of occupancy, which meant ownership of the land did not give the owner the right to disturb the occupancy of Indians living on the land. Americans often ignored those provisions. Throughout the last thirty years of the nineteenth century, state and federal officials evicted Indigenous People across the state. The Indians living on Rancho San Jacinto challenged their threatened eviction in court and won. Cupeños did so, as well, but with a different outcome. In 1901, their case went to the US Supreme Court. The Court ruled that the right of Indian occupancy guaranteed in the original Mexican land grant had not carried over into the legal titles conveyed by the United States government as it should have. Furthermore, the court ruled, even if it had, Cupeños sacrificed any claim by abandoning the land and not pursuing the claim with the Public Land Commission, which had been established immediately after statehood. It was immaterial in the eyes of the Court that no one made Cupeños aware of the necessity of pursuing a claim they did not realize had been changed on land they had not abandoned.

The decision ultimately led to the eviction of approximately three hundred residents of the villages of Kupa, Santa Ysabel, Mataguay, San Felipe, Puerta La Cruz, San Jose, Tawhee, Puerta Noria, and Cuca. After nearly two years of resistance and challenges, US Marshals, in 1903, forcibly relocated Cupeños to Pala, a Luiseño reservation forty miles down the San Luis Rey River from the hot springs. The eviction of Cupeños captured national attention. The hot springs at Kupa were well known. Cupeños used them for their own purposes, grinding acorns on granite bedrock mortars, leaching acorn flour of its tannins in the hot springs, irrigating their crops, and bathing. Additionally, Cupeños charged non-Indians who desired access to the springs for their supposed health benefits. Thus, the springs served as a spiritual, economic, and agricultural asset. Cupeños bitterly opposed leaving the valley. Celsa Apapa's comments were widely reported and reprinted at the time:

> You see that graveyard out there? There are our fathers and our grandfathers. You see that Eagle-nest mountain and that Rabbit-hole mountain? When God made them, He gave us this place. We have always been here. We do not care for any other place. It may be good, but it is not ours. We have always lived here. We would rather die here. Our fathers did. We cannot leave them. Our children were born here, how can we go away? If you give us the best place in the world, it is not so good for us as this. The captain he say his people cannot go anywhere else; they cannot live anywhere else. Here they always lived; their people always lived here. There is no other place. This is our home.

President Theodore Roosevelt appointed a three-person commission to find a suitable new home for Cupeños. Former Cupeño captain Salvador Nolasquez and Ambrosio Ortega traveled with the commission, which was led heavy-handedly by Charles Fletcher Lummis. They visited twenty-eight properties, but Nolasquez and Ortega rejected them all because of "want of sufficient water for domestic and irrigating purposes and also for the want of sufficient agricultural land on which we could support ourselves." Lummis and others saw things differently. They sought a model reservation, naturally protected from settler incursions, and susceptible to modern agricultural practices through extensive irrigation. Despite the fact that they visited the same sites, the two parties saw them differently. Nolasquez and Ortega saw what was there. Lummis saw what he imagined the BIA could build.

A few years prior, Lummis had founded the Sequoya League to focus on fighting for Indian rights, as non-Indians saw them. He also worked closely with the Landmark's Club to preserve Southern California's architectural relics, such as the *asistencia* at Pala. In his work with the commission, the two efforts converged. Lummis stubbornly envisioned Pala as the ideal site for a model reservation, driven more by an image of Cupeños living peacefully as "relics" amid a preserved picture of California's imaginary past. Cupeños rejected Lummis, calling him the "thin liar."

In May of 1903, Captain Juan Maria Cibimoat and Salvador Nolasquez consulted with a San Bernardino attorney and attempted to meet with President Theodore Roosevelt. At the same time, the federal agents came to Kupa to begin the eviction process. Strong protests by the Cupeños forced the agents to wait until Cibimoat could be called back from San Bernardino. His return and adamant refusal to concede failed to prevent eviction. Marshals loaded the Cupeños' belongings into wagons and started the forced march.

Begun in tragedy, the three-day trip to Pala ended with a new disappointment. Tents, rather than houses, greeted Cupeños. Cibimoat described the valley, which many of them had not yet seen, as "no muy bueno." Other villages in the area, such as San Felipe, were removed to Pala later that year. Kumeyaay communities resisted forced relocation by joining Kumeyaay settlements farther south.

Cupeño resistance did not stop at Pala. Contrary to the government's plans for the reservation, Cupeño refugees demanded Pala be organized around a central village with separate agricultural land on both sides of the river. Rather than being allowed to begin construction of adobe homes, as they had at Kupa, or wooden cabins with local timber, the Indian Office ordered prefabricated cabins to be delivered from New York. The cabins arrived six months later and cost twice as much as local wood, or four times the cost of adobe. More important, the prefabricated cabins were entirely inappropriate for the diurnal variations of the local climate. Unlike thick adobe, which retains heat when the temperature plunges at night, and stays cool when it heats up during the day, the temperature variations cracked and warped the cabins' thin walls and roofs.

Pala required extensive irrigation to ensure agricultural productivity. Disputes over the labor required to build the irrigation system, and wages paid for on-reservation work, meant Pala was not the model reservation Lummis hoped it would be. Instead, reservation residents demanded higher wages and organized the Common Council, echoing similar developments across the state in the first decade of the twentieth century. Within two decades, some of the same forces that led to their eviction dammed the San Luis Rey River at the western edge of Warner's Valley, creating Lake Henshaw and causing the river to run dry much of the year downstream at Pala (fig. 17).

In Northern California, landless Indians presented a pressing case. The NCIA, affiliated with the WNIA, performed mission work in the north at Hoopa and Greenville. Their early efforts concentrated on establishing schools, but they found it difficult to expand their work because of a landless and necessarily mobile Indian population. The NCIA, founded in San Jose in 1894, sought to obtain land for Indians, partly to improve their condition and partly to improve the efficiency of their own work. In good progressive fashion, they hired Charles Kelsey, an attorney practicing in San Jose and a member of the Sequoya League, to conduct a study. In his research, he found mention of the treaties signed in 1851 and 1852. These treaties, long relegated to the Senate archives and forgotten by the public, represented fresh evidence. Kelsey and the NCIA organized the documents and pressed the issues with President Theodore Roosevelt during his 1903 visit to San Jose.

Kelsey and the NCIA argued the United States failed to properly extinguish title because it did not ratify the treaties. The federal government sold Indigenous Peoples' lands but did not compensate them. Therefore, the NCIA argued, the federal government had a duty to purchase land for Indians. Roosevelt, in turn, pressured the commissioner of Indian affairs for information on the treaties. The commissioner claimed that "no compensation has ever been made [to] the California Indians for their lands, as the Government seems to have followed the policy of Mexico, from whom it got its title to California, in not recognizing the Indians' right of occupancy." The commissioner ignored the obvious and well-established precedent in Mexican law that explicitly did recognize Indians' right of occupancy.

The Indian Rights Association and the NCIA pressured Senator Thomas Bard to find the treaties. In September of 1904, his secretary found

FIGURE 17. Workers reinforcing the first joint of a caisson on the Pala Reservation, ca. 1912. Department of the Interior, Bureau of Indian Affairs, Portland Area Office, Irrigation Division, 1950 to present.

them in the Senate archives. The treaties had been rejected in July of 1852, and the order of secrecy remained in place. By early 1905, they were effectively secret to anyone outside the Senate. In June of 1905, Bard introduced a Senate motion to have the secrecy removed and ordered the treaties printed. The discovery of the treaties brought the injustice back into public and congressional eyes and led to the appointment of Kelsey to investigate the conditions of the landless Indians. Kelsey's research led to the appropriation acts of 1905, 1906, and 1908, eventually making $150,000 available to purchase land for Indian rancherias.

The injunction of secrecy kept information out of people's hands. It also suggested shame or guilt. It is unlikely that Indian efforts to secure land would have succeeded without sympathy from Congress that the lost treaties' discovery provided. More important, the discovery and release contributed to the Indian mobilization across the state. Cahuilla Ignacio Costo testified at a later House Committee on Indian Affairs hearing, "We never heard that the treaties had not been ratified, and that is the reason we are forming this organization [American Mission Indian Cooperation Society] and working to have it presented to the Court of Claims."

In the late 1860s and early 1870s, the state legislature repealed the provisions that enabled the enslavement of California Indians, and the last wave of genocidal violence abated in California. Certainly, Americans committed egregious acts of violence against California Indians well into the twenty-first century, but as the Gilded Age progressed, Indigenous People and Americans contended with new ways of living with one another. Americans continued to dispossess Indigenous People, either through squatting or forcible removal. When the federal government attempted to step in to secure Indigenous People of lands, dilatory actions and incompetence undermined its efforts. The government's claim of plenary power did not match its inability to impose that power on the ground. In other areas, the federal government indeed imposed its plenary power over Indigenous People but predicated it on their perceived status as children in need of federal oversight.

Indigenous People continued to chart a path for themselves, often with limited options. They attempted to steer federal policies, such as allotment, in their best interests. They insisted that their systems of law and order continued to matter. Indigenous People looked for sympathetic allies, in the federal government and private sectors, to assist in their efforts to reclaim land. Most important, Indigenous People turned their own wage labor into ways to maintain community and sovereignty in an industrializing and urbanizing California. At the dawn of the twentieth century, Indigenous People and the federal government built on these efforts to create a land system unique to the United States.

SOURCES

The 1860 census figures come from Albert L. Hurtado, "California Indian Demography, Sherburne F. Cook, and the Revision of American

History," *Pacific Historical Review* 58 (August 1989), 332. Indians as domestic laborers from 1860 to 1880 in Los Angeles is from Albert Hurtado, "'Hardly a Farm House—A Kitchen without Them': Indian and White Households on the California Borderland Frontier in 1860," *Western Historical Quarterly* 13 (July 1982): 253, 255, 258.

Olegario Calac's petitions and actions can be found in Tanis C. Thorne, *El Capitan* (Banning, CA: Malki-Ballena Press, 2012), 41. For a deeply contextualized account of Olegario's leadership, see Richard Carrico, "The Struggle for Native American Self-Determination in San Diego County," *Journal of California and Great Basin Anthropology* 2, no. 2 (Winter 1980): 199–213. On "paying the criminals for their crimes" in Round Valley, and the confrontations between the Mendocino County sheriff and General Howard, see Kevin Adams and Khal Schneider, "'Washington Is a Long Way Off': The 'Round Valley War' and the Limits of Federal Power on a California Indian Reservation," *Pacific Historical Review* 80 (Nov. 2011): 587.

The information on Sam Batwi's life and Curtin's comments on Yana's drive to earn money come from Jeremiah Curtin, *Creation Myths of Primitive America: In Relation to the Religious History and Mental Development of Mankind* (Boston: Little, Brown, 1898), 517–19.

On Indian slavery in California see Michael Magliari, particularly "Free Soil, Unfree Labor," *Pacific Historical Review* 73, no. 3 (August 2004): 349–90; and Michael Magliari, "Free State Slavery: Bound Indian Labor and Slave Trafficking in California's Sacramento Valley, 1850–1864," *Pacific Historical Review* 81, no. 2 (May 2012): 155–92. On the larger context and demise of Indian slavery in California, see Stacey L. Smith, *Freedom's Frontier: California and the Struggle over Unfree Labor, Emancipation, and Reconstruction* (Chapel Hill: University of North Carolina Press, 2015), 182–92.

The quotations from the decision in *United States v. Kagama*, 118 U.S. 375 (1886) come from pages 379 and 383–85. Gelya Frank and Carole Goldberg's, *Defying the Odds: The Tule River Tribe's Struggle for Sovereignty in Three Centuries* (New Haven, CT: Yale University Press, 2010) contains a deep analysis of the *U.S. v. Whaley* decision. The quotation, "While the offenses committed by the defendants would, if committed by a white man, have been of course murder . . ." from the judge's sentencing, can be found on page 100.

The quotation asserting that Indian laborers were superior to Whites is from Richard Carrico and Florence Shipek, "Indian Labor in San Diego County, California, 1850–1900," in *Native Americans and Wage Labor:*

Ethnohistorical Perspectives, edited by Alice Littlefield and Martha Knack (Norman: University of Oklahoma Press, 1996), 213. Florence Shipek worked extensively on Native land tenure in Southern California. See her book *Pushed into the Rocks: Southern California Indian Land Tenure, 1769–1986* (Lincoln: University of Nebraska Press, 1988); on the idea of homesteading as a way to secure places of refuge, see page 37. On allotment in Hoopa Valley, see David Rich Lewis, *Neither Wolf nor Dog: American Indians, Environment, and Agrarian Change* (New York: Oxford University Press, 1994), 97–105; and David Rich Lewis, "Changing Subsistence, Changing Reservation Environments: The Hupa, 1850s-1980s," *Agricultural History* 66, no. 2 (Spring 1992): 34–51.

The dramatic Cupeño removal from Warner's Ranch received extensive coverage at the time, much of it sensationalized. Some good accounts include Valerie Sherer Mathes and Phil Brigandi, *Reservations, Removal, and Reform: The Mission Indian Agents of Southern California, 1878–1903* (Norman: University of Oklahoma Press, 2018), from which the quotes regarding lack of sufficient water, Lummis as a thin liar, and the judgment that the land is "no muy bueno," come (172, 174, and 178). The quote regarding the graveyard is from Charles Fletcher Lummis, "Exiles of Cupa," *Out West* 16, no. 5 (May 1902): 475. See also Joel R. Hyer's *"We Are Not Savages": Native Americans in Southern California and the Pala Reservation, 1840–1920* (East Lansing: Michigan State University Press, 2002); and a collection of Cupeño-language oral histories, *Mulu'wetam: The First People,* edited by Jane Hill and Rosinda Nolasquez (Banning, CA: Malki Museum Press, 1973).

For a thoughtful and incisive overview of the story of the rediscovery of the so-called secret treaties, see Larissa K. Miller, "The Secret Treaties with California's Indians," *Prologue,* Fall/Winter 2013, esp. 40; see also Harry Kelsey, "The California Indian Treaty Myth," *Southern California Quarterly* 55 (Fall 1973): 225–38. President Fillmore's "Third Annual Message" (Dec. 6, 1852) included the following line: "The Senate not having thought proper to ratify the treaties which have been negotiated with the tribes of Indians in California and Oregon, our relations with them have been left in a very unsatisfactory condition." Ignacio Costo's claim connecting the rediscovery of the treaties to the organization of the American Mission Indian Cooperation Society comes from US Congress, House of Representatives, Committee on Indian Affairs, *Indians of the United States: Investigation of the Field Service,* vol. 3 (Washington, DC: Government Printing Office, 1920), 1095.

Three useful, but problematic, works by Helen Hunt Jackson are *Century of Dishonor: A Sketch of the United States Government's Dealings with Some of the Indian Tribes* (New York: Harper and Brothers, 1881); "Report on the Condition and Needs of the Mission Indians of California" (with Abbot Kinney) (Washington, DC: Office of Indian Affairs, 1883); and *Ramona: A Story* (Boston: Roberts Brothers, 1884). For useful context on Jackson's efforts, including her letters, see Valerie Sherer Mathes, *Helen Hunt Jackson and Her Indian Reform Legacy* (Norman: University of Oklahoma Press, 1990); and Valerie Sherer Mathes, *The Indian Reform Letters of Helen Hunt Jackson, 1879–1885* (Norman: University of Oklahoma Press, 1998).

John Peabody Harrington's collection of linguistic notes offers a wealth of information. They have been collected and microfilmed as *The Papers of John Peabody Harrington in the Smithsonian Institution, 1907–1957*, vols. 1–10 (Millwood, NY: Kraus International). Volume 4 contains "A Guide to the Field Notes: Native American History, Language, and Culture of the Southwest," edited by Elaine L. Mills and Ann J. Brickfield.

Ishi Wilderness

Located in Tehama County, in the southwest corner of the Lassen National Forest, Ishi Wilderness is a specially designated wilderness area managed by the United States Forest Service. The federal government established Ishi Wilderness in 1984 under the authority of the 1964 Wilderness Act. Perhaps nowhere else in the state is the deep and tragic irony at the heart of the National Forest and Park system more obvious. Ishi Wilderness constitutes the center of the Yahi Yana world, particularly the drainage of Deer and Mill Creeks, where around five hundred Yahi Yana lived. The Yahi, as they were often called, were the southernmost band of Yana. Approximately fifteen thousand Yana, Maidu, Konkow, Nomlaki, Wintu, Atsugewi, and Achumawi lived on the land now constituting the National Forest surrounding Lassen Peak. This was not empty land. It was emptied. Settler violence destroyed the Yahi and decimated or removed many of the other peoples.

Famously, a fifty-year-old man who survived these attempts was captured in Oroville in 1911. Theodora Kroeber described this man in her 1961 book as "the Last Wild Indian in North America [who] startled the Modern World by accidentally wandering into it from the Stone Age." Kroeber's husband, University of California anthropologist Alfred Kroeber, gave the man the name Ishi, a bastardization of the Yahi word for man *(i'citi)*. In turn, Ishi preferred to call Kroeber "Big Chief," but the lack of an *F* in Yahi rendered that "Big Cheap."

FIGURE 18. Ishi Wilderness, by Kurt Thomas Hunt, June 2010. Licensed under
Creative Commons Attribution 2.0 Generic (CC BY 2.0).

The image of Ishi leaving behind a now empty wilderness has shaped
all of the many stories written or performed about him and his life
since. But that image erases more than it frames. Settlers killed his people and many of those who lived alongside them. Settler society later
designated their lands wilderness, where, in the words of the Wilderness
Act, "the earth and its community of life are untrammeled by man,
where man himself is a visitor who does not remain" (see fig. 18).

Wilderness is a powerful but pliable social construction in settler
societies. Wilderness *needed* human attention, whether as an arid wasteland where people journeyed in fear or as an abundant landscape that
served as the raw material for the creation of an earthly paradise. People needed to make the desert blossom or tame and subdue the forest.
The land was never empty. It was empty of the right kind of people.
Hence, the paradox—a place "untrammeled by man" that had to be
emptied of the "savages" who lived there.

Furthermore, the language describing wilderness in the 1964 act
ignored the reality that Indigenous People carefully tended the land.
Native burning practices prevented the buildup of fuel that makes mod-

ern wildfires so destructive. The 2018 Camp Fire destroyed the town of Paradise, twenty miles south of Ishi Wilderness, leaving thirty thousand people homeless and eighty-five dead. Native burning, pruning, and harvesting practices managed forests and encouraged growth of new resources.

To Natives, the area was not a wilderness. It was the land. When settlers arrived in the Lassen foothills in the 1840s, they brought the image of wilderness with them. Settlers believed they needed to tame the wilderness just as they believed they needed to conquer the Indigenous People who lived there. By the twentieth century, many settlers convinced themselves that they had succeeded, and they grew nostalgic for an imagined past that could act as a prophylactic against the ills of the modern, urban world.

Ishi walked between those two worldviews more than between two worlds. The first understood him as someone to be conquered. The second wraps him in the nostalgia of an imagined and simpler time. The land, emptied of its Indigenous occupants, provided, in the words of the Wilderness Act, "outstanding opportunities for solitude or a primitive and unconfined type of recreation." His story became famous, not because of what it said about him but because of what it allowed, and still allows, non-Natives to tell themselves about their past. When Ishi succumbed to tuberculosis in San Francisco in 1916, his death accomplished both tasks non-Natives assigned to him: he was conquered, and the land was emptied. His death, understood as both inevitable and natural, suggested the completion and justness of settler occupation of Native land. Only then was it possible, cognitively, for the creation of National Parks to preserve what never was, as opposed to giving land back to people who remained. Ishi's story—the real story—began thousands of years ago in a land crowded with people, coyotes, rabbits, ducks, lizards, and grizzly bears, where fire was an ever-present part of life. Ishi told a story in 1915:

> Stone said, "I will burn."
> "I will burn up," said the tree.
> The earth said, "I will get hot."
> Water said, "I will boil off into steam from the heat."
> "Indeed, this is how it is," said Coyote.
> And then there was the oak tree, bearing acorns.
> Coyote said to it, "Maybe you will burn up too?"
> "I will be attacked by fire. I'll burn on the outside but not the inside," it said.
> "Ah!" said Coyote.

The fire in the stones, the earth, and the steam point to the volcanic landscape surrounding what the Yahi called Waganupa, or Little Mount Shasta. Today it is known as Lassen Peak, named after a Danish trader whose eponymous cutoff on the trail to the Gold Rush brought thousands of settlers to the heart of Ishi's world. Waganupa is the southernmost peak in the Cascade Mountains, a volcanic range stretching southward from British Columbia. It formed around three hundred thousand years ago and was dormant for most of its recent history until eruptions in 920, 1666, and 1915. Yahi and other inhabitants of the region witnessed those eruptions, and as the mountain made and remade the land, it also shaped the stories its People told about it.

Creeks washed gold out and in the nineteenth century brought outsiders in. The creeks functioned as a network connecting villages and people to each other and to the "outside" world. A map Ishi sketched for Big Cheap featured the creeks prominently, connecting thirty-three villages and sites. The violence of settler society had already shocked that network by the time of Ishi's birth, in 1860. By the time he turned sixteen, a series of settler massacres had decimated the Yahi population. Ishi lived most of his adult life as a refugee with less than a dozen survivors—among them, his wife and immediate family.

What was so compelling and tragic about Ishi's story to the non-Natives who flocked to hear it was unremarkable to many of the other Indigenous People who live in the region. They lived tightly in the landscape, in villages or territories close to each other. They traded and fought, bore children and grudges, cursed and allied with those around them. They knew each other. It was crowded in places, and pulsing with people in between, moving along creeks and between meadows, harvesting acorns and grass seeds, hunting deer, catching birds, snaring rabbits, spearing salmon, roasting grasshoppers, and gathering berries, tules, sedge, redbud, and willow to make exquisite baskets. And they all faced the violence of murder, dispossession, and removal.

The northern Yana lived northwest of Waganupa, north of Battle Creek. Sam Batwi was born there around 1850 of northern Yana and Maidu ancestry and experienced the devastation of the Gold Rush first firsthand. Between 1850 and 1866, steady extermination campaigns by local White militias and the military killed most of his people and forced the survivors into reservations, like the Nome Lakee Reservation, where the Battle Creek Yana were removed in 1858. Others moved farther up into the mountains or, increasingly, into the protection of settlers for whom they worked. Batwi and his wife, Anna, were among those. By the 1880s they lived in Redding, where Sam worked as a ranch hand.

Mariah Bill was born around 1849 in Big Meadow, southeast of Lassen Peak in what is now northwest Plumas County. Today, Big Meadow is the bed of Lake Almanor, but when Mariah was a child, around one thousand Mountain Maidu under the leadership of Hukespem, also known as Big Meadow Bill, called the place home. In 1860, Mill Creek Yahis killed Hukespem's wife and Mariah's sister. Sometime soon after that, Hukespem married Mariah, but Big Foot, a Mill Creek Yahi leader, captured her and kept her as his wife.

The Mill Creeks earned a well-deserved reputation for fiercely defending their territory from any encroachment. These may have been Ishi's people. They attacked settlers and Indigenous neighbors alike. These attacks provoked disproportionate responses from settlers, particularly Indian killers like Hi Good, Sim Moak, and Robert Anderson. In 1865, the three men caught up with Mariah and the Mill Creeks at Three Knolls. When the attack began, she squeezed herself into a cave and remained hidden for two days, as the settlers killed dozens of Mill Creek Yahis. Ishi survived, along with a few members of his family.

When it was safe, Mariah made her way back toward Big Meadow, stopping first at the house of a settler woman for whom she had washed clothes. She "made a big paper placard and filled it with writing," and hung it on Mariah's back. It read: "Help me get home the Mill Creeks stole me. Now I'm going back to my home in Big Meadow." In September, Mariah returned to Big Meadow and reunited with Hukespem. In 1895, when their daughter, Josie, had a daughter herself, Big Meadow was still home to a vibrant Maidu community. But things were changing. In 1900, Josie's daughter Marie joined her brother and sister in the nearby Greenville Indian School. There, she was assigned the last name Mason. She later told the story of her first day. She spoke no English. A school matron stripped her and prepared to bathe her. The process reminded Marie of making acorn mush, and understandably, she fled, naked and on foot, until she commandeered a bicycle. She made it a mile before another student from the school caught up with her.

When Ishi traveled from Deer Creek to Oroville in 1911, he walked through a landscape already radically changed. In 1905, President Theodore Roosevelt authorized the creation of the Lassen National Forest, the same year that Pacific Gas & Electric formed. All National Parks and Forests dispossessed Indigenous People, and the electrical grid, stretching into the foothills and fueled by hydroelectrical power, flooded their land. A power company dammed the Feather River to create Lake Almanor for hydroelectric power generation. The allotments in Big Meadow that Hukespem had taken for his family were partially submerged, near the current town of East Shore. In the 1920s, the family sold their allotments to power and lumber companies for around twenty dollars an acre.

When he arrived in Oroville, starving and grieving the death of his family, Ishi was the last known speaker of the Yahi language. Anthropologists and linguists from the University of California rushed to capture the knowledge of what Big Cheap called a pure, uncorrupted wild man. The anthropologists reached out to Sam Batwi, who by that time had twenty-five years of experience working for the *saltu* (White man), who paid him for his knowledge of Yana language and culture, plenty of time for him to develop a good sense of the market for anthropological information, especially given the scarcity of knowledgeable informants. Linguist Edward Sapir complained to Kroeber about having to pay Batwi what he considered an outrageous wage for his knowledge of mythological texts. Batwi had experienced settler violence firsthand. He saw his people dwindle to the dozens. Batwi was understandably suspicious of settler society, as well as largely unmoved by Ishi's plight. He learned to look after himself, his people, and his culture by adapting and maximizing his labor power in the regional economy. If Batwi was, as T. T. Waterman described him, a "damned old crank" who was "hard to handle," it was not without reason.

Batwi traveled with Ishi to San Francisco, where the two developed a complicated relationship. Batwi may have resented the attention that Ishi received, while Ishi distrusted Batwi, telling him, "I know you are a man like myself. You have red skin and black hair. The *saltu* want me to tell you about myself and my people. . . . Sam, you are not my friend but the friend of the white man. I will not tell anything about myself." Batwi eventually returned to Redding, where he died in the summer of 1914. Ishi remained in San Francisco. Puyukitchum-Ipai-Mexican American artist James Luna imagined Ishi addressing the audience in his performance piece "Ishi: The Archive Performance":

> You never asked me if I liked living in your world, and I would have told you, I didn't like it. But I dare not say anything, because you might have sold me to another museum, or worse, the circus.
>
> I would have told you I didn't like living here because it was too busy. The noise never stopped. I didn't like your food. Too sweet. Gravy on every-

thing. I like my greens fresh from the ground. I like my meat almost raw. And I like my soups clear.

You asked me to show you many things and I did. I showed you how to hunt and what it meant to live on the land with nothing. And survive.

But there were things that I would not show you. I would not tell you the stories of our sacred places. Our sacred songs. What for? You would not understand them.

I can't go home. There is nothing for me now. So I wait. I wait. I wait for the day when I leave this world. And when I get there, mother and father will be there. And all my relatives. And she'll be there.

Every day the sun will be shining and there will be a beautiful breeze, and the birds will be singing, and the children will be laughing and playing. Listen.

And there will be good Indian food out, and plenty to eat for everybody. There'll be Salmon. There'll be Buffalo. There'll be Elk. There'll be wee-wish. Every night. Every night, there will be a full moon. And every so often a brother or sister will come down.

We have no word in the Yahi language for goodbye. What we say when we part: You stay, I go.

Ishi contracted tuberculosis and passed away in the spring of 1916. Doctors performed an autopsy and removed his brain, sending it to the Smithsonian, where it was stored in a steel vat, forgotten until tracked down by anthropologist Orin Starn in 1999. Ishi's dramatic story and the publicity surrounding his death contrasted with the quiet survival of other Indigenous People. The year after Ishi traveled to San Francisco with Big Cheap and Batwi, Marie Mason went to Carlisle Indian School in Carlisle, Pennsylvania; that was in 1912. The school's transportation budget was insufficient to pay her fare, so she saved money over the summer waiting tables at a restaurant in Susanville bearing a sign that read: "No Dogs or Indians." After three years at Carlisle, she returned to California and married Henry Potts, a Maidu man she knew from their time at Greenville. They lived in the area, raising five girls and running a hunting and fishing operation on Lake Almanor. In 1942, she moved to Sacramento to help care for her daughter, Pansy Marine, who was seriously ill. Their house became the headquarters of the Federated Indians of California. Another daughter, Kitty Flores, was the organization's publicity agent and editor of the newspaper, Smoke Signal. When she resigned, Marie Mason took over both roles. Under her leadership, Smoke Signal circulated internationally. She was a founding member of the American Indian Press Association and wrote a book recounting the history, lifeways, and culture of her people in 1977. She died the following year.

By that time, the forces that had brought Ishi Wilderness into existence were already well-formed. But it is important to consider that this protected wilderness area, named after an Indigenous Person and encompassing Yahi territory, is nonetheless an act of erasure and dispossession. There are no Yahi who live in Ishi's wilderness. In 2000, the Smithsonian repatriated Ishi's brain to the Redding Rancheria, home of the Yahi's linguistic relatives, the Pit River people. In 2000, Mickey Gemmill and other Pit River people buried Ishi's brain and ashes at an undisclosed location along Deer Creek, perhaps within the boundary of Ishi Wilderness.

SOURCES

Theodora Kroeber, *Ishi in Two Worlds: A Biography of the Last Wild Indian in North America* (Berkeley: University of California Press, 1961); Orin Starn, *Ishi's Brain: In Search of America's Last "Wild" Indian* (New York: Norton, 2005); Douglas Cazaux Sackman, *Wild Men: Ishi and Kroeber in the Wilderness of Modern America* (New York: Oxford University Press, 2010).

On wilderness, see Roderick Nash, *Wilderness and the American Mind,* 5th ed. (New Haven, CT: Yale University Press, 2014). The Wilderness Act was codified as Public Law 88-577 (16 U.S.C. 1131–36), section 2(a), passed Sept. 3, 1964.

Performances of James Luna's "Ishi: The Archive Performance" are available online. The story of Mariah and Marie Potts comes from Marie Potts, *The Northern Maidu* (Happy Camp, CA: Naturegraph, 1977); and the work of Richard Burrill, who administers the website www.ishifacts.com. Edward Sapir's opinion of the Yana comes from Regna Darnell's excellent biography, *Edward Sapir: Linguist, Anthropologist, Humanist* (Berkeley: University of California Press, 1990), 25–26. On Sam Batwi as a crank and hard to handle, see Thomas Buckley, "'The Little History of Pitiful Events': The Epistemological and Moral Contexts of Kroeber's Californian Ethnology," in *Volksgeist as Methods and Ethic: Essays on Boasian Ethnography and the German Anthropological Tradition,* edited by George W. Stocking Jr. (Madison: University of Wisconsin Press, 1996), 292.

7

Friends and Enemies

Reframing Progress and Fighting for
Sovereignty, 1905–1928

In the summer of 1906, the Northern California Indian Association (NCIA) held its first Zayante Indian Conference at the Zayante Inn, at the Mount Hermon camp near Santa Cruz. The NCIA organized the conference to promote uplift through assimilation for California Indians. Few Indigenous People attended. By the second conference in 1907, twenty Indigenous People from nine tribes signed "The Plea of the Indians," addressed to "the president, Congress, and the governor and people of California." The plea, according to historian Valerie Sherer Mathes, demanded "land for their homes, protection from the liquor traffic, a common school education for all Indian children, field physicians, and legal protection." The conference's report, reprinted in the Women's National Indian Association's (WNIA) journal, captured the sincere but dismissive and heavy-handed approach, describing "the discussions in the Indians' councils, held with no white assistance, [as] earnest and able." Early on, California Indians' interests diverged from the missionary zeal animating much of the reformers' actions, but California Indians recognized the value in collaborating with reform groups, such as the WNIA, to pressure the federal government to honor its commitments. In 1908, William R. Benson, a Pomo delegate to the convention from Ukiah, claimed, "The whites have kept us below the lowest human beings." Among other things, he said, "We need law and a lawyer; less talk and more deeds. We want to rise but must have help to do it."

In the first three decades of the twentieth century, California Indians created economic and political relationships with Americans to secure their lands and advance programs of self-determination. As in the late nineteenth century, Americans expressed an interest in California Indians. They wanted to buy baskets, put children in school, and transform them into farmers. California Indians accepted this help and interest. They made and sold baskets. California Indians demanded schools close to their communities and improved facilities in the nation's many boarding schools. They demanded access to lands for farming and irrigation. California Indians, though, demanded less talk and more action. Conferences, such as Zayante, which talked about Indigenous People, failed to meet their needs. Organizations, such as the Mission Indian Federation (MIF), founded by and for California Indians, emerged as tools to claim land and sovereignty. During the Progressive Era, California Indians pushed for land by finding non-Indian allies and leveraging their often misdirected and heavy-handed attention to support their fight to reclaim land, demand citizenship, and assert sovereignty.

Across the United States, Indigenous People advanced programs of economic and political self-determination. They adjusted their economies to allotment policies. Children went to faraway boarding schools. When they returned from the schools, graduates formed new political organizations, such as the Society of American Indians (SAI), formed in Ohio in 1911. The SAI paralleled the efforts of the National Association for the Advancement of Colored People (NAACP), formed two years earlier. Both organizations comprised middle-class professionals and their White allies. What happened in California was slightly different and offers a unique spin on these national stories. The diversity and density of California Indian communities, even after the devastation of the nineteenth century, meant that intertribal organization happened on a smaller scale and flowed through local communities, strengthening tribal identities.

By the fourth Zayante conference, in 1909, the program weaved displays of Indian culture, such as baskets and songs, into the pleas, prayers, and demands of previous conferences. Baskets in this context bridged the interests of reformers and collectors at the height of what ethnohistorian Daniel Usner called "canastromania," the craze for Indian arts and crafts, particularly baskets. The interest in California's cultural identity brought attention to California Indians. While much of the interest dismissed living Indigenous People and intended to trap Indigenous People in an imaginary past, Americans' interest in items made by California Indians nonetheless gave some Indians new economic and political opportunities to carefully and tactically leverage that interest to their advantage.

Pomo Mary Knight Benson delicately balanced self-determination and cultural preservation with programs of racial uplift. She, along with her husband, William Benson, mentioned above, achieved recognition for the quality of their baskets. Indeed, they exhibited their work at the 1904 Louisiana Purchase Exposition in St. Louis. Mary Knight Benson learned the art of Pomo basket weaving from her mother, Sarah Knight, an innovative weaver in her own right, whose work had been collected widely. The Bensons worked closely with Grace Nicholson from Pasadena, who capitalized on the interest in California Indian baskets and ephemera. They were likely the first California Indians to make a living *as California Indians* by selling cultural items they produced for the commercial marketplace.

The Bensons, along with Wiyot-Hupa Louise Hickox, Washoe Lena Dick, Paiute Lucy Telles, Pomo Elsie Allen, Wappo-Pomo Laura Somersal, and Pomo-Patwin Mabel McKay, produced highly sought-after baskets. Many of these baskets adapted traditional styles meant to highlight the artistry of the craft or appeal to the tastes of collectors. Examples of their work ranged from large conical burden baskets, hoppers, and winnowing trays used to carry and process acorns to thicker cooking baskets, women's caps, and intricate, often tiny, ceremonial and gift baskets decorated with bird feathers and beads (see fig. 19). Each of these basket makers, to varying degrees, saw her work as a mixture of preserving traditional practices and adapting those practices to the marketplace as a means of thriving in the twentieth century.

California Indians navigated the marketplace for their baskets more easily than they navigated the market for their lands and cultural patrimony. Reformers and anthropologists attempted to study and preserve what they considered a vanishing culture. Across the state, hobbyists, collectors, amateur scientists, and anthropologists all turned their gaze toward California Indian graveyards. Because California Indian culture maintained a segregated proximity to the dead, strict rituals governed interaction with the People who had passed on. Yuroks carried the dead out of the house through a hole in the wall made strictly for that purpose. They placed graveyards and cemeteries close to home to facilitate care for the graves and reinscribe their identity in that place. As such, settler demand for Indian land inevitably involved settler claims on the Indian dead. Dispossession meant the loss of control over gravesites,

FIGURE 19. Yosemite master basket weaver Lucy Parker Telles, a Mono Lake Paiute, who lived at Yosemite and Mono Lake. Telles was one of a group of Mono-Paiute women renowned for the artistry of their stunning baskets, many of which they sold to Yosemite visitors. Here, Telles poses with her beautiful thirty-six-inch basket, which took her four years to complete and captured first prize at the 1933 World's Fair in Chicago. Photo courtesy California State Archives, a division of the Secretary of State's Office.

making them targets. As Yurok elder Walt Lara Sr. claimed, "When you dig these things up and remove them from the grave, you're actually ripping [the dead] off of their inherited right with the Creator."

California Indians recognized the value of their knowledge of history. As we saw in the previous chapter, Yanas Sam Batwi and Betty Brown worked with University of California anthropologist Edward Sapir on his book *Yana Texts,* published in 1907. Batwi and Brown's attitudes initially discouraged Sapir: "The Indians available for my purposes are strangely independent, largely because of the great scarcity of farm hands hereabouts. . . . Over and above this they are an unusually suspicious set of men." As Batwi aged, there were fewer people with which to speak Yana. Eventually, he spoke only with his wife, causing his memory of the male dialect of Yana, spoken only between men, to fade. Those who knew him or worked with him remembered him as a skilled teller of stories. In addition to Sapir, Batwi worked for Jeremiah Curtin in 1898 and Roland Dixon in 1900 as a source of Yana oral tradition. He was well-known to those looking to study Yana heritage.

Yuki Ralph Moore similarly viewed his work with the anthropologist Alfred Kroeber as a way to supplement income from agricultural labor, while also preserving some aspects of Yuki culture. He previously farmed on the Round Valley Reservation and worked in the area's hop fields. In 1901, he began a working relationship with Kroeber, which lasted almost forty years. Periodically, Moore traveled to the Bay Area to provide Kroeber with information. The work also gave him the opportunity to meet other Indians and to demonstrate the skills of an aspiring tribal leader. Moore scheduled those work trips between agricultural seasons and earned $2.50/day plus travel and lodging expenses. Moore treated his relationship with Kroeber similarly to his relationships with other employers, like the farmers and ranchers in the region. Philip Sparkman owned a store in Rincon, a village in San Diego County populated by Luiseños and ranchers. Fascinated by the Luiseño language, he hired Indians to teach it to him. He methodically recorded his notes, which after his murder in 1907 were published by the University of California.

California Indians approached non-Indian interest in their culture as an economic tool. Similarly, many sought out educational opportunities, but they envisioned them as supporting very different goals than the Indian Office planned. In 1910, a Wintu group from a rancheria four miles north of Colusa under the leadership of Captain Tom Odock attended the fifth Zayante conference and demanded a teacher for the school there. Frederick Collett and his wife, Beryl Bishop, took the job. Within a few years, Indian groups organized at Colusa for training in economics, thrift, self-government, and literary activities, the last called, predictably, the "Ramona Society." According to Cornelia Taber, Captain Odock said, after a few years, "Now we is somebody. Got schoolhouse, teacher, preacher, meetin's [sic] and our own life. I have gone on ahead to find light for my peoples. I want them to follow as fast as they can. We've been in awful darkness. Now we see a light. I want we go ahead be like other folks; go make something of ourselves." We should use caution in assessing Odock's words, filtered as they were through the lens of those who recorded them. Even so, the implicit goals of community persistence and sovereignty clearly emerged.

Odock continued to argue for educational opportunities at conferences. For the 1911 Zayante conference, Indians met separately, three weeks after the non-Indians. They issued broad demands. Odock urged reformers and government officials to teach Indians basic skills and how to care for themselves and their homes. Odock, though, rejected the conference organizers' expected gender norms. *The Indian's Friend* reported, "The consensus of opinion was . . . that boys must also be taught to cook, set the tables, prepare and serve a meal, and also know how to keep the home in a clean and sanitary condition. Someone suggested that it would not be as necessary for the boys to do this sort of work as thoroughly as the girls, but the Indians strongly disagreed. The same standard of excellence must be insisted upon for the boys as for the girls."

The push for education exemplifies the tensions between Indian self-advocacy and the reformers' oppressive assimilationist efforts. The Office of Indian Affairs created day schools on reservations and rancherias to educate children. As with many of the BIA's efforts, the schools were chronically underfunded, understaffed, and overprogrammed with assimilationist curricula, leading many Indians to push for access to local public schools or to relocate to cities to access the public school system.

Off-reservation boarding schools have attracted a lot of well-deserved scholarly attention. Boarding schools were significant but embodied assimilationist uplift through industrial training. The federal government operated five boarding schools in California: Perris/Sherman (1892–present), Hoopa Valley (1893–1931), Greenville Indian Industrial Boarding School (1897–1922), Fort Bidwell Indian Boarding School (1898–1930), and Round Valley (1881–1914). In 1913, the BIA also opened the Fort Yuma school, across the Colorado River in Ari-

FIGURE 20. Perris Industrial School students with Superintendent Savage and family, as they visited Whittier State School, Santa Monica, Redondo, and Los Angeles during summer vacation, ca. 1900. *Left panel, standing, left to right:* Samuel Scholder (Mesa Grande), Martina La Chusa (Mesa Grande), John [Ortega] (Kupa), Valentine Lavos (Kupa), Carolina Nolasquez (Kupa), Tomas [Arviso] (Rincon); *seated and kneeling: left to right:* Ysabel Martinez (La Jolla), Marinciana Sabacio (Potrero), Inocencia Apapas (Soboba), Frances Majel (Rincon). *Right panel, standing, left to right:* Margerite Scholder (Mesa Grande), Felipa Amago (La Jolla), Ignacio [Costo] (Cahuilla), Claudina Calac (Rincon), Carmelita Silvas (Soboba); *seated and kneeling:* Marcelina Pico (Pechanga), Dimple (the dog), Mrs. Savage, Mr. Savage, Violette Savage, Leponcia Cavar (Rincon). Photo courtesy Huntington Library.

zona. Many California Indians also attended Carlisle in Pennsylvania; Chemawa in Salem, Oregon; Stewart in Carson City, Nevada; or other boarding schools across the nation. In 1890, the Catholic Church established St. Boniface in Banning (fig. 20).

The goals of industrial training clashed with those of uplift. The initial goal of assimilationist policy was to integrate Indians into American society, to "kill the Indian to save the man," in Carlisle's founder Richard Henry Pratt's infamous phrase. To do that, school officials placed great attention on eradicating aspects of Indian culture, from the way students dressed to the language they spoke and the traditions and practices they treasured. Ultimately, at its most charitable, the goal of assimilationist policy was to make Indians indistinguishable from non-Indians. By the second decade of the twentieth century, that gave way to the reality that industrial education became the goal itself rather than serving as a means of working toward uplift. Estelle Reel, the federal superintendent

FIGURE 21. Intermediate sewing class at Sherman Indian Institute, ca. 1915. Photo courtesy Los Angeles Public Library.

of Indian schools, claimed the Indian child "is of lower physical organization than the white child" and should be directed toward manual labor. She wrote that Indian girls should "become proficient in cooking, sewing and laundry work before [being allowed] to spend hours in useless practice upon an expensive [piano] which in all probability they will never own." At the Sherman Indian Institute, in Riverside, boys and girls participated in various forms of industrial training. Boys took classes in farming and girls in the domestic arts. During summers, boys found work through the outing program, working on citrus farms, and girls found employment as maids for middle- and upper-class families in Anaheim and other burgeoning cities. In other words, industrial training prepared California Indian children for jobs as farmhands and domestics—the same jobs their parents performed near reservations and rancherias (fig. 21).

The history of Indian boarding schools is clearly deeply complex. One could argue, as many have, that the schools were chronically unhealthy, underfunded, and overcrowded sites of forced indoctrination and the eradication of Native culture. And they were. Widespread and preventable illnesses and Indian deaths, harsh corporal punishment, and relentless daily regimens plagued the schools. But they were also fertile sites of growth, where powerful intertribal identities, and lifelong relationships formed. Schools improved the economic prospects of many Indian students. They were places where students laughed, loved, and learned. They were also places where Indians worked. School officials assumed Indian boys would build and maintain the schools and Indian girls would clean and cook in it. The "value" of work in the assimilation process extended beyond the school.

California Indians resisted assimilation at home as well, particularly in terms of the administration of reservation affairs. On the Cahuilla Reservation, Captain Leonicio Lugo's efforts to maintain independence ran headlong into the Indian Office's efforts to assert control over Indian affairs in the region. The remote reservation, and others in the Soboba jurisdiction, retained comparatively more independence from federal Indian Office oversight than did reservations closer to the coast. Lugo assumed the captaincy of the reservation from his father, just as the Indian Office attempted to replace captaincies with committees. His methods of leadership clashed with the superintendent's, Frances Swayne, whom the BIA appointed two years after Lugo assumed the captaincy. The new superintendent challenged Lugo's exercise of power, and Lugo responded with petitions and a visit to Washington. In 1910, Swayne removed Lugo from office and asserted paternalistic federal power over Cahuillas: "They really believe that because they agree together that they do not want a thing, that no one has a right to do that, and that if they decide to do a thing no one has [the] right to stop them."

The federal government sought to make Indian administration more efficient and to break up tribal politics and counter the power of captains through the establishment of reservation committees or councils. Across the United States, BIA officials supported Indigenous Peoples' efforts to create tribal councils. The BIA envisioned these councils would agree to the extraction of resources from reservations, whether these resources were land, coal, or oil. In California, councils usually consisted of six men, elected by the adult males of the reservation, but California Indians repurposed the organizations and asserted more autonomy than the Indian Office wished. As the councils grew more independent, the initial apparent sympathy in the goals of Indians, reformers, and in some cases the Indian office itself broke apart.

At Pala, Cupeños and Luiseños attempted to exercise control over the conditions of the reservation. They went on strike concerning hiring practices on reservation infrastructure projects, protested the layout of the village itself, and struggled over the type of housing to build there. Rather than augmenting the authority of the Indian Office, the Common Council provided a platform for residents to resist federal oversight. John Ortega served as the president of the Pala council. In 1913, he wrote and signed a petition urging that the BIA patent two thousand unallotted acres of the reservation to the tribe in trust. The government held the patent for the "so-called waste lands, or strictly speaking pasture lands" that they deemed of "such a rough and inhospitable nature as to make it unfit for allotment." The signatories of the petition wanted the land for use as grazing land and feared it "may be some day opened to settlement or otherwise be conveyed to outside parties regardless of the interests of the Pala Indian tribe." Collectively, the council resisted Indian Office efforts to control Indian space and lives. Many of the early members of the council went on to leadership positions in the MIF.

Development increased the pressure on Indian land, but California Indians took advantage of the employment opportunities development produced to protect their land base. While the Common Council opposed the construction of the road, the majority of Indians in the region engaged in periodic off-reservation wage work, and in 1912, a local agent pointed to the county's highway and the Escondido Ditch company as two of the largest employers of Indian men. It is likely that Indians represented by, or perhaps sitting on, the council themselves worked in the road construction they protested here.

At the Tule River Reservation, Yokuts judge Frank Manuel protested the Indian Office's collection of grazing fees paid by non-Indians to graze their cattle on the reservation. He reasserted the title of *tiya* (chief) and in 1913 petitioned the Indian Office in Washington. Manuel claimed that the money should go directly to the tribal government rather than the Indian Office because he saw the decision to allow cattle grazing as resting with the tribe.

In some instances, reservation resistance and autonomy turned violent. Tensions ran high on the Cahuilla Reservation, and to break the standoff, the Indian Office replaced the existing agent. In May of 1912, however, a gunfight occurred in which the superintendent, William Stanley, was shot and killed, and several people were wounded. Federal courts found six people, including Leonicio Lugo, guilty of murder and sentenced them to ten years in the federal penitentiary. The murder and conviction polarized Southern California. Many non-Indians perceived the killing as evidence of an impending regional Indian uprising. It gave the Indian Office justification to suppress Indian resistance and a ready-made litmus test for Indian "loyalty." At the same time, the gunfight mobilized and politicized many Indians who had tried to avoid these disputes. Lugo's nephew, Lupy, circulated petitions that demanded Indian citizenship as a means of escaping federal wardship.

Less dramatic or deadly, similar events took place across Southern California. At the Soboba Reservation, twenty miles to the north, allotment surveys began in 1912, and the superintendent pledged to do away with the old political leadership and appoint a six-man committee to streamline the process. Cahuilla Adam Castillo recalled a meeting in which the superintendent announced his decision but refused to let Luiseños speak by claiming, "This is no day for speeches." Many Soboba residents refused to recognize the authority of the new committees.

The California Indian population decline brought about by disease and murder reached its nadir of approximately twenty-five thousand around 1910. After that time, the networks of labor and community that developed to resist genocide matured. Increasingly, California Indian assertions of their rights aligned with national movements. Most Indians in the state held fast to a desire to nurture and protect distinctive Indian communities. As more non-California Indians moved into the state, and California Indians increasingly attended school or worked outside the state, their approaches diverged, and they disagreed about how to achieve their goals. Some saw assimilation as a way to protect elements of Indian sovereignty. Others saw sovereignty as a way to fight assimilation. In between the poles of that binary, the spectrum was as diverse as the people and their experiences.

In 1914, Pomo Ethan Anderson wrote to the superintendent of the Carlisle Indian School about the benefits of off-reservation boarding schools. Anderson, born in 1888 in Lake County, California, attended a local Catholic mission school through fifth grade. By 1910, he served as a liquor suppression agent for the Indian Office. Between 1910 and 1912, he attended Carlisle, where he was an honor student who excelled on the debate team. After returning to Lake County in 1912, he took up farming on an allotment he selected on land purchased by the federal government as part of the efforts led by Charles Kelsey in 1906. In writing the superintendent, Anderson expressed pride in his accomplishments and training at Carlisle, saying he was "making good use of the education I received while at Carlisle and also the experience which I was trained to under the Outing system," which placed Indian students in seasonal or temporary jobs outside the school. He made it his "duty to explain to some of my young friends that Carlisle needs them to go there with a purpose and that all the advantages to make them better men and women can be found by enrolling as students at the dear school."

Anderson attempted to secure funding to pay for a trip to bring new students to Carlisle and to travel on his own to Wisconsin, Pennsylvania, and Washington, DC. He intended the trip to work "in the task to uplift my people as what Carlisle will hope to see me do" and included a visit to the White House for "certain purposes" and attendance at an Indian conference in Madison, Wisconsin. The superintendent declined his requests.

As evidence of his post-Carlisle success, Anderson pointed to his work with the Mt. Hermon Association, which hosted the Zayante conferences. Anderson saw their efforts and his participation in them as contributing to his people's uplift. He clarified that several younger Indians attended the meeting, inspired by his and his colleagues' experiences at Carlisle. These young men and women wanted to attend the school to learn a trade so that they could "labor close to their homes." Anderson promised that "1914 is a year of bright prospects for our tribe."

Anderson used the language of "uplift" familiar to the BIA but described something different from what the BIA envisioned. Laboring close to home would enable his "tribe" to prosper and strengthen its hold on the land. This was not assimilation as the Indian Office imagined. Anderson's involvement with the Zayante conferences after 1912 put him right in the middle of a network of Indians beginning to organize regionally. The same month Anderson wrote to the superintendent at Carlisle, the Indian Board of Cooperation (IBC), which developed out of the Ramona Society that Frederick Collett created at Colusa, filed articles of incorporation. By 1915, members elected Anderson to serve as secretary for the IBC.

Five hundred miles to the south, Cupeño Nicholas Peña, a 1905 Carlisle graduate, raised hay and beans on his own unpatented allotment on the Pala Reservation. He, too, was engaged in what the Indian Office understood to be uplift efforts at Pala. Peña was born at Kupa, the small village surrounding what came to be called Warner's Hot Springs, in 1879. His mother was one of the original defendants in the lawsuit that resulted in the Cupeño eviction of 1903. In 1912, he won the "best irrigated field" award at the annual Pala fiesta. The following year found him serving as the chairman of the Pala Common Council.

The stories of Anderson and Peña, and countless others like them, highlight the ways that California Indians incorporated some elements of BIA policy, while resisting the totality of the assimilationist model it envisioned. Both benefited from the education they received at Carlisle. Both were understood to be, in the language of the time, "progressive Indians," a loaded term, which generally referred to their willingness to adopt practices of non-Indian life. Their stories illustrate the degree to which the BIA privileged the experiences of men and sought to impose a settler gender system onto California Indian life. Both envisioned a *tribal* future but saw it playing out in distinct ways. For Anderson, a tribal future meant citizenship and full access to mainstream society as a way to uplift the tribe, as well as securing ownership of his small allotment to ensure his own financial security. For Peña, a tribal future meant organizing on the reservation to assert sovereignty against the power of the federal government.

In early September of 1916, Anderson and George Vicente went to the Lake County Courthouse in Lakeport to register to vote. The county clerk, Shafter Mathews, denied their effort on the grounds that, as Indians, they were not citizens of the state. Working with several regional Indian activists, and with the legal support and funding of the IBC, Anderson sued Mathews. The case became a test case for determining California Indian citizenship. The California Supreme Court agreed to take the case of *Anderson v. Mathews.*

Anderson and his attorneys based their argument on three claims: that Anderson was a citizen because he was *not tribal,* that is, that he had abandoned his tribal identity; that he had been allotted, which should confer citizenship to the allottee; and that he had been made a citizen by being born in California after the treaty ending the Mexican-American War in 1848, which had made citizens of his ancestors. Because of the complications in tracing the paper trail of his allotment, the attorneys abandoned the second claim. Neither party spent much time arguing about the existence of Anderson's tribal relations, largely because both sides agreed:

At the time of the treaty of [Guadalupe Hidalgo, Anderson's] ancestors were wild and uncivilized Indians settled in and permanently inhabiting Indian villages in the region now forming Lake county. Then and for several years thereafter they lived in tribes and maintained tribal relations, *the nature of which is not stated. The name of the tribe is not given. It does not appear that it was known by any name.* The United States has never made any treaty with the tribe, or with any tribe of which it ever formed a part, or with the particular group or village of Indians with whom the plaintiff associates and resides. It does not appear that the original tribe had any form of government, laws or regulations of any kind. He is one of a group of Indians residing in

Lake county, and who, although surrounded by white neighbors, practically associate exclusively with each other and with other Indians in that and adjacent counties. They have no tribal laws or regulations, and no organization or means of enforcing any such laws or regulations.

Given the agreement about the apparent lack of a clear tribal *government*, the briefs turned to tribal *culture* and included discussions of what Pomos of Lake County ate, how they dressed, whether they fished or hunted, all of which were used as markers of "civilization" and, therefore, the existence of a tribal culture. Elsewhere, the IBC attorney representing Anderson claimed:

Eating of fish, fresh or dried, certainly does not deprive any of the right to vote; and we see no reason why the eating of acorns should. When the writer of this brief in his boyhood lived in the part of the state where these Indians were and are, he ate acorns sometimes, and would be glad to have some now if the choicest varieties that grow there could be obtained. Yet, if eating them would deprive him of citizenship, he would like to be so informed so he may refrain.

The briefs for both parties, however, focused on complicated legal arguments surrounding the claim that the Treaty of Guadalupe Hidalgo conferred citizenship on Anderson. In 1917, the California Supreme Court dismissed those arguments and issued its ruling, arguing that because there was no tribal authority over Anderson, and that he had taken up "civilized" life, he was born under the jurisdiction of the United States under the Fourteenth Amendment and was therefore a citizen. In short, according to the court, Indians were citizens if they lived away from a reservation and acted like non-Indians.

Contrary to the brief his attorney presented, Anderson possessed a clear tribal identity, Pomo. It is telling that the brief they submitted claimed the name of the tribe was "not given." Anderson likely recognized his tribal identity as not antithetical to US citizenship. He pointed to the "bright prospects for [his] tribe" three years earlier. But the court saw tribal identity in opposition to US citizenship and distinguished between Indians living on reservations, for whom it could be argued there was an extant tribal government, and those who lived off or without reservations. In essence, the court equated tribal sovereignty with territorial claims. For someone like Anderson, while he lacked the tribal structure the government recognized, he retained the notion of tribal identity and territoriality.

Those who held on to reservation land now found it much harder to claim citizenship. Reservation politics often served as evidence for a tribal identity and functioning government. Furthermore, allotment often bogged citizenship claims down in a byzantine bureaucratic process. As was the case across most of the reservations in the central and southern part of the state, BIA infrastructure projects on reservations complicated things. Irrigated fields, which the Common Council established to promote assimilation and Peña used to win an award in 1912, stood in the way of his citizenship.

This is a complicated but necessary detour. In August of 1914, Congress changed the way the Indian Office funded irrigation projects. To prevent Indian Office monies going to construct irrigation projects that, when land was taken out of Indian hands, ended up supporting non-Indians, the new legislation attached a proportional share of the cost of the overall project as a lien on the land it irrigated. As an example, for an irrigation project covering one hundred acres and costing $100,000, the BIA attached a $100 lien to each acre of irrigated land. California Indians had to pay that debt before the BIA could finalize any transfer of property. Most critically, the legislation worked retroactively. The BIA suddenly encumbered Indians' land with a debt that California Indians had no role in creating but had to clear before they could sell it. In 1918, Cupeño Enrique Owlinguish was about to graduate high school at the Sherman Institute. His eight acres of land, only four of which were irrigable, possessed a value of $1,200 and a $700 lien. Those debts increased, reaching close to the per acre value of the land by the early 1920s. The debt often trapped Indians into holding on to land, as they could not sell it or secure additional loans to make it productive. Luiseño Saturnino Calac rightly referred to the debts as "a shadow overhanging us."

In 1917, the commissioner of Indian affairs issued a major new policy that gave "full and complete control of all their property" to "all able-bodied adult Indians of less than one-half Indian blood," by declaring that they were "competent," lifting all restrictions on their land and issuing them a fee patent. The goal was to save the federal government money, while promoting "self-respect and independence for the Indian, [and promoting] the ultimate absorption of the Indian race into the body politic of the Nation." The policy made blanket judgments of Indian competence based on the dubious idea of blood quantum. BIA officials required Indians with a higher blood quantum to demonstrate their competency through a hearing.

Given the arid climate of the southern part of the state, and the critical role of irrigation, many Southern California Indians with high blood quantum holding an allotment to irrigated land found themselves labeled "incompetent" and in debt. In 1920, Peña pointed out he was not currently a citizen because he had not yet been declared competent as his land was still restricted. He wanted to become a citizen and claimed he was willing to pay taxes and the reimbursable debt on his land to do so. Unfortunately, Peña claimed he was unable to do so with the small piece of land he had been allotted, and the threat of having to pay taxes on his land without income to do so made citizenship a losing proposition. Given the California Supreme Court ruling, his involvement in a tribal council meant that the Anderson decision did not apply in his case.

Anderson and Peña wanted citizenship, but Peña's involvement with the federal government interfered. Thus, a federal policy intent on assimilating Indians into citizenship made it harder to do so, and those Indians who were further from the oversight of the federal government found it easier. Federal policy inadvertently helped to protect an Indian land base in reservations but undermined its own assimilationist program.

Neither assimilation nor allotment made citizens, although across the state, federal officials restarted allotment projects on several reservations in the 1910s. At Hoopa Valley, in 1895, the BIA made 395 allotments of approximately ten acres each but failed to finalize them through a trust patent. Instead, land allotments languished as tentative for years. As more allottees died leaving unclear inheritance, and the population expanded, it became impossible for the Indian Office to move forward in approving the allotments. In 1911, Hupas formed a Business Council and demanded that the federal government redistribute the land more equitably. In 1915, the Indian Office agreed and resurveyed the valley into four-acre plots. Andrew Mesket and James Jackson Sr. protested the tiny allotments. Fearing that any land that was not allotted to Hupas would be made available to non-Indian settlers, Hupas pressed for allotment of the full reservation, not just the valley floor. Again, the Indian Office agreed, and in October of 1918, allotment began of plots of four acres of valley land and twenty acres of timber or grazing land for every individual on the 1895 list and their children. By the end of the process, the BIA made 414 allotments, and the Indian Office Competency Commission found half of those allottees competent to receive a fee-patent.

Allotment produced mixed results. In some cases, allottees used their land to assimilate in keeping with BIA policy. But the growing number of additional allottees, the unclear divisions associated with inheritance, the disputed water rights, and the leases signed by non-Indians all complicated matters. Even as the Hupa pushed successfully for allotment patterns that ordered Hupa life toward the elected Business Council, frame houses, plowed fields, and wage labor, the tribe's rituals and customs persisted. Hupa tribal historian Byron Nelson Jr. recalled that "the people's quiet, persistent refusal to abandon ancient beliefs had itself become a way of life in Hoopa Valley." Allotment and the assimilationist policies it entailed sat alongside traditional practices.

Across Southern California, renewing the allotment process followed a similar pattern. In 1917, the BIA resurveyed unapproved allotments from the late nineteenth century, which it distributed to heads of households alone, into smaller allotments, and assigned them to individuals. Families with young children stood to receive numerous allotments, while older individuals, the people who had received allotments in the earlier surveys, now found their share of the land reduced.

Additionally, federal policy complicated itself by its inclination toward trust patents. Despite the fact that the BIA deemed half of the allottees at Hoopa Valley eligible for a fee-patent, by the time the interior secretary approved the allotments four years later, 90 percent were twenty-five-year trust-patents. Additionally, the BIA opened the valley to mineral exploration, and miners who leased land from the tribe to look for gold and coal encroached on proposed allotments. On Southern California reservations, where farmers needed irrigation, the reimbursable debt problem all but locked up allotments in trust status.

Ultimately, allotment failed to accomplish its stated goal. It failed to attach Indians to land as subsistence and small market farmers as a way to civilize and prepare them for citizenship. In California, allotment inadvertently allowed some Indians to claim or hold on to land, giving them a base from which to engage the wage-labor market on different terms than those available to landless workers. Allotment gave Indians a place from which to assert power. By 1916, California Indians received two dollars a day to work on road-building projects, or four dollars a day if they brought their own team of horses, something few could do. Across the southern part of the state, roadwork occasionally took the entire male population of communities away from reservations for extended periods of time. An Indian agent claimed that "practically all of the Indians are at work on the County roads . . . [and] this work is a direct benefit to the Indians not only by furnishing them employment, but giving them an outlet to market."

That outlet to market opened opportunities, and land facilitated Indian access to it. While the Indian Office saw allotment as a way to attach Indians to the soil, it often cut the other way. In the late nineteenth century, Luiseño Robert Magee followed his non-Indian father into the small-scale beekeeping business in Temecula. Magee used his ten-acre allotment on the Rincon Reservation to house his apiaries. The BIA challenged his efforts. Beekeeping did not fit the ideal of the agricultural model of assimilation. With the early twentieth-century decline of the bee business, Magee left his allotment in the care of his family. He moved to Pauma, and then Pechanga, where he married a Cahuilla woman.

Over the next decade, Magee moved among the region's numerous reservations, as well as towns such as Lakeside, Riverside, and Temecula, with relative ease. He claimed rights through his wife to land on the Pechanga Reservation, and his own on Rincon. Magee decried the poor quality of the allotments available in Southern California and added that their small size trapped those wishing to farm. The size meant they were too small to raise enough grain to feed horses or to generate enough revenue to justify purchasing a tractor. As a result, neither he nor his people wanted to "make horses or oxen of ourselves." In Temecula and Lakeside, Magee worked as a stonecutter at local quarries. That experience helped him rise to manage a large quarry in Riverside that shipped paving stones primarily to San Francisco and Los Angeles.

Indians' work—domestic, factory, or field, as well as making baskets, picking hops, shearing sheep, informing anthropologists, managing stone quarries, gardening—put them in contact with other Indians from the region and their occasional "friends." One such person was Jonathan Tibbet. Like Frederick Collett, Tibbet took a complicated interest in Indian affairs. A White real estate agent and booster in Riverside, he wrote to Cahuilla Julio Norte of the Malki Reservation, asking him for help in 1918. Tibbet outlined his plan to create the Southern California Pioneer Association and its Memorial Museum in Riverside. His museum would integrate the stories of "the Indians, Pioneers and the Padres." Specifically, Tibbet proposed to create a "Temporary Indian Branch," with land set aside at the museum for "an Indian Village where they [Indians] can live their old simple lives once more," alongside "old time pioneers" in log cabins. His vision of a peaceful past belied historical reality but struck a different chord with Norte. Tibbet described an Indian space, although quite marginalized, where "control of the Indians will be in their own hands, by their electing a Capitan, and a council of their own people." What for Tibbet was nostalgia, for Norte and many other Indians was an opportunity to expand and strengthen Indian sovereignty. Norte and Cahuilla Joe Pete, captain at Torres, saw an opportunity and traveled to Riverside.

Norte and Pete's immediate concern involved recent efforts by the BIA to restart allotments across the region's desert reservations. Norte planted an orchard on three acres of his previous allotment selection on the Malki reservation sometime around 1912. Fruit trees rarely produced a marketable crop in fewer than five years, making Norte understandably concerned about a new allotment causing him to lose that six-year investment just as it began to yield. Fifty years old at the time, Joe Pete led a draft resistance movement during WWI and wrote several Indian Office officials and local politicians, complaining about the living conditions on the reservations and the increasing debt accruing to allotments because of the reimbursable irrigation expenditures. His work aroused considerable local attention and earned him the label "trouble maker."

Norte accepted the offer, and membership in the temporary Indian branch grew. By January of 1920, the organization morphed into the Indian Federation of Southern California and soon thereafter was renamed the Mission Indian Federation, with Norte as the grand president, Cahuilla Lupy Lugo as the first vice president, Cahuilla Adam Castillo as the second vice president, Joe Pete as chief inspector, and Tibbet as grand counselor, the organization's only non-Indian member. They held a well-publicized meeting at Tibbet's home in Riverside, where they drafted a constitution and outlined a broad policy of activism under the general motto "Human Rights and Home Rule." The following year, federal officials indicted the fifty-three members of the organization on charges of "conspiracy to defraud the United States government by obstructing officials of the Indian department, defeating the exercise of governmental functions by superintendents and agents, and of conspiracy to alienate the loyalty and confidence of the California Mission Indians in the government."

Nicholas Peña joined, as well, and in 1922 described the purpose of the organization as "to take up all the difficulties that the Indians have . . . and present it to the Government to see if the Government will help them out." In a general sense, the federation resisted the BIA and its policies but not out of opposition to "progress" per se. Instead, the federation wanted Indian control over Indian progress, something the Indian Office failed to recognize as progress at all. Additionally, the federation's "traditionalism" often meant more opportunities for women in leadership roles than within the progressive policies of the BIA. Luiseño Trinidad Mojado, from northern San Diego County's La Jolla Reservation, acted as a spokeswoman for the federation. She engaged in several actions on the reservation to stop allotment and prevent those allotted from using their land.

While Tibbet's motives were suspect, and the MIF resembled Frederick Collett's equally paternalistic Indian Brotherhood of California (IBC), the MIF was distinct in some important ways. Human rights and home rule brought together power and rights and grafted both onto existing Indian power structures. Whereas the IBC united Indians to "uplift the race" through legal challenges, the MIF emerged in the southern part of the state, where many Indians still retained a diminished land base in the form of reservations. The MIF, therefore, focused on revitalizing tribal governments by building on the extant structure of the Indian Office. The Indian Office was the network, not the source of power. Power came from tribal governments. Omaha Thomas Sloan, the past president of the SAI, who relocated to Southern California, became a fierce opponent of the federation. In 1929, in testimony given in an equity suit brought against the federation, he said, "I would like for you, Adam [Castillo], to understand, and those of you who are here, that you are a dirty, rotten bunch, and that all of you, and the officers of that organization, ought to be in the jail or the penitentiary." By fusing tribal and bureaucratic organizations, the MIF forged a powerful, and threatening, regional pan-Indian alliance focused on sovereignty and home rule, which functioned as a controversial alternative to both the Indian Office and mainstream national organizations like the SAI.

Unlike Collett, Tibbet, the MIF's controversial grand counselor, served as the only non-Indian member of the federation. The presence of Indians in all other positions of leadership in the federation, and the presence of federation-affiliated leaders in many of the reservations across the southern part of the state, meant the MIF quickly addressed issues that Indian members held dear, particularly efforts to restrict the power of the Indian Office and to stop allotment.

As laid out in its 1920 constitution, the MIF attempted to "secure by legislation or otherwise all the rights and benefits belonging to each Indian, both singly, and collectively; to protect them against unjust laws, rules and regulations; to guard the interests of each member against unjust and illegal treatment." In distinguishing Indians' rights as individuals and a collective, the MIF's constitution recognized the tensions that pulled on Indian communities, between identity defined collectively and determined by relationships to other members of one's village, band, tribe, or reservation, and identity defined by the racial or cultural characteristics of individual Indians. Contrary to what the Indian Office understood, Indian resistance to federal policy was not, in this case, resistance to individuation in defense of Indian communalism.

Rather, the MIF nurtured an emerging racial identity, which intermediated between these tensions and demanded rights on both accounts. The organization's constitution outlined a strategy to protect the area's reservations from federal abuse and mismanagement, while also urging that "all matters pertaining to the Mission Indian Federation must be handled in a broad, comprehensive sense. We are working for the Indian Race and must never lose sight of these facts." In short, they saw that working on behalf of the reservations in Southern California was benefiting the Indian race as a whole.

Adam Castillo emerged as the most prominent Indian representative of the organization for the next twenty years, literally its face on the federation seal. Born in 1885 on the Soboba Reservation in what is now Riverside County, Castillo grew up at a time when the reservation's boundaries remained in flux and when federal court decisions over Indian land tenure and allotment reoccurred. Castillo, like many Indians in the area, felt his status as ward and the federal government's power over his life in very palpable ways.

After living and working in and around Redlands for a few years, Castillo returned to Soboba in 1915 and began petitioning the Indian Rights Association and the Indian Office in Washington, DC, for help in establishing the reservation's boundaries and preventing Indians from other reservations and villages from receiving allotments at Soboba. Within a few years, Castillo embraced a much more expansive approach to his activism. In 1917, Castillo was elected Indian judge. In 1919, he organized the nascent federation movement, and by 1922 he became the organization's grand president.

The Indian Office failed to see the MIF as anything other than the corrupt work of a White interloper, inherently at odds with the generally "progressive" nature of many of the members. With increasingly provocative rhetoric, a claimed membership of two thousand, and one-dollar-per-month dues, the MIF threatened the Indian Office's control.

By bridging the reservation-based political culture of Indian resistance, and regional efforts at legal and political reform, the MIF gave some Indians who attained a level of economic or cultural competency in the non-Indian world a way to return to Indian country and integrate the two. For Indians who rooted their identity in local, village relationships, the MIF provided a way to reclaim authority from the Indian Office and deploy it against the non-Indian powers who worked against them. The MIF provided a way to push for reservation-based political and economic control.

Castillo looked back to the missions as models for reservations but in a different way than those who saw them as sites of efficient Indian labor. He claimed that "during the rule of the Padres the Indians lived in their own villages, elected their own head men, or chiefs, their captains, their judges. They made and enforced their own village laws and generally handled their own village affairs." He outlined a prototypical kind of sovereignty: "We have depended on state laws to protect us in our rights to hold land, and the state has failed. We have depended on the Federal laws and they have failed." As a result, "we have a right to elect our own tribal officers [and] ask to be allowed to see what we can do to help ourselves."

Not all who initially joined remained with the MIF. In May of 1920, Lupy Lugo left soon after the MIF formed and joined with Ben Amago, William B. Nelson, and Ignacio Costo, among others, to form the short-lived American Mission Indian Cooperative Society (AMICS). They envisioned this society as an alternative to the MIF. While the AMICS did not last long, a strong undercurrent of Indian resistance to the MIF's growing power did.

By 1920, schools provided additional ways Indigenous People could organize to help themselves. Despite the schools' assimilationist curricula and the unhealthy, disease-ridden physical environment, California Indians transformed boarding schools into sites of power. Boarding schools emerged as nodes in networks Indians built and increasingly incorporated Indians from all over the Southwest.

By 1920, Sherman became the largest Indian school in the state. Although boasting a capacity of seven hundred students, enrollment regularly exceeded that. The curriculum changed significantly after it moved to Riverside in 1903, increasingly shifting away from an assimilationist civics focus toward industrial education to prepare Indians for wage labor in the non-Indian world. In the decade preceding 1920, approximately 150 of a possible 3,000 students, graduated. Of those who graduated, roughly three-fourths of them took "their place as citizens off reservation." Commonly, graduates held jobs in housekeeping, ranching, day labor, nursing, stock raising, and military service. The majority of the students who did not graduate returned to the reservations.

In an attempt to balance the crosscutting goals of assimilation to White society and industrial training, the schools employed a "half-day" system in which morning classroom instruction preceded "practical" afternoon industrial training. Additionally, the Indian Office assumed the best way to prepare Indian children was to have them build and maintain the school and spend summers working "out" of the school in non-Indian communities (fig. 22). In that way, the "outing program" at Sherman and other Indian schools across the state acted as regional employment agencies. The ostensible purpose of the program was the assimilationist uplift the BIA thought would follow as Indians associated more closely with mainstream White society through summer work. Beginning in 1918, the Indian Office opened outing centers in Berkeley and Los Angeles, as well as Phoenix, Tucson, Reno, and other western cities. Staffed by matrons, the outing centers functioned as employment agencies focusing on finding domestic work for Indian women. But informally, the centers functioned as settlement houses and meeting places for Indian men and women who moved to cities. As with allotment, federal policies in regard to work did not assimilate Indians but instead provided them with a network they used to protect their land, culture, and sovereignty.

As with boarding schools and cooperation with "friends," Indians possessed a "clear-eyed" ambivalence to the outing program. In many cases, it functioned as a coercive system of employing Indian children and controlling the low wages they received. The supervising agent or superintendent carefully guarded Indian students' access to money; they held two-thirds of the wages earned by Indians in the outing program. In 1928 and 1929, Yuki Rachel Logan, a student at Sherman, worked as a domestic servant in Southern California. Employers did not pay Logan directly but sent checks to the school superintendent, who held the money for the students to use to return home at the end of their time at the school. Similarly, Paiute Josephine Natchez was paid twenty-five dollars a month for her labor as a domestic worker in San Francisco. Her employer sent two-thirds of that amount to the superintendent of Stewart Indian School, where Natchez was a student and the remaining one-third to the outing matron, who had to approve any withdrawal Natchez made. In other instances, Indians utilized the opportunities outing work provided to seek employment on a temporary basis. In that way, these jobs were not isolated sites of confinement but functioned as a "way station" or "migratory hub" to provide access to more jobs, housing, skills, and education across the region.

The outing program served as something of an institutional analogue to the informal labor networks in which California Indians had engaged for decades. In the twentieth century, many of those networks connected Indians to cities. The Quechan and Mojave women who left their reservations along the Colorado River to take domestic work in Los Angeles are but one example. In 1909, Quechan Bertha Baker

FIGURE 22. Sherman students with garden tools, ca. 1915. Photo courtesy Los Angeles Public Library.

moved to Los Angeles, where she served as an unofficial informal coordinator, working with BIA officials on the Fort Yuma Reservation, intervening when problems arose, and helping secure new positions for others who came later.

Word of mouth built extensive labor networks. Pomo-Patwin Mabel McKay worked in San Francisco, washing dishes in a Japanese restaurant, and then as a nanny, caring and cleaning for a White family. At the suggestion of her boss, McKay left that position to make more money cleaning a brothel for five dollars a day. She also traveled to Portland and Seattle, working odd jobs as she traveled to pay her way, before eventually returning to Lake County.

In the early 1920s, a growing chorus of criticism against the BIA launched a series of congressional investigations. In the spring of 1920, the House Subcommittee on Indian Affairs held hearings across the state. Indians voiced their concerns regarding allotment, irrigation, debt, insecurity of reservation boundaries, the lack of land, citizenship, voting rights, and education. Some of these efforts yielded results. By 1920, Representative John Raker, a Democrat who represented northeastern California's second district, submitted legislation seeking compensation for the land lost by California Indians when the United States Senate rejected the 1851 treaties. Although the legislation did not initially pass, the Indian Board of Cooperation (IBC) launched a campaign to support and further the effort. Charles Kelsey, among others, saw it as an "excuse and means of raising their [Collett's] salary." The IBC collected dues, and Collett traveled to Washington, DC, to push for compensation.

The IBC also supported the claims of Pomo Virgilia Knight, who, in 1923, successfully sued for the right to attend the Carroll District public schools. Her father, Stephen Knight, described it this way:

> We were six years trying to get the [BIA] day school in the Indian village where I lived. We appealed, attended conference after conference, and we never could do anything, until finally . . . through the Catholic Church we appealed to Senator Phelan, and he took action and we finally got our day school. But after sending our children to this day school for a number of years, we came to the conclusion that a Government day school is no place to educate your children. So . . . we went to work and tried to turn the Government day school into a district school, to be supervised by the county school authorities. In this we failed for a while, but finally we brought suit against the trustee of our school district to take our children into their white school.

That same year, the IBC Indian Auxiliary at Big Pine (in Owens Valley) demanded access to the public school for Paiute Alice Piper and six others. The trustees of the school refused, and the IBC took the case to the California Supreme Court, which upheld Piper's right to attend the school. It ruled that as a citizen, she did not belong to an organized Indian tribe with a treaty relationship with the United States. As a citizen, the public school could not deny Piper access to public education.

The same day that the California court issued its Piper decision, the US Congress passed the Snyder Act, conferring citizenship on all Indians born in the United States. By that point, approximately two-thirds of Indians in the country had already become citizens through allotment, military service, marriage to a White citizen, or other means. Citizenship did not mean Indians no longer faced segregation in education or restrictions in voting. It did, however, clarify their status, provided some legal traction, and motivated a number of Indians to act. Within the MIF, citizenship offered a new tool in asserting sovereignty and control over reservations vis-à-vis the Indian Office. Within the IBC, the Snyder Act emboldened many Indian members and coincided with increased exposure of the controversies in Collett's private life. A former IBC staff member brought charges against him, claiming that he had misused organizational funds. Leaders of many of the Indian

Auxiliaries grew frustrated with Collett's leadership style and the controversies surrounding him.

In 1926, members of the IBC Indian Auxiliaries, led by Pomos Stephen Knight and Albert James, broke with Collett and formed the California Indian Brotherhood (CIB). Eventually Ethan Anderson joined and took on a leadership position. The CIB developed a strong presence in Northern California and built on preexisting Indian networks facilitated by the IBC. They pressed for educational access and sought compensation for lost treaty land.

In 1927, the push for compensation for lost lands began to make headway. The California Jurisdictional Act of 1928 defined California Indians as all Indians living in the state on June 1, 1852, and their descendants. The act authorized the attorney general of California to bring a lawsuit in the US Court of Claims for the land covered by the eighteen unratified treaties. Valued at $1.25 an acre, the money, should it be awarded, would be held by the US Treasury in trust, not distributed through per capita payments. To determine eligibility, the act authorized the BIA to create a statewide roll. Beginning in 1928, federal employee Fred Baker traveled across the state, assisting Indians in applying for membership on the official roll. By the time it closed in 1933, the roll contained 23,542 California Indians. The process proved deeply problematic and often failed to accurately record Indians living off reservation, on reservations other than "their own," out of state, or in mixed-tribal relationships. The roll created frozen, rigid categories of Indian identity that failed to recognize the complexity and mobility of California Indian life. These details had consequences.

Indians acted on the promise of citizenship in other ways. In late 1925, MIF member Vidal Mojado and six representatives of the La Jolla and Rincon Reservations brought an equity suit against the Southern Sierras Power Company (SSPC). The suit alleged the company attempted to construct a telephone line across the reservations without their permission. Earlier that year, the Federal Power Commission granted the SSPC a license to construct and operate a power line across the reservation. In October, Indians ejected SSPC's employees from the reservation and removed the company's telephone poles, some of which they had contracted to install. The Indians brought a legal action to secure a court order to prohibit the company from returning to construct telephone lines and requiring they pay damages for the completed construction.

The nine Indians named in the suit argued that the 1924 Indian Citizenship Act invalidated previous laws, which gave authority to approve infrastructure projects on reservations to the secretary of the interior. As citizens, the plaintiffs argued that the SSPC's actions constituted trespassing because it failed to secure approval from the Indians themselves.

The SSPC claimed it did not trespass because the Indians did not own the lands. Rather, the land was patented to the band and held in trust by the US government, from whom the SSPC had received permission. Furthermore, the SSPC countersued on the grounds that Indian citizenship in no way affected previous legislation, and Indians conspired to interfere with their rights. In February of 1926, the judge agreed with the SSPC and denied that the Indians owned the land; they therefore did not have the power to grant rights of way. The judge issued a permanent injunction against all members of the Rincon and La Jolla Bands against any further act disturbing the SSPC in its actions.

Complications emerged. According to several participants, sometime in 1924, a meeting took place in a barn on the reservation. Indians, the federal Indian agent, and attorneys representing both the Indians and the power company agreed the company would pay the Indians $2,500 for the right of way across Indian land. The money went to the attorney who assisted the federation in bringing the suit. On the surface, this may appear as yet another in a series of legal actions benefiting the attorneys more than those who brought the charges. But the action demonstrated an opportunism and assertiveness that characterized a shift in Indian activism in the twentieth century. Both Vincenti Albanes and Bruno Sovenish worked for the power company, placing poles across the reservation. Both were also coplaintiffs in the lawsuit filed by Vidal Mojado against the power company. In using a settlement payment for rights-of-way to fund a subsequent lawsuit that sought to deny those rights, while working for the company that they sued for the work they themselves completed, the Indians of the region adeptly used the legal system to their advantage. Even if they did not win the court case, they leveraged settler interest in Indian land and resources and tacked against that pressure in ways that differed from ways available to Indians in the nineteenth century.

In 1928, the Senate Subcommittee on Indian Affairs held hearings in Riverside on the condition of Indians of the region. Mojave Bessie Edgar lived in Oakland at the Industrial Home for the Adult Blind. She and her two sons received ten-acre allotments at the Colorado River Reservation. The Indian agent placed Edgar in the home for the blind and leased her land, first to an agricultural company growing cotton, then to a ranching company. While the agent sent the lease money to the home, she nonetheless mopped and scrubbed floors to pay her board. Edgar asked the subcommittee for control over her leasing income.

Stephen Knight read a statement on the conditions of California Indians. He advocated for a distribution of land to Indian communities and government guarantee of access for Indian children to White schools. Lupy Lugo spoke angrily about a conversation regarding the surveys and allotment at the Cahuilla Reservation when Commissioner Cato Sells visited in 1919:

> I asked him . . . what you going to do? He said he could do nothing, and he asked me if we had ever made a petition. Would only take a 2-cent stamp to send the report to Washington. I am not speaking only for this reservation; generally for everybody. These Indians in the same shape all over southern California, it has been going on for many years. . . . He asked me if a report had ever been made. I showed him. I said I am sure you are not going to do anything. We have been trying for 20 years. He said yes he could not do anything.

Similarly, Cupeño Andrew Moro, a 1905 graduate of Carlisle Indian School, returned to the Pala Reservation. His peers elected him to the Common Council to raise land issues. When the BIA patented his allotment in 1915, Moro leased it and left the reservation for Los Angeles where he worked as a gardener. He also served as the second vice president of the MIF, and the president of the federation's Los Angeles branch, organizing among Indians and non-Indian supporters throughout the 1920s. Here, as it did in many instances, the federation divided the Moro family. Andrew's older brother, Domingo, served as the Mission Indian Agency chief of police for Pala and was tasked with upholding the authority of the Indian Office. In his testimony, Andrew Moro complained about the ambiguous status of California Indians. The Indian agent told them they were citizens, "but he don't say why we have the agent over us if we are citizens."

In the twentieth century's first two decades, California Indians, government officials, and American reformers looked for ways to uplift California Indian people. The Bureau of Indian Affairs realigned land to promote self-sufficient farming and school curricula to foster individualism. American reformers attempted to alleviate poverty and assimilate California Indians into the body politic. California Indians, though, did not envision uplift in the same way. They desired to take greater control over their lives, to live as both Indian and American. They worked in California's growing agricultural and industrial economy, formed their own organizations to advocate for land and sovereignty, and pushed back against the federal government's failure to uphold the trust relationship. These efforts continued as the nation careened toward a depression and rebounded with another effort to take California Indian lands.

SOURCES

The details of the 1906 Zayante conference come from Valerie Sherer Mathes, *Divinely Guided: The California Work of the Women's National Indian Association* (Lubbock: Texas Tech Press, 2012), 136–37; and the "Annual Report of the Women's National Indian Association," Thirteenth Annual Meeting, Dec. 7, 1909, 19. The comments by William Benson, Robert Parrish, and Ephraim Cummings come from "The Third Zayante Conference," *Indian's Friend*, Sept. 1908, 2. Cornelia Taber's recollection of Captain Tom Odock's comments is in Cornelia Taber, *California and Her Indian Children* (San Jose: Northern California Indian Association, 1911), 47. On the standards for boys and girls in the 1911 conference, see "The First Indian Conference at Guinda, Cal.," *Indian's Friend*, Oct. 1911, 2.

The term *canastromania* comes from Daniel Usner, "An Ethnohistory of Things: Or, How to Treat California's Canastromania," *Ethnohistory* 59 (Summer 2012): 441–63. On the desecration of graves by collectors, see Walt Lara Sr., "Respect for the Dead," *News from Native California* 9, no. 4 (2006): 21.

Edward Sapir's opinion of the Yana comes from Regna Darnell's excellent biography, *Edward Sapir: Linguist, Anthropologist, Humanist* (Berkeley: University of California Press, 1990), 25–26. On Estelle Reel, see K. Tsianina Lomawaima, *They Called It Prairie Light: The Story of Chilocco Indian School* (Lincoln: University of Nebraska Press, 1994), 93; and Clifford E. Trafzer, Jean A. Keller, and Lorene Sisquoc, *Boarding School Blues: Revisiting American Indian Educational Experiences* (Lincoln: University of Nebraska Press, 2006), 179.

On Lugo's petitions, and the Cahuilla Uprising, see Tanis Thorne, "The Death of Superintendent Stanley and the Cahuilla Uprising of 1907–1912," *Journal of California and Great Basin Anthropology* 24, no. 2 (2004): 234, 241–42, 247. The six appealed the conviction in *Apapas v. US*, 233 US 590 (1914).

John Ortega's petition, written while he was serving as president of the Pala Council, can be found in Walter Runke to Robert Valentine, April 8, 1913, NARA-Riverside, Bureau of Indian Affairs, Record

Group 75 (hereafter NARA, BIA, RG 75), PALA, Letters Sent to Commissioner of Indian Affairs, box 375, book 1. On the off-reservation work on the county highway and Escondido Ditch, see Walter Runke, "Narrative Annual Report," *Superintendents' Annual Narrative and Statistical Reports from Field Jurisdictions of the Bureau of Indian Affairs,* microcopy 1011, NARA, BIA, RG 75, 1912, roll 99, 15.

Adam Castillo's quote from the superintendent that this is no time for speeches is from his testimony in *U.S. v. Albanes,* reporter's transcript, vol. 26, NARA-Riverside, Records of the District Court of the United States, RG 21, Southern District of California, Southern Division, 1929–1938 (San Diego) (hereafter *US v. Albanes),* box 3, folder A2 [13/14], 2749.

Dickinson College maintains the Carlisle Indian School Digital Resource Center, which has digitized Ethan Anderson's student file. For the correspondence quoted here, see Ethan Anderson to Supt. Friedman, Feb. 15, 1914; Anderson to Oscar Lipps, Supt. Carlisle, August 7, 1914; Anderson to Supt. Friedman, Feb. 15, 1914; Student File, Carlisle Indian School, NARA, RG 75, Series 1327, box 77, folder 3700. The long quotation about the absence of Anderson's tribal relations is from *Anderson v. Mathews,* 163 P. 902 (1917), the Brief of the Petitioner, p. 4 (emphasis added). The quotation regarding eating acorns comes from the Closing Brief of the Petitioner, pp. 5–6. The Opinion of the court stated, "He voluntarily lives separate and apart from any organized tribe, he works, dresses, eats and lives with and maintains his lawful wife and his family, after the manner of civilized peoples" (Opinion, 9).

Saturnino Calac's comment about debt being a shadow overhanging allotments and Robert Magee's comment about not wanting to make horses or oxen of themselves come from a transcript of remarks at a conference between George Von Baux, the Chairman of Commission of Indian Affairs, and Indians gathered at Rincon Reservation on April 17, 1925. It was included as exhibit 1 in *US v. Albanes,* exhibits A-2-M, box 1A, folder "San Diego A-2-M exhibits 1–46."

Indian Commissioner Cato Sells's competency policy was laid out in Cato Sells, "Declaration of Policy in the Administration of Indian Affairs," *Indian's Friend,* May 1917, 5. Byron Nelson Jr.'s recollections about the Hupa's quiet, persistent refusal to abandon traditional beliefs comes from his book, *Our Home Forever: The Hupa Indians of Northern California* (Hoopa, CA: Hupa Valley Tribe, 1978), 162. The claim that "practically all of the Indians are at work on the County roads" comes from a letter from Thomas F. McCormick to Cato Sells, August

24, 1916, NARA, BIA, RG 75, fu PIS-1018, Reports: Correspondence 1910–20, PS 1903–21.

Many scholars have written about the Mission Indian Federation, but it awaits a definitive history. On Jonathan Tibbet and his relationship with the federation, see Walter Robert Baggs, "An Unfortunate Kind of Leadership: Jonathan Tibbet and the Mission Indian Federation" (master's thesis, University of California, Riverside, 1978). The letter regarding the temporary Indian branch he proposed is reproduced as appendix C. See also Richard A. Hanks, *This War Is for a Whole Life: The Culture of Resistance among Southern California Indians, 1850–1966* (Banning, CA: Ushkana Press, 2012); Heather Marie Daly, "American Indian Freedom Controversy: Political and Social Activism by Southern California Mission Indians, 1934–1958" (PhD diss., University of California, Los Angeles, 2013); Rose Delia Soza War Soldier, "'To Take Positive and Effective Action': Rupert Costo and the California Based American Indian Historical Society" (PhD diss., Arizona State University, 2013); and T. Robert Przeklasa, "Reservation Empire: The Mission Indian Federation and Native American Conservatism" (PhD diss., University of California, Riverside, 2015). The account of Julio Norte and Joe Pete's deliberation and decisions, along with a wealth of information on Indian affairs in the early twentieth century, can be found in House Committee on Indian Affairs, *Indians of the United States: Investigations of the Field Service, Hearings,* vol. 3, 66th Cong., 2nd Sess., 1920, 1117. On Joe Pete's history as a "trouble maker," see Christian McMillen, *Making Indian Law: The Hualapai Land Case and the Birth of Ethnohistory* (New Haven, CT: Yale University Press, 2007), 24. For newspaper coverage of the 1921 indictment against fifty-three members of the Mission Indian Federation on charges of "conspiracy to defraud the United States government . . . ," see "53 Indicted in Alleged Conspiracy of Indians," *Los Angeles Herald,* Sept. 23, 1921, A3. The federation's constitution was reproduced in *U.S. v. Albanes,* box 1A, folder "San Diego—A-2-M Exhibits 46–72"; and as part of the National Archives' exhibit, *Documented Rights.* Nicholas Peña's claim that the federation's goal was to take up the difficulties that the Indians had comes from *The Indian,* April 1922, 17. Adam Castillo's interpretation of California history comes from Adam Castillo, "The Story of the Indian Federation," NARA, BIA, RG 75, Mission Indian Agency / Central Classified Files, box 16, F(3) 091, 1.

The information on graduation and postgraduation options after Sherman comes from the United States House of Representatives,

"Indians of the United States: Investigation of the Field Service: Hearings by a Subcommittee of the Committee on Indian Affairs" (Washington, DC: GPO, 1920), 1075. Kevin Whalen's thoughtful description of the clear-eyed approach Native students took to outing work comes from his book, *Native Students at Work: American Indian Labor and Sherman Institute's Outing Program, 1900–1945* (Seattle: University of Washington Press, 2016), 155. See also Caitlin Keliiaa, "Unsettling Domesticity: Native Women Challenging U.S. Indian Policy in the San Francisco Bay Area, 1911–1931," University of California, Department of Ethnic Studies, Institute for the Study of Societal Issues, Graduate Fellows Working Paper Series, May 8, 2017, 1–49; Clifford E. Trafzer, *Fighting Invisible Enemies: Health and Medical Transitions among Southern California Indians* (Norman: University of Oklahoma Press, 2019); Trafzer, Keller, and Sisquoc, *Boarding School Blues;* and Matthew Sakiestewa Gilbert, *Education beyond the Mesas: Hopi Students at Sherman Institute, 1902–1929* (Lincoln: University of Nebraska Press, 2010).

Charles Kelsey's quote about Frederick and Beryl Bishop Collett's motives comes from Charles Wollenberg, *All Deliberate Speed: Segregation and Exclusion in California Schools, 1855–1975* (Berkeley: University of California Press, 1978), 92. For Stephen Knight's long quote about his daughter's attempt to attend Carrol District schools, see George Harwood Phillips, *The Enduring Struggle: Indians in California History* (San Francisco: Boyd and Fraser, 1981), 64. See also Nicole Blalock-Moore, *"Piper v. Big Pine School District of Inyo County:* Indigenous Schooling and Resistance in the Early Twentieth Century," *Southern California Quarterly* 94 (Fall 2012): 346–77.

Lupy Lugo's recollection of his conversation with Cato Sells comes from the extensive hearings before the Senate Subcommittee of the Committee on Indian Affairs, published as *Survey of the Conditions of the Indians, Hearings on S. Res. 79, part 2, 70th Congress, 2d Session* (Washington, DC: Government Printing Office, 1929), 743–44, 746.

Riverside

Riverside is a borderland, a place where peoples, cultures, and political powers meet. Tongvas (Gabrielino) to the west; Payómkawichum (Luiseño) to the southeast; Iviatim (Cahuilla) to the east; and Yuhaviatam (Serrano) to the north and northeast all occupied vertically organized territories, stretching from foothills and mountains down to the creeks and the Santa Ana River, where their territories met. Within these cultures, the variety of terrain allowed each to weave the region's resources into a resilient lifeway.

Despite the presence of a reliable water supply and an Indigenous population, both elements the Spanish looked for in selecting mission sites, the Spanish and Mexican government never built a mission within the Santa Ana River watershed. In 1776, Franciscans built San Juan Capistrano, just to the south, in Acjachemen (Juaneño) territory. Perhaps because of the absence of an actual mission, the settler cities situated alongside the river, Santa Ana and Riverside, appropriated the missions' imagery and iconography. None more so than Riverside.

In the early nineteenth century, Mexican officials quilted the region with ranchos, most devoted to raising cattle for their hide and tallow. Some of Mission San Gabriel's extensive ranch lands reached into the region. After secularization, Juan Bandini assumed the duties of administrator of the former Mission San Gabriel. In that capacity, he secured for himself the extensive Rancho Jurupa on the west side of the Santa Ana River, just south of the mountains that now bear that name. Other ranchers followed, and settlers from New Mexico and elsewhere established villages at Agua Mansa and La Placita, north of downtown. By the mid-nineteenth century, the region's ranches and farms interrupted the seasonal networks of indigenous economies. Settlers' livestock destroyed Indigenous food supplies and interfered with their hunting and gathering sites.

In 1862–63, smallpox hit the area hard, killing Chief Juan Antonio and many other Cahuilla living at Sahatapa, in San Timoteo Canyon, east of Riverside. Winter floods and summer drought destroyed much of the livestock industry and opened up large tracts of land suitable for irrigation. The decline of the mining industry across the state freed up the capital necessary for investment in such irrigation efforts. Initial attempts at agricultural settlement in Riverside failed, until 1873, when Eliza Tibbets planted Washington navel orange saplings. The climate and availability of water facilitated the agricultural colonization of the valley and led to a major citrus boom, which spread across the region. In short, citrus became Riverside's new religion, its orchards and processing facilities the new missions.

Attracted to the availability of work, Indigenous People moved to the city. Cahuillas settled at the Big Spring Rancheria near present-day Fairmont Park, just northeast of "Indian Hill Road," which now circles the hill in the foreground of the photograph (see fig. 23). Mount Rubidoux is in the background. Residents of Big Spring Rancheria, and other area settlements, worked picking and processing fruit, on infrastructure projects, and in light industry and domestic work. At the time of the city's incorporation in 1883, Indigenous People across the region were fighting to retain their land against settlers and increasingly relying on wage labor to assist in those efforts.

In Riverside, the bureaucratic hand of the federal government acted alongside the mythology of the region's past, the greed of its boosters, and the earnestness of its reformers. Founded in 1892, the Perris Indian School moved to Riverside in 1902 and became the Sherman Indian Institute. The relocation resulted from the confluence of labor, culture, nostalgia, and activism. Beginning in 1897, the superintendent of the school redirected outing work from Perris to Riverside to provide a cheap and abundant labor supply to citrus growers as a way to sow support for the school's move to Riverside. It succeeded. A. B. Miller's Fontana Farms Company used Sherman students' labor extensively, making it one of the largest integrated agricultural operations in the state. Hupa-Whilkut Edith Fogus remembered that "the students who stayed

FIGURE 23. Cahuilla Indian village, ca. 1880s, in Riverside at the Big Spring Rancheria near Mount Rubidoux, Santa Ana River, and Fairmont Park. Photo courtesy Huntington Library.

there [in the summer] worked for people around Riverside. There were a lot of ranchers growing oranges. There was nothing but orange groves around the place." The orange groves, and the Indian labor that made them possible, facilitated contact between Sherman students and their friends and relations at home. Cahuilla Robert Levi recalled meeting other Cahuilla students in the orange groves to sing Bird Songs and share food from relatives.

As a borderland, Riverside staged its imaginary past with astonishing success. The superintendent of Sherman worked with Frank Miller, owner of the Glenwood Mission Inn, to connect workers and growers, and with Charles Fletcher Lummis's historic preservation society, the Landmark's Club, to secure land and support for the construction of a new school. Built in the mission style, Sherman Indian Institute opened in 1903. Its architecture complemented that of Miller's newly renamed Glenwood Mission Inn.

Miller possessed a deep interest in history and, more important, he had an astute business sense. He recognized the commercial benefits of nostalgia and knew of the success of the Lake Mohonk Conference of the Friends of the Indian, which began in 1883. The Quaker twin brothers Alfred and Albert Smiley organized the annual meeting at a resort hotel they owned in upstate New York, but within a few years, they made Redlands in San Bernardino County their winter home for health purposes. Miller hoped to replicate that model locally.

In 1903 or 1904, Miller approached both Albert Smiley and Charles Fletcher Lummis about a series of annual Indian conferences at his Glenwood Mission Inn. Tellingly, Lummis saw the idea of the conference as supporting his efforts at historical preservation, not the Sequoya League, the organization he established in order "to make better Indians." In an undated letter from 1904, Lummis called the idea "a very good thing" to support the work of the Landmark's Club.

In April of 1908, approximately 150 people, luminaries from the nation's education, religious, and reform movements, as well as approximately fifty Indians from across the state, met for three days in Riverside. David Starr Jordan, president of Stanford and an avowed eugenicist, presided. Local dignitaries, activists, and Indian Office employees gave brief speeches. It is unclear what exactly the Indians who attended heard. Based on the program and the numerous local newspaper articles covering the event, it is clear the conference primarily aimed to build on Charles Kelsey's recent investigations to secure land for the landless Indians, many of whom lived in the northern part of the state.

Most curious, perhaps, the gathered Indians ended the first day's session with an address by New York Presbyterian minister George Spining. His talk, entitled "The Re-discovery of the Red Man," likely struck the Indians as simultaneously familiar and odd. In it, he recounted his work alongside Kelsey and his subsequent efforts to raise awareness nationwide of the conditions facing California Indians. While some Indians were likely pleased to see their demands more broadly disseminated, one wonders how they must have felt about being "rediscovered."

During the closing day of the conference, Miller changed the name of the inn yet again to capitalize on the conference, christening it the "Indian Mission Inn." Miller, an early proponent of the Mission Revival style, saw its potential to attract tourists and businesses. Miller established the San Gabriel Mission Play, which used the manufactured history of the state to craft a narrative of the inevitability of Anglo possession. Millions of people viewed the play. The image of the idyllic, orderly missions as a prelapsarian mythology became a core element in the state's marketing image. For instance, the Placentia Orchard Company, based out of Fullerton, called one of its orange varieties "Chapman's Old Mission Brand." The crate labels, plastered on the wooden boxes used to ship the fruit, featured a whitewashed mission set against an idyllic orange grove and three missionaries hovering over the no-doubt-delectable fruit.

A committee of Indian attendees at the 1908 conference composed of DJ Tortuga, Lupy Lugo, and H. Gulle heard something different than Miller intended. They prepared two resolutions thanking Miller for his hospitality, as well as for "naming his hotel the *Mission Indian Inn*" (emphasis added). This is a critical difference. Miller wanted the Indian Mission Inn to reflect its iconic mission architecture and to function as a reference to the moment in history when the Spanish had attempted to convert Indians. In fact, he soon dropped the word *Indian* from the name. But Southern California Indians understood it as referencing them—a living people, the Mission Indians. Lugo went on to argue for greater control by Mission Indians over reservations across the region, traveling to Washington, DC, and circulating petitions to garner support.

In 1920, the Bureau of Indian Affairs reestablished the consolidated Mission Indian Agency at Riverside. With Sherman, the Mission Inn, and the agency, the city became a cultural borderland where nostalgia and bureaucracy ran headlong into Indians themselves seeking to better their conditions. Students at Sherman worked throughout the region's houses and farms. The Mission Indian Federation held its first meeting in the Riverside home of Jonathan Tibbet that year. The city became the epicenter of the struggle between the federal government's Indian policy and Indians across the region.

In 1954, Cahuilla Rupert Costo, who attended Riverside City College between 1926 and 1928, emerged as an important advocate for the creation of the University of California, Riverside (UCR). He and his wife, Jeannette Henry Costo, devoted themselves to the cause of American Indian history. In 1986, they created the Costo Chair of American Indian Affairs and eventually donated their papers to establish the Rupert Costo Library of the American Indian at UCR. The library and the endowment that supports it have made the university a critical site in the story of California Indians. The California Center for Native Nations is an outgrowth of the Costos' influence at UCR. The Center supports interdisciplinary research and community programming on issues relevant to California Indians. Its various projects have included a collaborative effort with Sherman Indian High School, as the school has been known since 1971, and the Sherman Indian Museum to capture and preserve the story of boarding schools in American history, as well as symposia on contemporary Native art and culture.

SOURCES

On the Cahuilla, see John Lowell Bean, *Mukat's People: The Cahuilla Indians of Southern California* (Berkeley: University of California Press, 1974); John Lowell Bean and Katherine Siva Saubel, *Temalpakh: Cahuilla Indian Knowledge and Usage of Plants* (Banning, CA: Malki Press, 1972). On the Spanish arrival to the region, see Lisbeth Haas, *Conquests and Historical Identities in California, 1769–1936* (Berkeley: University of California Press, 1996). On the Smiley brothers, see Clyde A. Milner II, "Albert K. Smiley: Friend to Friends of the Indians," in *Churchmen and the Western Indians, 1820–1920,* edited by Clyde A. Milner II and Floyd A. O'Neil (Norman: University of Oklahoma Press, 1985), 143–75. Details on the planning for the 1908 meeting come from the Charles Fletcher Lummis Manuscript Collection, held by the Southwest Museum in Los Angeles. See particularly Frank Miller to Lummis, Feb. 4, 1901; and Lummis to Miller, n.d. [1904], both in Charles Fletcher Lummis Manuscript Collection, Correspondence series, ms.1.1.3089A. For Lupy Lugo's activities, see Tanis Thorne, "The Death of Superintendent Stanley and the Cahuilla Uprising of 1907–1912," *Journal of California and Great Basin Anthropology* 24, no 2. (2004): 233–58. On the relationship of Riverside, Sherman, and its students, see Clifford E. Trafzer, Matthew Sakiestewa Gilbert, and Lorene Sisquoc, eds., *The Indian School on Magnolia Avenue: Voices and Images from Sherman Institute* (Corvallis: Oregon State University Press, 2012). On the Mission Indian Federation, see sources in chapter 7.

8

Becoming the Indians of California

Reorganization and Justice, 1928–1954

In May of 1928, Congress passed an enabling act to allow the "Indians of California" to sue the federal government for the land lost because of the eighteen unratified treaties signed in 1851 and 1852. To limit the scope of the action and consolidate lawsuits, the act provided the first legal definition of the Indians of California: "all Indians who were residing in the State of California on June 1, 1852, and their descendants now living in said state." Lawmakers hoped this would prevent a flood of lawsuits parcel by parcel, rancheria by rancheria, village by village, tribe by tribe. The act authorized the lawsuit, which became known as the California Indian Claims Case, often referred to by its docket number: K-344. The case wound its way through the courts until a 1944 decision.

There have always been Indians in California, and despite their distinctiveness, the conditions they faced often shared important characteristics. But the idea of a category, much less a *legal* category encompassing all of the state's far-flung and various Indigenous Peoples, was a new and contested notion. The "Indians of California" resulted from decades of activism and various networks of education and mutual support in response to attacks on their existence and livelihood in the late nineteenth and early twentieth centuries. The Indians of California increasingly pressed their collective issues through the courts, laws, at state fairs, and the state capital, and in defense of the land itself. The category did not subsume individual, village, rancheria, reservation, or tribal identities. Instead, the name provided yet another aggregate conceptual category to organize and strengthen local activism.

In the middle of the twentieth century, the various people that the federal government subsumed under the moniker "Indians of California" responded to and shaped the ebbs and flows of federal Indian policy. Across the state, officials clamored to dam rivers and flood reservation lands in the name of urban development. During the Great Depression, the federal government initiated what it considered a new phase of federal Indian policy—the Indian Reorganization Act. The government promised the new act ensured the independence of California Indians and other Indigenous People in North America. In Southern California, Indigenous People questioned those beliefs. Finally, in the 1950s, policies swung back toward those of the 1920s, attempting to absorb Indigenous lands and sovereignty through the ominously titled "termination" policies. Throughout the era, California Indians charted their own path to secure land and sovereignty.

Indigenous People were bound up in California's image of itself, which was one of the state's most valuable export commodities in the 1920s and 1930s. The region's Mediterranean climate, landscape, and architecture, as well as its increasing prominence in the global economy, contributed to the production of the "Spanish fantasy past." Business, culture, and political leaders highlighted California's imaginary Spanish past to promote their vision of nostalgia for a vaguely European heritage and the tourism it supported. That story also helped to erase the diverse present by relocating people of color to the past. The gauzy stories of happy and orderly early California featured prominently at international expositions held around the region. These expositions announced California's promising future, yoked to an imaginary past. The Panama-Pacific International Exposition of 1915 in San Francisco and the Panama-California Exposition of 1915–16 in San Diego celebrated California's growth, especially because of the increased maritime trade brought about by the completion of the Panama Canal in 1914. Both expositions presented to the world a highly idealized version of California as paradise, with its Indians an important part of that *past*, not the present. Later expositions and fairs, such as the Long Beach Pacific Southwest Exposition of 1928 and San Diego's California-Pacific International Exposition of 1935–36, continued this theme.

Indians from around the state and region found work at the fairs and expositions, building the Painted Desert exhibit in San Diego in 1914–

15 and performing as "show Indians" in the pageants recounting California's history. They also produced items for display and sale. In the 1910s and 1920s, the market for California Indian baskets changed. As the collector's craze for baskets declined, Wiyot-Hupa Louise Hickox and Washoe Lena Dick led the way to finding retail outlets to sell their baskets and to promote their work at fairs and expositions. Hickox learned weaving from her mother, Elizabeth, and her grandmother, Polly Conrad Steve, who survived the notorious Indian Island massacre in 1860, when she was twelve years old.

Pomo-Patwin Mabel McKay appeared at the California State Fair and at various times at the California State Indian Museum, where she displayed her exquisite work. At the state fair in 1929, fair officials forced her to wear a skimpy beaded and fringed buckskin dress. After McKay reluctantly put it on, she asked wryly, "Do I look like an Indian yet?" In 1934, she appeared in the *Sacramento Union*, again dressed in a stereotypical Indian costume that bore no resemblance to Pomo culture. McKay displayed some of her well-known laconic wit when asked, what, besides basket weaving, the Pomos do. "Just live," she answered.

In McKay's case, tensions between "traditional" and "market" considerations revealed themselves. McKay was a Dreamer and a sucking doctor in the Bole Maru religion. Her great uncle, Richard Taylor, led the revivalist religious movement that became Bole Maru in the nineteenth century. While McKay grew up around very accomplished basket makers, including her aunt Laura Somersal, she learned weaving in her dreams. Baskets served a critical function in her healing practice, and McKay steadfastly refused to sell those baskets. At the same time, she often took commissions at demonstrations such as the 1929 State Fair.

Indians saw attending the fair *as work*—perhaps unsavory at times but work that had value. Margaret Harrie, a Karuk basket maker, single mother, and *pikváhaan* (storyteller), wrote to Grace Nicholson:

> I send you this little red basket just for [a] present. . . . My little girl made it. . . . I sell my baskets to you very cheap. [T]hat black basket cost very high [b]ut I send it to you very cheap [b]ecause I think you are my friend. . . . We do not get our straw to fix the basket with up here. We get our straw down the Klamath River they do not grow up here so we have a hard work in getting them I have a hard living Because I have childrens to take care of all by myself. P.S. I forgot to tell you that my baskets were all $28.75 worth.

Harrie established a trade relationship with Nicholson for very practical economic reasons and pointed out the importance of site-specific harvesting. She pursued a similar strategy later when the anthropologists began to show interest. Around 1930, Harrie worked with Hans Uldall, a Danish linguist, reciting the story of "Coyote and Old Woman Bullhead." Whether it was baskets or stories, Harrie recognized the value of her culture, to herself and to others.

California Indian baskets are ecologically sensitive and site specific. While weavers have adapted new plants and forbs into their baskets, the sedge, redbud, willow, and other materials that formed the core of the craft were susceptible to environmental change. Urbanization pushed increasingly complex water projects farther into the state's interior. California's map is dotted with sites where urban, industrial, or agricultural demand for water came at the expense of Indian communities: Hetch Hetchy Valley was flooded to provide water to the city of San Francisco; Owens Lake was drained to provide water to the city of Los Angeles; Capitan Grande was flooded to enable the city of San Diego to grow.

California Indians sat at the center of some of the most well-known histories of water disputes in the state, but they are commonly sidelined in the narratives constructed about them. For example, long a staple case study in environmental history, the story of the flooding of the Hetch Hetchy Valley is often depicted as a victory of conservationists over preservationists and an important step in the beginning of the modern environmental movement. The valley, however, was also Miwok land. Both the Ahwahnechee and the Tuolumne Bands of Sierra Miwok claimed the valley in summer and fall. John Muir praised the valley's "natural" beauty, calling it an "acorn orchard." Orchards are not natural, and neither was the valley's landscape, which Ahwahnechee and Tuolumne managed through controlled burns to increase seed output and fern growth. In addition to increasing the deer population, regular burning also reduced underbrush and contributed to the growth of the black oak trees, whose acorns formed a critical component of the Miwok diet.

The actors in the story, as it is normally told, are San Francisco city officials, the secretary of the interior, President Theodore Roosevelt, and John Muir. They all wrestled for control of the valley throughout the first two decades of the twentieth century. Some saw in it a solution to the city's growing water problem, while others saw it as a place of great natural beauty deserving protection. That distinction pitted a reflective, aesthetic use of the valley for leisure against the "daily comfort and welfare of 99 percent." The Miwok absence in the story highlights a central tenet of the environmental movement in California—namely, that preservation often, if not always, involved removing Indians from their land or severely reducing their ability to use it. In 1919,

FIGURE 24. View of the dry lake bed of Owens Lake, looking north, with cracked pink clay due to high amounts of halophilic archaebacteria. Photo by Vahe Martirosyan, April 2019. Licensed under Creative Commons Attribution-ShareAlike 2.0 (CC BY-SA 2.0).

construction of the dam began, and within a few years, waters submerged the vast "acorn orchard."

One of the most dramatic examples of urban infrastructure intervening in the Indigenous landscapes occurred in the Owens Valley in the eastern part of the state. Owens Lake lives on as a vestigial legacy on digital street maps, but it has long since disappeared. The lake dried up in 1926 (see fig. 24). The Owens River flows south through the slender valley, fed from the Sierra Nevada on its west and the White Mountains and Inyo Mountains on the east. Owens Valley Paiutes built a comprehensive irrigation system with lateral aqueducts running off of the east-west flowing creeks to grow seed grasses and edible tubers. As a result, before American settlement, the valley supported a Paiute population of between one thousand and two thousand people.

Beginning in the mid-nineteenth century, American settlers, attracted by the valley's suitability for ranching, encroached on Paiute settlements. In a familiar pattern, settler cattle destroyed grasses and tubers, and ranchers increasingly appropriated the water, without which the valley floor would become a semiarid dustscape. In 1862, tensions exploded into violence when settlers pushed Paiutes to the north end of the valley. Owens Valley Paiutes and Shoshone Bands from the east united under the leadership of Joaquin Jim and pushed the settlers back, reclaiming the valley for a brief time in the spring. By summer, the US Army moved in to starve the Paiutes out. They destroyed grain stores and ditches and forced the Paiutes into the mountains. Fighting continued through a peace treaty, eventually leading to the forced removal of almost one thousand Paiutes from the valley to the Sebastian Indian Reserve near Fort Tejon.

Ultimately, the war cost the lives of more than two hundred Paiutes and around thirty American settlers. The army remained in the valley for more than a decade to defend settler possession. By the beginning of the twentieth century, Paiutes made up around 20 percent of the local population but a majority of the labor force in the valley's ranching economy. Ranchers depended on Paiute labor and mountain water and therefore resisted efforts to remove Paiutes to reservations farther south or to give them a solid legal claim to control their own resources.

All of this changed when the city of Los Angeles came to the valley. Beginning in 1905, the city, desperate for additional sources of water to accommodate its rapidly growing needs, began to surreptitiously purchase land in the valley to get control of the water rights attached to it. Within a few years, the LA Department of Water and Power (LADWP) began to construct an aqueduct to carry the river water more than two hundred miles south to the growing city. By 1913, the city had fully diverted the river into the aqueduct. As much as settler society dispossessed the Paiute residents of the valley, the LADWP effectively dispossessed the dispossessors, who themselves depended on Paiute labor. By the mid-1920s, resistance by valley residents again turned violent, and they dynamited the aqueduct on several occasions. Nonetheless, by 1926, the lake dried up, leaving a toxic salt flat and layers of animosity and anger. The story, often told as a fight between small farmers and ranchers and the city of Los Angeles, took place on Paiute land and reinscribed the colonial process as it erased the wage labor that enabled Owens Valley Paiutes to retain a tenuous grip on their homeland.

Beginning in 1925, Paiutes who received individual allotments, and were able to sell their land, recognized the value of their water rights as Los Angeles attempted to increase the volume of water it took from the valley. But rather than selling their land and water rights individually, Paiutes banded together and proposed a land exchange. They proposed giving up allotted individual plots of land in return for community tracts. At first, the city of Los Angeles resisted the proposal and attempted to pressure individual owners into selling. Paiutes persisted, and as a result, Los Angeles officials abandoned the plan.

By 1932, the city agreed to the land exchange, and in 1937, Owens Valley Paiutes traded Los Angeles previously allotted land for the land that became the Bishop, Big Pine, and Lone Pine Reservations, allowing Paiutes to retain tribal land in the valley. The land exchange did not include water rights, which Paiutes retained to be negotiated later when the city of Los Angeles secured necessary approval. In the interim, Los Angeles promised to deliver water to the Paiutes. That has yet to happen. As of August of 2020, the Owens Valley Indian Water Commission is still fighting for the rights guaranteed by the 1937 legislation.

A map of reservoirs in California follows the contours of Indigenous land. Nowhere is this clearer than in San Diego County. In 1919, Congress authorized the construction of a dam on the San Diego River through an agreement with the city of San Diego and the BIA. The dam was designed to create a reservoir to store water for the city's growing needs. The Capitan Grande Indian community opposed the dam. Their resistance prolonged but did not prevent the construction, which began in 1931. Members of the Capitan Grande community split into three groups over their forced removal: approximately 35 percent of the 153 members of the community moved in early 1932 to newly constructed, architect-designed "model" cement block houses with indoor plumbing at Barona. Approximately 15 percent of the community, the *shaahook* (or "ten"), took their per capita shares in cash and left the reservation. The remaining 50 percent held out, refusing to move or allow officials to relocate their graveyard unless the BIA purchased a nearby ranch for their relocation. With the dam completed in October of 1934, the BIA relented and purchased the land that became the Viejas Reservation. Bureaucratic delays hampered their move. Ventura Paipa complained, "Here it is 1936, winter is upon us, and through unnecessary delay and lack of attention to our planning by the Bureau, we are facing a chance for a POOR CROP next year [with families] still living in barns with little or no protection from the winter snows sure to come." By 1938, water filled the El Capitan Reservoir, and the former residents of the lake bed relocated to new reservations. Residents at Barona and Viejas successfully pushed to retain control over the portion of their former reservation that remains above water as a nature preserve.

This pattern of flooding Indian lands for the "greater good" of non-Indian peoples repeated itself across California time and time again. Between 1923 and 1961, major dams built on the Colorado, Feather,

Merced, Sacramento, San Joaquin, Stanislaus, Trinity, and Tuolumne Rivers flooded lands of the Chemehuevi, Hupa, Maidu, Miwok, Paiute, Wintun, Yokuts, and Yuroks, among others. The state left few rivers untouched. Forty of the fifty largest lakes in the state are man-made reservoirs, and every one of them flooded Indigenous land. A hydrological map of the state is a map of Indian dispossession. In the 1950s, the Bradbury Dam on the Santa Ynez River created Lake Cachuma. In her poem "Indian Cartography," Ohlone-Costanoan-Esselen poet Deborah Miranda describes the dam's effects:

> A small blue spot marks
> Lake Cachuma, created when they
> dammed the Santa Ynez, flooded
> a valley, divided
> my father's boyhood: days
> he learned to swim the hard way,
> and days he walked across the silver scales,
> swollen bellies of salmon coming back
> to a river that wasn't there.
> *The government paid those Indians to move away,*
> he says; *I don't know where they went.*

Most poignantly, Miranda points to the land under the surface of the water, "not drawn on any map." A map of California highlighting reservoirs *is* a map outlining theft and erasure of Indian land.

John Collier and the work of the Indian New Deal offered a similar example of heavy-handed, overzealous, and conflicted interest in Indian affairs that Indians could, to varying degrees, manipulate to their advantage. Collier, a staunch critic of the federal government, began his involvement in Indian affairs with the Pueblos and their fight for religious freedom and land in the early 1920s. His work propelled him to join the American Indian Defense Association, which made him a full-time critic of the Indian Office, and he increasingly included California Indian issues in those critiques. In the late 1920s, he spearheaded investigations into corruption within the Indian Office. In 1933, Franklin D. Roosevelt tapped Collier to become commissioner of Indian affairs.

Collier imagined vibrant Indian communities as antidotes to the problems of modern life. That is, he saw Indian communities *as he imagined them* as valuable to non-Indians. As such, Collier believed someone needed to protect Indian communities. He proposed the Indian New Deal for that purpose. It consisted of two parts. First, Collier ensured that American Indians gained access to public works jobs, principally through the Indian Division of the Civilian Conservation Corp. On reservations throughout the American West, American Indians built much-needed infrastructure: roads, trails, dams, fences, and telephone lines. On the Round Valley Reservation, Concows Claude Hoaglin and Francis Crabtree built a footbridge across the Eel River so that their families could cross over to a railroad depot during the winter. Public works jobs also existed on the Hoopa Valley Reservation and the Mission Indian Agency. Yet government work still bowed to the pressure of agricultural interests in the state. California ranchers and farmers insisted that public work not conflict with agricultural work, so public work was often unavailable in late summer and early fall, when farmers needed California Indians to harvest crops.

Second, Collier sponsored a grandiose bill to enable economic development and political reorganization in Indian Country. Also known as the Wheeler-Howard Act, the Indian Reorganization Act (IRA) promised a new day for American Indians. Collier traveled the country advocating for the legislation while Congress debated the bill. He hosted several conferences in the American West, where Native People could learn about the bill and possibly offer suggestions. Many Indians welcomed the support that attention brought to their communities and welcomed Collier's plan to end allotment of Indian land, but they chafed at the one-dimensionality and heavy-handed nature of his vision, as well as the forceful ways in which consideration of the bill dismissed tribal communities' say in the process.

California Indians attended two of the congresses: one at the Chemawa Indian School in Salem, Oregon, and another at the Sherman Indian Institute in Riverside. California Indians reacted to the Wheeler-Howard Bill in diverse ways, determined in part by the fact that tribal land buffeted Indians from the effects of the economic depression by providing a temporary escape from the wage labor economy. In general, California Indians in the north supported the IRA because their land was more loosely held and often in broken, small plots, and the organizational aspects of the IRA furthered their goals of securing land. In the southern part of the state, where larger reservations were more common, communities more likely opposed Wheeler-Howard because they perceived it as isolating them from the rest of the state. Thus, the California Indian Brotherhood (CIB) largely supported the legislation, but the Mission Indian Federation (MIF) opposed it, calling it segregationist and communistic.

Pomo Stephen Knight, speaking at the Chemawa conference, claimed:

> The Sacramento [Agency] Indians are unanimously in support of this proposed bill. . . . I have always been independent and free and will always want to be that way. We find large reservations that are like a checker-board where the white man have gotten possession of the largest part of the reservation. Some reservations are composed mostly of inherited land; if this [reservation allotment] policy should continue for the next two or three generations, most of the Indians will be out on the road. . . . I found white men in possession of the cream of the land, while the Indians had rock piles, etc. Do [we] want to continue that policy? I, myself, say no. . . . I know of the fight that the Commissioner of Indian Affairs has put up on behalf of the Indians. I have enough faith and confidence in that man that I would support any proposal he might put up for the welfare of the Indians of America.

And at the Sherman meeting, Cahuilla Rupert Costo said the money available was insufficient to buy land: "That is quite communistic isn't it? Communism, socialism. Going right back to that, taking away all the rights belonging to everyone. Can't own anything for ourselves. Isn't that right?" He also questioned the purported independence the bill offered: "After delving into it I find we will always be under the Department of the Interior and the Commissioner. Self-government, but you will always be under the Commissioner and Department of Interior. Sounds good, but it is so good it takes away my personal rights, sends me back to [the] reservation, keeps our children out of public school. I do not want to do that, I want to be as other people."

Leon Palawash, of the Pauma Reservation, pointed to the unsettled compensation case over the unratified treaties as a reason to oppose hasty approval of the IRA: "I am speaking for the Indians of the State of California. . . . We will not endorse the Wheeler-Howard Bill. We have a committee in Washington who are now introducing all claims of Indians of the State of California for just settlement. Therefore, you gentlemen may return to Washington and expedite the just settlement to the Indians of the State of California of claims in Washington." Vivian Banks, from Pala, echoed his sentiments: "My people are opposed to this bill. They do not think it is fair. No other bill should be brought before them until the Court of Claims bill is settled if it takes 100 years to settle it."

Often, support was ambivalent. Ramón Ames, captain of the Barona community at Capitan Grande, claimed, "I am not well educated. . . . I have not been to college. . . . But I have had experience among my white brothers. I have listened to what they have said. The bill [IRA] is pretty good in some places, but I cannot say whether it is good or not. I would like to take more time to study it. I could not favor this bill just now."

In June of 1934, Congress passed a watered-down version of the bill. The IRA ended allotment, outlined the process for restoring some lost tribal land, and made revolving credit at low interest rates available to acquire new land to be put into trust. It also established a process for drafting tribal constitutions and creating tribal governments. The new tribal governments combined corporate charters and village democracies. They were often an alien and poor fit for existing structures of tribal power, especially on larger reservations that lacked the unity of a small village. Indian peoples could avail themselves of the act's provisions by holding referenda to form tribal governments and corporate entities under new tribal constitutions. But the IRA would not take effect if a majority of the "adult Indians" on a reservation voted against its application. Efforts to influence the vote included having opponents arrested, rendering them unable to participate in the referenda, and, more commonly, counting those who *did not vote* as voting *in favor* of the legislation, a policy that went against the basic practices of both Indian decision making and American democracy. Across the nation, around 70 percent of tribes approved the IRA.

The act layered new divisions over fractured communities and sharpened many that already existed. Forty-four California Indian rancherias or reservations voted to accept the IRA, while forty-five voted to reject it. Three reservations cast no votes, which, according to the regulations governing the referendum, meant a total of forty-seven accepted the IRA. Organization was slow. By 1947, only thirteen of those forty-seven produced tribal constitutions approved by the secretary of the interior.

The Tule River Indian Tribe is a good example of this process. In 1856, the United States established the Tule River Reservation. Various bands of Yokuts lived there on unallotted lands. In November of 1934, approximately half of the eligible voters did not participate in the referendum on the Indian Reorganization Act. Of the other half, fifty voted yes, and two voted no, so the referendum passed. In an administrative sense, the IRA subsumed the Yokuts' Band identities into the new Tule River Indian Tribe, led by a nine-person Tribal Council. The new tribal government offered benefits to the tribe in terms of protecting tribal land, but it also imposed majority rule rather than consensus decision making and increased the powers of the tribal government over reservation residents. Tribal leaders limited membership in the tribe to those born to parents whose names appeared on the official census roll used to establish eligibility for the referendum and who lived on the reservation. These policies concerning ancestry and place of living excluded many Yokuts who lived off the reservation. In the end, by focusing or concentrating power within the reservation, the IRA helped preserve Tule River land by ending the potential threat of allotment and making money available for development projects. Development came at a cost to traditional patterns of identity and decision making, at Tule River and across the state.

While California Indians debated the IRA's merits and limits, the United States entered a world war, which fundamentally altered California. Shipyards in Los Angeles and Richmond, and airplane factories across the southland, built the war-making machine. Millions of people moved from across the state and nation to work in the war industries. Numerous California military bases and camps funneled millions of soldiers, sailors, and other support staff through the state. The military presence in Oakland, San Diego, and Los Angeles expanded significantly alongside overall wartime urban growth. Indians from across the nation were in the middle of all of these changes. They were factory workers, migrants, soldiers, sailors, and nurses. Born in 1941 and raised in the Acoma Pueblo village of Deetzeyaamah in present-day New Mexico, Simon Ortiz, barely old enough to recollect the Second World War, remembered the soldiers he waved to as they left the village for California. He especially recalled the stories they brought back home with them when the war ended. Ortiz recalled that California played a major role in the minds of many fighting in Europe and the Pacific: "Young men and women went to California for US military training, usually Fort Ord and Camp Pendleton, and then they were shipped out from California seaports in San Diego or Oakland." Among returning military service people, stories of California were entangled with those of the Pacific theater. All the stories "seemed to feature California prominently because it was a place you went to on the way to a destination, or it was the destination itself."

For California Indians, as for all who served, the war changed their lives. Mountain Maidu-Pit River-Washo-Modoc Leonard Lowry, from the Susanville Indian Rancheria, described himself as "just a rookie trying to look like a soldier" when he arrived at Fort Ord in 1941. He served in the Thirty-Sixth Infantry Division throughout the Pacific. When the war ended, he had earned the rank of colonel, as well as two Silver Stars, five Purple Hearts, a Legion of Merit, and a World War II Victory Medal. He went on to earn a Distinguished Service Cross, making him one of the most decorated Indians in US history. He shared many of his stories with his daughter, painter Judith Lowry. In 1976, he founded the Lassen County American Indian Organization.

Many California Indians served the war effort at home. At the beginning of the war, the Sherman Institute initiated an expedited welding program to train workers for the defense industry. Karuk-Shasta Josie Valadez from Susanville was a senior in high school at Sherman when the war started. She joined the welding class and, after passing her test, welded aircraft parts for Solar Aircraft in San Diego. Hupa-Whilkut Edith Fogus also took the welding class her senior year and moved to San Diego for work. She shared an apartment with Yurok Georgiana Trull, who had returned to Sherman six years after graduation for the welding training. She described it as "something exciting to do, and I wanted to be a patriot." Both welded at Solar on the swing shift, from 4 p.m. to 11 p.m. Fogus described the work as monotonous: "You might drop asleep because everything was the same every time. You did the same thing over and over again." But she and Trull enjoyed their time in the city. Trull recalled that "San Diego was a lot of fun. We worked hard, but we had good times."

All of David and Geneva Risling's eight children served in the war effort. Vivian, Roselyn, and Viola welded and built dry docks in Humboldt Bay. Anthony Risling worked in the Bay Area in a war-related industry. Jack, David Jr., Baron, and Leslie all served in combat. Baron was a pilot who died in a test crash. Leslie enlisted in the army and fought in the Battle of the Bulge. Jack was drafted but joined the navy. He recalled, "When they drafted us, [we] were all 'white' on the paper. We were Indian again after the war. After the war I found out we weren't supposed to even carry weapons! But we were Indian again after we got out." Throughout the war, he and David, who also joined the navy, crossed paths: in New York City, Hawaii, and on Iwo Jima, where both participated in the Battle of Iwo Jima. Jack recalled that visiting his brother "meant quite a bit":

> Dave was a captain and his ship was nearby ours at Iwo Jima. At first with all the shooting and such we couldn't visit, but after it was kind of secured we would visit with each other on weekends. He would always come visit me and have meals. I didn't have to go to the officer's quarters.
>
> We used to argue ever since we were kids, and we were arguing once on the ship and it was getting late at night. Somebody hollered from the next bunk, "Pull your rank on that guy!" Dave said, "I can't, he's my older brother!"

David Risling Jr. went on to leverage his experience in the war to further his activism on behalf of Indian education and rights. Many of the congressmen he worked with were veterans as well. He recalled, "I would start with someone I knew and we'd talk about the war and our kids. Then they'd say to call if I ever needed them. It was the same with people here in the state. Most were service people." David went on to become a powerful advocate for Native education.

The war also opened a new round of political organizing. In 1942, California Indians won a symbolic but nearly empty victory in the courts. The court of claims ruled in favor of the Indians of California in the lawsuit they brought in 1928 to recover the value of land lost because of unratified treaties. The judgment was issued two years later, compensating the Indians of California $17,053,942. But the government deducted "offsets" of $12,029,100 for the expenses associated with administering California Indian affairs, leaving $5,024,842.

In 1946, some veterans of the IBC and CIB, along with some who were new to activism, formed the Federated Indians of California (FIC). Among those involved in the founding were Central Sierra Miwok William Fuller, Pomo Ethan Anderson, Central Sierra Miwok John Porter, Nisenan Maidu Martha Lemay, Pomo Stephen Knight, Tolowa Bertha Stewart of the Del Norte Indian Welfare Association (DIWA), and Pomo Arthur Treppa. Fuller and Stewart led the organization. They sought per capita distribution of the $5 million judgment from the 1928 case, but more critically, they wanted to pursue a lawsuit in the newly formed Indian Claims Commission involving the land taken from California Indians not covered by the treaties. In 1946, California Indians launched this lawsuit, which eventually encompassed more than twenty different petitions.

Challenges to Indian identity gave those who opposed the lawsuits a way to resist or delay. One example was congressional pressure for a new census of California Indians before allowing the lawsuit to go forward. Testifying in 1947, Bertha Stewart, who served as secretary for the FIC, pushed back. She urged Congress to distribute per capita payments using the roll already created for the 1928 case. Stewart argued the Indians had already paid for a roll through the federal government's administration fee deducted in the 1944 settlement. The case reached a compromise settlement. The 1963 settlement awarded $29 million for 64,425,000 acres of land, or forty-five cents per acre. In 1972, based on new rolls, more than sixty-nine thousand Indians received payments of slightly less than $700 each. It was another victory that failed to honor the extent of the loss Indians had faced.

The networks built by Indian activists to inform and advocate for the case and California Indian issues in general emerged as far more important than the settlement itself. Mountain Maidu Kitty Flores, an elected publicity agent for the FIC, arranged a meeting with California governor

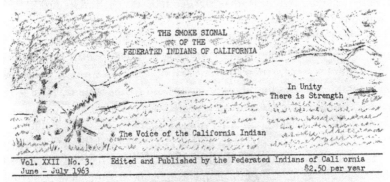

THE SMOKE SIGNAL
OF THE
FEDERATED INDIANS OF CALIFORNIA

In Unity
There is Strength

The Voice of the California Indian

Vol. XXII No. 3.	Edited and Published by the Federated Indians of California	
June - July 1963		$2.50 per year

U. S. GOVERNMENT GUARDIAN OF INDIANS

Indian people were not subject to carrying on demonstrations demanding so called rights yet they had every reason to.
They did put up a fight when all their buffalo were killed, their food storages burned and their lands taken from them.
The settlers did not consider the Indians as human beings. They were treated like wild beasts and were called savages. When the Indians won a battle it was called a massacre but when the so called civilized race won, it was a battle.
Today the Indian is still on the loosing end.
As guardian, how is Uncle Sam guarding the interest of the Indian nieces and nephews?
Treaties made with Indians are no longer respected. Promises are ignored. Recent land settlements made with other Indians have been a "give away".
Is California lands to be another "give Away"?
The Indians of California are not resorting to a demonstration to get a "just settlement". They are hopeful that the Claims Commission and the Attorney General of the United States will be liberal in settling with the Indians of California.

FIGURE 25. The front page of Marie Potts's *Smoke Signal of the Federated Indians of California*, June-July 1963. Photo courtesy Terri Castaneda.

Earl Warren at Sutter's Fort in Sacramento during the state's centennial celebration of the discovery of gold. Aware of the importance of media coverage of the event, she billed it as a "peace pipe ceremonial" and encouraged FIC members to wear tribal regalia, playing to non-Indian stereotypes to raise visibility. Warren spoke out publicly in favor of Indian justice in the courts, and Flores capitalized on that news. In the conformist, anticommunist postwar years focused on economic prosperity, many in the FIC saw success in presenting a "safe" activist image.

A fatal traffic accident cut short Flores's activism. Her mother, Mountain Maidu Marie Mason Potts, assumed the responsibilities as publicity agent. A graduate of Carlisle Indian Industrial School in Pennsylvania, Potts single-handedly produced the FIC newspaper *Smoke Signal*, which was mailed across the country and eventually internationally to soldiers serving abroad (see fig. 25). While its distribution was widespread across the country, the fact that approximately half of the recipients on the mailing list lived in rural areas without numerical addresses stands as a measure of the depth of its penetration into Indian communities.

Wartime service politicized other California Indians. Max Mazzetti was born in Los Angeles to a Luiseño mother and Italian father in 1922. At the age of six, Mazzetti moved to the Rincon Reservation. He attended Sherman, then joined the navy and fought during the Second World War. Like many veterans, Mazzetti returned from the war to find his options proscribed by federal policies. Upset with federal Indian policy, he became active in tribal politics and served as tribal chairman from 1947 to 1960. In line with many critics of Indian policy, Mazzetti bemoaned the intractable problems of incomplete and contradictory surveys, water and mineral rights, and liens on Indian land. As a recipient of the newer allotments on the Rincon Reservation, which cut against the larger but unapproved allotments based on surveys done in the late nineteenth century, he found himself in opposition to the Mission Indian Federation.

Beginning in the 1950s, there was growing demand for rights nationwide, and California played an important role in that effort. Advocates of school desegregation won their first major legal victory in *Mendez v. Westminster* (1947), and two major court decisions upholding Japanese internment during the war helped set the stage for demands for changes afterward. The National Congress of American Indians (NCAI), founded in 1944, quickly emerged as the most important and powerful national Indian organization. The NCAI sought to help the general public better understand, as they said, "the Indian race," preserve tribal culture, promote the common welfare of Indians, and defend treaty rights. In that capacity, the NCAI often criticized the BIA. In the late 1940s and 1950s, American Indians across the country looked to the NCAI for support as they faced dramatic changes in federal Indian policy.

In another important way, California's unique circumstances contributed to these developments in Indian policy. In 1950, President Harry Truman appointed Dillon Myer commissioner of Indian affairs. Myer had served as director of the War Relocation Authority from 1942 until it was dissolved in the summer of 1946. In that capacity, he oversaw the controversial process of relocating Japanese Americans from temporary holding facilities along the Pacific coast to more permanent internment camps in the interior of the country. A number of these camps were in California Indian territory, such as Manzanar, in Paiute territory in the Owens Valley, Tule Lake in Modoc lands in the far northeast of the state, and Poston on the Colorado River Reservation. Reservation residents were skeptical but open to what the camps could

FIGURE 26. Mrs. Ruby Snyder, Chemehuevi Indian,
Poston, Arizona. Created by Clem Albers. Photo courtesy
Bancroft Library, University of California, Berkeley.

mean for them. At Poston, the War Relocation Authority planned large-scale irrigation works to support the agriculture necessary to produce food for the detainees. The Mojave and Chemehuevi welcomed the development. Chemehuevi Ruby Snyder said, "I hear that the Japanese are wonderful farmers. I would like to go down to see how they grow things" (fig. 26).

Myer was motivated to move Japanese American internees out of the camps to assimilate them into American society. Under his direction, the WRA contracted to provide agricultural workers, sent some internees to eastern colleges, sent others to the armed forces, and resettled many to cities away from the coast. By 1946, through the use of informants and loyalty oaths, Myer and the WRA forcibly relocated fifty thousand Japanese and Japanese Americans. Myer also oversaw the closure of the camps themselves at the end of the war.

Myer's tenure at the WRA provided a blueprint for his approach to the BIA and aligned with the postwar moment of cultural conformity. He saw the Indian Reorganization Act as a "glass case policy," which preserved Indians as "museum pieces for future generations to enjoy." He saw the basic paradox in the federal trust relationship, that the obligation to protect tribal property came at the expense of Indian personal freedom. Myer sought to ensure the latter through the abandonment of the former. It was an optimistic and naive plan.

Myer claimed the guiding principle of the BIA under his leadership was "self-determination for Indians." He promised to "lead the Indian people in the mass out of the shadow of Federal paternalism into the sunlight of full independence." Such language struck a chord with the NCAI and many Indians in California. Earlier that year, the MIF sent a small contingency to Washington, DC, to demand an end to Indian "serfdom" and "slavery" under the BIA. In November of 1950, Myer and other BIA officials attended a meeting at Los Coyotes Reservation with more than four hundred Indians representing twenty-two reservations across California. There, he urged termination of Indian tribes as quickly as was feasible.

In April of 1952, Myer drafted termination legislation for 115 rancherias in California. The bill met with stiff opposition from the NCAI and other groups, which argued the legislation gave too much power to the secretary of the interior and set a bad precedent for future efforts. Steve Ponchetti of Santa Ysabel argued that "our reservations are very poor. We are asking [for] time to get ourselves prepared before we lose the protection of the Indian Bureau." Juanita Ortega of Pala worried that the legislation would mean seeing "our young people on the roadside of this state as paupers." Cahuilla Cruz Siva wrote to President Truman that if termination went forward, the "Indians of California would be turned out, stock and barrel on impoverished land . . . and they would not only be expected to make a living on it . . . but would be bound by law to make enough money from it to pay taxes."

Even after Myer lost the confidence of major American Indian rights organizations and the new Eisenhower administration removed him from office, termination legislation went forward. Despite widespread Indian opposition, support grew among non-Indian politicians. In August of 1953, Congress passed House Concurrent Resolution 108, which declared the policy of the federal government "as rapidly as possible, to make the Indians within the territorial limits of the United States subject to the same laws and entitled to the same privileges and responsibilities as are applicable to other citizens of the United States, to end their status as wards of the United States, and to grant them all the rights and prerogatives pertaining to American citizenship."

Two weeks later, Congress passed Public Law 280 (PL 280), transferring legal jurisdiction on tribal land from the federal government to California, Nebraska, portions of Wisconsin, Minnesota, and Oregon, and eventually Alaska. Congress instituted PL 280 without tribal consent, something Myer viewed as too costly to obtain. The NCAI opposed the legislation, arguing, "Shouldn't Indians have the same right of self-determination that our government has stated . . . is the inalienable right of peoples in far parts of the world?"

PL 280 did much more than frustrate California Indian efforts at self-determination. It also created a complex web of overlapping jurisdiction that bedevils Indian country to this day. PL 280 applied to statewide criminal laws, leaving some civil regulatory laws or local ordinances unenforceable by state governments. As a result, states were unable to enforce state environmental and land-use regulations in Indian country. Furthermore, the law did not eliminate tribal authority to establish tribal police forces to enforce tribal law. That, and a small number of specific crimes for which the federal government retained jurisdiction, meant basic law enforcement on tribal land often required the coordination of tribal, state, and federal officials.

In December, Mazzetti gathered more than three hundred California Indians, members of the NCAI and the FIC among them, at the Rincon Reservation and organized the California Indian Congress (CIC). Under the leadership of its first president, Pit River Erin Forest, the CIC vigorously lobbied the state of California to oppose termination legislation. They argued termination would harm Indian communities and produce an undue burden on the state in assuming responsibilities previously handled by the federal government, without a corresponding transfer of funds. Property, sales, and income taxes funded local law enforcement. Many California Indians were exempt from those taxes, while the state nonetheless provided the services the taxes normally funded.

By March of 1954, California Indian efforts convinced the California State Committee on California Indian Affairs to oppose the termination bills. In testimony before that body, Cahuilla Jane Penn, founder of the Malki Museum, argued:

> The Indian wants to hold his land, his home. He feels that this is his right. . . . He does not want to be forced. He wants within reason and initiative the same sound healthy living conditions and privileges as any other American citizen. If he is to lose certain protective rights, he wants to know, what, when, and how. The Indian does not appreciate mystery concerning his future and security any more than anyone else does. In short, the Indian wants justice whether under the heading of American Indian or American citizen. The "Indian Problem" is not unsolvable.

Clara Helms, from Soboba, made a common argument among many—namely, that termination could interfere with the ongoing lawsuit in the Indian claims court: "We of the Soboba Reservation, do not wish to have federal supervision terminated. . . . We fear the loss of our homes and lands on account of taxation. We wish to have our lands free from taxation forever but in the vent [sic] this [is] not to be, we wish to have our land and other problems satisfactorily settled before termination of federal supervision."

The MIF supported the bill. In 1952, its counselor testified: "either approve this bill and thus recognize California Indians as human beings entitled to equality under the law, or . . . perpetuate and make permanent the iron rule of the Indian Bureau." In the 1954 hearings in California, the MIF submitted a letter claiming the "Indian Bureau policy has always been, and remains so at this hour here in California, to force all Indians back into tribal life and to keep him a ward of the government, a system of state control. This is real communism and America has become justly alarmed."

In 1956, Pala tribal chairman Robert Lovato claimed that "the majority of California Indians have not asked for termination because they do not understand what it means or what problems will come up. . . . They have not had enough opportunity to study the proposed bills. Federal and state governments should not hurry the process. . . . We Indians like to go slow."

The federal government worked slowly and often begrudgingly to honor its commitments to California Indians. Local, state, and federal governments worked much faster to take California Indian land and water to facilitate urban and industrial growth. California Indians fought persistently for justice, often leveraging the law and courts to their advantage. In the late 1920s, California Indians sued the federal government over the unratified treaties. In 1944, they won the case. California Indians continued to mobilize their communities to protect their land and livelihoods. New Deal public works jobs afforded California Indians the opportunity to improve reservation infrastructure. California Indians who accepted the Indian Reorganization Act slowly and tentatively formed new tribal councils and governments. The battle over the California Indian land claims and wartime service energized new and old pockets of California Indian activism. The battle for and against termination steeled California Indian political leaders. The federal government settled the second lawsuit brought by the Indians of California in 1963, more than one hundred years after the land's theft. But termination efforts begun in the early 1950s took effect within a decade. Unfortunately, justice moved slowly, but change came quickly. As the 1960s dawned, California Indian efforts to defend their communities flourished into a spectacular new era of political activism.

SOURCES

The act that defined the Indians of California and authorized their lawsuit was codified as the Act of May 18, 1928 (45 Stat. 602). See Kenneth M. Johnson, *K-344: or, The Indians of California vs. The United States* (Los Angeles: Dawson's Book Shop, 1966). On the second lawsuit initiated in 1946, see Robert Heizer and Alfred Kroeber, "For Sale: California at 47 Cents Per Acre," *Journal of California Anthropology* 3 (Autumn 1976): 38–65.

The best source on the life, wisdom, and humor of Mabel McKay is Greg Sarris's biography, *Mabel McKay: Weaving the Dream* (Berkeley: University of California Press, 1997). Her question, "Do I look like an Indian yet?" can be found on page 83. McKay's comment that Pomos "just live" comes from "Indian Basket Weaving Demonstrated," *Sacramento Union*, Jan. 23, 1934. Margaret Harrie's letter to Grace Nicholson is from Daniel Usner, "An Ethnohistory of Things: Or, How to Treat California's Canastromania," *Ethnohistory* 59 (Summer 2012): 455–56.

Hetch Hetchy and the aesthetic use and leisure vs. the "daily comfort and welfare of 99 percent" is from Robert W. Righter, *The Battle over Hetch Hetchy: America's Most Controversial Dam and the Birth of Modern Environmentalism* (New York: Oxford University Press, 2006), 195.

Ramón Ames's request for more time to study the IRA and Ventura Paipa's complaint about a poor crop in 1936 are found in Tanis Thorne, *El Capitan* (Banning, CA: Malki-Ballena Press, 2012), 139 and 166. Claude Hoaglin and Francis Crabtree's work on a footbridge over the Eel River comes from William J. Bauer Jr., *We Were All like Migrant Workers Here: Work, Community and Memory on California's Round Valley Reservation, 1850–1941* (Chapel Hill: University of North Carolina Press, 2009), 187–94.

On the Indian Reorganization Act, an excellent source is Vine Deloria Jr., ed., *The Indian Reorganization Act: Congresses and Bills* (Norman: University of Oklahoma Press, 2002), from which many of the statements quoted here come. Stephen Knight's comments at the Chemawa conference can be found on page 136. Rupert Costo's comments about the communistic nature of the IRA and about being sent back to the reservation can be found on pages 244–45. Leon Palawash's and Vivian Banks's comments demanding an expedited settlement to the Claims case before considering the IRA can be found on page 253. See also Graham D. Taylor, *The New Deal and American Indian Tribalism: The Administration of the Indian Reorganization Act, 1934–1935* (Lincoln: University of Nebraska Press, 1980).

Simon Ortiz's recollection of California during the Second World War is from Simon Ortiz, foreword to *Urban Voices: The Bay Area American Indian Community,* edited by Susan Lobo (Tucson: University of Arizona Press, 2002), xvii–xviii. Chag Lowry's collection of detailed and thoughtful interviews with more than fifty veterans represents a tremendous amount of work of incalculable value. For the recollections of Leonard Lowry, Josie Valadez, Edith Fogus, Georgiana Trull, Jack Risling, and David Risling Jr., see Chag Lowry, *Original Patriots: Northern California Indian Veterans of World War Two* (Eureka: Chag Lowry, 2007).

Terri Castaneda's ongoing work on Marie Potts has provided rich insight into the context of her life and work. We look forward to her forthcoming book. The anecdote about Kitty Flores's "peace pipe ceremonial," as well as much of the information on Marie Potts's work, comes from Terri Castaneda, "Making News: Marie Potts and the *Smoke Signal* of the Federated Indians of California," in *Women in Print: Essays on the Print Culture of American Women from the Nineteenth and Twentieth Centuries,* edited by James P. Danky and Wayne A. Wiegand (Madison: University of Wisconsin Press, 2006).

Dillon Myer's comments about a "glass case policy" are from Kenneth R. Philp, "Dillon S. Myer and the Advent of Termination: 1950–1953," *Western Historical Quarterly* 19 (Jan. 1988): 41. His claim that the guiding principle was "self-determination for Indians" and "sunlight of full independence" comes from Dillon Myer, *The Program of the Bureau of Indian Affairs* (Washington, DC: Government Printing Office, 1951), 13, quoted in Philp. Robert Lovato's comments on Indians wanting to go slow is from Roberta Ulrich, *American Indian Nations from Termination to Restoration, 1953–2006* (Lincoln: University of Nebraska Press, 2010), 114.

Heather Marie Daly's doctoral dissertation, "American Indian Freedom Controversy: Political and Social Activism by Southern California Mission Indians, 1934–1958" (University of California, Los Angeles, 2013), provides a thorough analysis of the responses of thirty-two tribal communities across Southern California to the effects of the Indian New Deal and the challenges posed by House Concurrent Resolution 108 (67 Stat. B132). The Mission Indian Federation's claim about serfdom and slavery is from page 105. Steve Ponchetti's comments asking for time to prepare themselves for loss of BIA protection, and Juanita Ortega's concern about legislation making paupers of young people, can be found on pages 119–20. Cruz Siva's letter to President Truman comes from page 133. Jane Penn's comments that the Indian Problem is not unsolvable are from page 187. Clara Helms's comment that Soboba wishes to have lands free from taxation forever is from page 192. The Mission Indian Federation letter opposing BIA policy as "real communism and America has become justly alarmed" is quoted on page 205.

Public Law 280 is complex. Some of the best work on the inner workings of the law come from legal scholars. An excellent and sophisticated overview is Carole E. Goldberg and Duane Champagne, *Captured Justice: Native Nations and Public Law 280* (Durham, NC: Carolina Academic Press, 2012). The National Congress of American Indians' opposition to PL 280 on the basis of inalienable rights comes from Paul C. Rosier, *Serving Their Country: American Indian Politics and Patriotism in the Twentieth Century* (Cambridge, MA: Harvard University Press, 2009), 174.

Bertha Stewart's demands that California Indians have already paid for the creation of an administrative roll and should not pay for another is from United States Congress, Senate Subcommittee on Indian Affairs of the Committee on Public Lands, "California Indians," (Washington, DC, June 19, 1947), 4. The Mission Indian Federation's support of termination legislation as a way to end the "permanent . . . iron rule" of the BIA is from United States Congress, House Committee on Interior and Insular Affairs, Subcommittee on Indian Affairs, "State Legal Jurisdiction in Indian Country: Hearings on H.R. 459, H.R. 3235, and H.R. 3624" (1952).

The journalist Carey McWilliams is credited with coining the phrase "Spanish fantasy past," and he elaborated on it in Carey McWilliams, *Southern California Country: An Island on the Land* (New York: Duell, Sloan and Pearce, 1946); and Carey McWilliams, *North from Mexico: The Spanish-Speaking People of the United States* (Philadelphia: J. B. Lippincott, 1949). See also, David J. Weber, *The Spanish Frontier in North America* (New Haven, CT: Yale University Press, 1992), 351–55; and Phoebe Kropp, *California Vieja: Culture and Memory in a Modern American Place* (Berkeley: University of California Press, 2006), 47–156.

Los Angeles

When one of the authors of this book first moved to Los Angeles in 1994, he was struck by how often people asked where he was from. He soon realized it was not because his status as a recent transplant was obvious but because it was simply a normal part of everyday conversation when meeting people in Los Angeles. The old joke that no one in LA is actually *from* LA is a dangerous myth. And it is totally untrue. It erases Indigenous People and the idea of indigeneity itself.

But so many people move to LA to make it one way or another. And no city in the nation has consistently reinvented and repackaged itself better than Los Angeles. The mix—of erasing indigenousness and reinventing and reclaiming a multicultural past—has made Los Angeles a very distinct kind of Native space. Understanding it as such requires that we see it as a place native to some and a place that other Native People made their own—a place as important to Indigenous People as it is to the people indigenous to it.

The Los Angeles basin is the center of the Tongva world. For the Chumash, Tataviam, Serrano, and Acjachemen, the Los Angeles region is a critical part of their territories, although each of those stretched beyond what one would call "Los Angeles" today. Indigenous People from across the state who moved to Los Angeles, by force or by choice, met Indigenous Peoples from across the nation and the world. In short, Los Angeles was and is a place where Indigenous People met other Indigenous Peoples.

Today, Los Angeles County has one of the largest American Indian populations in the United States, but that population is made up largely of Indians *from outside the LA basin and California.* The Tongva called the region Tovaangar, and it included all of the Los Angeles basin, portions of the San Fernando Valley, western San Bernardino County, and south to the drainage of the Santa Ana River. Across the region were more than one hundred villages, most situated adjacent to the basin's rivers, creeks, and springs. Juyubit, located along Coyote Creek in present-day Buena Park, was one of the largest villages. Hotuuknga, along the Santa Ana River near present-day Yorba Linda, was another. Povuu'nga, where the Cal State Long Beach campus is today, emerged as an important site in the development of Tongva culture, in part because of its association with Wewyoot, Attajen, and Chinigchinich, but also because of its deep connections to Pimu (Catalina Island), connecting the mainland Tongva world to the Pacific. Other far-flung connections and legacies lived on in place-names: Asuksangna, a large settlement along the upper San Gabriel River, from which Azusa derived its name, and Kuukamonga, a village at the foothills of the San Gabriel Mountains near the site of present-day Rancho Cucamonga.

The story of Yaanga and Kuruvungna are illustrative. Yaanga, the largest Tongva village, sat just above the floodplain of the Los Angeles River, south of Olvera Street, near where the iconic Metropolitan Detention Center sits today. In 1771, the Spanish established the mission of San Gabriel along the Rio Hondo adjacent to village of 'Lisanchanga. When floods destroyed the mission buildings in 1776, the Franciscans chose a new site farther north, adjacent to the larger village of Shevaanga. In 1781, a diverse group of settlers—Spanish, mestizo, Indian, and African—established *El Pueblo de la Reina de Los Angeles* just uphill from Yaanga, about ten miles west of the mission.

Franciscans brought Indigenous People to Mission San Gabriel. The Early California Cultural Atlas project used mission baptism records to track this movement and animated the results. Initial relocations to San Gabriel came from villages in the general vicinity, especially larger towns such as Juyubit and Yaanga. Indigenous People moved to the mission from more distant towns in clusters suggesting adverse circumstances affecting those choices. Mission San Juan Capistrano (1776) and Mission San Fernando (1797) further disrupted California Indian life in the basin. Franciscans' efforts to seek converts followed the raw logic of numbers, not the territorial boundaries of Indigenous People. Moving People from one area to another challenged the territorial sovereignty of the Tongva. Motivated in part by frustration at the number of Indians from outside the region being pulled into the mission, the Tongva attacked Mission San Gabriel in 1784.

By the 1830s, Tongvas had effectively abandoned both Yaanga and Juyubit. During secularization, however, Yaanga grew as refugee Indigenous People—survivors of the missions, those displaced from their homes inland, or those who had moved closer to the growing settlement—reoccupied the site. While the village itself did not survive, the site of "El Pueblo" nearby did, and it grew into an important part of the city's cultural landscape.

Kuruvungna served as an important village adjacent to natural springs along the Santa Monica fault line in West Los Angeles. Unlike Yaanga, the site of the village has been preserved through the efforts of Tongva activists in the twentieth century. Kuruvungna still had a substantial population in the early 1810s, whereas other villages had largely been depopulated. During the next decade, the residents of the village left, mostly by forced relocation to the mission at San Gabriel. The springs continued to flow. Over time, the city developed westward through stages, from agriculture, to film lots, real estate, and industrial development. The springs, along with most of the naturally flowing water of the Los Angeles basin, was contained in channels and culverts. In 1923, the city built a new high school on the site of the springs and, in the process, found evidence of what was obvious to many Tongva still living in the area. The site had been an important village. City officials built University High School around the springs.

In the late nineteenth century, Indigenous People came to Los Angeles to work in the citrus orchards, vineyards, or other agriculture, the railroads that followed, and the domestic jobs that followed on the heels of the wealth made from those industries and real estate. In the twentieth century, the oil boom and the aviation and defense industry transformed the city. The iconic film and entertainment industry, what Angelenos still call "*the* Industry," framed the stories told of Los Angeles and particularly about Indians in the United States. The movies came to Los Angeles because of the light, the diversity of the landscape, and the consistency of the climate. These same characteristics contributed to the abundance that made the region such a densely populated place for such a long time. The beaches, grasslands, rivers, snowcapped mountains along the northern rim of the basin, the pine forests on their slopes, and the high desert beyond provided a diverse diet to the Tongva and made for diverse settings for films.

In the early twentieth century, when westerns dominated the emerging movie industry, Inceville Studios hired several Plains Indians, many of whom had worked in traveling "Wild West shows." They came to be known as the "Inceville Indians" for temporarily living on the studio property in a "teepee village." Lakota writer, activist, and tribal leader Luther Standing Bear worked extensively with Buffalo Bill Cody and his traveling show. In the 1910s, Standing Bear came to Hollywood as a consultant for the studio but soon turned to acting. His first film was, fittingly, *Ramona* (1916). He acted in more than a dozen films and, along with other Indian actors in Hollywood, founded the War Paint Club, which later became the Indian Actors Association (IAA) and functioned both as an employment agency and activist organization demanding more accurate portrayals of Indians.

Clearly, most Indians moving to Los Angeles did not find work in the Industry. Many of the seven hundred California Indians listed as residents of Los Angeles in the 1928 special census likely had experiences closer to that of Kumeyaay Romaldo LaChusa, from Mesa Grande. He was born in 1883 and was one of the first student to enroll at Sherman Indian Institute in Riverside. By 1917, LaChusa lived near downtown Los Angeles and worked as a landscape gardener. He married twice, both times to California Indians: Annie and, later, Margaret from the Torrez-Martinez Reservation.

By 1930, only a quarter of the Indians living in Los Angeles were from California. In part, this was because California Indians could maintain a permanent residency at their home village, rancheria, or reservation, while spending time working in Los Angeles. But it was also because Los Angeles was a place California Indians went to disappear. Carolina Burbee is an example. In the 1928 special census, she self-identified as Pechanga, but in the 1930 census, she was listed as White. Similarly, Belva Helm King identified in the 1928 census as Agua Caliente Indian, but the 1930 census recorded her as Mexican, with a Mexican father and California mother.

In the 1930s, an intertribal culture emerged in Los Angeles, structured around organizations such as the IAA, American Indian Progressive Association, Wigwam Club, California Indian Land Rights Association, and National Justice to the American Indian. The Los Angeles Indian Center served as the hub, linking these organizations' efforts to prominent Indians in the movie industry and coordinating powwows and fundraising. By the late 1960s, the Indian Center coordinated a different powwow every Saturday night for nine months out of the year (fig. 27).

FIGURE 27. Gathering at Los Angeles Indian Center. Photo courtesy *Los Angeles Daily News* Negative Archive (Collection 1387), Charles E. Young Research Library, Special Collections, UCLA.

But the multiethnic, intertribal culture of Los Angeles had a dark side. The federal government's termination and relocation policies brought Indians from across the West to the city. The Los Angeles Field Relocation Office oversaw the relocation of thirty thousand Indians and provided them with vocational training and temporary housing. By 1952, Indians dominated the line work at North American Aviation.

Kiowa author N. Scott Momaday's Pulitzer Prize–winning novel *House Made of Dawn* chronicles the experiences of a fictional transplant to Los Angeles. After serving in the Second World War, Abel, the novel's protagonist, returned to his home at the Jemez Pueblo in New Mexico. Broken from the war, he descends into alcoholism and is eventually arrested for murder. After serving his sentence, Abel moves to Los Angeles in the early 1950s. There, he struggles to fit in, both with the city's Anglo culture and the Indian subculture around Bunker Hill. Abel's life spirals downward, and he eventually returns to Jemez. Kent MacKenzie's 1961 film *The Exiles* captured Bunker Hill's Indian subculture, following a group of transplanted Indians over the course of one night, drinking at the Indian bars, Café Ritz, and the Columbine and singing traditional songs in Chavez Ravine.

After the 1950s, the city's Indian population grew dramatically— from fewer than nine thousand in 1960 to roughly twenty-eight thousand in 1970, and sixty-one thousand in 1980. By 1970, Los Angeles ranked second only to the Navajo Reservation in terms of the number of American Indians. In December of that year, approximately one hundred Indians protested at the Southwest Museum of the American Indian in Mount Washington, demanding the removal of American Indian remains and sacred relics. In response, the director of the museum covered some exhibits with sheets, but the protests continued. In March of 1973, Marlon Brando refused his Academy Award for best actor in *The Godfather* to protest the depiction of Indians in film and to draw attention to the occupation of the town of Wounded Knee, South Dakota, by American Indian Movement and Oglala Lakota activists. In his stead, he sent Apache actress Sacheen Littlefeather to read a statement. Indians occupied the Oscars.

Indians occupied Los Angeles' cultural scene in other ways, too. In 1988, movie cowboys Gene Autry and Monte Hale founded the Gene Autry Western Heritage Museum. In its early years, Autry celebrated the cowboy culture depicted in the films that made its founders famous. Thirty years later, a lot had changed. In 2018, Southern Cheyenne W. Richard West Jr. became the president of the renamed Autry Museum of the American West. Born in San Bernardino, but raised in Oklahoma, West had been the founding director of the National Museum of the American Indian in Washington, DC. During his tenure at the Autry, the museum presented a retrospective of Wiyot artist Rick Bartow, whose ancestors had survived the Wiyot massacre of 1860, and an exhibit devoted to the baskets of Pomo-Patwin Mabel McKay.

Despite the transformation of cultural institutions like the Autry, local activists still had to work to reassert their presence. Tongva Angie Behrns attended University High in the 1960s, where she remembered the springs there as an idyllic shaded space where students ate lunch. Returning for a reunion in 1991, she expressed shock to find the site full of trash and graffiti. She recalled, "I felt like a knife had been plunged into my stomach. I was totally sick at what I saw." She actively worked to protect and preserve the springs, especially in the face of impending development plans for an underground parking garage that would have stopped its flow entirely. In 1994, the group she organized incorporated as the Gabrielino Tongva Springs Foundation and has managed and preserved the springs since.

The Tongva are not among the more than one hundred federally recognized tribes in California. Their lack of recognition partly explains their undervisibility in comparison to other tribes, which are able to leverage gaming revenues toward cultural preservation projects. On the campus of Pitzer College, in Claremont, Southern Cheyenne artist Edgar Heap of Birds' work, part of his "Native Hosts" series, disrupts efforts to erase the Tongva, by identifying Tongva villages as "hosts" for California, which he writes backward, in effect, to turn the erasure back on the state. Tongva-Acjachemen artist L. Frank Manriquez described the heroism of the Tongva people in the present: "To have survived and to still call yourself indigenous to a place, belonging to a place, and this is that place . . . that's pretty strong. That takes something very special."

SOURCES

There is no shortage of scholarship on Los Angeles. The majority of it, however, only glances at the region's Indigenous People. Some notable exceptions are Diana Meyers Bahr, *From Mission to Metropolis: Cupeño Indian Women in Los Angeles* (Norman: University of Oklahoma Press, 1993); Nicolas G. Rosenthal, *Reimagining Indian Country: Native American Migration and Identity in Twentieth-Century Los Angeles* (Chapel Hill: University of North Carolina Press, 2014); Claudia Jurmain and William McCawley, *O, My Ancestor: Recognition and Renewal for the Gabrielino-Tongva People of the Los Angeles Area* (Berkeley, CA: Heyday, 2009); and Joan Weibel-Orlando, *Indian Country LA: Maintaining Ethnic Community in Complex Society* (Champaign: University of Illinois Press, 1999).

Of the many books that discuss the region's Indigenous People as part of a larger project, see William Deverell, *Whitewashed Adobe: The Rise of Los Angeles and the Remaking of Its Mexican Past* (Berkeley: University of California Press, 2004); John Mack Faragher, *Eternity Street: Vio-*

lence and Justice in Frontier Los Angeles (New York: Norton, 2016); Phoebe S. Kropp, *California Vieja: Culture and Memory in a Modern American Place* (Berkeley: University of California Press, 2008), 207–60; Kelly Lytle Hernández, *City of Inmates: Conquest, Rebellion, and the Rise of Human Caging in Los Angeles, 1771–1965* (Chapel Hill: University of North Carolina Press, 2017); and David Samuel Torres-Rouff, *Before L.A.: Race, Space, and Municipal Power in Los Angeles, 1781–1894* (New Haven, CT: Yale University Press, 2013).

The Early California Cultural Atlas project is part of the Huntington Library's Early California Population Project. Steven Hackel is its general editor. "The Great California Indian Migration" can be found on its website, https://lanaic.lacounty.gov/the-great-indian-migration-los-angeles-1772-1840. Population figures for Los Angeles come from the US Census Bureau, American Community Survey, *2013–2017 ACS 5-Year Estimates, Los Angeles County.* The quotations from Angie Behrns are from Michael Ashcraft, "Savior of the Tongva Springs Retires from Foundation," *Santa Monica Patch,* Nov. 11, 2015. L. Frank Manriquez's comments come from an oral history, part of the California Museum's exhibit "California Indians: Making a Difference," March 25, 2011.

9

Reoccupying California

Resistance and Reclaiming the Land,
1953–1985

Stewarts Point Rancheria sits high on a heavily wooded ridge between two forks of the Gualala River, about four miles inland from the coast and one hundred miles north of San Francisco. In 1916, the Kashaya Pomo moved there to occupy forty acres the federal government purchased for them. There, they built a roundhouse associated with the Bole Maru (Dream Dance) religion, which moved through Pomo territory in the 1870s after a Long Valley Cache Creek man named Richard Taylor gathered more than a thousand Indians on the shores of Clear Lake for a revivalist ceremony associated with the Ghost Dance. Participants took the practices back to their home communities. Annie Jarvis led the Kashaya Dreamers at Stewarts Point and emphasized the integrity of Kashaya culture by advocating isolation from non-Indians, speaking out against gambling and drinking, and urging Kashaya to keep their children at home rather than sending them to boarding schools.

Jarvis's isolationism persisted until Essie Parrish, who started Dreaming around 1915, became the community's spiritual leader in 1943. Parrish was a renowned sucking doctor, so called because she sucked the illness or poison out of her patients. Aided by her singers, she healed patients across the state. Parrish guided Stewarts Point through a dynamic period in Kashaya life. The small community's location kept the 150 or so Pomo relatively isolated from the changes affecting California Indians. Nonetheless, they were not immune to the challenges facing all people in the region. During the Second World War and after, many Kashaya left Stewarts Point to serve in the military or take up jobs across the region, especially in the city. Beginning in the 1950s, Mormon missionaries made inroads into the community, followed soon thereafter by evangelical pentecostal Christians. While Stewarts Point did not face termination under the 1958 California Rancheria Termination Act, erasure threatened nonetheless.

Parrish approached her community's situation differently than Jarvis had. With her husband, Sidney, as tribal chair, Parrish sought to preserve a living, dynamic, contemporary Kashaya culture. The prospect of drawing a boundary around the rancheria and keeping "outside" influences out vanished. Those influences existed inside the community, where Kashayas made them their own, much like they had made over the Bole Maru eighty years before. Parrish urged the community to engage them as an act of preservation. In 1957, she began to collaborate with Robert Oswalt and other anthropologists and linguists at the University of California. Parrish hoped that Oswalt's attention, and that of other anthropologists, would help preserve Kashaya culture in the face of change. In this spirit, in 1963, Parrish allowed a filmmaker associated with the university's American Indian Film Project to film the second night of a healing ceremony she conducted. The footage shows Parrish, dressed in white, assisted by three singers, treating a patient in the roundhouse at Stewarts Point.

The Kashaya experience was distinct among Pomo, and even more so regionally and statewide. But those differences suggest important patterns. Kashaya efforts to resist erasure by presenting a living, contemporary culture emphasized that they are still here. And insisting on the Kashaya way, even as some of those ways changed, echoed the efforts of many other Indians across the state to resist erasure through termination, relocation, and the general assault of non-Indian culture on Indian life.

The 1950s were a deeply conflicted time. The Cold War and growing cultural ferment by groups marginalized by mainstream society polarized the nation's politics and popular culture. Television's emergence provided a simplistic and conformist national image of mainstream popular culture, while simultaneously giving the civil rights movement national media exposure, helping to challenge the universality of White mainstream society.

While this national context is important, California Indian experiences and demands do not quite fit the images many have of the midcentury tensions between a mainstream culture of conformity and economic prosperity and social protests demanding cultural or political rights. Early twentieth-century Indian activism was often separatist and engaged in protecting Indian culture rather than demanding inclusion. The fight over termination in the mid-1950s reenergized many Indians toward self-determination. Thus, as the civil rights movement began in earnest, demanding inclusion and desegregation, Indians were already mobilizing toward self-determination, using the rhetoric of the Cold War and emergent democracies around the globe, as their model. In this, Indians' political activism in the 1950s clashed with the classic civil rights movement of the decade. Indians demanded health, welfare, education, land, language, culture, legal rights, and the ability to control those themselves.

Two events that began after World War II increasingly affected California Indians. The Second World War certainly transformed California cities. It initiated massive industrial development and human relocation from across the nation and the state. Plentiful jobs in the burgeoning wartime economy and the momentum those industries created persisted after the war. Spurred in part by those experiences, the federal government initiated a policy of relocating American Indians from their reservation homelands to urban areas. The BIA established Los Angeles, San Jose, Oakland, and San Francisco along with five other cities across the West and Midwest as relocation sites for Indians from across the nation. The BIA Relocation Program, designed to promote the assimilation of Indians into urban society, secured housing and provided job placement and financial support for Indians who left reservations. Between 1955 and 1962, the Indian population of the San Francisco Bay Area quadrupled, from twenty-five hundred to ten thousand. By 1970, it ranked as the third-largest urban Indian population in the United States, at twenty thousand. Los Angeles grew in a similar manner. Eventually, proponents of relocation believed, American Indians would melt into the urban populace.

In 1958, the federal government tried again to terminate California Indians' tribal status. This effort continued the national attempt to terminate tribes, which had begun in 1953, but met with stiff resistance in California. Targeting small rancherias rather than larger reservations, the 1958 California Rancheria Act abolished the trust status of tribal land and divided it among the adult Indian population or sold it, the proceeds going to a corporate entity that the Indians created. The act also ended the relationship between rancherias and the federal government. In return, the federal government pledged to complete surveys of rancheria land to ensure clear boundaries, to improve roads and bring them to comparable standards for state roads, to install or repair irrigation systems, to assist Indians in protecting their water rights in court, to cancel reimbursable debts for existing projects, and to resolve any lingering disputes that might affect property distribution. In addition, the federal government pledged to create a "special program of education and training designed to help the Indians earn a livelihood, to conduct their own affairs, and to assume responsibilities as citizens without special services because of their status as Indians." Based on those promises, rancheria communities put together termination plans and submitted them to the BIA. If approved, the BIA returned the plan to the rancheria for approval by a majority of the Indians who stood to receive land. Initially, Congress restricted the act to forty-one rancherias, but in 1964, Congress amended the act to apply to all the state's reservations and rancherias. Eventually, forty-six rancherias opted for termination on the promise of the government fulfilling its obligations.

The hollow nature of the federal government's promises quickly became evident. Many Indians complained that the federal government failed to include them in termination plans, did not inform them of termination, or told them termination was mandatory. Road and irrigation projects, as well as education and job-training programs, never materialized. Many of the individual parcels of land, especially with inadequate roads and incomplete irrigation works, were unworkable properties, which California Indians sold to pay property taxes.

In some ways, the distinctions between terminated and nonterminated communities were not as different as one might imagine, at least in the early years of the termination effort. Both faced attempts to erase and erode culture. Both faced challenges to their survivance. Some rancherias opted for termination because they saw their best hope in preservation and persistence outside of a relationship with the federal government. Those who rejected it did so because they saw the opposite. Both found the deck stacked against them in similar ways.

During the 1950s, California Indians reclaimed land and rights. Cahuillas Jane Penn and Katherine Siva Saubel worked with anthropologist Lowell Bean in the late 1950s. By 1964, they founded the Malki Museum on the Morongo Reservation in Banning to preserve Cahuilla culture, echoing, in a different voice, Essie Parrish's work at Stewarts Point. The Malki Museum grew to include an extensive exhibit of California flora and by 1979 began publishing the *Journal of California and Great Basin Anthropology.*

That same year, Cahuilla Rupert Costo and his wife, Cherokee Jeannette Henry Costo, founded the American Indian Historical Society

sympathies, job opportunities, and social relationships. Bars, pubs, and taverns often served that function for immigrants, whether the Irish pub in Boston or New York City or the Polish bar in Chicago in the nineteenth century. But if the bars gave urban immigrants a place to meet, they also attracted the attention of the police and made Indians easy targets for shakedowns and racial profiling. The sense of community that bars provided must also be weighed against the toll that these hardscrabble places took on the people who frequented them. Most cities in California possessed at least one so-called Indian bar. In Los Angeles, Café Ritz and the Columbine on Main Street catered to Bunker Hill's Indian community. By the late 1960s, Sixteenth Street in the Mission District emerged as the center of the San Francisco Indian community. Richard Oakes, an Akwesasne Mohawk who moved from New York to San Francisco in 1967, tended bar at Warren's Slaughterhouse Bar, owned by a Klamath couple and serving a primarily Indian crowd.

Indian centers hosted monthly powwows and meetings of intertribal organizations. In Oakland, the Intertribal Friendship House, founded in 1955, hosted a standing Wednesday night dinner, which became a vital source for information for the growing East Bay Indian community (fig. 28). The San Francisco Indian Center (SFIC), founded about the same time, facilitated Indians' arrival in the city. In 1957, the eleven-year-old Cherokee Wilma Mankiller's family relocated to San Francisco from Oklahoma. She recalled how the SFIC compensated for the federal government's failed promise of housing. Through the SFIC, her family found temporary housing in the Tenderloin District and more stable housing in Daly City the following year. By 1963, when Mankiller became actively involved in the SFIC's work, the number of Indian-run organizations in the Bay Area had increased from two to sixteen.

The centers also provided spaces for tribal groups to meet. The Los Angeles Indian Center (LAIC) was one of the most successful. Established in the 1930s, it took the lead in organizing arts and crafts, dancing, a youth club, and other activities after World War II. The LAIC also provided social and welfare services funded, in part, through its association with the American Friends Service Committee (AFSC). In the 1950s, the LAIC moved into its own downtown building and expanded its recreation programs. It began publishing *Talking Leaf,* a monthly newsletter that coordinated powwows and publicized other events of interest to the region's Indian community. The center hosted visiting Indians from boarding schools who worked in Los Angeles for the summer, delegations from the National Congress of American Indians and other

FIGURE 28. Three teenagers at the Intertribal Friendship House in Oakland California, ca. 1972. Photo courtesy of Ilka Hartmann.

organizations who were in town for events, Indians serving in the military passing through Los Angeles to or from the war in Korea, and Indians in town to work in the movie industry. As such, the LAIC promoted a broadly pan-Indian identity. A 1952 powwow promotion claimed, "Anyone who wishes can join in the fun, so let's be Indian!" Softball, basketball, and other sports leagues grew out of the LAIC and eventually became the American Indian Athletic Association in the early 1960s.

Unlike Indian bars, Indian centers and organizations could avail themselves of meager funding opportunities. In January of 1964, President Lyndon Johnson declared unconditional war on poverty. Later that year, Congress established the Office of Economic Opportunity (OEO), whose mission was to promote job training and mobilize community resources to break the "cycle of poverty." One of the key aspects of the OEO was the Community Action Programs, whose grants provided assistance, employment services, or other measures to help eliminate poverty. One of the most controversial and critical elements of the program was the requirement that grants be "developed, conducted and administered with the maximum feasible participation of residents of the areas and members of the groups served," which often upset established urban power dynamics, bypassing city councils and local political elites to inject federal dollars into the hands of organizations made up of and serving poor

FIGURE 29. Lillian Finnell *(left)* and Nancy Carrier, VISTA volunteers, and a group of Indian children on an outing to the Los Angeles Zoo, 1966. Photo courtesy *Los Angeles Times* Photographic Archives (Collection 1429), Charles E. Young Research Library, Special Collections, UCLA.

people of color. One such program was Volunteers in Service to America (VISTA), often described as a domestic peace corps. Volunteers committed a period of time to serve in impoverished communities (fig. 29).

The LAIC received an OEO-CAP grant in 1964, enabling it to hire a full-time staff of seven, secure a more suitable building, and lessen its reliance on fundraising. The expansion enabled it to serve not only as a provider of services but as a coordinator of activities and services going on across the region. For example, by the late 1960s, the LAIC served as a clearinghouse for information on, and provided rides to, the different regional powwows that took place every Saturday night across the Los Angeles area from September to May.

FIGURE 30. Group photo of attendees at the California Indian Education Conference, California State University, Chico, 1970. Marie Potts *(first row, third from left)*, Morgan Otis *(first row, fourth from left)*, Dave Risling *(second row, far left)*, Dr. Rose *(second row, second from left)*, Jim Meyers *(second row, last)*, Mr. and Mrs. Tom Merino *(third row, second and third from left)*, and others attending conference. Photo courtesy Meriam Library, California State University, Chico.

In addition to bars and community centers, a new landscape emerged on California's college campuses. Campus student movements erupted earlier in the decade, most notably in the Bay Area with the Free Speech Movement at UC Berkeley in 1964. In 1967, Hupa-Karuk-Yurok David Risling Jr. organized a statewide conference on Indian education at Stanislaus State College, and later that year, he organized the first Indian-controlled conference on California Indian education in North Fork. In 1950, Risling graduated from California Polytechnic College, San Luis Obispo, and had taught at Modesto Junior College since then. Out of the two conferences, Risling organized the California Indian Education Association (CIEA), which helped promote the need for Native American studies programs like those that were eventually created at UC Berkeley, Long Beach State, Sacramento State, UCLA, and UC Davis (fig. 30). But Risling, working with Renape-Lenape Jack Forbes, who established UC Davis's program, went further. Just as much as they believed it was critical to ensure Indians had a presence in the state's higher education landscape, they also pointed to the need for "an institution of higher learning *both Indian-controlled and Indian-centered.*" This belief mirrored the demand for both inclusion and sovereignty for which many California Indian activists had argued since the late nineteenth century.

In 1971, Risling and Forbes led the effort to found Deganawidah-Quetzalcoatl University. The name reflects the desire that the university embrace a broad notion of indigeneity. *Deganawidah* refers to the Iroquois figure who helped found the Haudenosaunee in the twelfth century. In the 1960s, Chicanx activists adopted the Aztec god Quetzalcoatl as a symbol of their efforts to reclaim the Southwest as the land of Aztlan, from which the Aztecs migrated south to Mexico. A group of early supporters, including Pit River Mickey Gemmill, occupied the six-hundred-acre site of a former army facility near Davis. Eventually, the federal government conditionally granted control of the site to the college. College leaders later shortened the name to D-Q University after the descendants of Deganawidah requested that his name not be used in a profane context.

To combat the alienation so common among Anglo-educated Indian students returning to tribal communities, D-Q University sought to provide training in education, law, arts, and social work within the context of the tribal communities to "large numbers of Indians in an environment suitable for the development of self-confidence, both individual and collective." Forbes saw this as potentially "*the* major effort in the 'war on poverty' in so far as tribal groups are concerned. It also could signal the dawn of a new age in which tribes take their place as worthy members of a modern world community." D-Q became a two-year college, which educated thousands of students before losing accreditation and closing in 2005 because of the loss of federal funds. Risling also helped to create California Indian Legal Services (CILS), an organization that provided legal services for California Indians. Within a few years, the CILS procured funding to nationalize its effort and created the Native American Rights Fund. Both organizations helped to fund subsequent efforts to challenge termination in California.

By the summer of 1968, California Indian Country, and the nation, and perhaps the world, was pregnant with change. That year, the state of California and the Army Corps of Engineers proposed to build the Dos Rios Dam on the Eel River, which would flood the Round Valley Reservation. The Army Corps of Engineers pledged to build recreational facilities and a museum on the shores of the new Lake Covelo to provide tourism and recreational income for the Round Valley tribal government. Tribal secretary Ida Soares and newly elected tribal president Norman Whipple, who fought in the Korean War, did not believe the army. Why would they? The federal government had failed to provide similar infrastructure to the Pomos and other terminated tribes in the state. Soares and Whipple developed an effective public relations campaign, comparing the flooding of the reservation to other campaigns of ethnic cleansing in California and US history. Their arguments found a sympathetic ear with Governor Ronald Reagan. "We're not going to flood [the Indians] out," Reagan declared in 1969. The late 1960s, then, represented a different historical moment. For much of the twentieth century, California Indians protested the building of dam projects in the state, which meant the ethnic cleansing of people, the destruction of traditional harvesting sites, and the covering of graves. Now, the tide changed; Americans began to give California Indians a more sympathetic hearing.

Similar political activism developed in the cities. During the previous decades, Indians had remade cities into Indian spaces by building networks and forming communities. Bars, Indian centers, campus organizations, neighborhoods, and other organizations became the nodes of those networks. In September of 1968, San Francisco police officers arrested Richard Oakes after a fight. The San Francisco Police Department, recognizing his charisma and sway in the city's Indian community, tapped him to serve as a community organizer to mitigate violence between Indians and Samoan gangs.

The East Bay emerged as an important site for organization. As summer turned to fall, students carried the unrest back to campus. At UC Berkeley, Shoshone-Bannock LaNada Means (now War Jack) occupied an abandoned bungalow on campus to demand a Native American student center. In November of 1968, a coalition of student activist groups led by the Black Student Union went on strike at San Francisco State College (now University) to protest the firing of an adjunct English instructor and Black Panther member. The strike lasted four and a half months. Students from across a spectrum of ethnic and racial groups organized under the title "Third World Liberation Front." The strike spread across the region, with a strong presence at UC Berkeley. As a direct result of the strike, both SFSU and UC Berkeley established ethnic studies departments, which began operation in 1969. The militant, separatist movements like the Black Panthers resonated with ongoing efforts by California Indians to demand sovereignty, and that spirit infused the new ethnic studies departments.

The SFSU Ethnic Studies department received OEO grant funds to recruit and support more than thirty Bay Area Native students for its first class. Richard Oakes was among them and eventually became a leader in the Student Coalition of American Natives there. At UCLA, Edward Castillo taught in the newly formed American Indian Studies Center. He was barely older than his students, most of whom were Indians from other states and many of whom believed Indians had disappeared in California. He and his students began planning an action to protest the disturbance of Indian burial sites, an increasingly common occurrence as a result of large urban construction projects. They intended to dig up the grave of a well-known nineteenth-century Indian fighter to bring attention to the practice.

In October of 1969, a fire destroyed the San Francisco American Indian Center. That event set in motion a series of events that captured nationwide attention and galvanized a large swath of Indians in California. Their actions exposed fissures that ran through the state's changing Indian community. In response to the loss of the Indian Center, Bay Area activists picked up an idea that had been floating around San Francisco since the Alcatraz Federal Penitentiary closed in 1963. Beginning that year, some Indian activists in the city advocated for Native control of the island, based on an 1868 treaty between the Lakota and the federal government, which allowed Indians to claim unused federal lands. Between 1964 and 1969, there were several plans and attempts to take over and occupy the island.

In light of the destruction of the Indian Center and burgeoning campus protests, local opinion shifted slightly. On November 9, 1969, Richard Oakes and three other Indians jumped from a yacht they commissioned to pass by the island. They swam to shore and claimed the island by right of discovery, the same doctrine used by the English and other European colonial powers to claim ownership of North America. The next morning, television crews recorded Oakes reading the "Proclamation to the Great White Father" to Thomas Hannon, the regional administrator of the Government Services Administration, the federal entity controlling the island. Red Lake Chippewa Adam Fortunate Eagle wrote the document for a 1964 attempt to take control of Alcatraz.

The document made great political theater. It offered a treaty to "the Caucasian inhabitants of this land," promising to purchase the island for "twenty-four dollars in glass beads and red cloth, a precedent set by the White man's purchase of [Manhattan] about 300 years ago." They pointed out the $1.24 per acre they offered was "greater than the $0.47 per acre the White men are now paying the California Indians for their lands." Essentially flipping Indian-White relations on its head, the treaty promised to establish a "Bureau of Caucasian Affairs" and offer Caucasian inhabitants Indian religion, culture, and education to "raise them and all their White brothers up from their savage and unhappy state" to the Indians' level of civilization.

Often lost in the political theater, then and now, are the last five points of the document, which outlined the creation of a Center for Native American Studies, an American Indian Spiritual Center, an Indian Center of Ecology, a Great Indian Training School, and an American Indian Museum. From the perspective of the twenty-first century, many of these demands seem tame, especially from the shadow of the Smithsonian's National Museum of the American Indian on the mall in Washington, DC, and the numerous Native American Studies centers at universities around the nation. At the time, though, the declaration demanded a revolution in Indian affairs and the treatment of Indigenous People.

It was a telling clash of cultures. Oakes, a former ironworker, was brash, confident, and direct, with an unshaven face and untamed hair. Hannon was the picture of 1960s government bureaucracy in a thin black tie, horn-rimmed glasses, and flattop haircut. News cameras and microphones crowded around them. After Oakes finished reading the document, Hannon asked Oakes and other Indians what they intended to do next. Oakes answered, "I guess we can go home." Hannon asked if they needed a lift, and Oakes readily accepted.

The surviving news footage of the event looks staged. Oakes and the Indians who organized and occupied the island knew the value of publicity. The theater of protest was a staple of college campuses at the time. For many non-Indians, especially those not on college campuses, this was the first indication that Indians in the Bay Area and across the nation were organizing. As Indians and scholars have pointed out, Alcatraz was not the beginning. It was the moment that decades of organizing effort punctured the mainstream news media's attention. Oakes's speech was important precisely because of the attention it received among Indians and non-Indians alike.

After leaving the island on November 10, Oakes began a publicity tour to college campuses across the state, visiting UC Riverside, UC Berkeley, San Francisco State, UCLA, and other campuses. At each, he met with students and faculty of the newly established Native American Studies programs. After Oakes visited Edward Castillo's class at UCLA, the students abandoned their planned protest against disinterment of Indian graves. Within days, half of the students in the UCLA Native American Studies program drove up to the Bay Area, where they picked up Castillo at the airport and joined the planning efforts for the occupation.

In early November, the protesters planned to maximize media coverage and ensure they could make this occupation stick. The organizers prearranged with local news media to televise their actions. On November 20, more than eighty Indians, including college students, and two federal informants took a chartered boat from the Sausalito Marina to the island. Oakes, Castillo, John Trudell, Adam Fortunate Eagle, Wilma Mankiller, LaNada Means, and others led the effort, calling themselves the Indians of All Tribes. Leaders expected Bay Area police to resist their occupation and possibly arrest them. Instead, the federal caretaker of the island brought them coffee and offered the women in the group access to the toilet and shower. Taking place a few days before Thanksgiving, the local media jumped on the story. A Chumash elder gave a blessing for a large Thanksgiving dinner held by the Indians on the island.

The occupiers worked to organize impromptu housing on the island, as well as handling the flood of media attention, the arrival of other supporters, and donations from around the nation. They organized a mainland office and an Intertribal Council on the island, including Oakes, Castillo, Seminole Al Miller, Ho-Chunk Ross Harden, Luiseño Dennis Turner, and Cherokee Jim Vaughn. Tensions emerged between older occupiers and college students and between those with ties to the area and those without. The prospect of Native control of Alcatraz excited many Indians but rankled some from California. Castillo recalled, "At that time, all of California's professional Indian leadership positions were held by Indians from out of state. This grated on those of us who were from California tribes, but the non-California Indians could not comprehend our concern. More troubling still, these leaders would be claiming California Indian land based on a treaty the government had made with the Lakota Indians!"

California-based organizations, such as the Federated Indians of California, CILS, or CIEA worked for decades to resolve issues of land, compensation, and educational reform. They challenged the limitations placed on the distribution of the award in the ICC case. They organized and coordinated legal challenges to the Rancheria Termination Act, which eventually coalesced into the 1979 class action lawsuit, *Tillie Hardwick v. the United States*. Their interests often differed from the demands of urban Indians. Some of them possessed California connections, but most did not. The stories of two women illustrate how those tensions played out on a personal level.

By the mid-1960s, Pomo Anne Marrufo, a single mother with six children, struggled to make it in San Francisco. Born in 1941 at the Stewarts

Point Rancheria, perhaps Marrufo became swept up in many of the other pressures that pushed and lured Indians to the city. She leaned heavily on the support network that developed in the Mission District. Either at Warren's Slaughterhouse Bar or perhaps the Indian Center, she met Richard Oakes, and they married within a year. Oakes took great pride in her children, adopting them and joking they were "Pomohawks." Anne and Richard attended area powwows, where they met Adam Fortunate Eagle.

Cherokee Wilma Mankiller was a few years younger than Anne Oakes. She was born in 1945 in her family's allotment in rural eastern Oklahoma. When the family followed the BIA's relocation policy to San Francisco, Mankiller was struck by urban life and by her sudden racialization as alternately Black or Indian. In addition to the support of the SFIC, the family also appreciated the "sanctuary" of the Intertribal Friendship House in Oakland. After graduating from high school in 1963, she became involved in the region's burgeoning activism, supporting the efforts of Cesar Chavez to organize farmworkers, as well as the efforts of the Black Panthers in Oakland. At the SFIC, she met Richard and Anne Oakes, and the occupation of Alcatraz provided the action that galvanized the community identity she found so critical to her development. She spent time on the island but mostly worked on the mainland at the temporary SFIC, where the occupation's command post was located.

After the November 20 occupation, Anne and the kids joined Richard on Alcatraz, with tragic consequences. In January of 1970, their twelve-year-old daughter, Yvonne, fell from an unprotected stairwell and died. Largely unsubstantiated rumors of foul play circulated. Anne and Richard left the island with their kids, but Richard remained centrally involved in the effort. His departure exacerbated the tensions between what Castillo called a small faction of "older, frustrated, unemployed semiprofessionals" and the college students who made up most of the leadership. The problems involved the control of donations pouring in and how to manage the media attention. After Oakes's departure, "it was clear to many of us that our original idealism was being replaced by cynical and frankly embarrassing self-declared 'leaders' whose interests were more financial and political in nature."

Tensions worsened with local Indian communities. The AIHS did not support the Alcatraz occupation. Ohlone Philip Galvan, secretary of the AIHS, organized a petition among Ohlone, which he sent to Richard Nixon in January of 1970. It argued that the Indians of All Tribes, who claimed they spoke for all Indians, did not. Galvan claimed they had no right to speak on behalf of the Ohlones and called the occupation "wrong" because the occupiers were "mainly from other states, other tribes and reservations."

Rupert Costo also pushed back against other heavy-handed pan-Indian action in the region. Ojibwe Dennis Banks emerged as an early leader of the American Indian Movement (AIM), which Americans associated with the Alcatraz occupation, although it was not directly involved. Banks and others also took up the case involving the repatriation efforts of Ohlone remains from construction sites in San Jose. They did so without Ohlone consent, something Costo opposed, claiming it was a question of tribal sovereignty over pan-Indian activism.

Anne and Richard returned to Stewarts Point, but Richard did not stay put for long. In March of 1970, the United Indians of All Tribes, based in the urban Indian and Indigenous population of Seattle, Washington, recruited him to assist in their takeover of Fort Lawton, an abandoned military base near Seattle. That same month, Richard and eleven others occupied the BIA office in Alameda, California, where police officers arrested them. Later that month, the Elem Pomo asked Oakes for assistance in their protest against a proposed Army Corps of Engineers dam on the Eel River, which would have inundated the Round Valley Reservation.

In May, Oakes returned to Elem Pomo land, this time Rattlesnake Island in Clear Lake, a sacred burial site on which a lumber company proposed to build a vacation resort. Oakes brought support from the United Indians of All Tribes and, along with members of the Elem Pomo community, occupied the island, setting up temporary residence there. The lumber company recognized the fight ahead and decided to negotiate with the Pomos and their allies.

Pit River Mickey Gemmill, a fellow SFSU student and tribal chairman of the Pit River Rancheria who participated in the initial D-Q occupation, invited Oakes to take his fight to the countryside by assisting the Pit Rivers in their battle with the federal government. The tribe refused the forty-seven cents per acre that the ICC case awarded for the land lost in the nineteenth century. Instead, they demanded the land itself—all 3.5 million acres of it—as well as the profits that the land had generated for its corporate owners since 1853.

In June of 1970, Gemmill, Richard, Anne, and around two hundred members of the Pit River community and their allies tried to occupy Mt. Lassen National Forest. Armed federal marshals met them. Pit River Raymond Lego took the lead and shrewdly called off the occupation. They left in a caravan, driving to a vacation campsite owned by Pacific Gas and Electric (PG&E), located within the 3.5 million acres the tribe claimed. In addition to the camp, the Pit Rivers claimed land owned by Southern Pacific Railroad, Pacific Telephone and Telegraph, Hearst Publications, United Fruit Growers, US Plywood, and Publisher's Forest Products, a subsidiary of the *Los Angeles Times*. Historian Sherry Smith called the dispute a "David and Goliath . . . Indians versus American corporate power."

Richard, Anne, their young son Joseph, and a caravan of approximately seventy-five others arrived at the PG&E camp. Lego urged the crowd, "Don't feel like you're a stranger here. This is your land. This is my land." The camp was luxurious compared to much of the housing at the Pit River rancheria. Anne took kids swimming; other children played among the pine trees. When the sheriff came to arrest them, the occupiers assisted him in the effort to test the legitimacy of PG&E's claim in court. They planned to argue one cannot trespass on one's own land. Joseph watched his parents, his father grinning as the police arrested, handcuffed, and took them to Redding, where folk singer Buffy Sainte-Marie covered their bail.

Only when they arrived in Shasta County court did PG&E realize they had been played. Aubrey Grossman, the attorney who came to prominence representing the Indian occupiers of Alcatraz, laid out the Pit Rivers' claim. PG&E contemplated dropping charges to avoid a court ruling in the Indians' favor. Pit River Indians renewed their occupations, sending small waves of occupiers back as a warning that without trespassing charges, PG&E should expect them to stay. A standoff ensued: Indians trying to get arrested and deputies alerted by PG&E that they should not arrest anyone for trespassing. As reported by a local newspaper, Oakes asked one of the officers what it would take to get arrested:

"I don't know. You tell me," the officer said, "We just might do something if anyone enters a cabin." It was all very friendly. Oakes explained the Indians' position. "But it's already in court. What are you going to gain by getting more people arrested?" the officer asked. "Think of the public that's paying for these courtroom and enforcement expenses," he added. "The taxpayers will get mad at PG&E, not us," another Indian predicted. "No, the public will get sick of the Indians," the deputy replied. "Your move," said Oakes, grinning. The patrol car left. "Now it's our move," Oakes told the Indians . . . [and with] no arrests the group decided to call it a day. Oakes pronounced the final benediction: "The game is being called on account of the rain."

Grossman continued to press the case that not only should his clients not be charged with trespassing, but the judge should charge PG&E with trespassing on Indian land. When the judge declined, Gemmill,

Lego, Oakes, Grace Thorpe (Sac-Fox), and Charlie Buckskin (Pit River) decided to make a citizen's arrest of the PG&E president at the company's office in San Francisco. The effort failed. The group held a strategy session to plan their next steps, which, after the others returned home for the night, Oakes and Gemmill continued at Warren's Slaughterhouse Bar. A Samoan from the neighborhood, with whom he previously quarreled, attacked Oakes with a pool cue, fracturing his skull and causing blood clots in the brain. Oakes spent the next two months hospitalized and never regained the full use of the left side of his body.

Before the attack, Oakes asked for "back-up from friendly freaks or anyone else" who wanted to help the Pit River cause. The call was successful, but not all the help was welcome. Countercultural groups from the Bay Area, such as Wavy Gravy and the Hog Farm, joined in the effort, in their own way. Hog Farmers, who lived in a hippie commune, saw the occupation as part of a larger countercultural struggle over environmental causes and social values. When Hog Farmers arrived at Pit River, they promptly stripped naked and swam around in the river, upsetting many of the local Indians, who saw their behavior as disrespectful. Additionally, the hippies' actions provoked law enforcement, but they were less likely to be arrested than the Indians, and being arrested for charges other than trespassing was counterproductive.

Hog Farmers returned to San Francisco and, with the Native American Studies program at UC, held a Summer Solstice fundraiser concert for the Pit River defendants. The Grateful Dead, New Riders of the Purple Sage, and Osceola performed, with Pit River tribal members describing their grievances between songs. Money was split between the legal defense fund and Oakes's hospital bills.

After checking himself out of the hospital in late August, Richard, with Anne, rejoined the Pit River effort. In October, one hundred Indians, including Anne, Richard, Gemmill, and Lego occupied Forest Service land near the "four-corners" intersection of Highways 299 and 89 in Burney. In response, approximately one hundred heavily armed federal, state, sheriff, and Forest Service officers arrived to arrest them. The occupiers refused to leave, and in the ensuing "Battle of the Four Corners," officers heavily beat many Indians.

Officials arrested more than two dozen Indians. Again, attorney Aubrey Grossman took the case. Wilma Mankiller volunteered in the legal fight and devoted herself to research related to the court case. Mankiller later wrote that she really came to understand treaties, federal Indian law, and the contours of sovereignty from a legal perspective through this experience. That work led eventually to her position as director of the Native American Youth Center in East Oakland.

Worried about Richard's health, Anne persuaded him to return with her to Stewarts Point. But again, Richard remained active across the region. In November of 1970, he led three actions, including occupying an abandoned CIA listening post near Santa Rosa and a former Foreign Broadcast Information Service monitor station near Healdsburg. In late November, Oakes brought the struggle home to Stewarts Point. The California Highway Department planned to widen a road through the rancheria without compensating the Kashaya for the expropriated land. Richard led a group of approximately twenty-five in blocking the road. They posted a sign: "Stop pay toll ahead, $1.00. This is Indian Land." Some who stopped recalled Oakes's direct politeness in explaining the purpose of the roadblock, helping change tires, and joking with the California Highway Patrol when they came to arrest him: "What took you so long? You can never find an officer when you need one." Officers arrested Oakes for felony robbery and blocking a public roadway. A judge dropped the first charge when he paid back the tolls but set the trial for the second charge for September of 1971.

When Oakes returned to the rancheria and was arrested again for the same activity, Kashaya chief James Allen and the tribal council chastened him for exposing the tribe to jeopardy they could not afford. Anne continued to worry about Richard's health. In January of 1971, a surgery to insert a steel plate in his skull helped ease the pain from Richard's injuries. Homesickness, combined with Anne's realization that Richard would be unlikely to slow down in California, caused the Oakeses to move back to the St. Regis Mohawk Reservation in New York in early spring of 1971. The break proved helpful in his recovery, but, unable to find work and detached from their respective support networks of family and friends, they decided to return to Stewarts Point in late spring.

Negotiations brought the Alcatraz occupation to an end in June, nineteen months after it began. Jack Forbes claimed that Alcatraz was pivotal in forcing Indians to confront the tension between spiritual values and the drugs and alcohol so prevalent in the urban Indian communities. Castillo later claimed that Alcatraz was "more political theater than substance." But it was a powerful show, and it raised attention internationally. According to Forbes, it "liberated the psyche of native peoples, making it 'all right to be Indian, headbands and all' ... an experiment in native self-determination in a communal and political sense." It was a moment on the national stage. When Oakes learned the news of the negotiated end to the occupation, he famously claimed, "Alcatraz is not an Island. It's an idea." He envisioned the actions begun there spreading across the state and nation.

In September of 1972, Richard Oakes addressed the California Indian Land Claims Commission on behalf of Pit Rivers' dispute with the California Indian land claims settlement. Observers remembered his health had declined to the point that he was unable to walk to the stage to speak. Later that month, back home at Stewarts Point, Oakes confronted the manager of a local YMCA camp over his purported mistreatment of some local Pomo children. The manager claimed Oakes lunged at him, and, in purported self-defense, shot and killed Oakes. A jury agreed the manager had overreacted but pointed to Oakes's reputation to justify his claim of self-defense and acquitted him of voluntary manslaughter in March of the following year. Anne's attorney claimed the jury "thought they might have reacted the same way." Anne spoke out, calling the manager's acquittal "white man's justice." She also committed to carry on Richard's work. In early November of 1972, she filed suit in federal court on behalf of herself and twenty other Stewarts Point residents for the return of ten miles of coastline to the Kashaya. She claimed the suit was filed to "show white men that when they killed Richard Oakes they did not kill the idea to which he devoted his life."

The idea of Alcatraz motivated many others as well. Luiseño Dennis Turner, a student at UC Santa Cruz in 1969, became involved in activism through the California Indian Education Association conferences. He went to Alcatraz along with other students from the conference to use the publicity to advocate for better representation of Indian issues in programs, courses, and faculty hires. Turner went on to be the tribal chairman of the Rincon Reservation.

Eastern Pomo Luwana Quitiquit grew up in the Stockton Delta in a family of seventeen, all of whom were farmworkers. Her mother, from the Robinson Rancheria, raised her children intentionally in her Pomo traditions. In the fall of 1969, she was a twenty-six-year-old mother who worked at the University of California, Berkeley. She was one of the first to make the journey to Alcatraz Island, taking her young son with her. They remained on the island until the occupation ended. Quitiquit eventually returned to Berkeley, this time as a student, where she earned a degree in sociology in 1977. Two important threads of her life grew out of that period and intertwined: a deep attachment to preserving California Indian land as a way to protect Indian culture, and a strong commitment to promoting economic growth for Indian communities, particularly those that lacked federal recognition.

While a student at Berkeley, Quitiquit studied basket weaving with Mabel McKay, who, along with a few other California Indians, achieved widespread recognition for their baskets. McKay, as all basket weavers, possessed extensive knowledge of the gathering spots for basket-making material. She spoke of the grasses and plants talking to her as she gathered them, in some instances through the squeak or timbre of the grass when she ran her fingers along it. In other cases, it was through the muffled attack of the roots as they were pulled from the mud. Each told the gatherer when the plant was ready to be taken. Graton Rancheria tribal president Greg Sarris recounts the story of Mabel speaking to students at Stanford University. A student asked her about the plants she used:

"Do you talk to them? Do they talk to you?"
"Well, if I'm going to use them I have to talk, pray."
The woman paused, then asked, "Do plants talk to each other?"
"I suppose."
"What do they say?"
Mabel laughed out loud, then caught her breath and said, "I don't know. Why would I be listening?"

The other of Quitiquit's threads was economic development. In 1978, she helped form the Economic Advancement for Rural Tribal Habitats (EARTH) in Ukiah and served as its executive director for many years. In the early 1980s, EARTH worked to acquire federal and state money to buy land, repair housing, and build new homes and community centers on Northern California rancherias. They helped secure grants from the California Department of Housing and Community Development to assist local rancherias in rebuilding housing, which was critical for rancherias the United States terminated and which lacked access to federal funds. In addition, EARTH hosted conferences to promote tribal business development, linking tribal communities to corporate and government institutions, and to help conduct tribal resource assessments to promote tribal businesses such as timber, farming, and renewable energy.

Quitiquit continued to work in tribal economic development and eventually served as the executive director of the Ya-Ka-Ama (Kashaya for "Our Land") Indian Education and Development Center, on the grounds of the former CIA West Coast Foreign Broadcast Monitoring Station that Pomos had occupied in 1971. Since that time, the federal government has granted Pomos legal custodianship of the property. Pomos devoted the land to promoting self-sufficiency through a nursery, which specialized in native plants, particularly those used in basket weaving, as well as educational programs promoting Indian culture, vocational training, and economic development. When she retired from social work, Quitiquit returned to basket weaving, working to train and educate others.

Alcatraz impacted Wilma Mankiller as well. In 1977, she moved home to Oklahoma with her two daughters. While her daughters found the transition to life in rural Oklahoma a challenge, Mankiller thrived. She finished her college degree, worked as an economic stimulus coordinator for the Cherokee Nation, and directed a major community revitalization project involving water lines and home construction in an impoverished Cherokee community. Quickly proving herself, she became director of the Cherokee Department of Community Development, the deputy chief of the Cherokee Nation in 1983, and the tribe's principal chief in 1985. While not the first woman to lead a large tribe, she was the first woman to lead the Cherokee Nation, the second largest tribe in the US. During her ten years of leadership, she revitalized the Nation, expanded Cherokee self-governance and community development, and defended Cherokee national interests. She left office in 1995 as one of the most well-known Indian women in the US. Mankiller credited her time in California as critical to her identity as both Cherokee and Indian.

Alcatraz had other, less obvious impacts on California Indian life. The actions by California Indians to reclaim land in the early 1970s, some of which were directly motivated by actions such as the Pit River occupation, coalesced into a successful pattern. Rather than occupying land, Indians pushed for land and the restoration of tribal status through all three branches of the federal government: judicially through court cases challenging termination, legislatively through acts of Congress, and administratively through the BIA and Department of the Interior.

The CILS Rural Indian Land Project (RILP) focused its efforts on assisting California Indians in navigating the legislative and judicial process. In 1972, the California Superior Court ruled in favor of an action brought by the Ione Band of Miwok Indians with the assistance of the CILS-RILP. The ruling granted title to forty acres of land, which the tribe intended to take into trust. The BIA responded later that year, extending federal recognition to the band, a necessary precursor to taking land into trust.

In 1978, the BIA published new guidelines for recognition, making the administrative path far more challenging. Those guidelines required Native groups petitioning for recognition to "establish a substantially continuous tribal existence and [to] have functioned as autonomous entities throughout history until the present." Many tribes across the US found it difficult to demonstrate that continuity because an adaptive, dynamic strategy had been necessary to survive settler colonialism. In California, many Indigenous People hid their tribal identities in order to survive the genocide of the nineteenth century. Additionally, the extensive documentation required created a backlog of petitions awaiting a ruling by the BIA, often leaving petitioning tribes waiting decades for decisions. The Honey Lake Maidu from Lassen County spent years seeking federal recognition, only to eventually decide to withdraw their application because the process required them to contradict their cultural values.

Many of the lawsuits with which CILS assisted challenged the federal government over its failure to honor the provisions of the 1958 Rancheria Termination Act. In 1976, the Robinson Rancheria (Pomo) contested the right of Lake County to collect taxes on the rancheria, which the federal government had terminated in 1965. They filed a lawsuit against Lake County, and the secretary of the interior, arguing unlawful termination because of the federal government's failure to adhere to the terms of the law. In 1977, the district court restored their tribal status, effectively "unterminating" the rancheria. Within two years, other actions followed the same path: Hopland Rancheria (Pomo) in 1978 and Upper Lake Rancheria (Habematolel Pomo) in 1979.

Building on the successes of the previous years, Pomo Tillie Hardwick sought the assistance of CILS to file what became a class action lawsuit in 1979. The complaint, on behalf of Pinoleville and thirty-five other rancherias, formalized the legal challenge of previous cases: the federal government had failed to uphold its obligations for infrastructural development before termination, and as a result, the members of the rancheria communities had been unable to utilize the land in the promised manner yet were required to pay taxes as if they had.

In a landmark decision in 1983, the district court ruled in favor of the petitioners and restored seventeen rancherias. The case reinstated individual members of the rancherias as Indians and restored their tribal status. Additionally, tribal members could place land back into trust status. Based on the success of the class action lawsuit, many other rancherias and a few reservations launched their own legal challenges to termination. A second decision in 1987 expanded the number of tribes eligible for the relief outlined in Hardwick, eventually restoring more than forty rancherias. The United States restored some of those tribes but without land, such as the Wilton Rancheria (Miwok), Paskenta Band (Nomlaki), and Upper Lake Rancheria.

Although the courts provided a clear path toward restoration, the United States has yet to restore several rancherias that it terminated in the 1950s and 1960s, including the Mission Creek Reservation, Cache Creek Rancheria, and Mishewal Wappo of Alexander Valley. In some cases, the government's failure to honor its obligation was not as obvious as it was in *Hardwick*. In other instances, the tribes lack the resources to pursue the effort in court, especially when facing intense resistance by local non-Indian communities.

A time of legal victories and increasing power, the 1970s also saw the maturation of cultural efforts. Cahuilla scholar and activist Jane Penn, who was instrumental in founding the Malki Museum, traveled to Geneva, Switzerland, to attend the 1977 United Nations International Conference on Discrimination against Indigenous Populations. This was the first UN conference with indigenous delegates and produced the first draft of the document that eventually became the UN Declaration of the Rights of Indigenous Peoples, approved in 2007.

In March of 1972, Pomo Essie Parrish, and Pomo-Patwin Mabel McKay traveled to New York City to discuss the Bole Maru religion and their healing practices with students and faculty at the New School for Social Research (now, New School University). When Parrish died in 1979, Pomos padlocked the roundhouse at Stewarts Point, as she had instructed. Mabel carried on alone. McKay's life followed many contours important to California Indians. She was born in a small enclave of Pomo people in a tenuous land-tenure situation. She moved frequently, often to find seasonal agricultural work or as a domestic in San Francisco. After she began Dreaming, that often took her across the region and later the state to heal patients. For years, she worked at an apple cannery in Sebastopol alongside Essie Parrish, who got her the job.

So much of McKay's life was rooted in the land, the baskets that she wove and used in her healing, and the plants that constituted her medicine. That attachment motivated her to protest the construction of Warm Springs Dam, which would have flooded important sedge gathering sites. Figure 31 depicts her standing in front of an earthmover as part of that protest. The project had begun in the 1960s but was slowed down by a coalition of environmentalists and Indians. They secured an injunction to stop construction in 1974 on the basis of inadequate seismic studies, an underestimation of environmental damage, and the fact that the lake would flood ancient Pomo village sites. They raised attention through protests.

In response, the Army Corps of Engineers, which oversaw the project, proposed to pave over prehistoric sites to preserve them and erect a museum on the shores of Lake Sonoma. A spokesperson for a group

News from
NATIVE CALIFORNIA
VOLUME 2   NUMBER 4   SEPTEMBER/OCTOBER 1988 $3.50

Conversations with Mabel McKay

California Indian Boats

Can a Non-Indian Participate in Indian
Ceremonies? Dr. Coyote Responds

FIGURE 31. Mabel McKay, Pomo basket weaver, stands in front of a huge truck while
protesting the construction of a dam in the Dry Creek basin. Pomo basket makers have
long been recognized as some of the premier basket weavers in the world. Their baskets
are extraordinarily beautiful and encompass a variety of shapes, function, designs, and
styles of weaving. Photo courtesy Sonoma County Library.

promoting the dam argued, "Let's live for today. What could be a more fitting memorial to you than this dam and lake?" Bill Smith, Pomo spokesman, said, "You can't preserve history by destroying it. Instead of a museum by the lake, I suggest you put up another kind of monument for the Indians, a headstone to mark the death of the Dry Creek Pomos." At a public hearing, forty members of the Pomo Band and their attorney claimed that the Army Corps cultural resource management reports grossly underestimated the number of Pomo sites to be flooded but were "regularly hooted down [and told to 'shut up'] by an audience of about 300 mostly white Sonomans."

Despite opposition, the Army Corps built the Warm Springs Dam in 1982. Eventually, Lake Sonoma flooded the prehistoric village sites, but the Army Corps agreed to move some of the sedge fields. Consistently, California Indians have had to fight against a persistent effort to remove them from the land and erase their culture. They have adapted methods from other groups, cooperated with them when it suited their needs, but distanced themselves when they needed to protect themselves. The sedge fields will go on producing the material for baskets, and California Indians will continue to make them.

After World War II, the Indigenous People of California, as well as those in other parts of the United States, migrated to California's cities. San Francisco, Los Angeles, and others reverted to Indigenous spaces. Indigenous People congregated in bars and urban centers. They discussed their shared histories of settler colonialism over a beer or whiskey. They put on dance regalia and danced in powwows. Building on these intertribal connections, California Indians and Native People from other states engaged in direct action protest. They occupied lands in the Bay Area and northeastern California to point out the illegal way in which Americans took California's land. California Indians and American Indians brought these activist efforts to their communities. They battled against the pernicious policy of termination, eventually overturning much of it. As California Indians entered the last two decades of the twentieth century, they stood poised to continue efforts to reclaim land and sovereignty.

SOURCES

The material on the Kashaya rancheria at Stewarts Point comes from a number of sources, including E. W. Gifford, "Ethnographic Notes on the Southwestern Pomo," *Anthropological Records* 25 (Berkeley: University of California Press, 1967); June Nieze, "The Purchase of Kashaya Reservation," *Working Paper No. 7, Kashaya Pomo Language in Culture Project,* Department of Anthropology, California State College, Sonoma, 1974; Cora Du Bois, *The 1870 Ghost Dance* (originally published in 1939 by the University of California Press; repr., Lincoln: University of Nebraska Press, 2007).

Rose Delia Soza War Soldier's doctoral dissertation, "'To Take Positive and Effective Action': Rupert Costo and the California Based American Indian Historical Society" (Arizona State University, 2013) was very useful. Rupert Costo's concern about a "smoothing out [of] cultural differences," is from page 125. Philip Galvan's petition claiming non-Ohlones had no right to speak on behalf of Ohlones is from page 120.

Deborah Miranda's comments on the canonization of Junípero Serra are from "Serra the Saint: Why Not?" *Indian Country Today,* Jan. 26, 2015. Edward Castillo's recollections about teaching at the UCLA American Indian Center, his experiences on Alcatraz, tensions with non-California Indians, the political theater and his cynicism with it, all are from Edward Castillo, "A Reminiscence of the Alcatraz Occupation," *American Indian Culture and Research Journal* 18, no. 4 (1994): 121–22, 127.

The Los Angeles Indian Center's promotion "Let's be Indian!" and much of the context of the era is from Nicolas Rosenthal, *Reimagining Indian Country: Native American Migration and Identity in Twentieth-Century Los Angeles* (Chapel Hill: University of North Carolina Press, 2014), 118.

David Risling and Jack Forbes's comment about an *"Indian-controlled and Indian-centered"* institution of higher learning, and Forbes's comments about the "dawn of a new age" are both from Jack Forbes, "An American Indian University: A Proposal for Survival," *Journal of American Indian Education* 5 (Jan. 1966): 1, 7. For the Dos Rios Dam, see William J. Bauer Jr., "Not Dammed Indians: The Dos Rios Dam and the Politics of Indian Removal in 1968," paper presented at the annual meeting of the Historians of the Twentieth Century United States, Liverpool, England, June 2019. Jack Forbes's claim that Alcatraz "liberated the psyche of native peoples" is from Jack Forbes, "The Native Struggle for Liberation: Alcatraz," in *American Indian Activism: Alcatraz to the Longest Walk,* edited by Troy R. Johnson, Joane Nagel, and Duane Champagne (Urbana: University of Illinois Press, 1997), 129.

Video footage of the encounter between Oakes and Hannon from KRON-TV, as well as extensive archival footage of the Alcatraz

Occupation, is available through San Francisco State University's "San Francisco Bay Area Television Archive."

Historian Sherry Smith's comment about "Indians versus American corporate power" and Oakes's request for "back up from friendly freaks" come from Smith's book, *Hippies, Indians, and the Fight for Red Power* (New York: Oxford University Press, 2012), 166–67.

Richard Oakes's question to the Highway Patrol, "What took you so long? You can never find an officer when you need one," is from Paul Chaat Smith and Robert Allen Warrior, *Like a Hurricane: The Indian Movement from Alcatraz to Wounded Knee* (New York: New Press, 1996), 140. Kent Blansett's excellent book, *A Journey to Freedom: Richard Oakes, Alcatraz, and the Red Power Movement* (New Haven, CT: Yale University Press, 2018), contextualizes Oakes and his activism. The numbers and general details of the Alcatraz occupation are from pages 117–65. Oakes's address to the California Indian Land Claims Commission on behalf of Pit Rivers can be found on page 245. Oakes's famous statement—"Alcatraz is not an Island. It's an idea"—is on page 5. Anne's lawsuit to "show white men . . . they did not kill the idea to which he devoted his life" is from page 256. Raymond Lego's claim to PG&E—"This is your land. This is my land"—is from page 210. Oakes's comment "The game is being called on account of the rain" is from page 213. On Anne Oakes's reaction to the YMCA manager's acquittal as "white man's justice," see Bony Saludes, "Oakes Case, Not Guilty," *Santa Rosa Press Democrat*, March 18, 1973, 1–2.

On Mabel McKay listening to plants, see Greg Sarris, *Mabel McKay: Weaving the Dream* (Berkeley: University of California Press, 1994), 2.

The 1958 California Rancheria Act was codified as Public Law 85-671 (72 Stat. 619, 621). The Office of Economic Opportunity's requirements for maximum feasible participation can be found in Public Law 88-452, Title II, Part A, Section 202. On 1978 BIA guidelines for recognition, often referred to as Part 83, that require "continuous tribal existence," and functioning as "autonomous entities throughout history until the present," see 25 C.F.R § 83.3(a).

For the claim that a dam and lake would be a fitting memorial to Pomos, see the *Santa Rosa Press Democrat*, July 16, 1976. In response, Bill Smith's suggestion of a headstone instead of a museum, and efforts to quiet protestors by white Sonomans, is from Ernest Murphy, "Indians Challenge Army on Dam," *San Rafael Daily Independent Journal*, March 4, 1976, 7.

Berkeley and the East Bay

In early October of 2015, Bancroft Way, by way of Boalt Hall's court-yard on the University of California, Berkeley, campus, offered a spectacular view. Most people did not seem to notice, likely because the view is so often stunning and easy to take for granted. One saw San Francisco Bay three miles and three hundred feet down the hill. Across the bay, the towers of the Golden Gate Bridge and the Marin Headlands rose above the fog. People gathered at Boalt Hall for the thirtieth meeting of the California Indian Conference. Conference attendees radiated a triumphant mood. Panel sessions and addresses began with greetings and recognitions in Chochenyo, the language spoken by the Huchiun Ohlone people of the East Bay. For thousands of years, the Huchiun Ohlone took in similar views as they moved seasonally from permanent village sites along the shore of San Francisco Bay at Temescal Creek and Strawberry Creek, inland to meadows and oak groves in the hills. Now, Ohlone students, scholars, elders, and other native Californians moved from lectures, panel discussions, and keynote addresses in the law school and the University Club on top of the newly remodeled Memorial Stadium. The Elder's Hospitality Room, in the Chancellor's Box, provided tribal elders and special guests with refreshments and a place to rest and take in the panoramic views of Oakland and San Francisco. Luiseño-Cahuilla Edward Castillo led an excursion to Alcatraz Island. Puyukitchum-Ipai–Mexican American James Luna performed his piece "Native Stories." Graton Rancheria Greg Sarris and Ohlone-Costanoan

FIGURE 32. View of Berkeley and the San Francisco Bay Area from the Chancellor's Box at Memorial Stadium, University of California, Berkeley, Oct. 2015. Photo courtesy Damon B. Akins.

Esselen Nation Deborah Miranda delivered keynote addresses. The meeting felt like a reoccupation (see fig. 32).

For thousands of years, the Bay Area was one of the most densely populated regions on the West Coast. The People who lived there were the children of Coyote, who lived at Reed's Peak, and Eagle, who lived on Mount Diablo. Both possessed a view of the Bay Area similar to the one down Bancroft Way. After a great flood receded, Coyote and Eagle placed their children on the shores of the bay. At the time of European contact, at least fifty thousand people lived from the Carmel River to the San Francisco and San Pablo Bay area. They consisted of fifty or so small bands, who spoke at least eight mutually intelligible languages. There was more water then, and the Ohlone elevated their thirty to forty permanent villages above the marshland on shell mounds—huge piles of shells, earth, and ashes. Today, a memorial at the Bay Street Shopping Mall at the corner of Shellmound Street and Ohlone Way marks the Emeryville Shellmound, located where Temescal Creek empties into the bay. The West Berkeley Shellmound stretches a few blocks inland from where Strawberry Creek empties into the bay at the Berkeley Marina.

Beginning in 1776, Franciscans established a total of six missions in Ohlone territory, the first of which they named Mission San Francisco de Assisi (Mission Dolores) in San Francisco. Most Chochenyo speakers went to Dolores, and then San José, following its 1796 founding. After secularization, Mexican officials recognized Luis Maria Peralta's Rancho San Antonio land grant, which comprised more than forty-four thousand acres in what is now San Leandro, Oakland, Alameda, Emeryville, Piedmont, Berkeley and Albany. Ohlones worked on the rancho, herding the eight thousand cattle grazing on their lands and butchering the animals for the hide and tallow trade.

Spared the worst of the genocidal violence that decimated Indigenous People in other parts of Northern California, Ohlones faced erasure during the Gold Rush. In 1850, federal subagent Adam Johnston reported, "Of the numerous tribes which but a few years ago inhabited the country bordering on the bay of San Francisco, scarcely an individual is left." During the American period, affiliated Ohlone reoccupied old places. Ohlones reestablished a community at Alisal, in Pleasanton. Initially part of the Rancho Valle de San José land grant, in the late nineteenth century Phoebe Apperson Hearst, wife of mining magnate and US senator George Hearst, purchased the land. Hearst sympathized with Ohlones and allowed them to live and work at Alisal. Americans named the rancheria the Verona Station Community. Ohlones integrated the Ghost Dance and the World Renewal Ceremony with local dances and ceremonies. They remained connected to other nearby sites at Niles and Sunol. In 1906, Charles Kelsey, a lawyer from San Jose working with the Northern California Indian Association, conducted a survey of Northern California Indians and recorded the community as the Verona Band of Indians of Alameda County. He recommended the federal government buy land for them. The government did not. In 1919, Phoebe Hearst died, and the new owners evicted the residents of Alisal because they had no title to the land. Eventually, the property became the Castlewood Country Club.

Elsewhere in the East Bay, another group of settlers erased Ohlones. In 1873, the state moved the University of California to a site along Strawberry Creek, in Berkeley. The Hearst family donated a considerable amount of money to the university, a legacy that lives on in numerous buildings and structures bearing the family name. In 1901, Hearst founded the University of California Museum of Anthropology in the Parnassus Heights neighborhood in San Francisco to house Phoebe's extensive collection of Indigenous artifacts. The triangular relationship between philanthropists, academics, and California Indians built the museum and the university's academic reputation. The university established the first Linguistics Department in the nation. Some of the biggest names in the field, who worked closely with ethnologists like John Peabody Harrington from the Smithsonian, staffed its Anthropology Department. In 1925, Alfred Kroeber, the head of the department, declared the Verona Band extinct in his *Handbook of the Indians of California*. At the same time, Harrington recorded languages with Chochenyo speakers Angela (María de los Angeles) Colós and José Guzman. Today, Harrington's extensive collection of field notes on California Indian languages is vital to those trying to reconstruct these dormant languages. Kroeber later acknowledged his mistake but only after the superintendent in a regional Bureau of Indian Affairs office removed the tribe from the list of federally recognized tribes in 1927. In the 1930s, lack of official recognition removed the Verona Band from the Indian Reorganization Act process, which, while problematic, created ways for tribes to create tribal governments and acquired loans available for tribes to purchase land.

In 1931, the university's museum relocated to the Berkeley campus. In 1991, the university renamed the museum the Phoebe A. Hearst

Museum, which contains the second-largest collection of California Indian artifacts after the Smithsonian. The museum holds ten thousand ancestral remains, many excavated from the region's shell mounds, villages, and burial sites. Archaeologists exhumed some of the remains under the direction of Kroeber and other anthropologists at the university. The museum acquired many others from hobbyists and amateurs whose work can only accurately be labeled grave robbing.

The Second World War transformed the Bay Area yet again. The population grew dramatically, land prices soared, and the freeway system was grafted onto the land. In the early 1960s, the Oakland diocese of the Catholic Church sold a portion of Mission San José's cemetery, where many Ohlone ancestors are buried, to housing and retail developers. In 1964, the proposed route of Interstate 680 threatened to destroy the rest of the cemetery. Ohlone Dolores Marine Galvan pressured CALTRANS to change the route. Philip Galvan, Dolores's son and secretary for the San Francisco–based American Indian Historical Society (AIHS), launched a crusade to save the cemetery. In 1971, Cahuilla Rupert Costo and Cherokee Jeannette Henry Costo, founders of the AIHS, brokered a deal with the diocese to transfer ownership to the AIHS, who in turn, deeded the land to a new entity: the Ohlone Indian Tribe Inc.

Cultural revival occurred all around the region. In 1969, the first Native American Studies program in the United States was founded at San Francisco State University. This and other newly established regional Native American Studies programs helped forge tentative and complicated alliances among academics, activists, tribal members, the counterculture, and the educational institutions where these groups increasingly met. In 1985, Native students and activists worked with the Anthropology Department, the Native American Studies Program, the Linguistics Department, and the Lowie Museum of Anthropology at UC Berkeley to organize the first California Indian Conference. The conference sought to provide an opportunity for scholars working on California Indian topics to share their research. A mixture of academics and public officials from colleges and universities, museums, and public history sites across the nation presented brief talks. While a few California Indians gave presentations at the conference, their presence was primarily as *subjects* of study. That changed the following summer, when the Lowie Museum sponsored a conference called "Weaving Ancient Traditions into the Fabric of Modern Indian Life" on campus. Conference organizers wanted to bring California Indian artists to campus to meet with educators and scholars. By the end of the decade, the annual

California Indian Conference wove these two threads together and quickly became a vital part of California Indian life.

Ohlones, too, revitalized culture and politics. Vincent Medina, who later opened Café Ohlone in Berkeley with Louis Trevino, acquired a copy of the Chochenyo dictionary. Working with that and the Harrington recordings, he began to piece together the dormant language, eventually studying linguistics at UC Berkeley. Medina helped to revive the language and eventually worked alongside his cousin, Andrew Galvan, as the assistant curator at the Mission San Francisco, the site of his six-time great grandfather's baptism. At Mission San Francisco, Medina speaks the Chochenyo language to visiting school children, who are often surprised to learn Ohlones still exist. Galvan and Medina publicly disagreed when, in 2015, the Catholic Church sought to canonize Junípero Serra, a process that began in 1985, when the pope declared him "Venerable." Galvan, an outspoken supporter of the effort, praised it. Medina, an equally vocal critic, claimed canonizing "the leader of the disastrous, genocidal California mission system is a way that the church further legitimizes the pain and suffering of Ohlone and countless other California Indians." Outsiders often describe disagreements within Indigenous communities as "factionalism" and proof of Indigenous political impotence. Instead, Medina and Galvan approached sovereignty and cultural preservation from different vantages. They agreed on the end result although they might not walk the same path to get there.

The same held true for land. The parking lot across from Spenger's Fish Grotto restaurant on Fourth Street in Berkeley is the last portion of the West Berkeley Shellmound that remains relatively undeveloped. It is also immediately adjacent to the Fourth Street Shops, and a coveted spot for developers. Plans for the construction of a five-story mixed-use residential and retail development on the site emerged in 2015. Fierce opposition by some members of the local Ohlone greeted the announcement. Chochenyo Ohlone Corrina Gould, of Indian People Organizing for Change, argued, "When it comes to sacred sites, we as a society should think about things in a different way. This was the very first place inhabited on the entire bay—that is something that should be worth saving." Vincent Medina pointed out, "We did not stand in opposition when you developed other parts of our land. We do not get in the way when you put up apartment buildings or shopping malls. But where we draw the line is when you propose to dig up and desecrate the most sacred places where our ancestors are buried." Some Ohlone supported the project. Andrew Galvan consulted on the project. In late 2018, Spenger's closed after 128 years. Its closure makes the property even more tempting to developers. In October of 2019, the court ruling on the West Berkeley Shellmound upheld the decision to reject the housing project. The judge wrote that "a historic structure does not cease to be a historic structure" simply because "it is ruined or buried." That principle, he argued "would exclude many of the world's most beloved archaeological treasures." Despite the decision, pressure to develop the area, and the fight against it, continues.

And yet, the East Bay remains a place that Indigenous People and their relations reoccupy. The California Indian Conference has been held at UC Berkeley six times. In 2020, the city of San Francisco and much of the East Bay went into quarantine because of the COVID-19 pandemic. Not long after, people reported seeing Coyote roaming the streets, looking for food and observing how the space changed since he arrived after the flood and bore children with Eagle.

SOURCES

The authors are indebted to Hupa linguist Kayla Begay for use of the term *dormant* when discussing California Indian languages. Rather than consider languages "dying" or "lost," Begay explains Indigenous languages are sleeping, waiting to be woken up. The authors also wish to thank the many people involved in the organization of the California Indian Conference.

For statements of erasure during the American period, see Adam Johnston to Orlando Brown, Sept. 16, 1850, *Report of the Secretary of the Interior, Communicating in Compliance with a Resolution of the Senate, a Copy of the Correspondence between the Department of the Interior and the Indian Agents and Commissioners in California*, Senate Executive Document, No. 4, 33rd Congress, Special Session (1853), 45; and Alfred Kroeber, *The Handbook of the Indians of California* (1925; New York: Dover, 1976), 464.

The controversy over the canonization of Junípero Serra was widely covered. For an overview that contains links to other important statements, see Carol Pogash, "To Some Indians in California, Father Serra Is Far from a Saint," *New York Times*, Jan. 21, 2015. Vincent Medina and Corrina Gould are quoted in J.K. Dineen, "Berkeley 4th Street Developer Plans to Use New Housing Law to Bypass Review," *San Francisco Chronicle*, March 9, 2018. On the recent developments regarding the Fourth Street development projects, see Allison Griner, "'On My Ancestors' Remains': The Fight for Sacred Lands," Aljazeera.com, Dec. 16, 2019.

10

Returning to the Land

Sovereignty, Self-Determination, and
Revitalization since 1985

As the sun set over the San Jacinto Mountains, a small group of people, perhaps one hundred, waited for the evening's entertainment to begin. A long workday over, everyone came together to enjoy one another's company by playing poker. Suddenly, thirty-five police officers, wearing armor and helmets with visors and brandishing firearms, broke into the facility and began yelling at the people. One of the officers put a girl in a stranglehold and another forced a boy to the ground, even though he pleaded, "I'm not going anywhere." The men dragged the children away, perhaps to the city jail, and gave citations to others. The police officers took everything, including the furniture and much of the group's money. John Paul Nichols, a non-Indian who managed the facility, concluded, "The war started." In a way, nothing was new in this story. In the past, armed non-Indian men stormed into California Indian towns, homes, and communities, threatened and perpetrated violence, and incarcerated California Indian children. But this incident occurred on October 18, 1980. Instead of signaling the attempted destruction of California Indian people through genocide and child slavery, the "war" that non-Indians initiated against California Indian gaming in 1980 ended with an affirmation of California Indian sovereignty and self-determination.

In the late twentieth century, California Indians reclaimed land and engaged in cultural renewal activities as a result of the nationwide expansion of Indian gaming. In 1988, the Supreme Court ruled that California's Cabazon and Morongo Reservations, located along the interstate highway between Los Angeles and Palm Springs, could operate gaming businesses without state and county officials' interference. Although the subsequent Indian Gaming Regulatory Act (IGRA) diluted the court's decision by mandating some state involvement, California Indians explored unprecedented economic opportunities to assert political power and expand ongoing efforts to revitalize their social and cultural practices. California Indians faced difficulties in their efforts to achieve sovereignty and self-determination. The state of California attempted to stymie Indian gaming. The United States government balked at recognizing and restoring tribal groups. Within California Indian nations, people debated the parameters of citizenship. Although *Cabazon* and subsequent federal legislation initiated new economic, social, and political opportunities, these actions did not break with the past. California Indians have continually changed their economic strategies to secure political sovereignty and maintain social cohesion.

In the mid-to late 1970s, American Indian governments looked for ways to increase revenue and employ tribal members. In part, federal Indian policy initiated these developments. In the 1960s, the executive branch of the federal government advocated self-determination, not termination. Under the Lyndon Johnson administration, tribal nations could contract directly with the Office of Economic Opportunity rather than deal with the Bureau of Indian Affairs (BIA).

California tribal leaders recognized the impact of two centuries of colonial policies that divested California Indians of land and resources. Nations in Southern California were especially keen to engage in economic development. Many Southern California reservations sit in arid parts of the state and are unsuitable for agricultural production. But Southern California is a tourist hotspot. Twenty-two California Indian nations formed Indian Campgrounds Inc. to cater to tourists and campers traveling to and through Southern California.

Still, efforts to develop tribal economies and social services emerged unevenly. The federal government put obstacles in front of tribal leaders. The Viejas Band of Kumeyaay Indians, located approximately forty miles from downtown San Diego and thirty miles north of the US-Mexico border, proposed a processing facility for undocumented immigrants. "With families in custody," Anthony Pico explained, "most of the time the men and women would go to different institutions. Children, if they were there, they would go to different institutions. Families were split up." Designed to keep families together, the Viejas facility secured investors, but the federal government dragged its feet in approving the project. Pico estimated the BIA spent eighteen months reviewing the project, and the investors pulled out.

Courts, too, put up roadblocks to California Indian economic development. In 1979, the Cabazon Band of Mission Indians, whose reservation sits in Riverside County, opened a smoke shop and did not charge state taxes on cigarettes and liquor sold to nontribal members. The following year, the Supreme Court ruled states could charge taxes on those products sold on reservations to nonmembers. The Court decided American Indian smoke shops marketed an "exemption from state taxation," not an actual product. California Indian nations, as well as American Indian nations across the country, faced obstacles to their ongoing efforts of economic development. The trust relationship and excessive federal oversight made for a dilatory federal government, and federal courts stymied efforts of American Indians to expand their sovereignty. California Indians then turned to a new, and eventually controversial, opportunity.

In the early 1980s, American Indian nations began to engage in gambling-related businesses. American Indian–owned bingo halls and card rooms often flouted state laws by offering prizes on more days and in excess amounts than state laws allowed. States went to court to challenge the right of American Indian nations to operate gambling businesses. Federal district courts ruled laws concerning bingo and card rooms were "civil/regulatory" not "criminal/prohibitory," and thus states could not enforce their laws. In other words, most states "regulated" gambling; they did not prohibit it. Therefore, states could not enforce their gambling restrictions on sovereign tribal lands.

Losses in federal courts did not deter California state officials. On October 16, 1980, the Cabazon Band of Mission Indians opened a card room in Riverside County. Two days later, Indio City police officers, dressed in riot gear, arrested one hundred people and closed the card room for violating a city ordinance. Cabazon officials sued the city of Indio, and federal courts sided with Cabazon. In 1983, the Riverside County Sheriff's Office issued citations to thirty Cabazon officers for reopening the card room and confiscated cash. Cabazon and the Morongo Band of Mission Indians, also located in Riverside County, appealed to federal courts, ultimately producing one of the most significant legal decisions in federal Indian law.

In early 1987, the Supreme Court heard arguments in *California v. Cabazon Band of Mission Indians*. Twenty-five states supported California's position that tribal gaming "frustrated" state gambling policies and might permit organized crime to infiltrate their states. Cabazon countered that California lacked jurisdiction because Congress never specifically authorized state oversight and that Riverside County regulated gambling since five card rooms already operated in the county. In a six-to-three decision, the Court found in favor of Cabazon. The Court declared that "tribal sovereignty is dependent on, and subordinate to, only the Federal Government and not the States." The Court also noted that President Ronald Reagan had recently reaffirmed the federal government's support of "encouraging tribal self-sufficiency and economic development." "The Cabazon and Morongo Reservations contain no natural resources which can be exploited," the Court explained. "The tribal games at present provide the sole source of revenues for the provision of tribal services. They are also the major sources of employment on the reservations. Self-determination and economic development are not within reach if the Tribes cannot raise revenues and provide employment for their members."

Simultaneous with Cabazon's struggle with city and county officials, the United States Congress debated how to regulate Indian gaming. In 1983, Senator Morris Udall of Arizona called for a law to enable tribes to engage in gaming as long as they did not violate federal or state laws. Senator Harry Reid of Nevada and Representative Norman Shumway of California called for greater state regulation of gaming. Representatives and senators were in the process of designing a strict bill regarding gaming when the Supreme Court handed down *Cabazon*. After *Cabazon*, Senators Daniel Inouye and John McCain developed compromise legislation, and in 1988, President Reagan signed the Indian Gaming Regulatory Act. The act divided gaming into three categories. Class I games were "traditional forms of Indian gaming" and regulated solely by tribes. Tribes and the newly formed National Indian Gaming Commission regulate Class II games, such as bingo and nonbanked card games, such as poker, where the player plays against other players. Class III games included banked card games, blackjack, for instance, where the player plays against the "house," or casino, and slot machines. For tribes to operate Class III games, the most lucrative, Congress required they negotiate compacts with state governments, which the Department of the Interior would approve. The Indian Gaming Regulatory Act also exempted tribal nations from the Johnson Act of 1951, which prevented electronic games on federal lands. Finally, the act required that states "negotiate in good faith" with tribal nations.

California's governor and attorney general quickly tested the meaning of "good faith."

After *Cabazon* and the IGRA, more California Indian nations entered the gaming business. Anthony Miranda of the Pechanga Band of Luiseño Indians said, "We were operating out of trailers, still putting together trailers. . . . I teased everybody that if we would have learned how to stack trailers on top of each other, we would have built our hotel already." California Indian tribes expanded beyond card rooms and bingo to operate video gambling games, which they argued resembled the machines dispensing California state lottery tickets. Pechanga, for instance, increased their video gambling games from two hundred games to thirteen hundred by 1995.

Republican governor Pete Wilson disagreed with the tribes' assertions and refused to negotiate compacts with California Indian tribes. Much of Wilson's socially conservative base opposed the expansion of Indian gaming and supported his hard-line stance against California Indian tribes. Furthermore, California Indian tribes routinely supported Democratic candidates for state and federal office. Wilson argued that video poker and similar games violated state laws. In October of 1991, Attorney General Dan Lungren urged local and county officials to use "appropriate action" against what he considered illegal gambling. On the night of November 3, Fresno County sheriff's deputies seized ninety-three "slot-type gambling machines" on the Table Mountain Rancheria. Three weeks later, Rancheria and Fresno County officials agreed on a 240-day moratorium on raids and arrests.

Federal officials also intervened in California Indian gaming. Federal law officials threatened to raid California Indian casinos, arguing they violated the Johnson Act of 1951, which prohibited "gambling devices" on federal lands. Anthony Miranda recalled the US attorney issued a cease-and-desist order to the tribe. Rather than arresting people or confiscating machines, the district attorney "[issued] arrest warrants on the games themselves; each game has a VIN number, and they actually arrested the games themselves." For the most part, though, federal officials permitted existing games to operate while the issue remained in front of the California state legislature and federal courts.

California Indian tribes, of course, disagreed with the state and federal government. The Rumsey Band of Wintun Indians wanted to install stand-alone electronic gaming devices in its casino. Wilson and the Republican administration refused to negotiate a compact with those provisions. The Rumsey Band of Wintun Indians and nine California

Indian tribes sued Wilson for failing to negotiate a compact under the IGRA. The district court found in favor of California in *Rumsey v. Wilson*, arguing that the IGRA did not compel states to create compacts with American Indian nations.

Eventually, some California Indian tribes reached an agreement with the recalcitrant Wilson administration. In 1997, Wilson negotiated a compact with the Pala Band of Mission Indians. Pala was one of the largest tribes in the state but had not previously operated gaming and did not sue Wilson as part of *Rumsey*. Pala and Wilson took six months to reach a deal. In March of 1998, eleven other tribes joined Pala in signing a compact with Wilson. The compact allowed "lottery devices," which the Supreme Court had previously deemed legal, not slot machines, and capped the number at nineteen thousand in the state and 975 per tribe. Labor unions celebrated the compact because it required tribes to cover casino workers under the state's workers' compensation law and collective bargaining. The compact gave the other tribes in California sixty days to agree to the compact or face being shut out of the gaming industry.

The Pala Compact dismayed many California Indian nations. The compact undermined California Indian sovereignty since tribes could not negotiate compacts different from the Pala Compact. Anthony Pico, of the Viejas Band of Kumeyaay Indians, explained: "the Wilson administration wanted to have exclusive jurisdiction in regulating the games, and we said that Congress under IGRA had given that jurisdiction to tribes." Additionally, the Pala Compact threatened future revenues. Slot machines, banned in the compact, offer the highest financial return and profitability for casinos. In 1997 alone, California Indian tribes generated $1.4 billion in revenue. No one in Indian country wanted to foreclose future revenue.

In 1998, California Indian leaders went on the offensive. They placed a referendum on the state ballot, called Proposition 5, which required the state to negotiate compacts, allow slot machines, eliminate the cap on the number of machines in the state or per tribe, provide for revenue sharing with state and local governments as well as nongaming tribes, grandfather in preexisting games, and disallow workers to collectively bargain. Tribes argued gaming would rescue California Indians from poverty and benefit both county and state governments by generating new tax revenues and stimulating infrastructure spending. The tribes did not convince everyone. An antigaming political organization called the Coalition against Unregulated Gambling, led by Nevada-based casinos, labor unions, and the Walt Disney Company, raised $25 million to fight Proposition 5. California Indian tribes countered by spending more than $66 million. The tribes' spending and arguments worked. Sixty percent of California voted in favor of Proposition 5, a resounding victory for California Indian tribes.

Opponents of Indian gaming were not thwarted yet, however. A group consisting of unions, California card rooms, and Nevada casinos argued that Proposition 5 violated the state constitution and sued the state of California. In 1984, the state passed a constitutional amendment that banned Nevada- and New Jersey–style gaming in California. In *Hotel Employees and Restaurant Employees (HERE) v. Davis* (1999), the California State Supreme Court agreed with the gaming opponents and struck down Proposition 5.

Under the Wilson administration, which supported *HERE*, California Indian tribes possessed few alternatives. But Gray Davis, the newly elected governor of California, took a neutral stance in the legal battles and favored negotiating compacts with California Indian tribes. After a series of intense and heated debates, California Indian tribes and Davis agreed on a series of compacts that resulted in Proposition 1A, an amendment to the California Constitution. The new compacts capped the number of slot machines on a reservation at two thousand, limited tribes to two casinos, and required gaming tribes to share revenue with nongaming tribes. Proposition 1A carried 64 percent of the vote, another significant win for California Indian nations.

Since 1998, California Indians have explored unprecedented economic, social, and cultural opportunities provided, in large part, by gaming. The twenty-seven-story Morongo Casino and Resort looms over the San Gorgonio Pass like a neon Joshua Tree. Morongo leaders use gaming revenues to diversify their economy, partnering with Arrowhead Bottling Company to bottle and sell spring water and revitalize their language. In 2008, Morongo hosted "Prez on the Rez," in which eight candidates for the Democratic Party's nomination for president of the United States debated voting rights, campaign contribution spending limits, and running for office. Several hundred miles north of Morongo, the Round Valley Reservation's modest, one-story Quonset hut–like Hidden Oaks casino houses fewer slot machines but similarly enables the tribe to develop its economy and revitalize its culture. Hidden Oaks anchors a site that includes a convenience store and gas station and funds the reservation's youth programs and social services (see figs. 33 and 34).

FIGURE 33. Hidden Oaks Casino on the Round Valley Reservation. Photo by William J. Bauer Jr.

Gaming sparked other economic development projects on reservations and rancherias. The Cabazon Band of Mission Indians constructed a twelve-story hotel, complete with more than two hundred rooms and conference space to house their two thousand slot machines. Cabazon attached a golf course and bowling alley to the resort. Beyond that, Cabazon owns a small industrial park, where they lease space to other businesses, and a biomass power plant. The Viejas Band of Kumeyaay Indians purchased three radio stations in San Diego. The Yocha Dehe Band of Wintu Indians (formerly Rumsey) operate Cache Creek Casino and Resort. Gaming revenues fund a fire station, tribal schooling for children through grade eight, and an organic farm that produces wine and olive oil. Indian gaming drives California's economy, in general, not just on reservation and rancheria lands. Casino resorts are often the largest employers in these areas. The Pechanga Band of Luiseño Indians employs more than fifty-two thousand non-Indians in Southern California.

In addition to business opportunities, tribes use gaming revenues to improve living conditions on reservations. Until the 1980s, the Viejas Reservation suffered from poor roads and infrastructure, largely because of a century of federal neglect. Viejas built roads, a reclamation and sewer plant, and connected all houses to water and sewer systems. Additionally,

FIGURE 34. Morongo Casino, Cabazon, California, March 2007. Photo by David Scriven.

the tribal government set up a home loan program, whereby tribal members could purchase new or remodel older homes. On the Pechanga Reservation, the tribal government instituted an education program, where tribal members could take advantage of a range of educational opportunities, from college to vocational training programs.

California Indian tribes promoted cultural revitalization activities. Throughout much of California's history, colonizing forces, such as Spain, Mexico, and the United States, attempted to eradicate Indigenous cultural practices. Franciscan priests and BIA officials discouraged Indigenous languages, ceremonies, and living patterns. Many tribal nations have sponsored projects to reawaken their languages, "because in the end," Anthony Pico of the Viejas Band of Kumeyaay Indians said,

FIGURE 35. Anthony Pico, PhD, tribal chairman of the Viejas Band of Kumeyaay Indians, speaking at the San Salvador Replica Ceremonial Keel Laying at the Liberty Station, San Diego, California, April 15, 2001. Photo by Dale Frost. Licensed under Creative Commons Attribution 2.0 Generic (CC BY 2.0).

"our language is going to save us" (see fig. 35). Every August, the Viejas Band holds a three-week cultural event. "We do dancing and singing," Bobby Barrett explained, "and teach our kids our native games that we grew up with." The Agua Caliente Tribe built a one-hundred-thousand-square-foot cultural museum, which hosts academic presentations and language classes and collects Cahuilla artifacts.

California Indians bought back lands that the United States took from them. In 1877, the United States created the Morongo Reservation by executive order. Like many reservations in Southern California, Morongo sits in an arid part of the state, which limited the ability of residents to fulfill the government's misguided efforts to transform California Indians into farmers. In the early twentieth century, land dispossession continued as the federal government allotted the reservation. Soon the reservation began to take on the checkerboard look of many reservations in the United States, featuring alternating sections of Indian- and non-Indian-owned land. Furthermore, the federal government failed to protect Morongo's borders. Non-Indians in Southern California came onto the reservation and dumped garbage and toxic chemicals. In 2003, Morongo tribal president Maurice Lyons began the land buyback program. The tribe bought up all of Millard Canyon, located near Banning. Tribal attorney Howard Dickstein said, "These land acquisitions are attempts to fulfill an emotional promise handed down for generations: If there is any way possible, we will get our land back."

Not all efforts to leverage gaming revenues toward land-buyback efforts have succeeded. The Pala Reservation has long sought to repurchase Warner's Hot Springs, from which the federal government evicted Cupeños in 1903. When the property declared bankruptcy, the tribe submitted the highest bid, but the judge overseeing the bankruptcy ruled in favor of a non-Indian development company.

California Indians also returned to reservations. Throughout the late nineteenth and twentieth centuries, federal policies and economic changes in the state pushed California Indians to leave their homelands. After Proposition 1A, California Indians could find jobs, social services, and cultural projects on their home reservations. On the Pechanga Reservation, the population increased from 100 in the 1960s to 346 in 2000. The growing number of California Indians on reservations reversed more than a century of federal Indian policy and state dispossession.

Although the citizens of California expressed support for California Indian gaming in the votes on Proposition 5 and 1A, some began to question the expansion of gaming. In 2003, after a recession caused by the bursting of the "dot-com" bubble and an energy crisis in the state that tripled electricity bills, Californians voted to recall Governor Gray Davis and replaced him with the actor Arnold Schwarzenegger. During the campaign, Schwarzenegger followed in the footsteps of other Republicans, such as former Governor Wilson, and attacked California Indian tribes as a "special interest" group strangling California. On September 22, 2003, with sinking poll numbers, Schwarzenegger lashed out against California Indians. "It's time for [California Indians] to pay their fair share," he declared in a political ad. Elsewhere in the state, columnists argued California Indian gaming tribes had "gone too far." Schwarzenegger's anti-Indian language helped to buoy his candidacy and sweep him into office.

Many heralded Schwarzenegger's victory in the recall election a defeat for California Indian tribes. Victor Rocha, of the Pechanga Band of Luiseño Indians, observed, "We kind of got too big for our britches, politically speaking, and Schwarzenegger shoved it down our throats. But we learned a very valuable lesson." Rocha saw a silver lining in Schwarzenegger's victory, arguing the loss made California Indian tribes more politically savvy. To shore up California's budget deficit, Governor Schwarzenegger approached California Indian tribes, seemingly backtracking on his campaign's anti-Indian stance. He offered tribes the ability to add slot machines in excess of the currently negotiated compacts if they paid a double-digit tax on the new machines and deposited the funds into California's General Fund, not the Indian Gaming Revenue Sharing Fund. Morongo, Agua Caliente, Pechanga, and Sycuan jumped at the opportunity. The new compacts generated $350 million per year for California's general fund, which helped erase the deficit.

The Rincon Band of Luiseño Indians, however, opposed Schwarzenegger's efforts to compel California Indians to provide more revenue to the state. Rincon leaders attempted to negotiate a new compact with the Schwarzenegger administration that would have added nine hundred slot machines to the tribe's sixteen hundred. Of the $40 million in new revenues, however, Schwarzenegger's proposed compact with Rincon would have reserved $38 million for the state's general operating budget and only $2 million for the tribes. Rincon leaders believed the proposal illegally taxed Rincon, since compacts should only cover the direct impact of casinos on a local area. They sued the governor. Rincon eventually won two of the cases, with federal courts holding that revenue sharing should not be part of gaming compacts. After the victory in *Rincon,* in 2015, Auburn Rancheria renegotiated a compact with the new governor, Jerry Brown, which reduced Auburn's obligation to the state budget by two-thirds and redirected revenues to local concerns and nongaming tribes.

Many non-Indians in California approached tribal casinos in a not-in-my-back-yard way. Californians accepted casinos in Southern California's deserts or rural Northern California mountains but not in urban areas. This battle became especially pronounced in Sonoma County. In 1920, the federal government had purchased fifteen acres in Graton for "homeless" Indians living in the communities of Marshall, Bodega, Tomales, and Sebastopol. Seventy-five people, largely Coast Miwok and Southern Pomo, moved to the land but found only three acres were inhabitable. In 1958, BIA officials found only three families at Graton. In 1966, the United States terminated the Graton Rancheria and turned over the land to the last remaining family. By the 1990s, the original rancheria dwindled to a single acre, owned by the daughter of the original designee. Graton Indians, led by Miwok-Pomo novelist Greg Sarris, embarked on a campaign to restore their tribal status. They argued that restoration of their tribal status would mean access to federal health care and education opportunities, not necessarily gaming. In 2000, President Bill Clinton signed legislation to restore Graton Rancheria's trust status. Soon after, Graton launched efforts to build a casino in

Rohnert Park. An opposition group, called "Stop the Casino 101," responded with lawsuits. The tribe, now led by Tribal Chairman Sarris, reached an agreement with county and city officials, in which Graton purchased 254 acres outside of Rohnert Park. After the land was put into trust, Graton broke ground on its Graton Resort and Casino, which opened in 2013.

California Indians also engaged in internal debates about who belonged in a tribe and how to determine citizenship in their respective nations. In some cases, California Indian tribal governments chose to disenroll tribal citizens. As of July of 2016, thirty California tribes undertook just such disenrollment. Debates regarding the practice have been especially acrimonious. Often, tribal governments justify it by arguing they are correcting mistakes from past censuses—that the Bureau of Indian Affairs (BIA) should never have included the disenrolleds' ancestors on tribal rolls in the first place. In 2004 and 2006, the Pechanga tribal government removed 315 descendants of two individuals from tribal rolls, claiming the BIA relocated these people to the reservation in the 1880s, but they were not members of the Pechanga Band of Luiseño Indians.

Opponents argue money and political power determine disenrollments. Pechanga allocates some of its gaming revenue to all tribal members, as per capita payments. Before disenrollment, Pechanga tribal members received $15,000 per month; after disenrollment, tribal members received $40,000 per month. In addition, some disenrolled citizens alleged then-chairman Mark Macarro purged members of the tribe to consolidate his political base and ensure reelection. Chairman Macarro, however, argues money and politics had little to do with disenrollment. "This has never been about money," he said. "This is about the integrity of tribal citizenship at Pechanga. If there was a corn field instead of a casino, these same challenges would have taken the same path to the same conclusion." Disenrolled citizens counter that they lose revenue, access to health care and housing, education benefits, and ties to their people and homeland.

Some disenrolled tribal members challenged the decisions of tribal governments in state and federal courts. In 2011, the Pala Reservation's tribal government altered its tribal rolls and reduced an older citizen's blood quantum. Then, Pala disenrolled 150 of that person's descendants. Some of the disenrolled tribal members sued tribal leaders, alleging the tribal government prevented the BIA from exercising its trust relationship with all tribal members. *Aguayo v. Jewell,* and a related case called *Alto v. Jewell,* progressed through the federal courts. At each step, the courts sided with Pala. The Supreme Court declined to hear the case, upholding the lower courts' decisions. Gabe Galanda, a lawyer and enrolled member of the Round Valley Indian tribes, breathed a sigh of relief when the Court decided not to hear *Aguayo:* "Indian Country dodged a bullet. No tribal politicians should ever again tempt SCOTUS to ask and answer the question, 'Who's a tribal member?' In other words, disenrollment must stop before SCOTUS or the Congress is allowed to ask and answer that existential question for Indian Country. Rest assured we wouldn't like their answer."

As Galanda notes, tribal membership is a sovereign right of all American Indian nations. American Indian nations choose their criteria for determining citizenship. So, if tribes can disenroll members, they can also pass laws preventing future disenrollment. In 2013, on the eve of opening its casino resort, 85 percent of the Graton Rancheria voted to amend its constitution and prevent future tribal governments from disenrolling citizens. "We saw the money coming," said Tribal Chairman Greg Sarris. "We saw the changes coming. We saw the challenges and we said, 'Let's do something that could prohibit disenrollments in our tribe.'"

Furthermore, tribal governments can restore citizenship status. In 2009, the Robinson Rancheria Pomos, located in Lake County, disenrolled tribal members who were descended from people who were not included on a 1980 tribal census, which, at the time, served as the basis for tribal membership. Opponents contended that politics lay at the root of disenrollment. Eddie Crandell ran for tribal chair against incumbent Tracey Avila. Crandell won the election, but the tribe threw out the results, enabling Avila to retain her seat. Robinson then changed its membership criteria and purged sixty-seven people, many of whom had supported Crandell in the election. Karen Ramos had lived on the rancheria for twenty-four years, and she lost her home. "We were tribeless," Julie Moran, Ramos's relative, said. "It really did take away who we were." Avila remained tribal chair until 2013, when she passed away. In 2015, Crandell won election as tribal chair and began the work of overturning disenrollment. The disenrolled members petitioned the BIA to overturn Robinson's decision, but the BIA refused to intervene. Crandell and other tribal members worked behind the scenes to lay the groundwork for reenrollment of tribal members. In February of 2017, Robinson Rancheria voted fifty-four to twenty-five in favor of bringing back tribal members. Moran expressed joy to be reenrolled but acknowledged that the pain of what happened in 2008 stung two of her relatives, who chose not to petition for reenrollment.

Unacknowledged tribes engaged in similar struggles regarding Indigenous identity. There are several reasons tribes lack federal recognition in California. For the Verona Band of Indians in Alameda County, for instance, federal officials failed to put land in trust for them, although other officials recognized them as a tribe and in need of land, and University of California anthropologists declared they were extinct. Furthermore, as in the case of the aforementioned Graton Rancheria, the federal government engaged in an expansive termination campaign in the 1950s and 1960s, effectively eliminating Indigenous People with small land bases.

Since 1978, the federal government developed procedures for unrecognized tribes to gain federal recognition. Congress can issue a law granting recognized status. United States courts, such as in *Tillie Hardwick,* can also recognize a tribe. The Federal Acknowledgment Process requires tribes to constitute a distinct community and exist from historical times, exercise political influence over members, possess membership criteria, and include people who are not members of another tribe. These stipulations require tribes to conduct lengthy and often expensive research in their histories and cultures. As of April of 2020, three California Indian tribes have a petition in front of the Office of Federal Acknowledgment (OFA): the Southern Sierra Miwuk Nation, the Amah Matsun Band of Ohlone-Costanoan Indians, and the Fernandeño Tataviam Band of Mission Indians. One tribe—the Juaneño Band of Mission Indians, Acjachemen Nation—needs to supplement its petition.

The story of the Muwekma Ohlone Tribe illustrates the perils of federal acknowledgment. In the 1980s, Rosemary Cambra became the tribal chair of the Muwekma Ohlone Tribe. Cambra possessed a long history of sometimes controversial activism. In 1969, she rushed to Alcatraz to participate in the takeover. The experience set her on the path toward political power. In 1985, she became infamous in Indian affairs when TV cameras caught her attacking an anthropologist with a shovel for being insensitive about tribal remains at a construction site in San Jose. Cambra pled guilty to assault and served time in jail and probation. Although she became a hero among some activists, she lost her nursing license and her livelihood. In the late 1980s, *before* the Native American Graves Protection and Repatriation Act (NAGPRA), and without the power of federal recognition, Cambra negotiated an agreement with Stanford University to repatriate seven hundred ancestral remains.

Under Cambra's leadership, the Muwekma Ohlone Tribe sought restoration of its federal recognition. In 2002, federal officials denied the request, despite previous recognition and no evidence of the tribe's termination. In 2006, the Muwekma Ohlone Tribe appealed but, five years later, lost again. The tribe's fight for the restoration of its status is ongoing. The Muwekma effort to gain federal recognition has little to do with gaming. The tribe initiated the effort in the early 1980s. Furthermore, federal recognition would provide the protection of NAGPRA. Cambra claimed that when recognition occurs, "one of our first priorities will be to direct our attention to UC Berkeley and open discussions with them about how best to return our ancestors' remains for proper burial."

Although gaming impacted California Indian country positively, it is by no means the only way California Indians pursued land, cultural renewal, and sovereignty. Yuroks, Karuks, and Tolowas use the Siskiyou Mountains of northwestern California as a site for preparing for world renewal ceremonies. Religious leaders follow the Thkla-Mah, or Ladder Path, into the mountains to prepare for the Brush Dance, Jump Dance, and White Deerskin Dance, as well as to receive instruction for healing. "There are a number of prayer seats along the river," Yurok Chris Peters said. "The most important ones are in the high country areas, the Burl's Peak and the Doctor Rock–Chimney Rock areas. These are where high mountain medicine people go for fasting and praying. They make the connection that unites them as individuals with all of creation and with all of their spiritual needs."

In 1947, President Harry Truman designated parts of the area as the Six Rivers National Forest. Thereafter, the National Forest Service allowed clear-cut logging. By the 1970s, the Forest Service prepared to develop the area called the High Country, home to three spiritually significant peaks—Doctor Rock, Chimney Rock, and Peak 8—by paving a six-mile section of gravel road between the small towns of Gasquet and Orleans. Yuroks, Tolowas, and Karuks, joined by conservationists, protested the road and the proposed logging development near Chimney Rock. The Northwest Indian Cemetery Protective Association (NICPA) assumed a prominent role in the case. Founded in 1970 and led by Milton Marks, Walt Lara Sr., and Joy Sundberg, the NICPA watched over grave looting in Northern California. The NICPA and other California Indians argued the road and logging development infringed on their First Amendment rights and the American Indian Religious Freedom Act. Karuk elder Charlie Thom testified in *Lyng v. Northwest Indian Cemetery Protective Association,* "They're putting through the GO Road. . . . That road goes right past Chimney Rock, Doctor Rock, Little Medicine

Mountain, [and] Flint Valley. Those are places where we can shoot medicine right down into the Brush Dance hole."

Lower federal courts sided with the NICPA, and the case eventually went to the Supreme Court. The high court reversed the lower court decisions. Supreme Court Justice Sandra Day O'Conner upheld the federal government's ability and right to use its own land as it sees fit, even if that use infringes on American Indian religious practices. Although California Indians lost the Supreme Court case, Congress blocked any development around Chimney Rock when it designated the area a wilderness.

Beginning in May of 2001, women and men at the Hoopa Valley Reservation revitalized a Hupa women's ceremony called the Flower Dance. Hupas hold the Flower Dance at a young woman's coming of age. During the late nineteenth and early twentieth centuries, federal and state genocidal and assimilation policies undermined the practice of the Flower Dance. Male anthropologists, such as Alfred Kroeber, considered the Flower Dance a relic of a primitive past and indicative of the Hupas' less civilized nature. In the late twentieth and early twenty-first centuries, Hupa women Melodie George-Moore and Lois Risling brought back the ceremony. Hupa scholar Cutcha Risling Baldy documented the revitalization. Since the first ceremony, more Hupa girls requested the ceremony, and Hupa people developed new songs.

Elsewhere in Northern California, Native People commemorated the traumatic events in their past. In 1863, the United States forcibly removed 460 Concows and Maidus from their homeland near Oroville and Chico, California. The army imprisoned the Concows and Maidus in a corral outside of Camp Bidwell. Subsequently, malaria swept through the People waiting for the forced march. On September 4, 1863, the army began to march the Concows and Maidus the one hundred miles from Camp Bidwell to the Round Valley Reservation. Only 277 Concows and Maidus arrived at Round Valley two weeks later. The rest remained behind on the trail, too sick to continue. Oral histories of the ethnic cleansing recalled soldiers killing the elderly, women, and children.

Native People at Round Valley and Chico held this memory. In 1968 and 1969, Round Valley tribal leaders reminded the state of California of this ethnic cleansing when the state and Army Corps of Engineers proposed building a dam on the Eel River, which would have flooded the reservation and relocated the Round Valley People. In 1993, Round Valley tribal member Gaylan Azbill worked with the National Forest Service to mark the trail with interpretive signs. Three years later, at the conclusion of that effort, the descendants of the survivors of the ethnic cleansing began an annual walk along the route. In 1996, people gathered at California State University, Chico, to hold the first walk. The Nome Cult Walk has been instrumental in the process by which Round Valley Indians heal historical trauma. Gaylan Azbill said, "There's a lot of hurt, a lot of pain [in Round Valley]. We can't change what happened, but we've got to heal sometime. I think the dedication will have some closure for us." Arlene Ward, then chair of the Mechoopda Tribe of the Chico Rancheria, said that her grandfather would not attend the first Nome Cult Walk: "He would not come. He said it would be like going to a funeral." For others, the Walk has been a way to unite the Round Valley community, much like the Flower Dance at Hoopa. Fred Downey, a Round Valley tribal member, added, "We're able to walk together and be a loose-knit family again. The positive thing from this walk is the healing. We can learn a great deal and our kids can learn a great deal." Additionally, Round Valley Indians established intergenerational connections on the Walk. Kenneth Wright, former chairperson of the Round Valley Reservation, said that "it is important that our youngest members take part in this annual event." Shortly before her death, in 2011, Anita Rome, the last living descendant of someone who was forcibly removed by the United States in 1863, greeted her children, grandchildren, and great-grandchildren who participated in that year's Walk.

In the early 1980s, California Indians did not magically reappear with the advent of Indian gaming. Rather, the economic and political efforts to maintain connections to the land since 1985 rested on the efforts that began in the 1870s, as California Indian People, communities, and nations recovered from genocide, ethnic cleansing, and slavery. Influenced by national events, California Indian nations took the lead on advancing Indian gaming all the way to the Supreme Court. They struggled to carve out sovereign space with the state of California, eventually securing the support of the state's citizens to manage and operate gaming facilities. Gaming and nongaming tribes then advanced more and more efforts to revitalize cultures and secure land. These efforts have not been without contest. California citizens balked at the rate of gaming's expansion, and California Indians debated notions of national citizenship and belonging. Yet, as California Indians chart new paths in the twenty-first century, they remain committed to maintaining and securing their connection to the land.

SOURCES

There is a growing body of literature examining the history of Indian gaming in the United States, in general, and California, in particular. These studies tend to focus on the development of laws, court cases, and policies. See Ralph Rossum, *The Supreme Court and Tribal Gaming: California v. Cabazon Band of Mission Indians* (Lawrence: University Press of Kansas, 2011); Dale Mason, *Indian Gaming: Tribal Sovereignty and American Politics* (Norman: University of Oklahoma Press, 2000); Kevin Bruyneel, "The Colonizer Demands Its 'Fair Share,' and More: Contemporary American Anti-tribalism from Arnold Schwarzenegger to the Extreme Right," *New Political Science* 28 (Sept. 2006): 303–12; and Aaron Peardon, "Jackpot! A Legal History of Indian Gaming in California" (master's thesis, University of Nevada, Las Vegas, 2011). Some studies emphasize California Indian perspectives and practices. Suzette Brewer and Cheryl Cadue's edited volume of oral histories, *Sovereign: An Oral History of Indian Gaming in America* (Albuquerque, NM: Ipanema Literatures, 2009), was invaluable to this chapter. See also Nicolas Rosenthal, "Dawn of a New Day? Notes on Indian Gaming in Southern California," in *Native Pathways: American Indian Culture and Economic Development in the Twentieth Century*, edited by Brian Hosmer and Colleen O'Neill (Boulder: University of Colorado Press, 2004), 91–111; and Carole Goldberg and Duane Champagne, "Ramona Redeemed? The Rise of Tribal Political Power in California," *Wicazo Sa Review* 17 (April 2002): 43–63.

Scholars debate the impact of the *Cabazon* decision on the Indian Gaming Regulatory Act. Mason argues that "the cumulative effect of federal court rulings ending in the *Cabazon* decision . . . finally spurred Congress to action" (Mason, *Indian Gaming*, 53). Carole Goldberg and Duane Champagne agreed: "The *Cabazon* case and other Indian and state gaming conflicts around the country led the tribes and states to the Indian Gaming Regulatory Act of 1988 (IGRA)" ("Ramona Redeemed?" 46). Rossum, however, counters that it is an "exaggeration" to suggest that the IGRA was "Congress's reaction to *Cabazon*" (Rossum, *Supreme Court*, 149).

Newspapers devoted considerable space to reporting on Indian gaming. See stories in the *Los Angeles Times*, Indianz.com, *San Diego Union-Tribune*, and *Sacramento Bee*, among others. Tribal governments provide information on economic, cultural, and social programs on their websites. For representative websites, see those of the Yocha

Dehe Wintun Nation (www.yochadehe.org/heritage/history) and the Federated Tribes of Graton Rancheria (https://gratonrancheria.com).

For a scholarly analysis of disenrollment see David E. Wilkins and Shelly Hulse Wilkins, *Dismembered: Native Disenrollment and the Battle for Human Rights* (Seattle: University of Washington Press, 2017). As with gaming, state and national newspapers have covered disenrollments. One can find coverage in *Indian Country Today,* Indianz.com, and *L.A. Weekly* (for Pechanga); the *Press Democrat, Willits News,* and *Lake County News* (for Robinson Rancheria); and the *Press Democrat* (for Graton Rancheria).

For the Muwekma Ohlone battle for federal recognition, consult Les Field, with Alan Leventhal and Rosemary Cambra, "Mapping Erasure: The Power of Nominative Cartography in the Past and Present of the Muwekma Ohlones of the San Francisco Bay Area," in *Recognition, Sovereignty Struggles, and Indigenous Rights in the United States,* edited by Amy E. Den Ouden and Jean M. O'Brien (Chapel Hill: University of North Carolina Press, 2013); Les W. Field, "Unacknowledged Tribes, Dangerous Knowledge: The Muwekma Ohlone and How Indian Identities are 'Known,'" *Wicazo Sa Review* 18 (Oct. 2003): 79–94; and Les Field, Alan Leventhal, Dolores Sanchez, and Rosemary Cambra, "A Contemporary Ohlone Tribal Revitalization Movement: A Perspective from the Muwekma Costanoan/Ohlone Indians of the San Francisco Bay Area," *California History* 71 (Oct. 1992): 412–31.

Peter Nabokov provides an overview of *Lyng v. Northwest Indian Cemetery Protective Association* in *Where the Lightning Strikes: The Lives of American Indian Sacred Places* (New York: Viking, 2006).

For the revitalization of women's coming-of-age ceremonies, see Cutcha Risling Baldy, *We Are Dancing for You: Native Feminisms and the Revitalization of Women's Coming-of-Age Ceremonies* (Seattle: University of Washington Press, 2018).

For the Nome Cult Walk see *Chico Enterprise Record,* August 8, 1996; and Lee Romney, "Retracing the Grim Past," *Los Angeles Times,* Sept. 19, 2004.

Returns

In January of 2019, the City of Eureka approved the return of 202 acres of Indian Island to the Wiyot Tribe. The transfer was the third in a series that began in 2000 and restored approximately 95 percent of the island to tribal control. The first was the purchase of the site of Tuluwat, one of two historic Wiyot villages on the island and the spiritual center of the tribal universe for more than a thousand years. In private hands, non-Indians used the site as a boathouse. Discarded toxic batteries and leaking fuel had contaminated the soil, and erosion and looting had disturbed the thousand-year-old, six-acre shell mound adjacent to the site, which included numerous gravesites. Tribal Chair Ted Hernandez said, "It's sacred land. This is our sacred property. It's where our ancestors are. That's where our ancestors are buried, and that's what we recognize it as. It's the center of our world."

While this marks what is, perhaps, the first instance of a municipality returning land to its Indigenous occupants outside the context of a lawsuit, the Wiyots' story up to that point was tragically familiar. In an early morning raid in February of 1860, American settlers attacked temporary campsites on the island with axes, hatchets, and clubs, killing almost all of the mostly women and children who had gathered on the island for the weeklong World Renewal Ceremony. This was the third or fourth attack on Wiyot settlements in the area in a twenty-four-hour period. The total number killed is unknown but certainly reached the hundreds, constituting the majority of the Wiyots living in the Eureka area.

After the attackers left, Wiyots returning from the mainland found a few survivors among the dead: an older woman stuck in the mud and singing a mourning song, and small children, among them an infant crying in his dead mother's arms. She had been killed along with the rest of his family, but the infant, Jerry James, survived.

The Indian Island massacre almost wiped out the Wiyots. The federal government removed the survivors, first to Del Norte County near Oregon, but they returned. Then the Wiyots were moved to the Hoopa Valley Reservation in northern Humboldt County, but they came home. Then they were moved to the Round Valley Reservation in Mendocino County, but they returned home again. Many Wiyots lived hiding "among the willows." Eventually, a church donated twenty acres of land south of Eureka to the tribe, which became the Table Bluff Reservation. In 1961, the federal government terminated the tribe. The following year, Della Prince, the last documented fluent Wiyot speaker, died. Wiyot people and history followed a familiar narrative in California; despite their efforts, they seemed to be vanishing.

In 1970, Albert James, president of the Far West Indian Historical Center Association, and grandson of Jerry James, suggested it was time for the Wiyots to get Indian Island back. The goal of the organization was to construct an Indian Historical Center on the island, including an auditorium, museum, and library. The city of Eureka made a small step in that direction, voting to officially rename the island "Indian Island" rather than retain the name Gunther Island, a tribute to an American settler who occupied the island after the 1860 massacre.

The effort to reclaim the island coincided with and mutually reinforced the effort to regain federal recognition. Efforts across the state resulted in a series of lawsuits against the federal government for the restoration of tribal status. In 1981, the Supreme Court settled the case in favor of the Wiyots at Table Bluff. The BIA reinstated the tribe, a gesture that helped in their efforts to push for the return of the island.

Albert James's niece, Jerry James's great-granddaughter, Cheryl Seidner, moved back to Eureka from San Francisco and pestered her mother, Loreta, and grandmother, Hazel, to tell her the stories of her people. She learned that the Creator put the Wiyot there. The Creator sent rains and flooded the earth. All of creation perished except for a boy and a girl, who survived the flood, secure in a big basket, sewn up tight, and stocked with provisions by their mother. When the water receded, they found themselves at Indian Island.

Cheryl Seidner described her family's attitude toward history as matter of fact. Her parents were generous and welcoming, but she summarized their outlook as blunt: "Things happen. You die." Her great-grandfather survived, and it was up to his ancestors to go beyond that. She was not supposed to be here but was. So, she worked with others to raise money selling T-shirts, baked goods, and posters, and asking for donations at university events and meetings of organizations such as the National Congress of American Indians.

In 1992, the boathouse on the island shut down. In 1996, Seidner became the chairwoman of the Wiyot Tribe. She organized candlelight vigils to raise consciousness of Wiyot history around the region, and she built relationships among Indian and non-Indian residents of Eureka. A flurry of intense fundraising efforts in the late 1990s eventually raised the $106,000 to buy the 1.5-acre site of Tuluwat in 2000.

The return of the site to Wiyot hands allowed the tribe to protect the shell midden from further erosion, but the toxic chemicals, fuel, and metals of the boatyard had contaminated the land. The tribe secured grants from the Environmental Protection Agency and the California Integrated Waste Management Board. An acre and a half is slightly larger than a football field. A team of specially trained archaeologists, wearing white hazmat suits and looking like astronauts on a construction site, sifted through the entire site with shovels. They screened every shovelful of dirt for artifacts. Eventually, the archaeologists removed eighty-eight fifty-five-gallon drums of contaminated waste from the site. Two forty-yard-long dumpsters of metal were removed and recycled. Given the proximity of the shell midden, and the numerous grave sites, a consultant on the project described it as like excavating a contaminated site at Arlington National Cemetery. The tribe rebuilt the shoreline to prevent further erosion and replanted indigenous plants.

Under Seidner's leadership, the tribe continued to press for the transfer of the rest of the forty acres north of State Highway 255. In the summer of 2004, the deeds were signed and gifts exchanged, transferring the land to the tribe. In 2017, the EPA gave the tribe the "excellence in site reuse award," the first time a tribe anywhere in the United States had received such recognition. In January of 2019, the city of Eureka returned the bulk of the island south of the highway. The Tuluwat project embodies survivance and eschews the narrative of victimhood and, as Seidner described it, shows that "we aren't shadows today. We are not forgotten. . . . We are still here. We are still a people. We still *cast* a shadow."

The tribe's restoration of Indian Island shows in stark relief the differences between the Wiyot approach to stewardship and the all-too-familiar and often destructive settler concept of landownership, as exemplified by the boathouse. It also provides healing to the Wiyots, as well as the non-Indian people of the region. In March of 2014, the tribe performed the World Renewal Ceremony for the first time since the 1860 massacre. Some of the ceremonial knowledge, regalia, and language was dormant, but the tribe worked with elders, written records, and neighboring tribes to awaken it. Seidner and the new tribal chair, Ted Hernandez, took on the role of medicine for the ceremony—she for the women, he for the men.

Ojibwe Bob Anderson, director of the Native American Law center at the University of Washington School of Law, points out that the transfer of Indian Island back to the Wiyots, and how they have managed it, is "a big deal [because] it sets an important precedent for other communities that might be thinking about doing this." He cites it as a "significant example of the sort of forward-looking, modern good relationships between tribal government and non-tribal governments. . . . It seems to me this could be a shining example of what's possible."

What is possible is also visible in the California Indian History Curriculum Commission, founded in the summer of 2016 by Rose Borunda, Gregg Castro, and others. Their work in developing a curriculum that is accurate and respects the distinctiveness of specific tribal identities counters the often general stories of Indians in California schools. It turns a dismissive but ubiquitous narrative into a broad foundation on which to build a statewide effort to reorient students' understanding of the people on whose land they live.

And what is possible is proof that the story is not over, that we are in the middle of it. It also shows that out of the tragedy comes the promise of survivance and the power to make that promise real. Like Mvskoke-Creek poet Joy Harjo wrote in "Anchorage":

And I think of the 6th Avenue jail, of mostly Native
and Black men, where Henry told about being shot at
eight times outside a liquor store in L.A., but when
the car sped away he was surprised he was alive,
no bullet holes, man, and eight cartridges strewn
on the sidewalk
all around him.
Everyone laughed at the impossibility of it,
but also the truth. Because who would believe

the fantastic and terrible story of all of our survival
those who were never meant
to survive?

SOURCES

Thadeus Greenson, "We Are Coming Home: The Unprecedented Return of Indian Island to the Wiyot Tribe," *North Coast Journal* 30, no. 4 (Jan. 24–30, 2019); Cheryl Seidner, interview by Paul Nelson, Sept. 8, 2015, paulenelson.com; Joy Harjo, "Anchorage," in *She Had Some Horses* (New York: Norton, 2008), 4.

Index

All place names are in California unless otherwise noted.

Kupa, Cupeño village of, 150, 185, 186
Kuruvungna, Tongva village of, 263, 264
Kuukamonga, Tongva village of, 263
Kwtsaan People, 32. *See also* Quechan
Kwaw (Atsugewi Creator), 9

La Jolla Reservation, 219, 226–27
La Placita, village of, 234
LaChusa, Annie (Indigenous Californian), 265
LaChusa, Margaret (Torrez-Martinez Cahuilla), 265
LaChusa, Martina (Kumeyaay), 207*fig*
LaChusa, Romaldo (Kumeyaay), 265
Lake County, 163–64, 166, 211, 214, 293, 319
Lake County Courthouse, 213
Lake Mohonk Conference of the Friends of the Indian, 235
Lakeport, 213
Lakeside, 218
Lakota People, 137, 180, 265, 267, 282, 284
Landmark's Club, 186, 235–36
lanl hanp ("acorn sing" ceremony), 23
Lara, Sr., Walt (Yurok), 205, 321
Larkin, Thomas, 118
Las Vegas, Nevada, 15
Lassen County, 293
Lassen County American Indian Organization, 251
Lassen Cutoff, 168
Lassen, Mount, 21, 26. *See also* Lassen Peak
Lassen National Forest, 193, 197, 286
Lassen Peak, 193, 196, 197. *See also* Lassen, Mount
Lasuen, Fermin, 65
Lavos, Valentine (Cupeño), 207*fig*
Lego, Raymond (Pit River), 286–88
Leivas, Matthew (Luiseño), 15
Lemay, Martha (Nisenan Maidu), 252
Lemoore, 14
Levi, Robert (Cahuilla), 235
Lewis (Yokaya Pomo leader), 163
Liborato (Huchiun fugitive), 81
Lippett, Francis, 152
Lisanchanga, Tongva village of, 263
Little Medicine Mountain, 321
Little Mount Shasta, 196. *See also* Wagunupa
Little Temecula Ranch, 115
Littlefeather, Sacheen (Apache), 267
Livermore Valley, 131

livestock, 107, 109, 110, 112–15, 162; and effects on flora and fauna, 234, 243; Spanish, 68; Russian, 101
Locolumne Yokuts People, 131–32. *See also* Yokuts
Logan, Rachel (Yuki), 223
London, England, 89, 92, 94, 95
Lone Pine Reservation, 245
Long Beach Pacific Southwest Exposition (1928), 240
Long Beach State University, 279. *See also* California State University, Long Beach
Long, L. F., 163
Lopez (Native child enslaved in Mendocino County), 143
Loreto, Mexico, 54
Los Angeles, 9, 16, 33, 66, 96, 111, 112, 117, 128, 129, 131, 147, 150, 152, 170, 172, 181, 218, 223, 224, 228, 242, 244, 245, 250, 254, 262–68, 272, 274–77, 296, 330; Indigenous Peoples' culture in, 140; Indigenous Peoples' labor in, 139; slavery in, 141; violence against Indigenous People in, 140
Los Angeles Basin, 16, 263, 264
Los Angeles County, 170, 179, 263
Los Angeles Department of Water and Power, 244
Los Angeles Field Relocation Office, 266
Los Angeles Indian Center, 265, 266*fig*, 276–78
Los Angeles Star, 140
Los Angeles Times, 287
Los Coyotes Canyon, 150
Los Coyotes Reservation, 256
Louisiana Purchase Exposition (1904), 203
Lovato, Robert (Pala), 258
Lowie Museum, 303
Lowry, Judith, 251
Lowry, Leonard (Mountain Maidu-Pit River-Washo-Modoc), 250
Lugo, Antonio, 150
Lugo, Leoncio (Cahuilla), 209–11
Lugo, Lupy (Cahuilla), 211, 219, 222, 228, 237
Luis (Native *alcalde* of Mission San Francisco), 81
Luiseño People: and anthropologists, 205; beekeeping, 218; ceremonies of, 24, 25; creation story of, 14; and dispossession, 176; and emancipation, 110; and Garra Revolt, 150; and irrigation projects, 178; land tenure, 114–15, 171–72, 175;

Founded in 1893,
UNIVERSITY OF CALIFORNIA PRESS
publishes bold, progressive books and journals
on topics in the arts, humanities, social sciences,
and natural sciences—with a focus on social
justice issues—that inspire thought and action
among readers worldwide.

The UC PRESS FOUNDATION
raises funds to uphold the press's vital role
as an independent, nonprofit publisher, and
receives philanthropic support from a wide
range of individuals and institutions—and from
committed readers like you. To learn more, visit
ucpress.edu/supportus.